The
BOOK OF
BUSINESS WISDOM

The
BOOK OF
BUSINESS
WISDOM

Classic Writings by the Legends
of Commerce and Industry

Edited by Peter Krass

John Wiley & Sons, Inc.

New York • Chichester • Weinheim • Brisbane • Singapore • Toronto

Copyright © 1997 by Peter Krass.
Published by John Wiley & Sons, Inc.

Library of Congress Cataloging-in-Publication Data:

The book of business wisdom : classic writings by the legends of
    commerce and industry / edited by Peter Krass.
        p.   cm.
    Includes index.
    ISBN 0-471-16512-3 (cloth : alk. paper)
    1. Success in business.   I. Krass, Peter.
HF5386.B66   1997
650.1—dc21   97-15014
                                                                          CIP

Printed in the United States of America

10   9   8   7   6   5   4   3   2   1

Contents

Contents

Contents

Contents

Contents

Introduction

Imagine yourself stomping into Jack Welch's office and demanding his secrets for dynamic leadership; or, marching into Andy Grove's office for a discourse on management theory; or, slipping into Carl Icahn's office and soliciting his ideas on finance. Why stomp, march, and slip? Because it is unlikely we will be invited. Of course, if we were to invite ourselves into their offices, we would undoubtedly be escorted out by two burly security guards and the F.B.I. would be running a background check on us within the hour. But just imagine having the opportunity to sit down not only with today's captains of industry, but yesterday's icons as well. What advice would Andrew Carnegie, John D. Rockefeller, and J. Paul Getty give us on leadership, management, finance, and other components essential to achieving success? *The Book of Business Wisdom* provides this enchanting opportunity.

Success! A multibillion dollar industry has been created around this word. Motivational speakers command huge appearance fees. Institutions have been built around business gurus. Authors attempting to crack the secrets of success have used every metaphor imaginable to depict their ideas. And all of these innovative and sometimes useful books, seminars, and mere premises have been selling like hot cakes since the dawn of free enterprise. But, in truth, who better understands the necessary qualities to succeed than the most successful captains of American industry? They are not pretenders to the throne; they embody the essence of American commerce and industry, and their brilliance abounds in this anthology.

The key to this project was finding poignant material written by these magnates that offers practical advice and insights into fundamental business methods. This book is not about inspirational fluff, nor does it include glossed over, massaged material that reads like an excerpt from an annual report. By nature, these captains of industry were dynamic characters, and I wanted essays that captured their persona and displayed their vitality through their words. For example, Getty was a flamboyant character and as you read his selection, you will discover extravagant language and images that reflect who he was. Jack Welch, on the other hand, is a blunt, no nonsense kind of guy. He uses phrases like, "Big, bold changes . . . exposing people . . . judging ideas . . . insatiable passion for winning . . ." The introductions for the authors also give you a flavor of their character, and a sense of the perspective from which they were writing.

Another important criterion in selecting the pieces was that they had to be universal in nature, not restricted by time or place. Carnegie expounding upon labor problems of the 1880s would be of little use today. His selection is a speech he gave at Curry Commercial College in 1885; he could well be speaking to both students and businesspeople today. Carnegie discusses the importance of smashing routines and making new rules. Except for a few semantical differences, he is clearly discussing the notion of reengineering, a critical catchword of the 1990s. Carnegie also asserts the need to break orders and boss your boss as soon as you can when seeking to improve business methods, otherwise known as empowering the employee in the 1990s. Of course, when it came to empowering unions, he and others were not exactly enthusiastic; however, you have to appreciate the sophisticated and universal ideas that guided these magnates more than a hundred years ago. The same universality is discovered in all the selections, regardless of the author's occupation or year written, from J. Ogden Armour (meat packing in 1917) to J. Irwin Miller (diesel engine maker in 1959) to Victor Kiam (Remington razors in 1986) to Edward C. Johnson, III (Fidelity Investments in 1996).

As the search for material expanded, it became obvious that there was a plethora available at the turn of the twentieth century. The major reason is without a doubt the impact of America's industrial revolution. America, up until the industrial revolution, was far more concerned with the conduct of life rather than business. God still came before Mammon and the almighty dollar. In economic terms, the aggregate value of U.S. manufacturing (plant and production) in 1860 was less than that of England, France, or Germany, respectively. However, by the early 1890s, the value almost equalled the three countries combined. Seemingly overnight, America became conscious of her industrial might and the need for more sophisticated means of doing business. The industrial leaders had an audience as Mammon usurped God. In addition, Horatio Alger, who was born in 1832, pioneered the genre of business literature, writing more than 135 books on the theme of success. His hard working heroes rose from rags to riches in such novels as *Fame and Fortune, Struggling Upward,* and *Strive and Succeed.* A market was born.

The preceding point is exemplified by the fact that more than a third of the authors included in this collection were conducting business at the height of the industrial revolution. I discovered an incredible amount of rich material from which to select in the years 1920 through 1924, as these men reflected on the fruits of their labor and contemplated the business landscape post World War I. As you scan the contents, you might notice some names conspicuously missing, such as J. P. Morgan. Unfortunately, Morgan chose to burn most of his private and business papers, and left little for historians and students of business. You may also find names that you are not familiar with, but you will know the companies they led: for example, Marvin Bower was a managing partner of McKinsey & Company, Crawford H. Greenewalt was the chairman of Du Pont, and John L. McCaffrey was the chairman of International Harvester. These men and others have been recognized as outstanding businessmen and express exceptional ideas with real style.

The material has been arranged into eight parts or themes, in order to maximize the functional use of the collection. *How to Get Ahead* addresses the qualities necessary to negotiate successfully the business world and to scale the corporate ladder. *The Importance of Character* is not a lecture from the temperance society; this section delves into what it means to have backbone and grit. The Dynamics of *Leadership* and *The Essentials of Good Management* speak for themselves. *Selling Skills and Customer Focus* is decidedly not for salespeople alone. Everybody is always selling himself to somebody for some reason, and therefore this section is of great import. In addition, many of these authors often integrate a number of tangential ideas into their main themes. For example, Thomas J. Watson not only discusses salesmanship, but also the mental posture required for any employee to succeed. He gives practical examples of daily rituals on how to achieve that posture.

Independent Thinking and Individuality in the Corporate World is a powerful section that deals with the reality of working within the rigid structure of a corporation, and surviving with your integrity intact. Although many of us do work for someone else, the collection of characters in *Gunslingers and the Entrepreneurial Spirit* makes it must reading. They provide insights that are universal and beneficial to every individual and business enterprise. The same goes for *Philosophy from Wall Street*. After reading Baruch and company, you'll not only know how to avoid a bad investment, but you'll learn quite a bit about American business from the viewpoint of the investor.

This collection is about everything for everybody. Regardless of your position in life, my advice is simply to read the book from cover to cover. The design of the book also offers the enjoyable opportunity to pick and choose your way through this prestigious group of authors. By the time you have finished this collection, I sincerely believe it will have answered the many questions you would have had if you had been given the opportunity to sit down with the authors included here. As you read the selections, allow these captains of industry to come alive in your mind; hear the vitality of their character; listen to their distinct voices and unique ideas; but, also search for and understand the common threads they share.

The
BOOK OF
BUSINESS WISDOM

PART I

HOW TO GET AHEAD

ANDREW CARNEGIE
1835 – 1919

Carnegie, who has been characterized as "impulsive, haughty, idealistic, warm, loyal, and shrewd," was born in Scotland and immigrated with his family to the United States when he was 12 years old. His first job was as a bobbin boy, earning $1.20 a week. At 16 Carnegie became a telegraph operator for the Pennsylvania Railroad, where he stayed for 12 years. He then struck out on his own and started the Keystone Bridge Works, envisioning the need for steel bridges. Eventually, Carnegie concentrated on steel production, later buying an oil company, a railroad, and steamships. When he sold the Carnegie Steel Company for $250 million in 1901, it accounted for 25 percent of all steel sold in the United States.

Carnegie attributed much of his success to the men around him. At one point he wrote an epitaph for his grave that read, "Here lies one who knew how to get around him men cleverer than himself." In life and in death, Andrew Carnegie has been called both a tyrant and a saint. As a businessman, Carnegie's idea of conciliation with competitors was their complete surrender to his demands. As an employer, he squeezed all that he could from his employees, offering them wage packages that in effect amounted to "tails I win, heads you lose." During the Homestead Steel Workers' strike of 1892, Carnegie remained at a safe distance in Scotland while 300 Pinkerton guards were hired in an attempt to crush the workers. The conflict ended in a bloody battle and remains a black mark on Carnegie's legacy.

However, Carnegie was considered a saint for giving away more than $325 million to charitable causes before his death, including 7,000 church organs. Carnegie, along with John D. Rockefeller, was the first to make a big business of philanthropy. He also cared deeply for the education of youth; therefore, he not only endowed libraries and universities, but also actively wrote and spoke on social issues. *The Road to Business Success* is from an address given to the students of Curry Commercial College, Pittsburgh. In this poignant speech, he elaborates on his famous axiom, "Always break orders to save owners," and discusses the critical importance of independent action.

The Road to Business Success
Andrew Carnegie

I can give you the secret. It lies mainly in this. Instead of the question, "What must I do for my employer?" substitute "What can I do?" Faithful and conscientious discharge of the duties assigned you is all very well, but the verdict in such cases generally is that you perform your present duties so well that you had better continue performing them. Now, young gentlemen, this will not do. It will not do for the coming partners. There must be something beyond this. We make Clerks, Bookkeepers, Treasurers, Bank Tellers of this class, and there they remain to the end of the chapter. The rising man must do something exceptional, and beyond the range of his special department. HE MUST ATTRACT ATTENTION. A shipping clerk, he may do so by discovering in an invoice an error with which he has nothing to do, and which has escaped the attention of the proper party. If a weighing clerk, he may save for the firm by doubting the adjustment of the scales and having them corrected, even if this be the province of the master mechanic. If a messenger boy, even he can lay the seed of promotion by going beyond the letter of his instructions in order to secure the desired reply. There is no service so low and simple, neither any so high, in which the young man of ability and willing disposition cannot readily and almost daily prove himself capable of greater trust and usefulness, and, what is equally important, show his invincible determination to rise. Some day, in your own department, you will be directed to do or say something which you know will prove disadvantageous to the interest of the firm. Here is your chance. Stand up like a man and say so. Say it boldly, and give your reasons, and thus prove to your employer that, while his thoughts have been engaged upon other matters, you have been studying

---

The rising man must do something excep- tional, and beyond the range of his special department. HE MUST ATTRACT ATTENTION.

---

during hours when perhaps he thought you asleep, how to advance his interests. You may be right or you may be wrong, but in either case you have gained the first condition of success. You have attracted attention. Your employer has found that he has not a mere hireling in his service, but a man; not one who is content to give so many hours of work for so many dollars in return, but one who devotes his spare hours and constant thoughts to the business. Such an employe must perforce be thought of, and thought of kindly and well. It will not be long before his advice is asked in his special branch, and if the advice given be sound, it will soon be asked and taken upon questions of broader bearing. This means partnership; if not with present employers then with others. Your foot, in such a case, is upon the ladder; the amount of climbing done depends entirely upon yourself.

One false axiom you will often hear, which I wish to guard you against: "Obey orders if you break owners." Don't you do it. This is no rule for you to follow. Always break orders to save owners. There never was a great character who did not sometimes smash the routine regulations and make new ones for himself. The rule is only suitable for such as have no aspirations, and you have not forgotten that you are destined to be owners and to make orders and break orders. Do not hesitate to do it whenever you are sure the interests of your employer will be thereby promoted and when you are so sure of the result that you are willing to take the responsibility. You will never be a partner unless you know the business of your department far better than the owners possibly can. When called to account for your independent action, show him the result of your genius, and tell him that you knew that it would be so; show him how mistaken the orders were. Boss your boss just as soon as you can; try it on early. There is nothing he will like so well if he is the right kind of boss; if he is not, he is not the man for you to remain with—leave him whenever you can, even at a present sacrifice, and find one capable of discerning genius. Our young partners in the Carnegie firm have won their spurs by showing that we did not know half as well what was wanted as they did. Some of them have acted upon occasion with me as if they owned the firm and I was but some airy New Yorker presuming to advise upon what I knew very little about. Well, they are not interfered with much now. They were the true bosses—the very men we were looking for.

There is one sure mark of the coming partner, the future millionnaire; his revenues always exceed his expenditures. He begins to save early, almost as soon as he begins to earn.

Boss your boss just as soon as you can; try it on early. There is nothing he will like so well if he is the right kind of boss; if he is not, he is not the man for you to remain with—leave him whenever you can, even at a present sacrifice, and find one capable of discerning genius.

No matter how little it may be possible to save, save that little. Invest it securely, not necessarily in bonds, but in anything which you have good reason to believe will be profitable, but no gambling with it, remember. A rare chance will soon present itself for investment. The little you have saved will prove the basis for an amount of credit utterly surprising to you. Capitalists trust the saving young man. For every hundred dollars you can produce as the result of hard-won savings, Midas, in search of a partner, will lend or credit a thousand; for every thousand, fifty thousand. It is not capital that your seniors require, it is the man who has proved that he has the business habits which create capital, and to create it in the best of all possible ways, as far as self-discipline is concerned, is, by adjusting his habits to his means. Gentlemen, it is the first hundred dollars saved which tells. Begin at once to lay up something. The bee predominates in the future millionnaire.

Of course there are better, higher aims than saving. As an end, the acquisition of wealth is ignoble in the extreme; I assume that you save and long for wealth only as a means of enabling you the better to do some good in your day and generation. Make a note of this essential rule: Expenditure always within income.

You may grow impatient, or become discouraged when year by year you float on in subordinate positions. There is no doubt that it is becoming harder and harder as business gravitates more and more to immense concerns, for a young man without capital to get a start for himself, and in this city especially, where large capital is essential, it is unusually difficult. Still, let me tell you for your encouragement that there is no country in the world where able and energetic young men can so readily rise as this, nor any city where there is more room at the top. It has been impossible to meet the demand for capable, first-class bookkeepers (mark the adjectives), the supply has *never* been equal to the demand. Young men give all kinds of reasons why in their cases failure was clearly attributable to exceptional circumstances which render success impossible. Some never had a chance, according to their own story. This is simply nonsense. No young man ever lived who had not a chance, and a splendid chance, too, if he ever was employed at all. He is assayed in the mind of his immediate superior, from the day he begins work, and, after a time, if he has merit, he is assayed in the council chamber of the firm. His ability, honesty, habits, associations, temper, disposition, all these are weighed and analysed. The young man who never had a chance is the

---

There is always a boom in brains, cultivate that crop, for if you grow any amount of that commodity, here is your best market and you cannot overstock it, and the more brains you have to sell, the higher price you can exact.

---

same young man who has been canvassed over and over again by his superiors, and found destitute of necessary qualifications, or is deemed unworthy of closer relations with the firm, owing to some objectionable act, habit, or association, of which he thought his employers ignorant.

Another class of young men attribute their failure to employers having relations or favourites whom they advanced unfairly. They also insist that their employers disliked brighter intelligences than their own, and were disposed to discourage aspiring genius, and delighted in keeping young men down. There is nothing in this. On the contrary, there is no one suffering so much for lack of the right man in the right place, nor so anxious to find him as the owner. There is not a firm in Pittsburg to-day which is not in the constant search for business ability, and every one of them will tell you that there is no article in the market at all times so scarce. There is always a boom in brains, cultivate that crop, for if you grow any amount of that commodity, here is your best market and you cannot overstock it, and the more brains you have to sell, the higher price you can exact. They are not quite so sure a crop as wild oats, which never fail to produce a bountiful harvest, but they have the advantage over these in always finding a market. Do not hesitate to engage in any legitimate business, for there is no business in America, I do not care what, which will not yield a fair profit if it receive the unremitting, exclusive attention, and all the capital of capable and industrious men. Every business will have its season of depression—years always come during which the manufacturers and merchants of the city are severely tried—years when mills must be run, not for profit, but at a loss, that the organization and men may be

---

"Don't put all your eggs in one basket" is all wrong. I tell you "put all your eggs in one basket, and then watch that basket."

---

kept together and employed, and the concern may keep its products in the market. But on the other hand, every legitimate business producing or dealing in an article which man requires is bound in time to be fairly profitable, if properly conducted.

And here is the prime condition of success, the great secret: concentrate your energy, thought, and capital exclusively upon the business in which you are engaged. Having begun in one line, resolve to fight it out on that line, to lead in it; adopt every improvement, have the best machinery, and know the most about it.

The concerns which fail are those which have scattered their capital, which means that they have scattered their brains also. They have investments in this, or that, or the other, here, there and everywhere. "Don't put all your eggs in one basket" is all wrong. I tell you "put all your eggs in one basket, and then watch that basket." Look round you and take notice; men who do that do not often fail. It is easy to watch and carry the one basket. It is trying to carry too many baskets that breaks most eggs in this country. He who carries three baskets must put one on his head, which is apt to tumble and trip him up. One fault of the American business man is lack of concentration.

To summarize what I have said: Aim for the highest; never enter a bar-room; do not touch liquor, or if at all only at meals; never speculate; never indorse beyond your surplus cash fund; make the firm's interest yours; break orders always to save owners; concentrate; put all your eggs in one basket, and watch that basket; expenditure always within revenue; lastly, be not impatient, for, as Emerson says, "no one can cheat you out of ultimate success but yourselves."

I congratulate poor young men upon being born to that ancient and honourable degree which renders it necessary that they should devote themselves to hard work. A basketful of bonds is the heaviest basket a young man ever had to carry. He generally gets to staggering under it. We have in this city creditable instances of such young men, who have pressed to the front rank of our best and most useful citizens. These deserve great credit. But the vast majority of the sons of rich men are unable to resist the temptations to which wealth subjects them, and sink to unworthy lives. I would almost as soon leave a young man a curse, as burden him with the almighty dollar. It is not from this class you have rivalry to fear. The partner's sons will not trouble you much, but look out that some boys poorer, much poorer than yourselves, whose parents cannot afford to give them the advantages of a course in this institute, advantages which should give you a decided lead in the race—look out that such boys do not challenge you at the post and pass you at the grand stand. Look out for the boy who has to plunge into work direct from the common school and who begins by sweeping out the office. He is the probable dark horse that you had better watch.

Extravagant parties mixed pleasure with business; Elizabeth Taylor was his one-time companion; his lifestyle provided fodder for the gossip columns; a billion dollar empire continued to grow; and the spendthrift Forbes enjoyed joking that he had acquired it all through "sheer ability—spelled i-n-h-e-r-i-t-a-n-c-e." He certainly inherited a sharp wit from his father, Bertie, but in fact, he accomplished much on his own. Forbes first demonstrated his grit in World War II, when he cheated on an eye exam to enter the army and then nearly lost a leg to enemy machine gun fire while searching for a missing unit. But it was not until after his older brother Bruce died in 1964 that Forbes took the helm of the family publishing business. He reflected, "The joy of being boss is what [chief executives] really like—the battle, the challenge. They are free spirits who don't seem to be burdened down by responsibility."

Although *Forbes* magazine was on solid footing, the flamboyant new boss initiated a snappy and irreverent ad campaign. From it was born the famous slogan, "Forbes: Capitalist Tool." Of the caption, Forbes said, "It was humor, but it has its point and really rehabilitated the word *capitalist* when the word had almost become a cussword." The ad campaign put their sales over the top of their arch rival *Fortune,* and provided Forbes with the money to buy everything from Fabergé eggs to an island in Fiji (whose people he hoped to convert from "coconuts to credit cards, all in one generation").

For all his extravagance Forbes was a very business-oriented and observant man who keenly noted, "The most useful piece of equipment in [the office] remains the scrap basket." The same poignant wit is demonstrated in the two selections that follow, which he wrote for his own column in *Forbes*. The straightforward message for success and the importance of occasional failure is not lost in the playful language.

A Vital Ingredient of Sustained Success
Malcolm S. Forbes

A vital ingredient of sustained success is occasional failure. Decision making is a prime responsibility of those in top positions, and their batting average between right ones and wrong ones must be high.

Being right most of the time is pretty heady medicine. The higher one is, the less likely are subordinates and associates inclined to argue. Certainly, they are unapt to point out or remind the boss of his boo-boos.

Apparently, it is not a long leap from being right most of the time to the assumption that one is right all the time. At this point there is nothing as essential as an unmistakable mistake of some magnitude to restore the perspective that is needed to ensure continued success.

Joe Louis was long a champion as a result of being upended—once—by Max Schmeling. Floyd Patterson came back stronger than ever after Ingemar Johansson gave him a taste of defeat, but no continued appetite for it.

A big shot who has never laid an egg—in his insulated opinion—is in the position of a hen under a similar handicap, about to be made a meal of.

Dispensability Precedes Indispensability
Malcolm S. Forbes

All too often we loosely say of a man doing a good job that he is indispensable.

A flattering canard, as so many disillusioned retired and fired have discovered when the world seems to keep on turning without them.

It matters not how small or large the job you now have; if you have trained no one to do it as well, you're not available; you've made your promotion difficult if not impossible.

In business a man can come nearest to indispensability by being dispensable in his present job. How can a man move up to new responsibilities if he is the only one able to handle his present tasks? It matters not how small or large the job you now have; if you have trained no one to do it as well, you're not available; you've made your promotion difficult if not impossible.

You may think you've made yourself unfireable, whereas in reality you've made yourself unpromotable.

I can see the heads of all you nabobs bobbing in agreement.

I wonder, though, how many of you can honestly say you have had at least one man able to step into your shoes and do your job as well or possibly better? Try asking today each of the men who report to you for the names of the men under them qualified this very moment to take their job. On their answers you can judge their promotability.

Dispensability precedes indispensability.

Thomas Alva Edison
1847 – 1931

The famous motto that "Genius is one percent inspiration and 99 percent perspiration" belongs to Edison. He also believed he was merely "a plate on a record or a receiving apparatus" on which he would obtain impressions from the Universe and then "work them out." The self-educated inventor received, one way or another, quite a few impressions on his "apparatus" and was awarded more than 1,000 patents over his lifetime. Of course, it was the phonograph that made him an international celebrity at the age of 30. Shortly thereafter, J. P. Morgan himself summoned Edison to his Manhattan mansion to install the first residential lighting system running off an electric generator. Morgan was so impressed that he later bought the entire Edison Light Company and formed General Electric.

Edison, who is said to have invented the twentieth century, was also a businessman, concerned with everything from using effective advertising to keeping overhead costs down. For him, automation was the true catchword of the day; he believed that machines would emancipate the people, and once this occurred, a new and better age of thinking would evolve. His streamlined factories turned out not only products, but also protégés like Henry Ford, who typified the Edison employee: a man with much common sense and practical knowledge. Edison's screening of prospective employees was very intense. Over a particular two-year period, he interviewed 2,000 men and hired only 80 of them. Although many were educated at excellent universities, he found most of them lacking in the area of independent thinking.

Thinking was a recurring theme for Edison, and he had plenty of thoughts on a multitude of subjects, from attacking the rascals of Wall Street to debating who best sings *The Swanee River* (Edison himself was almost deaf). In his laboratory hung a sign with his favorite aphorism by Joshua Reynolds to remind his employees of his officially adopted work motto: "There is no expedient to which a man will not resort to avoid the real labor of thinking." In *They Won't Think,* Edison delves into his favorite subject and declares that there is more to exercising than sit-ups and push-ups. Unquestionably, he leaves the reader thinking.

They Won't Think
Thomas Alva Edison

Every man has some forte, something he can do better than he can do anything else. Many men, however, never find the job they are best suited for. And often this is because they do not think enough. Too many men drift lazily into any job, suited or unsuited for them; and when they don't get along well they blame everybody and everything but themselves.

Grouches are nearly always pinheads, small men who have never made any effort to improve their mental capacity.

The brain can be developed just the same as the muscles can be developed, if one will only take the pains to train the mind to think.

Why do so many men never amount to anything? Because they don't think.

I am going to have a sign put up all over my plant, reading "There is no expedient to which a man will not resort to avoid the real labor of thinking."

That is true. There is hardly a day that I do not discover how painfully true it is.

What progress individuals could make, and what progress the world would make, if thinking were given proper consideration! It seems to me that not one man in a thousand appreciates what can be accomplished by training the mind to think.

It is because they do not use their thinking powers that so many people have never developed a creditable mentality. The brain that isn't used rusts. The brain that is used responds. The brain is exactly like any other part of the body: it can be strengthened by proper exercise, by proper use. Put your arm in a sling and keep it there for a considerable length of time, and, when you take it out, you find that you can't use it. In the same way, the brain that isn't used suffers atrophy.

By developing your thinking powers you expand the capacity of your brain and attain new abilities. For example, the average person's brain does not observe a thousandth part of what the eye observes. The average brain simply fails to register the things which come before the eye. It is almost incredible how poor our powers of observation—genuine observation—are.

Let me give an illustration: When we first started the incandescent lighting system we had a lamp factory at the bottom of a hill, at Menlo Park. It was a very busy time for us all. Seventy-five of us worked twenty hours every day and slept only four hours—and thrived on it.

I fed them all, and I had a man play an organ all the time we were at work. One midnight, while at lunch, a matter

---

The brain that isn't used rusts. The brain that is used responds.

---

came up which caused me to refer to a cherry tree beside the hill leading from the main works to the lamp factory. Nobody seemed to know anything about the location of the cherry tree. This made me conduct a little investigation, and I found that although twenty-seven of these men had used this path every day for six months not one of them had ever noticed the tree.

The eye sees a great many things, but the average brain records very few of them. Indeed, nobody has the slightest conception of how little the brain 'sees' unless it has been highly trained. I remember dropping in to see a man whose duty was to watch the working of a hundred machines on a table. I asked him if everything was all right.

Yes, everything is all right, he said.

But I had already noticed that two of the machines had stopped. I drew his attention to them, and he was mortified.

The man who doesn't make up his mind to cultivate the habit of thinking misses the greatest pleasure in life.

He confessed that, although his sole duty was to watch and see that every machine was working, he had not noticed that these two had stopped. I could hie myself off and keep busy at thinking forever. I don't need anybody to amuse me. It is the same way with my friends John Burroughs, the naturalist, and Henry Ford, who is a natural-born mechanic. We can derive the most satisfying kind of joy from thinking and thinking and thinking.

The man who doesn't make up his mind to cultivate the habit of thinking misses the greatest pleasure in life. He not only misses the greatest pleasure, but he cannot make the most of himself. All progress, all success, springs from thinking.

J. Ogden Armour
1863 – 1927

Philip D. Armour founded the Armour meat packing business in 1867, after he had made a small fortune trading pork options at the end of the Civil War. The Chicago-based company soon became one of the world's largest processors of pork. "J. O.," as he was known to colleagues, inherited the family business when his father died in 1901. Prior to his death, Philip warned his son against the pitfalls of being born into a rich family (i.e., the propensity to become spoiled, lazy, and arrogant). Philip advised: "You have to take the curse off being a rich man."—a nice curse, if ever there was one. J. O. took the advice to heart and did not let the money ruin him; to the contrary, with a grand vision that "outstripped" that of his father, he transformed Armour into a conglomerate with over 3,000 products, handling everything from fertilizer production to processed foods. J. O. was recognized as "the largest merchant in Christendom or heathendom," and was for a while the largest individual employer in the country.

To the muckrakers of the time, he also represented heathendom, and Upton Sinclair's momentous novel, *The Jungle,* which depicted horrid working and living conditions in Chicago's meat packing district, was based on Armour & Co. J. O. threatened to file a libel suit against F. N. Doubleday, who published the story in 1906. However, J. O. eventually shook off the criticism and even forthrightly admitted, "I have no social ambitions. My ambition is to run Armour & Co. successfully. . . ."

Over the years J. O.'s business philosophy changed, perhaps as a result of *The Jungle* escapade. He realized that "Business can no longer be done with a club, but with a chemist—and a lawyer." He also came to place great emphasis on cultivating loyalty and enthusiasm among his workers. Toward that end, most executives were promoted from the ranks. J. O. was also far more endeared to those self-trained men who pushed themselves up from the bottom than those cut from the MBA mold. Self-training was one prerequisite to getting far, as opposed to just getting by. In *Armour Men Who Got Ahead—and Why,* J. O. outlines his other prerequisites for personal achievement and his responsibility for helping the employees fulfill their goals.

Armour Men Who Got Ahead — and Why

J. Ogden Armour

In a little town three hundred miles east of the Chicago stockyards an old hunter was telling his grocery store cronies one evening about the exciting chase of a fox by his hound the day before.

"They were streaking along," he said, "and every jump Bill was getting closer to the fox; but just when he was ready to pounce on him, the pesky little critter scooted right up a poplar an' — "

"Here! hold on!" shouted someone. "Foxes don't climb trees."

"Well," returned the hunter calmly, "*this* fox *had to.*"

I use Bill and the fox to illustrate something I have seen work out many times in the careers of successful men, particularly those who have come up from the ranks in our own organization. They met emergencies because they "had to," and the reason they "had to" was because they were given complete responsibility in the jobs they were holding down.

Some axioms are true; others aren't. One of the truest I know is the business saying that "the best trained man is the self-trained man." It is my belief that no man developed by a formula in a business organization can ever reach the power of one who is put on his own responsibility, knowing that his advancement depends on his own brains, foresight and application.

By this I do not mean that a business leader should let his men go along blindly. He must always give something of himself; he must teach them the overhand and crawl strokes where they knew only the breast stroke before. But in any office organization the man who has never had to stand squarely on his own feet is never in a position to march ahead.

Almost every executive in our company has risen from the ranks. M. D. Harding, general manager of our Chicago plant, started in as a boy of eleven—the youngest of a dozen children—as an office boy in our Kansas City plant. C. H. MacDowell president of the Armour Fertilizer Works, was my father's stenographer; William E. Pierce, who built our plant in La Plata, Argentina, began as a timekeeper. And so it goes all along the line.

When I am asked to explain the individual successes of some of these men I can say only that they were given full opportunity to do their work as they saw fit, and made answerable only for results. The men working with them had the same opportunities, but it was they who brought their faculties into a little fuller play. We try to run our business so that everyone, from the latest office boy all the way up the line, knows the business of the man just ahead of him. . . .

The man who has never had to stand squarely on his own feet is never in a position to march ahead.

All our department managers, having come up from the ranks themselves, naturally are interested in giving other men opportunities for self-development. The other day one of our executives came across a middle-aged fellow of unpromising appearance who was checking the loading of cars for the butter and egg department.

"How much are you paying this man?" he inquired of the foreman of this department.

"He is getting twenty cents an hour."

"Give him another job. This is the first stage in this particular operation that requires thinking. Anyone can lug boxes, but it takes a little headwork to keep tally of them. Put a young man here. Change the wages from twenty cents an hour to fifty dollars a month, so that the fellow who holds the job won't think of himself as a day laborer. Let him feel he is a regular monthly paid member of our organization— and you have a potential executive in the making."

Whenever men attract your attention so that you wish to promote them, seven times out of ten they will grow up to their job, even if they were not big enough to fill it when they were appointed.

A man who has developed personality, enthusiasm, loyalty and organization sense will pick up the necessary information in almost any position in which he is placed. . . .

GOOD MEN WILL PUSH THEMSELVES FORWARD

No business prestidigitation is sharp enough to lose a good man in the shuffle. The law of business works exactly opposite to the law of gravitation; it always draws to the top.

One day a young man came to Mr. O'Hern and said he wanted to get some experience among our branch plants. O'Hern asked him if he wasn't afraid he would lose his identity in the outside crowd and have to work a lot longer to get ahead.

"They can't lose me!" the young man declared. "I'll come back."

He is now the superintendent of one of our auxiliary plants.

Beyond the great advantage to a corporation in having executives trained up from its own ranks, there is the tremendous lift in the working force itself. Nothing will make more for loyalty and energy in an organization than the knowledge that employees are being promoted continually from the bottom. It gives men ambition, it gives them pride; and pride and ambition, as my father used to say, will keep a man working at top speed when money is merely a by-product.

Many men of average ability are kept from greater accomplishment through reluctance to put in a good assistant who may show up as more brilliant than they. Another common failing among executives is a disposition to do relatively minor duties, because it happens that they can do them better than anyone else in their organization. It is better for a man to accept efficiency ten or fifteen per cent below his own in such matters, and save his own time and ability for the really big things. These are two of the evils which we try to avoid here.

An object lesson along this very line was furnished by a machine shop into which one of our men happened to go the other day. He noticed a boy passing around among the workmen with a pail of drinking water.

"That's very thoughtful of you," he remarked to the foreman.

"Thoughtful?" the foreman smiled. "Perhaps. But it's more than that. The men's time is worth seventy-five cents an hour; the boy's time is worth twelve and a half cents an hour. Figure out for yourself just about how much it would cost the house if every man had to go after drinking water two or three times a day."

What Business Men Can Learn From Theatrical Producers

The capable executive is master of his time. He systematizes his minutes. Everything it is not absolutely essential for him to do he leaves to subordinates. It is better for him and better for them. In the long run, the most successful man is the man who gives the fewest orders.

Business men might learn from theatrical producers a useful lesson in the development of understudies. Few plays are ever put on the boards without an understudy for every important part. And yet some business organizations, either as a whole or in departments, are run on the "one-man plan." When this man drops out the whole structure totters.

We try to run things here so that every man knows the duties of the man just ahead of him. We encourage men to be inquisitive, and we satisfy their curiosity. Sometimes, if that man ahead is not looking sharp, he finds himself shoved out automatically by a pushing chap behind him. We try to guard against any such thing as an automatic foreclosure of opportunity to anyone.

The capable executive is master of his time. He systematizes his minutes. . . . In the long run, the most successful man is the man who gives the fewest orders.

The right sort of man doesn't have to find opportunities; he makes them. He may make mistakes, too, but that is all part of the venture. "Empty things don't slop over," as Henry Ward Beecher once remarked. What is more, I have found that when a man does make a mistake it does not pay to criticize him too severely. He will be afraid to assume responsibilities in another emergency. And responsibility is the thing that makes men.

Any man who is master of one thing is a success. Given a group of men, each master of one thing, and you have a successful organization. Such organizations are seldom a galaxy of scintillant stars. It is team work that counts. In baseball the star second baseman who fails to cover first when he should, is likely to draw a fine; if he makes that negligence a habit, he probably will be released. Champion ball clubs—those which share in world series purses—are usually made up of fair, reliable, strong-hearted players who work together like a machine.

The trouble with many brilliant men is that they "won't stay hitched," as my father used to say. We don't want fellows who have to play a solo. We put a man on his own responsibility as far as his own job is concerned; we encourage him to push on, but he must have organization sense and loyalty, or even brilliancy may be a handicap. A business organization should be as well coordinated as a symphony orchestra.

I shall never forget one lesson in loyalty and team work that I learned from my father many years ago. It came in the form of a letter to my brother and me, and although it referred directly to our business, its principles are broad enough to apply to any business. This is the letter:

A LETTER FROM P. D. ARMOUR

APRIL 1, 1895.

MY DEAR OGDEN AND PHIL:

Mr. Earling, superintendent of the C. M. & St. P. Railway, rode home with me from Carey's funeral yesterday, and in the course of conversation related a little incident to illustrate why railroads don't succeed better. It struck me very forcibly, and I think the meat of it will apply to the packing business.

He said that while he was in Minneapolis last week he stepped into a little cigar store near the depot and bought a couple of cigars. As he was lighting one he asked the man whether he was doing a good business. He said, yes; he had all the Milwaukee & St. Paul Railroad trade, and that was a very large volume indeed; in fact, it was practically all the business he had.

Then Earling asked him where he bought his cigars, and he replied, "In New York."

He then asked him how he shipped them, and he answered, "Via the Burlington Road."

"You *get* all your patronage from the St. Paul, and yet you *give* all your patronage to the Burlington, a road that you have never had a bit of trade from."

"Oh, well," said the cigar man, "I never thought anything about that. *I have never been asked by any of the St. Paul people to ship them via their road.*"

Mr. Earling said that fundamental principle was the same all through the railroad business—the men about the road did simply what they were told to do and what they thought was their duty, but they were not inventive in their heads nor tried to help the railroad. They never looked so far ahead as to see that by boosting the railroad for which they worked they also helped themselves.

Of all the great number of employees who supported that tobacco store, not one had ever asked the cigar man to send his business over the St. Paul Railroad. Of course, they were not the commercial men, exactly, of the road, but they thought nothing concerned them except their special duties and whatever was doled out to them.

Consequently, that was why railroads in a great measure fell short of giving the results to the stockholders that they might give, and, naturally, that meant they did not pay the men what they might pay them.

Now, I think this holds good all through Armour & Company to a great extent.

If every man about Armour & Company would pay a little attention to supporting and helping the House, it would go a very long way toward the success of the House: and no one connected with Armour & Company could go out of his way and show that he took an interest in their success but what the House would soon find it out.

It would be a very simple matter for any of our boys, on going into a store, if they didn't see our goods, to ask why, and if they could not find

25

out, it would be easy enough to report it to the commercial part of the house.

Sincerely yours,
PHILIP D. ARMOUR

Successful men show many contrasting characteristics — but the one quality which they never lack is thoroughness. Business is full of men who would be at the top if they had only learned to think their thoughts out to a conclusion. They know that 2 and 2 make 4, but they never stop to think 4 *what*.

Many of these half-way folks *get by*, but they never *get far*. There is always a premium in business on the man who does his work painstakingly, with completeness and finality; he is the man who will be trusted with more and more responsibility, up to the limit of his capacity. The man who informs himself adequately about his firm, its methods, its policies and its products, who does his work so well that no one need follow him up to patch the ragged edges, is on the safest, surest and shortest road to achievement.

I remember my father called one of his men into his office one day and asked him what figure the receipt of hogs had reached the day before in Kansas City.

"I don't know *exactly*," replied the man; "but I can tell you *about* what the figures were."

"Well, what were the Omaha figures?" went on my father.

"I know *about* what they were," was the reply.

My father wheeled around in his chair.

"Young man, get me those figures exact," he ordered: "Your guesses don't interest me in the least. If there's any guessing to be done around here, I'm a pretty good guesser myself."

In our business — and I take it that this is true of most business organizations — the man who succeeds is the man who "brings back the answer," not the approximate, but the right answer.

Sentiment in business was never more alive than it is to-day. Any able employer of labor knows that kindness and fairness build the cornerstone to a man's best effort. From a purely commercial standpoint, discarding all other reasons, they are the soundest investments in the world. You can buy a man's work, but you cannot buy his loyalty. That can be gained only by treating him fairly. I have declared repeatedly that any success which has come to me has been due almost entirely to the loyalty of my men and their eagerness to please me. I consider this sentiment of more value in dollars and cents than the entire financial investment in our business.

I do not want my men to work because they fear me, or because they are afraid of losing their jobs. I want them to work because they want to work, and because they would rather work here than any other place in the world. A man is no good to me unless he is necessary to Armour & Company, and we are necessary to him.

Business is full of men who would be at the top if they had only learned to think their thoughts out to a conclusion. They know that 2 and 2 make 4, but they never stop to think 4 what.

As a matter of practical business common sense, I make it a rule that my door shall always be open to my men, and any employee, down to the humblest day laborer, may feel free at any time to bring his troubles to me directly. My job would not be worth while under any other conditions.

In the last analysis, a business and an individual have much the same characteristics; they make friends and enemies in exactly the same ways, and nothing pays either quite so well as to be fair.

Schwab, in a speech to the students of Princeton University, said, ". . . there are other things in life than mere work. I believe an appreciation of the finer things in life. . . ." And shortly after assuming the helm at U.S. Steel in 1901, his fine living and gambling exploits in Monaco made newspaper headlines. Schwab was immediately in hot water with the board of directors, which included none other than J. P. Morgan. Of course, by "finer things" Schwab really meant art, literature, and music, which he believed would "help any man in his career." His reasoning was that by cultivating this appreciation of the fine arts, businesspeople improve their own imagination when it comes to problem solving and strategic planning.

Schwab's own meteoric rise to the top at the young age of 39 was largely due to his ability to maintain an excellent rapport with the hardened steel workers, which was sorely needed by management during a period of labor upheaval. His sensitivity to labor relations was revealed by another speech delivered at a convention many years later, in which he said, "I may induce you to buy large quantities of goods from me, but unless I can induce my organization, down to the humblest workman, to want to produce those goods economically and efficiently, my skill in selling you those goods is wasted."

Schwab left U.S. Steel after only a few years, not because of the gambling episode, but because "I could not do what I had been doing all my life. I was hampered by directors and other interests who did not give me sufficient play to be useful." Imagine how he would react to today's environment, in which a CEO's performance is often measured by the company's stock price. Schwab went on to head Bethlehem Steel, and built the modest company into one of U.S. Steel's most formidable competitors. He totally immersed himself in every endeavor undertaken, for he believed, "The man who has done less than his best has done nothing." In *Succeeding with What You Have*, Schwab debunks any myth that he was a genius of sorts and points to the qualities that are necessary to forge a successful career.

Succeeding with What You Have
Charles M. Schwab

For thirty-six years I have been moving among working men in what is now the biggest branch of American industry, the steel business. In that time it has been my good fortune to watch most of the present leaders rise from the ranks. These men, I am convinced, are not natural prodigies. *They won out by using normal brains to think beyond their manifest daily duty.*

American industry is spilling over with men who started life even with the leaders, with brains just as big, with hands quite as capable. And yet one man emerges from the mass, rises sheer above his fellows; and the rest remain.

The men who miss success have two general alibis: "I'm not a genius" is one; the other, "There aren't the opportunities to-day there used to be."

Neither excuse holds. The first is beside the point; the second is altogether wrong.

The thing that most people call "genius" I do not believe in. That is, I am sure that few successful men are so-called "natural geniuses."

There is not a man in power at our Bethlehem steel works to-day who did not begin at the bottom and work his way up, round by round, simply by using his head and his hands a little more freely and a little more effectively than the men beside him. Eugene Grace, president of Bethlehem, worked in the yard when I first knew him. Mr. Snyder was a stenographer, Mr. Mathews a draftsman. The fifteen men in direct charge of the plants were selected not because of some startling stroke of genius but because, day in and day out, they were doing little unusual things — thinking beyond their jobs.

American industry is spilling over with men who started life even with the leaders, with brains just as big, with hands quite as capable. And yet one man emerges from the mass, rises sheer above his fellows; and the rest remain.

When I took over the Bethlehem works I decided to train up its managers as Mr. Carnegie trained his "boys." So I watched the men who were already there, and picked out a dozen. This selection took months. Then I set out to build an organization in which we should be bound together in harmony and kindly cooperation. I encouraged my managers to study iron and steel, markets and men. I gave them all small salaries, but instituted a system whereby each man would share directly in the profits for which he himself was responsible. Every one of those boys "came through." They are wealthy men to-day; all are directors of the company, some are directors of the corporation.

MOST TALK ABOUT GENIUSES IS NONSENSE

Most talk about "super-geniuses" is nonsense. I have found that when "stars" drop out, their departments seldom suffer. And their successors are merely men who have learned by application and self-discipline to get full production from an average, normal brain.

30

The inventor, the man with a unique, specialized talent, is the only real supergenius. But he is so rare that he needs no consideration here.

I have always felt that the surest way to qualify for the job just ahead is to work a little harder than anyone else on the job one is holding down. One of the most successful men I have known never carried a watch until he began to earn ten thousand dollars a year. Before that he had managed with a nickel alarm clock in his bedroom, which he never forgot to wind. Young men may enjoy dropping their work at five or six o'clock and slipping into a dress suit for an evening of pleasure; but the habit has certain drawbacks. I happen to know several able-bodied gentlemen who got it so completely that now they are spending all their time, days as well as evenings, in dress suits, serving food in fashionable restaurants to men who did not get the dress suit habit until somewhat later in life.

Most talk about "super-geniuses" is nonsense. I have found that when "stars" drop out, their departments seldom suffer. And their successors are merely men who have learned by application and self-discipline to get full production from an average, normal brain.

Recently we have heard much about investments. To my mind, the best investment a young man starting out in business can possibly make is to give all his time, all his energies, to work—just plain, hard work. After a man's position is assured, he can indulge in pleasure if he wishes. He will have lost nothing by waiting—and gained much. He will have made money enough really to afford to spend some, and he will know that he has done his duty by himself and by the world.

The man who has done his best has done everything. The man who has done less than his best has done nothing.

Recently we have heard much about investments. To my mind, the best investment a young man starting out in business can possibly make is to give all his time, all his energies, to work — just plain, hard work.

Nothing is more fatal to success than taking one's job as a matter of course. If more persons would get so enthused over their day's work that someone would have to remind them to go out to lunch there would be more happiness in the world and less indigestion. If you must be a glutton, be a glutton for work. A trained ear can do tremendous business in the obstruction line. Sometimes it listens so intently for the toot of the quitting whistle that it quite loses the sense of spoken orders.

I have yet to hear an instance where misfortune hit a man because he worked overtime. I know lots of instances where it hit men who did not. Misfortune has many cloaks. Much more serious than physical injury is the slow, relentless blight that brings standstill, lack of advancement, final failure.

If more persons would get so enthused over their day's work that someone would have to remind them to go out to lunch there would be more happiness in the world and less indigestion.

The man who fails to give fair service during the hours for which he is paid is dishonest. The man who is not willing to give more than this is foolish.

In the modern business world "pull" is losing its power. "Soft snaps" have been sponged off the slate. In most big companies a thousand stockholders stand guard over the cashier's window, where formerly there were ten. The president's son starts at scratch. Achievement is the only test. The fellow who does the most work is going to get the most pay, provided he shows equal intelligence.

Captains of industry are not hunting money. America is heavy with it. They are seeking brains — specialized brains — and faithful, loyal service. Brains are needed to carry out the plans of those who furnish the capital.

The man who attracts attention is the man who is thinking all the time, and expressing himself in little ways. It is not the man who tries to dazzle his employer by doing the theatrical, the spectacular. The man who attempts this is bound to fail.

BENJAMIN F. FAIRLESS
1890 – 1962

Fairless was another great leader in the U.S. Steel tradition, which includes the commanding figures of Andrew Carnegie and Charles M. Schwab. He was elected president of the company in 1938, became chairman in 1952, and retired in 1955. During his 17 years at the helm, U.S. Steel experienced tremendous growth and by 1955 was producing more steel than was being made in the entire U.S.S.R. Fairless was also heavily involved with the government: He served on the War Production Board during World War II and later advised the Eisenhower administration on a host of issues, from studying foreign aid programs to monitoring the actions of the C.I.A.

By any measure, Fairless was an endearing public figure and a success. However, he humbly made it a point to say, "America is full of successful people you never heard of: men and women whom fame passed by . . . who perhaps have never known the luxury of more than a couple of extra dollars, but who, nevertheless, have gained happiness. . . ." He counted his father and uncle among them. His father was a coal miner in the tough mining town of Pigeon Run, Ohio. His uncle, with whom Fairless went to live after his mother became very ill, was a farmer and a country store keeper, and barely made ends meet. A young Fairless helped out by toiling on the farm, selling newspapers, and working as a janitor at the local school. In his spare time, he played baseball (little did he know that one day he would be part owner of the Pittsburgh Pirates).

Life was a struggle, but Fairless set his sights high, worked his way through college, and earned a degree in civil engineering. Then, of course, he realized his greatest dreams with U.S. Steel. America truly was a land of opportunity for him; however, he enigmatically said of his beloved country, "I don't hold with those who say, 'America must never change.' Our country has always changed. When it ceases to change it will cease to be America." In other words, do not be content with status quo. America must continue to evolve, to build new enterprises, and to offer new and greater opportunities. Fairless certainly knew how to seize an opportunity, and he depicts his ideas on getting ahead in *What Democracy Did for Me*.

What Democracy Did for Me
Benjamin F. Fairless

What is the recipe for successful achievement? To my mind there are just four essential ingredients: Choose a career you love. . . . Give it the best there is in you. . . . Seize your opportunities. . . . And be a member of the team. . . . In no country but America, I believe, is it possible to fulfill all four of these requirements.

I love the steel business. I've been in love with it ever since the day 35 years ago when, as a young engineer, I helped lay out my first open-hearth furnace. For me, steelmaking holds a fascination—a romance—unequaled by any other occupation.

Not everyone, I realize, shares my enthusiasm. Which perhaps is fortunate, else we might have too many steelmakers in this country and too few doctors, merchants, or college professors.

America has need of many different talents: The archaeologist, the bricklayer, and the accountant all have their contributions to make. Some men derive a thrill from raising wheat; others, from dissecting atoms, painting portraits, or selling automobiles. But no man can be truly successful unless his job arouses his enthusiasm. That's why it's so important for him to pick a field of endeavor he feels will be congenial.

The other day one of my friends sent his son to me for some advice about his future.

"I can't decide for you whether you belong in steel, or agriculture, or communications, or shipping," I told the boy. "I can't tell you that you ought to be a surgeon, or a lawyer, or an architect. That's up to you. A vocational counselor and aptitude tests may help you to choose intelligently; but the decision must be yours.

"My only suggestion would be that you select a field of activity that you think is capable of holding your interest for the next forty years. Once you're in it you may still find that you've made a mistake. In that case, I believe you should get out fast and into something that you like.

"There are countries where you couldn't do this. But in America, under our free-enterprise system, you still have the right to choose your own lifework."

Opportunity, for most of us, doesn't knock just once; she raps a continual tattoo on our doors. The pity is that much of the time we're either too preoccupied to hear or too lethargic to answer.

For generations the men of my family were all coal miners. In the old country that's the way it was: A son usually had no choice but to follow in his father's footsteps. My grandparents came to this country to better their lot; but they remained coal miners. My father, born in Wales, went to work in the mines at 12. Not until I was a grown man did he leave the pits and become a steelworker; he retired 13 years ago at the age of 70.

"Remember, Ben," he often told me as a boy, "nobody gets anything out of life unless he's willing to work hard and long for it."

I believe that's true. Once a man has picked a career, he's got to do his utmost, give it everything he's got.

In a race, why is one horse the winner? Because he's the better horse? Not necessarily. Perhaps he tried a little harder.

It seems to me that many people make the mistake of coasting—of attempting to get by with as little effort as possible. Others waste all their ammunition aiming at near-by targets for two-penny prizes, with the result that none of their bullets ever hit a worthwhile mark. I tried early in life to acquire the habit of doing everything I undertook to the utmost of my ability—whether it was building a fire, swatting a baseball, or passing an exam. I feel that this habit has served me well. . . .

I believe a third ingredient in any recipe for success would be that of seizing one's opportunities.

I know men who complain they "never had a break." I believe if they were honest with themselves they would probably find that their careers had been pockmarked by opportunities of which they failed to take advantage.

In America, everybody gets the breaks. Opportunity, for most of us, doesn't knock just once; she raps a continual tattoo on our doors. The pity is that much of the time we're either too preoccupied to hear or too lethargic to answer.

Of course, some breaks are bigger than others. My big break came the summer after I was graduated from Ohio Northern University. If I hadn't decided to see Coxey's Army off for Washington, I might still be a railroad man instead of a steelmaker.

It happened this way: I'd just been hired as a civil engineer by the Wheeling & Lake Erie Railroad when the word got round that "General" Jacob Coxey was about to lead a second march of the unemployed on the nation's capital. Coxey's headquarters at the time were at Massillon, Ohio, 7 miles from my home. I decided to see the show.

As my train neared the city, we passed a 1,000-acre field crisscrossed by railway spurs and muddy wagon tracks and dotted with the beginnings of some strange sort of building.

"What's going on here?" I asked the conductor.

"New steel plant," he informed me tersely, between chomps on his tobacco.

From that moment Coxey and his Army were forgotten. When the train slowed down, I dropped off and headed for the superintendent's shack.

The construction boss turned out to be a burly six-footer by the name of Mastersteck. I was undersized and skinny. He looked unimpressed when I told him I wanted to help him build the steel plant.

"Leave your name and address," he directed. "If I need you I'll get in touch with you inside a week."

A week, ten days, passed without the hoped-for letter. I determined on another trip to Massillon. Mastersteck, surprised, greeted me with open arms.

"I lost your address," he explained. "How soon can you start?"

That's how, back in 1913, I got into Central Steel quite literally on the ground floor.

As the company grew, my responsibilities grew with it. In 1926 Central Steel merged with United Alloy; in 1930 the new company combined with several others to form the giant Republic Steel Corporation. Fortune smiled on me each time. But none of it would have happened if, first, I hadn't been curious about Coxey's Army—or if, secondly, not hearing from Mastersteck, I hadn't decided to jog his elbow. . . .

Teamwork, to me, is the fourth requirement for achievement. Unless a person is a clam digger, a trapper, or an old-style pick-and-shovel prospector, it's virtually impossible these days to be a success all by oneself. Even scientific research, once the domain of cloistered individuals, has become a cooperative affair. Hermits have gone out of style; and in modern industry there's no room for the predatory lone wolf.

Other countries have organized their economy along authoritarian lines: at the top, a small, privileged group of whip-cracking bosses; below them, the rest of the people, whom they tell what to do and how to do it. In America, on the contrary, we believe in teamwork—in everybody's working together for the good of all. We apply teamwork in our homes, in our jobs, and in our running of the nation. Under our democracy the man who goes farthest is generally the man who contributes most to the welfare of the team.

Unless a person is a clam digger, a trapper, or an old-style pick-and-shovel prospector, it's virtually impossible these days to be a success all by oneself.

Teamwork involves split-second collaboration. It also implies a high degree of initiative and responsibility on the part of every player. No other game demands these qualities to the same extent as baseball. So it's only natural that baseball should have become our national sport.

I learned baseball on a vacant lot in Justus. I was the catcher, and for one year the captain, of my college nine. At Central Steel I helped to organize a semi-pro team which was called the Agathons. I played with them until the competition got too stiff, then retired to the managerial bench.

An organization like the United States Steel Corporation differs from a baseball club only in size and complexity. Basically, it meets its problems in the same way—by teamwork. I agree with Mr. A. W. Robertson, of Westinghouse, who stated in THE AMERICAN MAGAZINE last year, "Teamwork, not money, factory space, or tools, is what makes big business click."

I also agree with Andrew Carnegie, whose tradition my company inherits. The great Scotch steelmaster once said: "Take away all our trade, our avenues of transportation, our money. Leave us with nothing but our organization, and in four years we shall have re-established ourselves." Without organization, U.S. Steel would amount to little; and without teamwork, we would have no organization.

HENRY FORD, II
1917 – 1987

The grandson of Henry Ford successfully ruled over what has been labeled a Byzantine empire. As one biographer noted, "Alas, unlike his grandfather, Henry II preferred the good life of an international jet-setter, partying in the far corners of the world, drinking to excess. . . ." This indulgent behavior was most likely the extension of a spoiled childhood. In fact, few thought the young man would amount to much. However, when Henry II enlisted in the Navy during War World II against his powerful grandfather's wishes, he finally experienced true independence and understood what it meant to act responsibly.

Unfortunately, his father Edsel, president of Ford Motor Company, died shortly thereafter in 1943. Arrangements were quickly made for Henry II to leave the Navy and take a position in Ford's management. Frankly, old Henry was going senile and a family member was needed to watch over the business. Initially, the young man had no official title and no job description, so he spent a great deal of time wandering through the various factories and learning about the industry. He soon discovered numerous improprieties and basic mismanagement. At one point he remarked, "Can you believe it, in one department they figured their costs by weighing the pile of invoices on a scale." His grandfather, who was still chairman, had been running the company like it was a country store; it was time to clean house. Henry II actually took to packing a gun for protection against reprisals as he confronted individuals involved in dubious rackets.

Many were surprised by his earnestness in reversing the downward trends of the ailing company. One friend commented, "I think Henry II's principal adviser is the memory of his father." Edsel had, prior to his death, been a steady influence in the raucous kingdom. The young leader, however, knew he had to build a solid management team around him to help resurrect the Ford Motor Company. They redesigned their organization in part after Sloan's General Motors and succeeded in re-creating a powerhouse. One of Henry II's greatest strengths was having a good eye for talent (and hiring innovative men like Lee Iacocca). He shares his views on the characteristics that make an employee an asset to a company in *Business: An Introduction.*

Business: An Introduction
Henry Ford, II

In considering a man for a management job or for other work, every employer must ask himself, "Would this applicant, if hired, be an asset to my company?" We know many of the qualities that make a man an asset to a business. Here are the main ones.

- *Proficiency in your field.* Your college training is the company's justification for hiring you. But you should remember that when an employer thinks about an applicant's college training, he thinks about more than a major in one field. He thinks about the applicant's reading speed and comprehension; his ability to write the English language and his knowledge of the principles of mathematics. These form the hard logical base not only of a successful education but of a successful career as well. Naturally, the better prepared you are in accounting or public relations, engineering or market research, product design or law, the better are your chances of matching the description of the job that is open. Never forget, however, that specialized training alone is not enough. It may get you that first job; but if it is all you have to offer an employer, it may also bury you in that first job.
- *Social competence.* This is the kind of unsatisfactory term that always means too many things. Perhaps I

can clarify it somewhat by pointing out that the social skills a young man learns while in school will serve him well in a large corporation. The ability to cooperate with others in purposeful activity, congeniality, knowing how to follow and lead—all of these personal traits are important in school, and they are important in a company. I don't mean to suggest that an employer is going to be impressed automatically

---

Specialized training alone is not enough. It may get you that first job; but if it is all you have to offer an employer, it may also bury you in that first job.

---

by a long list of extracurricular activities. Your chairmanship of the dance committee speaks highly for you. But for an employer, your chairmanships in the professional and honorary societies speak more highly—and more to the point. They indicate that you possess the kinds of skills which are highly prized in a company.

- *Analytical power.* You exercise this power in the classroom to the extent that you gather evidence, interpret it and draw logical conclusions. You will also exercise it in business, but there will be a difference—a big one. When you apply the scientific method to a problem in a classroom, usually you don't apply all of it. In a mathematics class, for example, a teacher gives you the problem, and you work out the solution to it. In business, you often have to find the problem before you can even start thinking about the solution. In business, recognizing the problem is just as important as knowing the method that will solve it.

42

What an Employer Wants

- *Curiosity.* An employer is always on the lookout for questing minds. Many people with specialized training and the ability to reason can deal easily with accepted facts. Fewer people are blessed with the kind of curiosity that breaks up familiar patterns and starts fresh thoughts. This is the very source of innovation—the less costly manufacturing technique, the quicker accounting system, the more effective sales plan, the better design.
- *Integrity.* This is the quality that gives meaning to all the rest. You must have it first of all for yourself, of course, for without it no person is whole. But individual integrity also makes group integrity and this is essential to a company. It is the guidance-and-control system that directs company performance. And by its performance over the long haul, a company lives or dies.

The qualities employers seek are the concern and the result not so much of specialized education as of liberal education. They are the kind of qualities that will stand you in good stead, regardless of the kind of company you join. They are "transferable"—a favorite term of Theodore O. Yntema, vice president of Ford Motor Company and chairman of our Finance Committee.

Mr. Yntema believes that the liberally educated man not only has a sense of values thoughtfully evolved, a body of classified and ordered knowledge, and the capacity for finding satisfaction in work and play and the good things of life, but also has a collection of basic abilities and skills that are widely useful and transferable from one field to another.

"Many men," he says, "prepare for one career, but shift with little or no handicap to another. Executives move from one kind of job to another—often with greater success than if they stick to one specialty."

No matter what career you choose, you will get along best if you know how to maintain sound relationships with people, communicate clearly and listen carefully, organize your own activities and those of others, work hard and like it, and memorize faces, names and facts important to your job. The liberally educated man with these abilities and skills is prepared to fill almost any position with credit. . . .

You may have some concern that life in a large company will stunt your growth as an individual. Such a concern shows that you place high value on one of the most valuable of all human possessions—independence. But generally speaking it is an unwarranted concern. Most companies, far from being hostile and restrictive, have an environment that encourages the individual's development.

Talent, especially young talent, is absolutely necessary to keep a company strong and competitive. And there is such a tremendous demand for talent that it must be noted, must be encouraged, and must be used in the most responsible positions possible. Otherwise a company is guilty of improper use of its resources. Of course, there are instances where poor supervision temporarily blocks the development of a talent. But those instances are exceptions.

THE RULES DO MAKE SENSE

Again, you may fear that you will be required to conform to some overpowering corporate system that intimidates the individual. This kind of pressure, of course, exists to some degree in all organizations. In some it exists to a ridiculous degree. However, in most American companies a man's family life, his social ties, his political beliefs and his religious convictions are his own business. Most companies are interested in performance, not conformance.

In a business firm, as in other kinds of organizations— including the family, school, church and government—

there are certain rules that must be observed by everyone. This is not comformity. It is common sense. Efficiency dictates such rules, and without them no organization could stay organized, much less fulfill its functions. If, for example, you as a student attended a class every fourth time it met, turned in assignments on whim and otherwise ignored routine requirements, you would compromise the class's larger purposes—to disseminate specific knowledge to as many students as possible and to encourage constructive curiosity.

By the same token, if you as a young man in a company came to work irregularly, observed your own instead of the

---

A young man is always faced with the job of bringing a tremendous number of variables under control. Hunches won't do. Simple rules of thumb won't do.

---

company's deadlines and generally indulged in irrelevancies, you would compromise the larger purposes of the company—to produce quality goods or services at minimum cost and on schedule.

You might also remember this about efficiency: Doing routine tasks well and quickly, saves time, frees you to do other things. And the time you spend ranging after new ideas can be as vital to the company's well-being as it is to your individual well-being.

Even though you believe you have some idea of American business, its size and accomplishments and potentials, I think that you might be surprised at the tremendous number and diversity of opportunities for individuals in large companies today. At Ford, for example, we are concerned not only with our primary business of producing and selling cars and trucks, tractors and farm implements, parts and accessories, but also with electronics, communications, rocketry,

45

advanced weapons technology and space guidance systems. We are also studying the possibility of a space train which, as visualized now, will have three sections: up front, a command post; in the middle, a propulsion unit for orbital corrections; and back in caboose position a detachable living or laboratory car for maneuvering in space.

When you realize that just one company can be engaged in these diverse activities, you begin to get some idea of the extent of American business as a whole. There are any number of companies in America engaged in imaginative and multiple activities. That fact, along with the explorative temper of the times in which we live, means that there are opportunities for an individual to find a place to start and almost unlimited opportunities for him to grow.

How to Grow — and Why

It is not enough for me to admonish you to grow in order to keep up with what is happening. Let me also suggest the general direction of growth.

Every company is markedly different from any other. But no matter what company he may be in a young man is always faced with the job of bringing a tremendous number of variables under control. Hunches won't do. Simple rules of thumb won't do. These things may help, but what it really takes to achieve order and steady progress is system, and the young man must learn to master that system. The extension of his mastery over it — regardless of the level at which he works — is one measure of the young man's growth.

Lightning-fast communications, for example, regularly put information from around the world at his fingertips. Highly trained specialists tell him what is happening in the world and something of what will happen. And if the experts bog down, they can run alternative courses of action through computers and get quick, accurate answers that used to be available only after weeks or months or even years of strenuous work.

Learning the value and use of these aids contributes to the growth of a young man. But the greatest help of all to him, as he seeks control of the variables that confront him, is his own flexibility of mind which allows him to accommodate to rapid social and economic shifts that affect his company. It is important, therefore, that his mind be stored with knowledge acquired not just during the formal educational period but afterward too, through experience and independent reading. Language and marketing, literature and capital, philosophy and taxation, psychology and manufacturing—the more the young man in business knows of these and other branches of human knowledge, the more effective his work will be and the faster he will grow.

In so doing, a young man becomes a pro in one of the biggest, most exciting games in which humans engage. It is a game that requires his total professional involvement and a considerable share of his personal involvement. Commitment to his work will make the game fun for him. And it ought to be fun, for if he chooses a business career, he probably will be playing it for the rest of his professional life.

PART II

THE IMPORTANCE OF CHARACTER

Firestone wandered through a series of jobs, including that of a traveling medicine-extract salesman, before he founded his Akron, Ohio-based tire and rubber company in 1900. Goodyear and Goodrich were already well established in town and did not welcome the newcomer. The unwanted Firestone lost money the first few years and almost folded. Fortunately, Firestone's tire design excelled in an area that was a big issue of the day—keeping the rubber tire fastened to the rim. His big break finally came in 1906 when Henry Ford ordered 2,000 sets of tires, and the next year Firestone sold a total of 105,000 tires. The two men's relationship soon developed beyond rubber, and beginning in 1916, they went on a series of annual camping trips with Thomas Edison and John Burroughs, the naturalist.

John Burroughs, the camping party's man of letters, characterized Firestone as "the clean, clear-headed, conscientious type, always on his job, always ready for what comes. . . ." There is a caveat to what Burroughs meant by clean—Firestone was the only one of the campers who would not bathe in streams or lakes and insisted on a good hotel shower. Edison enjoyed ridiculing him about it.

While surrounded by these men of vision, Firestone realized that the definition of vision does not necessarily include some mystical quality. Rather, he reflected, vision "is not a dreaming forward. It is a thinking through with the values ever in mind." By "thinking through" Firestone meant developing a practical understanding of what the future would require. By "the values" he meant the best business principles that would be necessary to meet future requirements. His own vision included building rubber plantations in Liberia and Singapore, as he anticipated the critical importance of a vertically integrated and globally oriented business. To make his vision a reality, he took a very active role in hiring Firestone employees.

In *What I have Learned about Men*, he provides some unique ideas about interviewing prospective employees, but more important, he shares his insights into how to determine the nature of a person's character.

What I Have Learned about Men
Harvey S. Firestone

When people think of business as a mere matter of merchandise, of buying and making and selling goods, they overlook what is perhaps the most important, and certainly the most interesting, factor in the game. It takes *men* to produce merchandise. It takes *men* to sell it. To get the right kind of men is, therefore, the chief concern of every executive.

I have employed thousands of men and have picked scores for promotion. Of course, sometimes I have guessed wrong. There is no infallible formula for choosing them. But unless an employer can guess right in a majority of cases, he can scarcely hope to run his business successfully.

When I used to hire all my employees myself, I asked applicants a good many questions which some people might think irrelevant. I went back to a boy's grandparents. Who and what were they? Where was he born? What did his father do? How about school? Did he go through high school? If he didn't, why not? And all the time I was getting a line on his character. From his answers and the way he gave them I was learning whether he thought clearly and quickly, what was his training, what were his powers of reasoning and analysis. When I got through, I had a pretty good idea whether he was energetic, persistent, straightforward, and ambitious. If he had those qualities, he had at least the right stuff in him. Minor faults might be corrected. But the fundamentals were there.

And while I talked with him I watched his eyes and his hands. I always do that when I am trying to determine anybody's character. We all like a man to look us straight in the eye. Yet there is a difference in the way men do even this. Some of them do it because *they* are watching *you*. And that is all right, too, unless there is a sort of suspicion behind it. A man must, of course, "watch the other fellow," sometimes. But if suspicion and distrust are a part of his character it is pretty safe to conclude one of two things: either he has been fooled so often that he has come to expect it—in which case there is something wrong with him; or else he himself is looking for a chance to get the better of you. I like to see a man who is evidently studying a *proposition*. But when a man is watching *me*, either because he expects me to try "to put one over on him," or because he is looking for a chance to get some advantage for himself, I have a good many reserves about him.

There is one type of man that does not often look you in the eye and yet, in his case, it does not repel me. He is the thoughtful type. And he thinks better when he can detach himself from outside influence. He is very likely to be looking out of the window, or down at his hands, while you are talking. He is listening—and thinking. But when he does bring his eyes back to your face there is a quiet directness about his glance.

The way a man uses his hands is very significant. Suppose you are talking to an applicant for a position and, after you have explained what will be expected of him, he gives a flabby little wave of his hand and says, "I guess I can do it." Maybe I am wrong, but my feeling is that he is nothing but a guesser and not a very good one at that. If he involuntarily shuts his hand hard, as if he were gripping some material thing, and says, "I believe I can do it. I certainly will try!" I am inclined to think he will "take off his coat" and make a good job of it.

The man who is always tapping his fingers on something shows that he is of a nervous temperament. That, in itself, is nothing against him. Nervous energy is all right if it is expended in constructive action, in doing real things. But you have to be sure that the nervous man isn't the kind that simply stirs himself and everybody around him into a turmoil. He sets the water to boiling, but he doesn't do anything with the steam. It merely makes a cloud around him and his associates, makes them hot and uncomfortable, and finally evaporates without having developed any horse power. Such a man needs to concentrate his nervous energy on getting things done. Then he is likely to be what is known in business as "a driver" and may be a valuable asset in an organization. But you want to be sure of this before you take him.

An employer tries to be careful about hiring a man, in the first place. But I believe it is the experience of all managers and heads of departments that *promotion* may have even more important consequences, both for the man himself and for the business. Strange as it may sound, it is sometimes an actual injustice to a man to advance him. If he is promoted too rapidly, or is put into a position for which he is not fitted,

---

Nervous energy is all right if it is expended in constructive action, in doing real things. But you have to be sure that the nervous man isn't the kind that simply stirs himself and everybody around him into a turmoil.

---

he may fail to make good; and that failure may be a setback from which he will never recover.

The power of promotion is one of the gravest responsibilities an employer has to meet. If he makes a mistake, he not only does harm to the business but he also hurts the man he has advanced. Out of mere justice to his men, therefore, an employer should be careful in picking the ones he promotes.

When a man does fail to make good after promotion, I believe it is due to one of two causes: He may have been a success in a minor position, but is out of his depth in a higher one. He has been able to see clearly when he has had only one line of action to consider, but when he has to get "the big picture," he can't do it. He fumbles around, making decisions simply because he must do something or be hopelessly stalled.

A business won't stand still and wait while you dally around, wondering what to do. The different departments are like several horses pulling the same wagon. If one of them stops, the wagon is on his heels and the whole thing piles up in confusion. All of the departments are interdependent. You must keep raw materials coming in steadily to feed production. Labor and machinery must be provided to handle raw materials. Sales must take care of the production, and distribution must keep the current moving between these two. One department cannot slow up without affecting all the others. A man may fail, therefore, because he can't keep the pace or isn't big enough for the job.

But when this happens, when a man has been advanced and fails to make good, his career in that organization is generally ended. Not because the heads of it want to let him out, but because he doesn't want to drop back to his old place. You can't blame him. That is a pretty hard thing for a man to do. It hurts his pride and, whether rightly or wrongly, he thinks it hurts his standing with his associates.

I have had cases, however, where a man put his pride in his pocket, went back to the work which was congenial to him, and for which he was fitted, and in time made a greater success than was open to him in the line he had to give up. Because a man fails in one position is no disgrace. A baseball player may be a fine batter but a rotten pitcher. If he is tried out as a pitcher and fails, there is no reason for him to think his usefulness is ended. He may be worth even more as a batter—the thing he *is* fitted for.

One advantage in working with a big organization is that there are so many lines of activity in it that a man is pretty certain to find the one where he can make good. He can transfer within the organization; and if his ambition is greater than his pride, he will overcome an apparent setback

---

A business won't stand still and wait while you dally around, wondering what to do.

---

in one direction and forge ahead in another. But, because no man really enjoys a setback, and because it often discourages men and humiliates them, an employer is bound to be careful about promotion lest it may prove an injury rather than a benefit to an employee.

The other cause of this occasional failure to make good is that some men cannot stand success and the things which come with success, especially the added power over other men. It goes to their heads. They see themselves under a magnifying glass. They not only run their own job but jump over the fence and try to run some other man's job. The trouble with that type of man is not that he isn't equal to his work. He is big enough for the job. But he *thinks* he is *too* big for it.

An organization is fortunate when it has men in it who are big but have the wonderful faculty of keeping the brakes on their self-esteem. Some men are so sound and well balanced that they have the power of drawing strong men to them. They build up a force of live, enthusiastic, loyal co-workers; and I think they can do it because they have a reputation for justice and fair dealing. If a subordinate comes to them they give him a chance to talk. They don't take away his initiative by simply imposing their own will without any regard for him. They don't "spill their own ideas" in a rush and make him a mere machine.

A good executive has a certain amount of reserve. He gets other men's ideas but he doesn't do much talking about his own. The valuable executive is not expansive about his work; at least, not with his subordinates. He may be a good mixer, but he doesn't tell all he knows. He is fearless when it comes to action. But he is guarded when it is a matter of talk. He doesn't tell what he is *going* to do. He waits —and does it.

The man who is really valuable in an organization, whether he is a subordinate or an executive, is the one who realizes that it *is* an organization and that his own success must be built on the success of the men around him. You have got to pull with and for the other fellow. If you set a trained eight-oar college crew, for instance, to pull against one man in a boat by himself, there is no question as to which will go ahead of the other. Or, if you had the 'varsity eight in a race with eight other men who were pulling according to their own ideas, each with a different stroke, none of them paying much attention to the rest, the contest would be a joke.

The valuable executive is not expansive about his work; at least, not with his subordinates. . . . He doesn't tell what he is going to do. *He waits —and does it.*

It is just the same in business. You will go further and faster if you think about the man who is working with you. Some men are so anxious to get all the rewards for themselves that they defeat their own aims. A man who isn't willing to share his success with others won't have much success to put in his own pocket. That is why I like to know a man's attitude toward the people around him. If he hasn't any idea of team work, he would better stay in some minor position where it won't make so much difference if he does keep his eyes on just his own special job. For the higher a man goes, the more essential it is that he shall be able to cooperate with other men.

A man who wants to advance must learn two things about responsibility: He must learn to delegate certain duties to other men, holding them responsible for fulfilling these duties; and he must learn to hold *himself* responsible for his own work. The temptation is always "to pass the buck" to someone else.

Suppose a manager tells his immediate subordinate that he wants a certain thing done. Later, he finds that it hasn't been done and he calls for an explanation. The subordinate puts the blame on *his* subordinate; *he* puts it on somebody else; and so it goes: everybody "passing the buck" to the next one in the chain. A man must be responsible for himself and for the man below him; that man must feel the same double responsibility; and so on down the line.

It is an old saying that a chain is only as strong as its weakest link. A business organization is a series of these chains. If there are weak spots in any of them it impairs the strength of all the rest. Men who can't stand up and take responsibility are weak links.

One of the problems an executive has to face is how far he should go down into an organization in his active control of it. He knows that he should confine himself to the heads of departments and hold them responsible for everything that goes on under them—make them hunt for the weak spots in their particular chain. If he knows that things are going wrong in a department, he cannot send for a subordinate in that department and question him, because that would discredit the head of it. But if he makes a practice of going around through his plant, talking with the men everywhere, he can find out what is the trouble, and no one will know that he was hunting for a weak spot. Then he can talk things over with the responsible head.

I think most executives have to fight this temptation to go down into the organization themselves and deal directly with things. They have to train themselves not to do it. And this, by the way, is another point worth making. We talk about "the period of training," as if it were a sort of college course from which men were graduated with a diploma and a degree. Education doesn't end when a man leaves college, and neither does a man's business training end at any fixed point. I am learning things now as much as I ever did. And I am certain of one thing—no man can expect to train others if he has not trained himself.

I believe that the war will prove to have accomplished a splendid work in just this respect. The men who have gone into the army have learned things which will be of definite value to them in business. Thousands of them who did not appreciate the part which discipline and order and obedience play in the work of an organization are realizing it now as they see how essential it has been to the success of the army. They have learned team work on a gigantic scale. They have learned to take orders, to give orders, and to put things *across*. Some people have feared that our boys would be demoralized, from a business point of view, by this interruption of their civil life. I look for just the opposite result.

Take the one question of orderliness. My boy's room at college used to look as if a cyclone had gone through it. I tried to make him feel that an orderly room indicated an orderly mind. But I can't claim to have been very successful. Uncle Sam, however, has taught him, and a few million other young men, that lesson, and others even more important. Instead of their period of military service being a misfortune to them I think it is going to send back into the realm of business a mass of trained, self-reliant, energetic, healthy young men who will be invaluable in meeting the great problems coming after the war. One thing alone—the broadening of their ideas through this experience in other countries—will make them especially helpful in handling the export business, which is going to be of greater importance in this country than ever before.

No one can dismiss the subject of men as we see them in business without speaking of a certain class which is always saying: "What about *me?*" I refer to the men who tell you how long and how faithfully they have worked without getting anywhere in particular. They can't see where they have failed in themselves, and so they put the blame on circumstances, or on their employers. They say: "Everything was against me."

Well, hard work and faithful work isn't everything. Did you ever see a horse in threshing season on the farm? *He* works hard and faithfully; but he doesn't get anywhere! He goes round and round in his little circle. He puts in so many hours a day and keeps right on plugging. He is fed and watered, and goes back to his stall at night, and that's all there is to it.

There are thousands of men who work just that way. As a rule, I believe that the trouble with them is that they haven't any goal. They have not picked out an object to attain. The horse cannot help himself. He has no power of choice and of initiative. But the fine thing about a human being is that he *can* choose his goal, and set out to attain it, if he has the will and the necessary courage. If you find that you are going around in a little routine circle, your head down, just plugging, the only thing for you to do is to look around you, pick out a definite goal which you want to reach, and begin traveling toward it. It may not be some remote and difficult peak. It may be simply the top of the nearest hill. There are not many "air-lines" in business. It is a matter of climbing, not soaring. The essential thing is to pick out an objective and try to reach it. When you have gained that one, you can pick out the next higher one, and begin climbing toward that. But a man must have *some* goal to work for, or he is not likely to do much traveling.

We are always talking about "success," and we are likely to regard money as the gauge by which to measure it. In one way, money really is a good gauge, but I don't think it is always applied in the right way. I think the comparison should be made within the *same* class of work and not between *different* classes. I mean that we should compare a salesman with other salesmen, a clerk with other clerks, a banker with other bankers, and so on. We should not compare a clerk with a banker, a salesman with a manufacturer, an engineer with a merchant.

Ability is really merchandise. And the rarer the particular kind of ability, the higher the price it brings. Executives are scarcer than manual laborers. Inevitably, therefore, they command a higher price. If manual skill were scarcer than executive ability, the market price would be reversed.

But when you measure one man's success by comparing it with the success of a man in another kind of work, it is like comparing the relative price of, say, apples and cabbages. If you want to estimate the value of an apple, you must compare it with other fruits. Cabbages should be compared with other vegetables. And so on.

Ambition is something more than looking *at the point you want to reach. Ambition is taking off your coat and pulling and dragging your boat up the stream.*

If you want to determine the quality of your own success, compare yourself with the men who are doing the same kind of work you have set yourself to accomplish. What you are doing now may be only one stage of your progress. But if you are doing better work at this stage than others are, you are succeeding. If you are doing the work you are happy in and fitted for, the kind of work you want to stay in, and are doing it better than anybody else, I think you are a success. You may be plowing a field, or making a tire, or keeping a set of books. Whatever it is, if you are doing it to the top notch of skill and efficiency, and if it is the thing you are best fitted for, you are achieving success. And, using money as the gauge, you will almost certainly register higher than the men who are doing the same work less competently.

I think a truer measure of success, however, is accomplishment. Certainly it is a deeper source of satisfaction than money is. The man or the woman who doesn't accomplish anything doesn't get much out of life. I believe most men will make good if they find the work they are happy in doing.

The mere routine job-holders may seem to disprove my theory, but I don't think so. The fact is *they* are happy in just drifting. They go on year after year, in some minor position, always thinking they are *going* to pull up to something better, but never doing it. They are quite comfortable, the job is easy for them, and they just drift along. They don't get hold of the oars and brace themselves and pull up the stream with every ounce of energy. The drifters slip along until they float into some quiet by-water, or they go over the falls—and that is the end of them. Ambition is something more than *looking* at the point you want to reach. Ambition is taking off your coat and pulling and dragging your boat up the stream.

HAROLD GENEEN
1910 –

If Star Trek's Spock were to have a business management philosophy, it would be embodied by Geneen. The accounting and finance major was truly able to separate the profit motive from emotions. Pure logic ruled his world. When he was tapped for ITT's presidency in 1959, more than 80 percent of the multinational's revenues were derived overseas. Geneen, who deplored surprises, viewed Europe and the world at large as extremely unstable. His solution was a fast-paced game of divestiture and acquisition in order to become at least 50 percent reliant on more stable U.S. markets. In the process, he managed to pump annual sales from $766 million to $22 billion over time (putting a fair amount of loose change in his own pocket). He also inflicted on his people a doctrine and discipline that has been likened to the Catholic Church or the Communist Party—take your pick.

The rhetoric Geneen used was certainly militaristic, as he expected his managers to follow "a philosophy of aggressive anticipation of goals and problems and of effective advanced counteractions to insure our attainment of final objectives." Ultimately, Geneen understood that for a true multinational conglomerate to operate efficiently, control was everything. His managers were subject to continuous scrutiny within a system of checks and balances. For Geneen, "the highest art of professional management requires the literal ability to 'smell' a 'real fact' from all others." And when it came to reviewing his operations, he had a nose like an anteater. The French even labeled him "The Michelangelo of Management."

Perhaps in response to the critics' attacks on his autocratic methods, Geneen included a section on egotism in his book, *Managing,* that is reprinted in the selection that follows. In it he compares egotism to a disease more destructive than alcoholism and states that all levels of management are subject to it, not just the CEOs. Although Geneen warns against egotism, he also points out "A good measure of self-esteem and confidence is essential to anyone who would be a leader. . . ."

Not Alcoholism — Egotism
Harold Geneen

No matter how high one puts the figure, I am certain that the cost of alcoholism to American business is only a small fraction of the price companies pay for the phenomenon I think of as executive egotism. It is a problem as old as alcoholism, with probably the same roots growing out of deep personal insecurity. While egotism does not directly affect the health of the individual, it certainly can influence the well-being of the corporation, the people in it, and, by ripple effect, the productivity of an entire country. Potentially, it is much more dangerous than alcoholism to the well-being of a company. Unlike alcoholism, however, the problem of the executive egotist is *still* in the closet, a secret everyone knows, few talk about, and almost no one knows how to handle.

Whether in middle management or top management, unbridled personal egotism blindsides a man to the realities around him; more and more he comes to live in a world of his own imagination; and because he sincerely believes he can do no wrong, he becomes a menace to the men and women who have to work under his direction. Where such behavior impinges upon corporate or business affairs, the problem of how to handle an egotist is every bit as serious as that of alcoholism. The egotist may walk and talk and smile like everyone else; still, he is impaired as much by his narcissism as the alcoholic is by his martinis. He becomes unwilling to accept information which is contrary to some preconceived notion or image of himself held in his mind. The supreme egotist in corporate life believes that he is smarter than everyone else around him, that he is somehow "ordained" from on high to know the answer to everything, that he is in control and everyone else is there to serve him. To my mind, he is sick.

This kind of egotism is a far cry from the normal pride or self-esteem that resides in the heart of every man who has ever achieved anything. A good measure of self-esteem and confidence is essential to anyone who would be a leader, in corporate life or elsewhere. The corporate leader needs to exert his own personality in order to motivate people in the direction of an objective which, right or wrong, appears to him to be correct. But his leadership in getting things off dead center and moving is always subject to correction. He must be willing to admit a mistake, willing to listen to other points of view. Without trying to sound like a psychologist, it seems to me perfectly obvious that any normal person would remember his

---

Whether in middle management or top management, unbridled personal egotism blindsides a man to the realities around him; . . . and . . . he becomes a menace . . .

---

own humble beginnings, his mistakes of the past, and be open to criticism (even if he did not like it). He would want to be realistic in seeking the facts which would lead him to the best available answers. No matter how smart he thought he was, he would know that he was fallible, as well as susceptible to doubts and uncertainties. He welcomes ideas, suggestions, and information from others. He is aware and sensitive to what is going on around him. That would be normal.

Most executives I know strive not to be or to appear egotistical. Logic, purpose, objectivity are the qualities most managers seek to bring to the fore: good business is based upon those elements. The good executive screens his actions for any hint of personal prejudices and vanity. He does not become overly concerned about where he sits in a meeting or whether or not people rise when he enters a room. On the other hand, he won't allow anyone else to push his way ahead of him because he has to play the role that his position demands, lest he be seen as a soft leader. It is largely a matter of self-identity. It is one thing to know who and what you are, and quite another to go about *seeking* praise and adulation. Of course, everyone likes praise and becomes defensive when criticized. I've gone overboard on occasion in pushing my convictions upon a subordinate when I disagreed with him. But when it turns out that I was wrong, I go out of my way to make amends with that man either publicly or privately and I take corrective action for the future. Perhaps the fine line of distinction between self-identity and egotism is difficult to explain, but everyone involved can sense the difference.

It is often difficult to distinguish normal pride from egotism, particularly in the early stages of the symptoms. That is equally true of alcoholism. A pleasant drink at lunch does not make a man an alcoholic. Does two drinks indicate that he is on the road to oblivion? Would you pin a label on the man who had three martinis at lunch? It may be the first and only time that man has had three drinks at lunch. It is not the numbers that count, but the facts behind the numbers, the pattern in the behavior.

The successful corporate executive who has worked his way up the ranks takes pride in a well-appointed office, the use of a company car or a chauffeured limousine. There's nothing wrong with that. The corporate airplane does save him valuable time and energy. He would be less than normal if he did not enjoy reading about his or his company's accomplishments in the daily press or the weekly magazines. Nothing wrong with that at all.

But I have seen grown men become absolutely distraught and almost hysterical because the color of the carpet in their office was not the right shade, or the view from their window was not the view they wanted. Some of these men were second- and third-layer management. Vanity and egotism are not confined to chief executive officers. At the top

---

The good executive screens his actions for any hint of personal prejudices and vanity. He does not become overly concerned about where he sits in a meeting or whether or not people rise when he enters a room.

---

level, I've known some chief executives to compete with one another in the length and model of their limousines. In corporate aircraft, the Gulfstream III is now the status symbol, whether or not that particular plane fits the real needs of a company. The use of the Gulfstream III is defended on the grounds of "the company's image." Some companies compete for "image" with as much force and energy as they do for earnings, market share, and stock market price. That is ego gratification. I've heard a chief executive complain bitterly because another chief executive was getting a better "press" than he was. I've known of men who measure the space, rather than the content, of articles given to their companies in the New York *Times*. Some corporate vice presidents of public relations earn their keep both by competing in the market for column inches and by coddling and feeding the egos of their chief executives.

One should be gratified, I suppose, if the press seeks you out for your opinions, expertise, or whatever on a current general problem in your field, or if you are invited to address a convention of your peers and to impart the wisdom of your experience. If you are the head of a large public corporation, a certain amount of public service is expected of you. You are asked to give your time — really the company's time — to this or that needy cause. We all have our obligations to the well-being of society. Those of us who can should give. But it should always be recognized that such contributions come from the corporation and its shareholders. The time you give is taken away from the time you would otherwise be spending on company business and for which you are being paid by the shareholders. Even if your speech is given during the luncheon break or after business hours, a professional manager is paid for his full time, not nine to five. A speech, a fund drive, or a civic service venture, done well, consumes considerably more time in preparation and planning than the event itself. Again, there is nothing wrong in any of this, so long as one is realistic about the cost of the contribution. It is one thing to fulfill one's service obligations to the community; it's quite another to overdo such outside activities for personal recognition and adulation.

In recent years there has been more and more competition among business executives for recognition in such ventures beyond the call of business. They become ventures in ego massage. For the sweet sound of applause, for praise and personal recognition, many business executives devote inordinate amounts of time to outside activities, delegating to others the supposedly "routine" responsibilities of their businesses. Their egos have made them blind to the reality that their first and primary responsibility is to the company that signs their paycheck.

I remember one man who headed a major corporation for about twenty years who became so enamored of his own success and the benefits of scientific management that he spent an enormous part of his time going about the country making speeches on the subject. He was quoted widely in the press as the leading spokesman on the new age of scientific management. Behind his back, however, he became a joke inside and outside of his company because while he was out making speeches, it was obvious that he was not running his own company. It got to a point where he was spending more time speaking than showing up in his office. Probably he was unaware of what was happening; his ego had taken over. The end result was that his company got rid of him. His board of directors gave other reasons for his dismissal, of course, but his case was so egregious and well known that no one was fooled.

The cost and harm of ego inflation to the companies involved go far beyond lost work hours. That is like measuring the cost of alcoholism by the rate of absenteeism. At the management level, the alcoholic can do far more harm on the job than if he slept it off at home. The same is true of the egotist. All those ego-feeding activities—the long hours in the limousine, the skylarking in the corporate jet, the collecting of press clippings, the unnecessary speeches—feed the sickness and one way or another make a corporate problem out of what had been an otherwise perfectly competent, even brilliant executive.

The real harm is that unbridled personal vanity takes over, very much the way liquor claims the alcoholic, and the man involved becomes a victim of his own egotism. He begins to believe his own press releases and the accolades arranged for him by his own public relations people. He becomes so involved with himself and his own vanity that he loses his sensitivity to the feelings of others. He loses his common sense and objectivity. He becomes a potential menace in the decision-making process. All this does not become immediately apparent around the office. The egotist does not stumble about, knocking things off his desk. He does not stammer or drool. No, instead he becomes more and more arrogant, and some people, not knowing what is underneath such an attitude, mistake his arrogance for a sense of power and self-confidence.

But he cannot fool the people around him for long. That egotistic arrogance has a corrosive effect upon everyone who has to deal with him. While people tend to pity and sympathize with the plight of the alcoholic, they have the opposite feelings about the egotistical boss in their midst. They resent the boss who is cold, aloof, and all-knowing. They ridicule him behind his back and try to work around him. They see through him and recognize that his pose does not make him

---

Some companies compete for "image" with as much force and energy as they do for earnings, market share, and stock market price. That is ego gratification.

---

the leader he pretends to be. Once that happens, the whole structure and momentum of a management team, indeed the whole company, begins to fall apart. Oftentimes, the egotistical boss will sense that something is wrong, although he will never recognize the cause; he will press harder for the respect and adulation of his subordinates, and the more he presses, the less he receives. Thus, he becomes more arrogant and demagogic in his demands. His people resent him more and more. The situation becomes worse with time. As the management team is divided into enemy camps, the head man begins to surround himself with sycophants. He can tolerate only yes men.

It does not take long for this kind of attitude to work its way down through an organization. That kind of egotism will demean and destroy the collective effort of a company's management team. People become very wary of bringing such a boss any kind of bad news. He is too likely to shoot the messenger. In turn, that will have a curdling effect upon any degree of open communications in a company. Consciously or subconsciously, no one wants to take issue, much less argue, with a boss like that. He is as likely to fly off the handle and rant and rave as the worst alcoholic. No one can be sure what he will do. He is, as they say, drunk with power. His mind is set. His attitude is that he, not you, is the chief, his is the greatest brain in the world, so it must follow that if he decides to do something it must be right. He will announce his decisions, handing down manifestos in effect: "We will do this and we are going to do that and don't tell me that it's wrong, because you people don't know beans about the situation, and I do!" Obviously, the man has become an egotistical maniac, as out of touch with reality as the alcoholic. And in business as in life, reality has a way of catching up with people.

The egotist is a much more difficult executive to deal with than an alcoholic. Perhaps on the department or even division level of management someone could step in and quash such disquieting arrogance. But in the upper corridors of power it is extremely difficult to deal with unbridled egotism. Subordinates have to cope with it by "handling" such a boss gingerly. They will stifle their own innovative ideas in order to get along with him. They will offer only the mildest debate on any issue. They will learn how to cater to his whims, agree with him, praise him. They know or suspect that his decisions are based more upon personal considerations than on realism, objectivity, or facts. Pet projects get priority. Decisions which are almost impossible to implement are passed down to the troops and no one on the line understands the reason behind those decisions. They resent it like hell. At the peer level, whether it is the chief executive officer or a member of the board of directors, people generally are aware of enormous ego problems, but they don't know how to measure or to cope with them.

One situation in which a man's ego became caught in a large merger negotiation cost his company more than $100 million. Heading a team of negotiators, this man was so arrogant and insensitive to others in his approach to the transaction that the price of purchase rose more than $100 million from what it should have been. Everyone on his team was aware of what was happening—everyone, that is, except the man himself and he was their chief executive. Yet there was no way to quantify or to certify the intangibles involved. It is very difficult to fire a man because of his ego. The man's explanation to his board of directors was reasonable: he blamed the unreasonableness of the other side. Perhaps some of the board members suspected the truth, but no one raised a question about his handling of the merger. If they had learned, on the other hand, that the man had been drunk and had lost the company $100 million, or $50 million, or even $25 million, he probably would have been fired on the spot. But could anyone question an ego?

That may seem an extreme example. But such situations occur time and time again, even in lesser degree, and somehow no one attempts to put a price tag upon the number of deals that fell through because of one man's overextended ego, the amount of business lost because outsiders chose not to deal at all with a self-styled demigod. No one has as yet devised a reasonable basis for measuring what a company should have accomplished as opposed to what it did accomplish and how much of that lost potential was caused by the blinded, closed minds of men wrapped in self-love.

... the loss in performance, productivity, earnings in any company, division, or department subjected to the wiles and whims of an egotistical corporate executive would approach at least 40 percent.

Not until he is far gone does the egotist reveal plainly his overbloated opinion of himself. Like the alcoholic, he usually is adept at hiding his secret vice, covering his true thoughts by acting out the prescribed, correct behavior of executives on his level. But, as I said, reality catches up with him. Ultimately, it catches up with him in the performance of his department, his division, or his company. It cannot be otherwise, because the egotist, as a manager, is *impaired* in his judgments, in his relationships with others, in his ability to function.

I have the feeling that, generally speaking, people tend to tolerate this kind of egotism, where they would not tolerate a similar degree of alcoholism, because they have absolutely no idea of the very, very high cost it represents. I have no way of measuring it either, but from personal observations I would guess that the loss in performance, productivity, earnings in any company, division, or department subjected to the wiles and whims of an egotistical corporate executive would approach at least 40 percent. In other words, if it were not for that malfunctioning, damaging executive egotism, one might expect a 40 percent improvement across the board. The cost in lost performance is enormous.

If only people would recognize egotism as a disease, more could be done about it. But the vagueness and lack of measurement associated with a narcissistic personality have allowed this cause of mismanagement to continue as a secret loss in the business world. I suspect that it will continue to be tolerated.

Excess egotism is oftentimes based upon the utter fear of failure. Most people spend a good deal of their time developing skills to defend themselves against what they see as "failure." I don't think they really know what "failure" means,

---

Can you guard against the virus of personal egotism? Can you view with perspective the flattery and praise of sycophants? Can you discard the pleasant aspects of your position in the company for the more realistic problems facing you, which may be unpleasant?

---

only that they want no part of it. However, it is my observation that more people and more careers are "ruined" by success than by failure. I have seen people fail at one or another point in their careers, and go on to greater success than they had ever envisioned before.

People learn from their failures. Seldom do they learn anything from success. Most people do not spend any more time defining for themselves what "success" means than they do with "failure." I've seen absolutely sound, sensible, modest people go "bananas" when suddenly elevated to heights of power not formerly experienced. Reaching the starting gate of a new position is regarded by them as having arrived at their destination. They stop moving forward and bask in the sunshine of their prominence. Unfortunately, in the business environment, the performance of a top manager cannot be determined in his first year or two, or three. Such a man can devote his time to so-called broad concepts, theories, and fancy explanations. If he is close to retirement, he knows he will be long gone before his mark on the company can be evaluated. So how can he lose? He is the only one in the race. So he sees his role as guarding his image and he begins to believe his press clippings.

On a personal, individual level, the question becomes: Can you handle success? Can you guard against the virus of personal egotism? Can you view with perspective the flattery and praise of sycophants? Can you discard the pleasant aspects of your position in the company for the more realistic problems facing you, which may be unpleasant?

Success, it seems to me, is much more difficult to deal with than failure, because only you will know how you are handling it!

HORACE GREELEY
1811 – 1872

The legend surrounding Greeley varies greatly, from proclaiming him as obscenely rude, disheveled, and eccentric to being infectiously enthusiastic and a noble soldier for social reform. In depicting Greeley, a competitive editor said that he "is self-educated, and very imperfectly at that—has no great grasp of mind, no great political insight, and has his brain crammed with half truths and odds and ends of ideas." Little did the editor know that one day Greeley would have educational institutions named after him. Greeley's roots were in fact extremely modest, and his youth was spent on a run-down farm. He readily admitted that his father was slow and ignorant and that his mother was the kind of woman who could "outrake any man in town." Of himself Greeley proudly said, "I can write better slang than any editor in America." And the style worked.

After launching the *New Yorker* in 1834, and then the *New York Tribune* in 1841, Greeley found his groove as he fought for the underclass and emancipation. His fiery editorials labeled proslavery factions as "traitorous scamps" and "vagabond repudiators of obligations most sacred," and he almost single-handedly roused the North against slavery. His bold language sprung from the belief that an editor must "entertain and inspire." He also correctly surmised that "the subject of deepest interest to an average human being is himself." By combining poignant copy with his business philosophy that to succeed you must be adventurous, resourceful, and committed to the community, his *Tribune* became one of the loudest voices in a deafening New York.

Greeley's most famous homily is, of course, "Go West young man, go West!" In addition to this statement of where to seek opportunity in terms of geography, he had more tangible thoughts on succeeding in business. In the following selection, which is excerpted from a speech Greeley delivered, he defines the necessary characteristics of a "true business man." Although some of his colloquialisms suggest the prudish idealism of his time, his message is equally poignant over 100 years later.

Success in Business
Horace Greeley

I f I were asked to define a business man, I should say he was one who knew how to set other people's fingers at work—possibly their heads, also—to his own profit and theirs.

This may be in trade, it may be in manufactures, it may be in the mechanical arts, or in agriculture; but wherever the man, who, stepping into a new and partially employed community, knows how to set new wheels running, axes plying, and reapers and mowers in motion, and so of all the various machinery of production, transformation and distribution, or any part of it—he who knows how to do this with advantage to the community (as he can scarcely fail to do it), and with reasonable profit also to himself, that man is a business man, though he may not know how to read, even; though he may have no money when he commences; though he has simply the capacity—which some possess and more men aspire to—to make himself a sort of driving-wheel to all that machinery. If he has this, he is a true business man, although he may never have received anything more than the rudest common-school education. I have such men in my eye now; and they were not capitalists, the men I think of. They ultimately became so by means of business, but they did not become business men by means of their capital. . . .

THE ACQUIREMENT OF WEALTH

If I have been understood in this to give an undue prominence to the acquirement of wealth, I need only say that I have never considered the acquisition of an immense fortune desirable; but this I do hold, that thrift, within reasonable limits, is the moral obligation of every man; that he should endeavor and aspire to be a little better off at the close of each year. I never could sympathize with a large class who

---

There is now and then a case of brilliant rascality known among us; and . . . we are inclined, some of us, to admire it; but, after all, there are no cases, . . . wherein roguery has led to fortune.

---

are fond of saying, "I am proud of being a poor man." Doubtless, misfortune, calamity, sickness, heavy burdens, may justify men in being poor to the last days of their lives; but, after all, this universe is not bankrupt—we are not sent into it to fight a losing battle. It is possible, nay, it is feasible, for every man to be thrifty if he will be frugal, not only in his expenditures, but in the use of his time. If his time and means are profitably employed, I say there is no need of his being poor and needy to the end of life.

ELEMENTS OF BUSINESS SUCCESS

I close, then, with some suggestions as to what I consider the bases of a true business career—those which give reasonable assurance of a true business success. I place first among these, integrity; because I believe that there is to-day a good deal of misapprehension on this point. There is now and then a case of brilliant rascality known among us; and we hear of this, and talk of it; we are inclined, some of us, to admire it; but, after all, there are no cases, except very exceptional cases, wherein roguery has led to fortune. The rule is almost absolute, that our thrifty men have been essentially upright men. You will find few cases where the dishonest man has continuously flourished. There have been cases of his temporary, transient, meteoric success; but the rule is very uniform in its operation, that business success has been based on a broad platform of integrity. Next to that, I would place frugality, on which I have said as much as I mean to say. And next, general capacity—I mean natural capacity. I venture to say that all our successful men in business have been men of strong, original minds. It is perfectly idle, the popular conception that fortune goes by luck, or that weak men make it. Weak men make money. They do so in very rare instances; and there are abundant cases where strong men, having other desires, other aspirations, have not sought wealth. The rule is very general, however, that the men who have succeeded have been men of very strong natural powers. Then comes training—general and special education and system—and after that the energy of continuous application. There is nothing else wherein the rolling stone is so bare of moss as in business. The true business man must have the power of persistency in discouragement—of keeping on continuously in a good track, sure that he will come to the right result at last.

HENRY R. LUCE
1898 – 1967

In the 1950s Luce's magazines were increasingly accused of being "masterpieces of bias," and he the king of propaganda. His response was, "I am a Protestant, a Republican and a free enterpriser, which means I am biased in favor of God, Eisenhower and the stockholders of Time Inc.—and if anybody who objects doesn't know this by now, why the hell are they still spending 35 cents for the magazine." Luce was not short on opinion when it came to running his business, which included *Time* (founded 1923), *Fortune* (1930), *Life* (1936), and *Sports Illustrated* (1954). In selecting his staffs, he "forbade expertise," and instead opted for youth and enthusiasm, people who could keep up with his chain-smoking, shotgun speaking, high-energy persona. For example, he hired Archibald MacLeish, the respected poet, to report on business in *Fortune.*

Luce's view of the world was from the unique perspective of having been born to missionary parents in China. During the Boxer rebellion of 1900, the family barely escaped the massacre, but returned to continue their work. For the first 14 years of his life, Luce's image of America was influenced by glorious tales of Theodore Roosevelt and the country's God-given right to civilize the world. He then came to live in America, attended Yale University, and started to think for himself. Yale, at the time, was an institution described by one professor as educating "specifically for the harsh competitions of capitalism, for the successful and often unscrupulous pursuit by the individual of power for himself. . . ." Luce now had more than God and country to think about; there was money, too.

Yale's gospel of success was quickly adopted by Luce, who once remarked, "Business is what we [in America] believe in more than any other agency of society. . . . [B]usiness will never be run on a democratic basis. . . . [B]usiness must be aristocratic. There must be a top and, if possible, the best man must get there." And yet, the Christian values of Luce's religious upbringing remained an integral component to his model businessperson. In *The Character of the Businessman,* he explains what it means to be both virtuous and successful in the "Age of Abundance."

The Character of the Businessman
Henry R. Luce

T wenty-five years ago, Alfred
North Whitehead gave a lecture on "Foresight" at the Harvard Business School. In it he said: "A great society is a society in which its men of business think greatly of their functions."

If we are to have an Age of Abundance, the businessman must be worthy of his great vocation. He must be worthy of this calling in two senses: first, in the sense of his own personal character; second, in the sense of the general character of the worldwide fraternity of businessmen. You are responsible for yourself; you are also your brother's keeper. Let me put the matter more bluntly. In my judgment we shall win or lose the Age of Abundance to the degree that the businessman exhibits two basic virtues. The first is honesty— downright, old-fashioned truthtelling. The second is that businessmen must have clear convictions about the kind of society, the kind of system they want, and they must be willing to stand up and fight for these convictions. The businessman must have courage—the courage of his convictions.

Before dealing with these two virtues in the modern application, let us pause a moment to consider the character and reputation of the businessman generally in history. Perhaps the first thing to be said is that, at most times and places, the businessman has not been an attractive figure. The word "bourgeois" springs to mind. I was shocked the other day when I looked up the meaning of the word in Webster's dictionary. Let me say that I consider myself a bourgeois. And here is what I read about myself in Webster's:

> *Bourgeois* 1. Characteristic of the middle class. Hence: *a* Engrossed in material things; Philistine; often, conservative; hidebound. *b Colloq.* Common; boorish; stupid. *c* Capitalistic.

A shock indeed: to look into the mirror of a dictionary and find such an ugly face. In my dismay I rushed like a wounded child to the scholars. How could this be? I had been proud of my bourgeois ancestors. Was it not they who overthrew feudalism, formed the great nation-states of Europe under kings and emperors, and then overthrew the kings and emperors when kings and emperors stood in the way of human progress? Were not the burghers identified for 500 years—in France, in Holland and elsewhere—with the rise of the cities and their civilization, with parliamentary rule, with liberty under law, with exploration and discovery, with science and literacy?

The scholars came to my rescue—especially the Reverend Father R. L. Bruckberger,* a French Dominican who knows and loves both Europe and America. Father Bruckberger explained many things which I can but touch on here. For one thing he explained that it was Karl Marx and the *Communist Manifesto* that finally made "bourgeois" a dirty, stinking word. But what he was mainly concerned to explain was that in the word "bourgeois" you find just about the deepest difference between the experience of the Europeans and the experience of the Americans in the 300 years since my own ancestors crossed the sea. And, of course, in America we do not actually use the word "bourgeois"—except in

*Author of *One Sky to Share* (1956) and *Image of America* (1959).

little literary reviews; in America we say "middle class." We are a middle-class, that is to say a classless, country.

The businessman in America today enjoys a good enough position in our vast middle-class society—and it is, I think, important, even necessary, that the businessman in other countries should be respected and should feel at home in the nations that are everywhere being born or renewed.

But there is something else the businessman must realize: though generally in the past he has been associated with the rise of freedom and the progress of civilization, he has only a mediocre record in modern politics. Too many German businessmen were associated with Hitler. Too many businessmen were hand in glove with Fascism in Italy and elsewhere. Too many Japanese businessmen took the way of the sword. Too many American businessmen were isolationists before the war. In the past decade too few businessmen have really fought against Communism. Perhaps the most sensational record of political stupidity was made by the businessmen of Shanghai; they thought it would make no difference if Communists took over China. So now there aren't any Shanghai businessmen. No, the modern political record of businessmen is not good.

Now, to be sure, it is not the businessmen who run the politics of their nation or the world; they have their own vast and onerous job to do. But I do plead that in the coming Age of Abundance the businessman must learn a little greater wisdom about politics.

The whole business of the businessman is changing, and he with it. His ranks are being strengthened, not only by new risk-takers in the direct bourgeois line, but by the rise of the industrial manager. This new man, native to the age of large corporations and high taxes, has merged his high standards of efficiency with the capital of ownership, in such a way that business today has many attributes of a profession, and the businessman is or ought to be a respected servant of society well worthy of his hire. Owners and managers alike add luster to this new title of businessman.

I have said that I would speak of just two virtues. The first is honesty. This is an old-fashioned virtue—perhaps even a *bourgeois* virtue. We need it now more than ever—and in broader terms than ever before. As one travels around the world, or as one listens to businessmen speaking of doing business in various countries, one is appalled by the amount of dishonesty that infects the so-called free world. In so many places, bribery is taken for granted. In so many places, cheating on taxes is accepted as part of the way of life. I urge businessmen to stand against all this cheating. Of course, governments bear their heavy share of guilt for the dishonesty in the world. Historically it is governments that have been the great robbers of the people—through inflation and other forms of misgovernment. The Soviet Government has just publicly enacted the biggest steal of the decade; by defaulting payments on Soviet bonds, it robbed a generation of Russian workers of their alleged savings. Governments rob by inflation and by expropriation, but also each and every government restriction in the field of economics is an invitation to dishonesty. I ask businessmen to protest against all forms of corruption, legal corruption as well as illegal. I ask businessmen to refuse, even at personal cost, to participate in corruption.

The concept of honesty is necessarily broadened in our time. The radical doctrine I hold is that all business is invested with a public interest. Therefore all business must be open to public inspection. The annual reports of corporations should be models of candor even beyond the demands of legitimate public curiosity. The businessman's pride should lie in the fact that his every transaction can withstand the scrutiny of the law courts and the historians, and above all the daily scrutiny of his own conscience. The consequences of such open honesty will be so profound they cannot be exaggerated. For what the world needs today more than anything else is good faith and credence between man and man, between class and class (where classes exist), between nation and nation. Let us determine that we will so act as to establish, across all boundaries, one great web and frame of common honesty, openly demonstrated and proudly proclaimed.

I come now to the second great and immemorial virtue that the businessman is specially called on to display—the courage of his convictions. I assume all honest businessmen share a common belief in business—a belief, that is, that business is an honorable occupation, and that the best way to develop wealth and to spread it is through business. I suppose that most of us would agree that one great condition of healthy business is that our society should have a dependable currency, *sound* money. But do businessmen, even bankers, really fight for this absolute condition of our business economy? In my own country there are general cheers when the Federal Reserve Board relaxes credit. But when it tightens credit and thus tries to keep the boom under control, there is apt to be large outcry. Someone, it is said, is going to get *hurt*. Of course that is so. But, I submit, it is far better for a few people to get momentarily hurt through decent fiscal and credit policies than for everybody to get hurt through inflation and subsequent collapse.

In our time we businessmen have sought many ways to define the system we stand for. We have called it free enterprise or the people's capitalism. Permit me to suggest an older definition. What we must stand for and fight for is the *free market*—not just a free market for Europe, but a free market for the world.

For the market *is* the heart of our system, and let us be clear what we mean by it. Assuredly we do not mean a condition where businessmen can do just as they please. Nor do we mean that there is no room for social welfare. What we do mean is a system under which the overwhelming proportion of the world's goods and services are produced and distributed, not by government edict, but rather in response to choices freely made in the marketplace. We mean a system where the consumer, who is Everyman, is able to register *what* he wants, and we businessmen and entrepreneurs are *forced* in seeking our own gain to serve the public will.

J. C. PENNEY
1875 – 1971

The son of a Baptist minister, Penney's first business venture as a butcher failed because he refused to supply meat to hotels that sold liquor. In 1902 he started working for a dry goods store in Kemmerer, Wyoming, and was eventually allowed to buy into one third of the business; this opportunity of part ownership would prove to be a key element in his future success. Eight years later he had opened 13 stores of his own, calling them the Golden Rule Stores (Penney insisted that his employees never touch tobacco or alcohol). In 1913 the name of the stores was changed to J. C. Penney, and by 1917 he was operating 175 stores.

The rapid growth and financial success was achieved in part by requiring the store managers to own 33 percent of their store, an early form of franchising. The arrangement provided Penney with financing and provided the managers with a stake in the business's success, the importance of which Penney had learned back in Kemmerer. Penney's most ingenious revolution was the creation of a central warehouse and corresponding inventory control system, which greatly increased buying power and reduced overhead costs. What Penney considered to be "one of the greatest economic advantages of the chain store form of organization" his managers fought in the beginning. They argued that only they could gauge the demand and tastes of their customers at a given location, and therefore, should retain control over inventory. Penney was pleased with their response and concern for their customers because it proved he had chosen the right people to manage his stores.

Penney looked for very particular qualities in the people he hired, even paying close attention to their facial expressions and body language during interviews. He describes these qualities in *It Is One Thing to Desire—and Another to Determine*. Penney also defines the fine line between merely wanting success and willing it to happen through the force of character.

It Is One Thing to Desire — and Another to Determine

J. C. Penney

Last year, I, as an employer, talked with at least five thousand applicants for jobs. Many of these men were not out of work. They already had positions, but they wanted to make a change.

Part of my problem in picking those I wanted out of this mass of applicants was to find what was at the bottom of their desire for a new position. For that desire may be a sign of weakness or it may be a sign of strength.

If I can get the truth about this one thing, I shall have a pretty good clue to a man's value in business. In response to my questions, he may unconsciously show that he can't stand criticism, that he resents being asked to work hard, that he hasn't the grit to live on a small salary until he has made himself worth a big one. He may not be able to get along with other men. He may be looking for a soft snap, an easy boss. If he is guilty of any of these things, I don't want him.

But, on the other hand, he may want to change because he has come to the conclusion, after an honest effort, that his present job holds no future for him. He is willing to start at the bottom, to work hard, to get along on small pay; but he wants to see footholds above him by which he can climb. He may be in business where the very top isn't much of a height itself. He wants to go higher and he is bound to do it. *That* kind of a desire for change is a sign of strength—if it doesn't stop at being merely a desire.

I have to study very often the type of man who sticks at an unpromising job until he loses all hope, all initiative. And I want to say right here, if you can't see any future in your work, get out! Take a position at a lower salary, if necessary. If you lack the courage to make the plunge, all right! Stay where you are. But blame yourself, then; don't blame the job. And remember that "desire" is not "determination." They begin with the same letter—but they don't end on the same pinnacle of success.

You notice that I said to get out if you can't see any future in your job. As a matter of fact, there is a future in most jobs. But it probably isn't there for *you*, if you can't *see* it. You must have a vision before you of something toward which you are striving. And if, even after opening your eyes and *honestly* looking for something worth attaining, you still can see nothing ahead—then you never will go far.

Many times I have been sick at heart over the crushed, discouraged men who have come to ask timidly for a position. Unhappy, hopeless, they feebly beat their wings against the bars, trying to escape from their prison. Had they made the attempt when they first realized that their job held no future for them, they probably would have succeeded. But they lacked the courage. When they came to me, they were still moved more by desire than by determination. They *wanted* rather than *willed*. And their attempt to escape was almost pitiful.

Don't misunderstand me. I do not mean to say that if you are middle-aged, discouraged, in a rut, it is impossible for you to get out of it. Although as a rule I prefer to hire young men, I have taken on middle-aged men who had got into a blind alley, but, through some revival of will and courage, had broken through the wall that blocked their way and had come to me for a chance to begin in another direction. And they made good. Courage is a quality which grows with use. It may take nerve to give up a position where you are doing fairly well and to take a lower one, somewhere else. But if you have courage and ambition you can do it. The breaking away is the hardest part. But the man who does it when it does cost him an effort has the right stuff in him. The man who makes a change just *for* a change is merely a floater.

Real success has never yet been obtained except through sacrifice. My job is to try to develop men into good merchants; and someone asked me the other day how these men could help themselves in this process of development. My reply was:

"By study, more study, and then some more study."

I had the opportunity recently to look over the records of a New York business school which trains men by correspondence, and I confess that I was amazed at what I found. On its lists were over 1,300 presidents of corporations! There were 2,500 vice presidents; 2,000 treasurers, 5,000 secretaries, and 11,000 managers. Do you realize what that means? Here were more than 20,000 men who had reached positions of high authority in business, but who were still

---

It may take nerve to give up a position where you are doing fairly well and to take a lower one, somewhere else. But if you have courage and ambition you can do it.

---

eager to learn, to study, in order to become more efficient. That's the kind of stuff in a man which keeps him growing. It is perhaps a platitude to say that what you do in business hours does not count as much as what you do outside of them. But, like most platitudes, there's a lot of truth in it.

From among the five thousand applicants I examined last year I picked a hundred men. I was choosing them with a view to making them partners in our stores, but I think most employers also want men with the qualities for which I was looking. Of course I am glad to have a man understand the business. But there is something much more important than technical knowledge, and that thing is character.

One of the first tests to which I put an applicant is to make our offer just as unattractive as possible. I tell him baldly that he will have long, hard hours of work. I describe the dull little towns in which he may have to live. I emphasize the small salary on which he must start. I make everything, *except* the ultimate goal of a partnership, as little tempting as possible. If the man is the kind that thinks through to the end, sees what he wants to gain, and is willing to pay the price for it, I'll find it out then and there. Men often smile, when I have painted the prospect in dreary colors, and say, "You can't frighten me. I want that job!" And if they are that kind, then we want them.

If they flinch at the picture I draw, they are not for us. Sometimes they hem and haw and say, "Well, of course, I have my wife to consider. I don't know how she'd feel about living in a little town."

When they talk like that I mentally reject them. Unless a wife is right behind her husband, encouraging him and spurring him on, she is more of a handicap than a helpmate. As a rule, a man with a nagging, selfish wife is not a success. He is discouraged and discontented. So when men suggest that their wives may protest, I agree with them—and they

---

Jesus and Moses were two of the greatest sales-men the world has ever known. Just take one of the Bible's stated principles — . . . and see how it applies to business.

---

pass out of the door. I want a man who knows that his wife will go through anything to aid him in achieving success.

Another quality which seems to me very important in a man is that he shall be fair and generous in his dealings with others. Recently I heard a story which illustrates my point: It seems that the manager of a chain store had run out of a certain line of goods and had appealed to the manager of another store in the chain for a share of the supply which this second man had on hand. This man consented—but sent some goods of poor quality which *he* had not been able to sell. He thought he was being very shrewd. But if I had the chance I would fire that man. He was not square. He hadn't the instinct of fair dealing. You can't build a solid, substantial house with decayed planks, no matter what kind of a veneer is put over their rottenness. That man's action was rotten, even though it was veneered with temporary shrewdness.

I am not orthodox, in a religious way, but I like to employ a man with what I should call the mind and morals of a Christian. Somehow I think a man is better anchored who has a belief in a Supreme Being. His idea may not be the same as mine, but if he has one that really *means* something to him I find that he has a steadiness which other men lack.

I think it is a good thing for a man, a business man, I mean, to know something about the Bible. I was past thirty before I discovered that the Bible was a pretty fine business textbook! I do not mean to be irreverent when I say that Jesus and Moses were two of the greatest salesmen the world has ever known. Just take one of the Bible's stated principles—and there are scores of others which might be picked out—and see how it applies to business. I refer to the declaration that if a man would be first among you, let him become your servant. That principle is at the foundation of business success. I think it would be a good idea if the business colleges would include the Bible in their list of textbooks. I suppose its value lies in the fact that it teaches character, which is the very fundamental of success.

In personal interviews I always study a man's face, because his character is more or less plainly written there. I don't measure his eyebrows, or say that because his ear is formed like that of a criminal he must be dishonest. But experience has shown me that it pays to study a man's face.

If he is furtive, sneaky, and unreliable, his eyes betray him by shifting constantly. If he is mean, spiteful, hard to please, his lips are thin and compressed. And while a receding chin may label wrongly a man who is really strong and forceful, it is usually the mark of indecisiveness.

I do not mean to say that these points are infallible. One of the most depraved men I have ever known could look me straight in the eye without batting an eyelash. But he was the exception that proves the rule.

One time when it pays to watch a man is when you ask for his references. If you do it suddenly and catch him off his guard, a man who has nothing to conceal answers without

---

Every employer is always looking for men who really love to work. Yet work alone is not enough to make a man truly successful.

---

hesitation that he has worked for So-and-so. When men hesitate and look embarrassed it is the time to begin wondering why they do not speak up at once. We often find that such men have been discharged for reasons which they know would influence us unfavorably.

Men who talk too much or who jump at the chance too eagerly, without asking questions about the work, are also the kind of men to avoid. A boaster and braggart rarely make good. And another thing: the man who changes jobs without knowing all about his new job is not displaying very much sense. A man should ask questions and show intelligent interest in his new work.

Because I want men who have self-confidence I watch for signs of nervousness and timidity. I have found that many men come to an interview of this sort with a feeling of "Well, I don't suppose I'll get the job, but I might as well try." Such men, of course, make pretty poor salesmen. They are the kind who lack initiative, dash, personality and, almost always, ability. We don't condemn a man just because he is nervous, of course, but we do expect his nervousness to wear off when he has been talking a few moments.

Of course what we especially want is what you might call partnership material. And to fit this requirement men must be workers and salesmen, but also able *and willing* to train other men. This is the way I put the scheme to them.

Suppose you come to one of our stores and, after you have proved your ability as a salesman, you become head man, or assistant to the manager. While you have been working there the manager who trained you has been seeking the opportunity to open new stores in other towns. When he finds the right town, he recommends you as the prospective manager of this new store. If we approve the recommendation, we then put you in charge of a tryout store. If you make good, you become manager of one of our stores with the privilege of buying a one-third interest with the money loaned to you by me, or the senior partner. In other words, you are now a partner in a store.

Now begins the working of the endless chain. You, as manager, must train a head man in *your store,* and in time recommend him as manager for another which *you* desire to open. When he is placed in charge and makes good in a tryout store, he is then sold a one-third interest in a new store, and, as manager, proceeds to train another man. In this way, new stores are constantly being opened.

Every employer is always looking for men who really love to work. Yet work alone is not enough to make a man truly successful. Thousands of men can echo that, some of them very bitterly. *They* have worked, they say, but have not reached any real height of success. Unorganized work, work performed without an eye always fixed on the ultimate goal, is generally futile. A writer has said that a man of ordinary mind, body, and attainments, if inspired by some high ideal, accomplishes far more in life than the man of the finest mental and physical equipment *who drifts.*

Unlike the famous epigram of the cowboy who said, "I have always liked my business, but it has never attracted my attention much," a man's business *must* attract his attention. History has shown us that everything really worth while was accomplished because something did attract someone's attention *very much*. When Herschel, the astronomer, was working with his instruments, he often refused to take his hands from his work, even to eat his supper. So, in order that his work might go on, his sister Caroline often fed him with her own hands. Meanwhile, Herschel himself was so absolutely absorbed in his work that he did not even know he was eating. It is that type of concentration and unswerving purpose that wins in life.

In training men we always start them on a small salary, partly because we want to see how they will manage on it. We figure out what it will cost a man to live in a small town, and in accordance with what the volume of business justifies. How he gets along is not only a clue to his character but it shows what his business capacity is. If he finds ways and means to eliminate waste in his own affairs, to practice economy, to get good value for every dollar of his income, it is fairly safe to conclude that he will be able to run a business on those same sound principles.

In training men we always start them on a small salary, partly because we want to see how they will manage on it. . . . How he gets along is not only a clue to his character but it shows what his business capacity is.

We even make our managers live within their salaries, without drawing on their profits. Some men in business often get their pockets mixed, you know. Instead of living on the money in their own pocket, they draw some from the pocket of their business. Instead of running the business as something distinct, they confuse themselves with the business, and soon begin to think that they and the business are one; that the profits can be used as desired, and that the current cash is always available for their needs or pleasure.

Some managers, for example, want to buy a home or an automobile with the profits of the first year or two of the business. They do not realize that, though they have earned their dividend, the profits must stay in the business until it has flourished sufficiently to warrant the drawing out of a few thousand dollars. In addition, managers are expected to take their profits and open up new stores in which to put their head men. But, unless they are saving, this cannot be done.

In training men we have the unusual advantage of being absolutely confident that our managers will help us in every way possible. It is to their interest to do so, you see, because until they have a man properly trained they cannot put him in charge of a store. Therefore they encourage and aid him in every way, whereas under other systems a manager who sees a man coming to the front worries for fear he will take his job away from him. Then, instead of aiding him, he either discharges him or holds him down as much as possible, this naturally being to the detriment of the business.

Yet, while hard work and determination are factors, there are other things which must be considered. We ask our men if they are going along doing every day the things they did yesterday in the same old way, or whether they are studying, trying to improve themselves in order to prepare for the larger duties and responsibilities which may arise.

In twenty years, the entire personnel of an organization changes to a large degree. Therefore I ask a man if it is his aspiration to be the president, or one of the board of directors? Or, is he saying to himself, "Oh, there's no chance! I can never get there." If they are doing that, I point out that they certainly will *not* get there if they do not see the possibility and make the effort.

Each year, as I see more of men, my belief that encouragement and cheer always pay increases a hundredfold. Time and again I have seen men who were about to give up in despair get back on their feet simply by knowing that someone believed in them.

I remember once that a young man from my own home town was about to quit his job in one of our stores. His friends and my friends had told me, when I put him to work, that he had never been any good, and never would be. They even told *him* that fact; but wanting the chance to see for himself how he would turn out, he asked for a job and I gave him one.

In less than a year I heard how discouraged he had become. He was out in Idaho, in the dead of winter; and knowing the situation there at that time I sat down and wrote him a long letter, telling him I believed that he could make good and that I would be bitterly disappointed if he didn't.

As I afterward learned, the same day he got my letter a letter from his home town arrived scoffing at his pretensions of being a business man and telling him that he had better quit, and come home and have a good time.

He said that if my letter hadn't arrived the same day he would have given up the ship. Encouraged by my faith in him, however, he remained in Idaho and *won out!* To-day he is one of our most successful men.

To help men succeed, you have *got* to have faith in them. And you must let men know that you do believe in them. I remember another time when faith and encouragement helped another man to make something of himself. This man, put in charge of one of our stores, fell down on the job. He came to see me, and when I asked him if he thought he could make good if given another chance, he said he thought he could. Whereupon I offered him another job on the spot.

"But I haven't a cent in my pockets," he told me. "I can't even move my wife and children to that town."

I loaned him fifty dollars, and he packed up and went to the store to which I had sent him. Two months later, I got back my fifty dollars, and a few years later I was in their house having supper with them. Backed by faith and courage, he had achieved success and was on the road to prosperity.

But it wasn't until a friend of his told me that I learned how the fifty dollars had been paid back in two months. This man, his wife, and his children had lived on bread and water in order to return the loan.

Faith and encouragement will work wonders in a man. Yet there must be a foundation in the man himself to work these wonders *on*. Remember that it is *up to you!* If you are not getting along where you are, first study the whole situation honestly and see whether the trouble isn't with you and not with the job.

But if you make up your mind that the job *is* wrong, or, at least, the wrong one for you, and if you have the nerve and the will and the faith in yourself and in humanity to do it, *break away*, and start out for a goal *you* can *see* and one you will fight to reach.

There is much more to the man than the entertaining fable about an eccentric inventor who flew a kite in a lightning storm. New England Puritans aside, Benjamin Franklin was the first classic American entrepreneur and businessman, or tradesman as he was then known. It did not come easy. Franklin was a poor student who failed math, and at the age of 12 was forced into an apprenticeship under his older brother, a printer. He was supposed to serve as apprentice until he was 21, and according to the contract, only in the last year would he receive wages. By 17 Franklin had had enough and left Boston for Philadelphia. He would see his parents just three more times in his life, yet he had only kind words for them in his autobiography. "He [father] had an excellent constitution of body . . . could draw prettily . . . a mechanical genius, too . . . My mother had likewise an excellent constitution; she suckled all ten of her children." This practical language exemplifies Franklin's pragmatic mind.

Once in Philadelphia, Franklin worked for another printer before he founded the *Pennsylvania Gazette* in 1728 and built a renown print shop. He carefully cultivated his image as a businessman. "I took care not only to be in reality industrious and frugal but to avoid all appearances to the contrary. I dressed plainly; I was seen at no places of idle diversion. I never went out a-fishing or shooting; a book, indeed, sometimes debauched me from my work, but that was seldom, snug, and gave no scandal. . . ." The image served Franklin's ambitions and he built a media empire in his own right. He printed books, started *Gazettes* in Rhode Island and South Carolina, became the "public" printer for Pennsylvania, Delaware, Maryland, and New Jersey, and published the priceless *Poor Richard's Almanac* from 1732 to 1757.

The preface for the 1757 Almanac, *The Way to Wealth*, is considered by many to be Franklin's highest literary and philosophical achievement. Franklin himself makes the introduction to it: "These proverbs, which contained the wisdom of many ages and nations, I assembl'd and form'd into a connected discourse prefix'd to the Almanac of 1757, as the harangue of a wise old man to the people attending an auction. . . ."

The Way to Wealth
Benjamin Franklin

C OURTEOUS READER,

I have heard that nothing gives an author so great pleasure, as to find his works respectfully quoted by other
learned authors. This pleasure I have seldom enjoyed; for
tho' I have been, if I may say it without vanity, an *eminent
author* of Almanacks annually now a full quarter of a century,
my brother authors in the same way, for what reason I know
not, have ever been very sparing in their applauses; and no
other author has taken the least notice of me, so that did not
my writings produce me some solid *pudding*, the great defi-
ciency of *praise* would have quite discouraged me.

I concluded at length, that the people were the best judges
of my merit; for they buy my works; and besides, in my ram-
bles, where I am not personally known, I have frequently
heard one or other of my adages repeated, with, *as Poor Richard
says*, at the end on't; this gave me some satisfaction, as it
showed not only that my instructions were regarded, but discovered likewise some respect for my authority; and I own,
that to encourage the practice of remembering and repeating
those wise sentences, I have sometimes *quoted myself* with great
gravity.

Judge then how much I must have been gratified by an
incident I am going to relate to you. I stopt my horse lately

where a great number of people were collected at a vendue of merchant goods. The hour of sale not being come, they were conversing on the badness of the times, and one of the company call'd to a plain clean old man, with white locks, *Pray Father* Abraham *what think you of the times? Won't these heavy taxes quite ruin the country? How shall we be ever able to pay them? What would you advise us to?*—Father *Abraham* stood up, and reply'd, if you'd have my advice, I'll give it you in short, for *a word to the wise is enough,* and *many words won't fill a bushel,* as *Poor Richard* says. They join'd in desiring him to speak his mind, and gathering round him, he proceeded as follows:

Friends, says he, and neighbors, the taxes are indeed very heavy, and if those laid on by the government were the only

---

Sloth, like rust, consumes faster than labor wears, while the used key is always bright . . .

---

ones we had to pay, we might more easily discharge them; but we have many others, and much more grievous to some of us. We are taxed twice as much by our *idleness,* three times as much by our *pride,* and four times as much by our *folly,* and from these taxes the commissioners cannot ease or deliver us by allowing an abatement. However, let us hearken to good advice, and something may be done for us; *God helps them that help themselves,* as *Poor Richard* says, in his Almanack of 1733.

It would be thought a hard government that should tax its people one tenth part of their *time,* to be employed in its service. But *idleness* taxes many of us much more, if we reckon all that is spent in absolute *sloth,* or doing of nothing, with that which is spent in idle employments or amusements, that amount to nothing. *Sloth,* by bringing on diseases, absolutely shortens life. *Sloth, like rust, consumes faster than labor wears, while the used key is always bright,* as *Poor Richard* says. But *dost thou love life, then do not squander time, for that's the stuff life is made of,* as *Poor Richard* says.—How much more

98

than is necessary do we spend in sleep! forgetting that *the sleeping fox catches no poultry,* and that *there will be sleeping enough in the grave,* as *Poor Richard* says. If time be of all things the most precious, *wasting time* must be, as *Poor Richard* says, *the greatest prodigality,* since, as he elsewhere tells us, *lost time is never found again;* and what we call *time enough, always proves little enough.* Let us then be up and doing, and doing to the purpose; so by diligence shall we do more with less perplexity. *Sloth makes all things difficult, but industry all easy,* as *Poor Richard* says; and *he that riseth late, must trot all day, and shall scarce overtake his business at night.* While *laziness travels so slowly, that poverty soon overtakes him,* as we read in *Poor Richard,* who adds, *drive thy business, let not that drive thee;* and *early to bed, and early to rise, makes a man healthy, wealthy and wise.*

So what signifies *wishing* and *hoping* for better times? We may make these times better if we bestir ourselves. *Industry need not wish* as *Poor Richard* says, and *he that lives upon hope will die fasting. There are no gains, without pains;* then *help hands, for I have no lands,* or if I have, they are smartly taxed. And, as *Poor Richard* likewise observes, *he that hath a trade hath an estate,* and *he that hath a calling hath an office of profit and honor;* but then the *trade* must be worked at, and the *calling* well followed, or neither the *estate* nor the *office* will enable us to pay

---

... he that riseth late, must trot all day, and shall scarce overtake his business at night.

---

our taxes. — If we are industrious we shall never starve; for as *Poor Richard* says, *at the working man's house hunger looks in, but dares not enter.* Nor will the bailiff or the constable enter, for *industry pays debts, while despair encreaseth them,* says *Poor Richard.* — What though you have found no treasure, nor has any rich relation left you a legacy, *diligence is the mother of good luck,* as *Poor Richard* says, and *God gives all things to industry.* Then *plough deep, while sluggards sleep, and you shall have corn to sell and to keep,* says *Poor Dick.* Work while it is called today, for you know not how much you may be hindered tomorrow, which makes *Poor Richard* say, *one today is worth two tomorrows;* and farther, *have you somewhat to do tomorrow, do it today.* If you were a servant, would you not be ashamed that a good master should catch you idle? Are you then your own master, *be ashamed to catch yourself idle,* as *Poor Dick* says. When there is so much to be done for yourself, your family, your country, and your gracious king, be up by peep of day; *let not the sun look down and say, inglorious here he lies.* Handle your tools without mittens; remember that *the cat in gloves catches no mice,* as *Poor Richard* says. 'Tis true there is much to be done, and perhaps you are weak handed, but stick to it steadily, and you will see great effects, for *constant dropping wears away stones,* and by *diligence and patience the mouse ate in two the cable;* and *little strokes fell great oaks,* as *Poor Richard* says in his Almanack, the year I cannot just now remember.

Methinks I hear some of you say, *must a man afford himself no leisure?* — I will tell thee, my friend, what *Poor Richard* says, *employ thy time well if thou meanest to gain leisure;* and, *since thou art not sure of a minute, throw not away an hour.* Leisure is time for doing something useful; this leisure the diligent man will obtain, but the lazy man never; so that, as *Poor Richard* says, *a life of leisure and a life of laziness are two things.* Do you imagine

---

> *If we are industrious we shall never starve; for as Poor Richard says, at the working man's house hunger looks in, but dares not enter.*

---

that sloth will afford you more comfort than labor? No, for as *Poor Richard* says, *trouble springs from idleness, and grievous toil from needless ease.* Many without labor would live by their wits only, but they break for want of stock. Whereas industry gives comfort, and plenty, and respect: *fly pleasures, and they'll follow you. The diligent spinner has a large shift;* and *now I have a sheep and a cow, everybody bids me good morrow;* all of which is well said by *Poor Richard.*

But with our industry, we must likewise be *steady, settled* and *careful,* and oversee our own affairs *with our own eyes* and not trust too much to others; for, as *Poor Richard* says,

> I never saw an oft removed tree,
> Nor yet an oft removed family,
> That throve so well as those that settled be.

And again, *three removes is as bad as a fire;* and again, *keep thy shop, and thy shop will keep thee;* and again, *if you would have your business done, go; if not, send.* And again,

> He that by the plow must thrive,
> Himself must either hold or drive.

And again, *the eye of a master will do more work than both his hands;* and again, *want of care does us more damage than want of knowledge;* and again, *not to oversee workmen, is to leave them your purse open.* Trusting too much to others' care is the ruin of many; for, as the *Almanack* says, *in the affairs of this world, men are saved, not by faith, but by the want of it;* but a man's own care is profitable; for saith *Poor Dick, learning is to the studious,* and *riches to the careful,* as well as *power to the bold,* and *Heaven to the virtuous.* And farther, *if you would have a faithful servant, and one that you like, serve yourself.* And again, he adviseth to circumspection and care, even in the smallest matters, because sometimes *a little neglect may breed great mischief;* adding, *for want of a nail, the shoe was lost; for want of a shoe the horse was lost; and for want of a horse the rider was lost,* being overtaken and slain by the enemy, all for want of care about a horseshoe nail.

So much for industry, my friends, and attention to one's own business; but to these we must add *frugality,* if we would make our *industry* more certainly successful. A man may, if he knows not how to save as he gets, *keep his nose all his life to the grindstone,* and die not worth a *groat* at last. *A fat kitchen makes a lean will,* as *Poor Richard* says; and,

Many estates are spent in the getting,
Since women for tea forsook spinning and
 knitting,
And men for punch forsook hewing and
 splitting.

If you would be wealthy, says he, in another Almanack, *think of saving as well as of getting: The* Indies *have not made* Spain *rich, because her* outgoes *are greater than her* incomes. Away then with your expensive follies, and you will not have so much cause to complain of hard times, heavy taxes, and chargeable families; for, as *Poor Dick* says,

Women and wine, game and deceit,
Make the wealth small, and the wants great.

And farther, *what maintains one vice would bring up two children.* You may think perhaps, that a *little* tea, or a *little* punch now and then, diet a *little* more costly, clothes a *little* finer, and a *little* entertainment now and then, can be no *great* matter; but remember what *Poor Richard* says, *many a little makes a mickle;* and farther, *beware of* little *expenses; a small leak will sink a great ship;* and again, *who dainties love, shall beggars prove;* and moreover, *fools make feasts, and wise men eat them.*

Here you are all got together at this vendue of *fineries* and *knicknacks.* You call them *goods,* but if you do not take care, they will prove *evils* to some of you. You expect they will be sold *cheap,* and perhaps they may for less than they cost; but if you have no occasion for them, they must be *dear* to you. Remember what *Poor Richard* says, *Buy what thou hast no need of, and ere long thou shalt sell thy necessaries.* And again, *at a great pennyworth pause a while;* he means that perhaps the cheapness is *apparent* only and not *real;* or the bargain, by straitning thee in thy business, may do thee more harm than good. For in another place he says, *many have been ruined by buying good pennyworths.* Again, *Poor Richard* says, *'tis foolish to lay out money in a purchase of repentance;* and yet this folly is practiced every day at vendues, for want of minding the Almanack. *Wise men,* as *Poor Dick* says, *learn by others harms, fools scarcely by their own;* but, *felix quem faciunt aliena pericula cautum.* * Many a one, for the sake of finery on the back, have gone with a hungry belly, and half starved their families; *silks and sattins, scarlets and velvets,* as *Poor Richard* says, *put out the kitchen fire.* These are not the *necessaries* of life; they can scarcely be called the *conveniences,* and yet only because they look pretty, how many *want* to *have* them. The *artificial* wants of mankind thus become more numerous than the *natural;* and, as *Poor Dick* says, *for one* poor *person, there are an hundred* indigent. By these, and other extravagancies, the genteel are reduced to poverty, and forced to borrow of those whom they formerly despised, but who through *industry* and *frugality* have maintained their standing; in which case it appears plainly, that *a ploughman on his legs is higher than a gentleman on his knees,* as *Poor Richard* says. Perhaps they have had a small estate left them, which they knew not the getting of; they think *'tis day, and will never be night;* that a little to be spent out of *so much,* is not worth minding; (*a child and a fool,* as *Poor Richard* says, *imagine twenty shillings and twenty years can never be spent*) but, *always taking out of the meal-tub, and never putting in, soon comes to the bottom;* then, as *Poor Dick* says, *when the well's dry, they know the worth of water.* But this they might have known before, if they had taken his advice; *If you would know the value of money, go and try to borrow some;* for, *he that goes a borrowing goes a sorrowing;* and indeed so does he that lends to such people, when he goes *to get it in again.* —*Poor Dick* farther advises, and says,

> Fond *pride of dress,* is sure a very curse;
> E'er *fancy* you consult, consult your purse.

And again, *pride is as loud a beggar as want, and a great deal more saucy.* When you have bought one fine thing you must

*He is lucky who is made cautious by other men's perils.

buy ten more, that your appearance may be all of a piece; but *Poor Dick* says, *'tis easier to* suppress *the first desire, than to* satisfy *all that follow it*. And 'tis as truly folly for the poor to ape the rich, as for the frog to swell, in order to equal the ox.

> Great estates may venture more,
> But little boats should keep near shore.

'Tis however a folly soon punished; for *pride that dines on vanity sups on contempt*, as *Poor Richard* says. And in another place, *pride breakfasted with plenty, dined with poverty, and supped with infamy*. And after all, of what use is this *pride of appearance*, for which so much is risked, so much is suffered? It cannot promote health, or ease pain; it makes no increase of merit in the person, creates envy, it hastens misfortune.

> What is a butterfly? At best
> He's but a caterpillar drest.
> The gaudy fop's his picture just,

as *Poor Richard* says.

But what madness must it be to *run in debt* for these superfluities! We are offered, by the terms of this vendue, *six months' credit*; and that perhaps has induced some of us to attend it, because we cannot spare the ready money, and hope now to be fine without it. But, ah, think what you do when you run in debt; *you give to another power over your liberty*. If you cannot pay at the time, you will be ashamed to see your creditor; you will be in fear when you speak to him; you will make poor pitiful sneaking excuses, and by degrees come to lose your veracity, and sink into base downright lying; for, as *Poor Richard* says, *the second vice is lying, the first is running in debt*. And again, to the same purpose, *lying rides upon debt's back*. Whereas a freeborn *Englishman* ought not to be ashamed or afraid to see or speak to any man living. But poverty often deprives a man of all spirit and virtue: *'tis hard for an empty bag to stand upright*, as *Poor Richard* truly says. What would you think of that prince, or that government, who should issue an edict forbidding you to dress like a gentleman or a gentlewoman, on pain of imprisonment or servitude? Would you not say, that you are free, have a right to dress as you please, and that such an edict would be a breach of your privileges, and such a government tyrannical? And yet you are about to put yourself under that tyranny when you run in debt for such dress! Your creditor has authority at his pleasure to deprive you of your liberty, by confining you in gaol for life, or to sell you for a servant, if you should not be about to pay him! When you have got your bargain, you may, perhaps, think little of payment; but *creditors, Poor Richard* tells us, *have better memories than debtors;* and in another place says, *creditors are a superstitious sect, great observers of set days and times.* The day comes round before you are aware, and the demand is made before you are prepared to satisfy it. Or if you bear your debt in mind, the term which at first seemed so long, will, as it lessens, appear extremely short. *Time* will seem to have added wings to his heels as well as shoulders. *Those have a short Lent,* saith *Poor Richard, who owe money to be paid at Easter.* Then, since, as he says, *the borrower is a slave to the lender, and the debtor is to the creditor,* disdain the chain, preserve your freedom; and maintain your independency: be *industrious* and *free;* be *frugal* and *free.* At present, perhaps, you may think yourself in thriving circumstances, and that you can bear a little extravagance without injury; but,

> For age and want, save while you may;
> No morning sun lasts a whole day,

as *Poor Richard* says. — Gain may be temporary and uncertain, but ever while you live, Experience is constant and certain; and *'tis easier to build two chimneys than to keep one in fuel,* as *Poor Richard* says. So *rather go to bed supperless than rise in debt.*

> Get what you can, and what you get hold;
> 'Tis the stone that will turn all your lead into
> gold,

as *Poor Richard* says. And when you have got the philosopher's stone, sure you will no longer complain of the bad times, or the difficulties of paying taxes.

This doctrine, my friends, is *reason* and *wisdom;* but after all, do not depend too much on your own *industry* and *frugality* and *prudence,* though excellent things, for they may all be blasted without the blessing of heaven; and therefore ask that blessing humbly, and be not uncharitable to those that at present seem to want it, but comfort and help them. Remember *Job* suffered, and was afterwards prosperous.

And now to conclude, *experience keeps a dear school, but fools will learn in no other, and scarce in that;* for it is true, *we may give advice, but we cannot give conduct,* as *Poor Richard* says; however, remember this, *they that won't be counseled can't be helped,* as *Poor Richard* says; and farther, that *if you will not hear reason, she'll surely rap your knuckles.*

Thus the old gentleman ended his harangue. The people heard it, and approved the doctrine, and immediately practiced the contrary, just as if it had been a common sermon; for the vendue opened, and they began to buy extravagantly, notwithstanding all his cautions, and their own fear of taxes. — I found the good man had thoroughly studied my Almanacks, and digested all I had dropt on those topics during the course of five-and-twenty years. The frequent mention he made of me must have tired anyone else, but my vanity was wonderfully delighted with it, though I was conscious that not a tenth part of this wisdom was my own which he ascribed to me, but rather the *gleanings* I had made of the sense of all ages and nations. However, I resolved to be the better for the echo of it; and though I had at first determined to buy stuff for a new coat, I went away resolved to wear my old one a little longer. *Reader,* if thou wilt do the same, thy profit will be as great as mine.

I am, as ever,
Thine to serve thee,
RICHARD SAUNDERS

106

PART III

THE DYNAMICS OF LEADERSHIP

Ogilvy's knack for advertising and extravagant language is clearly illustrated in his recollection of his father's influence. "He sneezed louder than anyone I have ever known, ate spoonfuls of hot Colman's mustard without any apparent sign of distress, and climbed trees as fast as a chimpanzee. He did his best to make me as strong and brainy as himself. When I was six, he required that I should drink a glass of raw blood every day. To strengthen my mental faculties, he ordained that I should eat calve's brains three times a week, washed down with a bottle of beer. Blood, brains and beer; a noble experiment." Life was grand in Scotland until young Ogilvy was required to find work. His ability to focus was lacking initially as he bounced through several jobs, before emigrating to America in search of adventure.

Ogilvy found work with Dr. George Gallup, creator of the Gallup Poll. It was a learning experience. "Apart from polling, he [Gallup] taught me three things of consummate value: 1. 'Grant graciously what you dare not refuse'; 2. 'When you don't know the answer, confuse the issue'; 3. 'When you foul the air in somebody else's bathroom, burn a match and the smell will vanish.' " Well, knowledge comes in many forms. When war broke out with Germany, Ogilvy used his position with Gallup to gather information and advise the British Government on American opinions. He was soon invited to join Britain's Secret Service, and his first mission was to help ruin Latin American businessmen who were supporting Hitler. It was not until several years after the war, and after a stint as a farmer in Amish country, that Ogilvy finally concentrated his efforts and founded Ogilvy & Mather.

In building one of the largest advertising agencies in the world, Ogilvy rubbed shoulders with many captains of industry. One troubling observation he made was, "I seldom came across a top man who showed any ability as a leader. All too many of them, far from inspiring their lieutenants, displayed a genius for emasculating them." Rather than remaining merely a critical voice, Ogilvy provides his own formula for leadership in the following selection.

Leadership
David Ogilvy

I have had unique opportunities for observing men who manage great corporations — my clients. Most of them are good *problem-solvers* and *decision-makers*, but few are outstanding *leaders*. Some of them, far from inspiring their lieutenants, display a genius for castrating them.

Great leadership can have an electrifying effect on the performance of any corporation. I have had the good fortune to work for three inspiring leaders — Monsieur Pitard, who was my boss in the kitchens of the Majestic Hotel in Paris; George Gallup; and Sir William Stephenson of British Intelligence.

There has been a lot of research into leadership. It is the consensus among the social scientists that success in leadership depends on the circumstances. For example, a man who has been an outstanding leader in an industrial company can be a flop when he goes to Washington as Secretary of Commerce. And the kind of leadership which works well in a new company seldom works well in a mature company.

There appears to be no correlation between leadership and academic achievement. I was relieved to learn this, because I have no college degree. The motivation which makes a man a good student is not the kind of motivation which makes him a good leader.

There is a tendency for corporations to reject executives who do not fit their conventions. How many corporations would promote a maverick like Charlie Kettering of General Motors? How many advertising agencies would hire a 38-year-old man whose curriculum vitae read: 'Unemployed farmer, former cook and university drop-out?' (Me in the year I started Ogilvy & Mather.)

Great leaders almost always exude self-confidence. *They are never petty. They are never buck-passers. They pick themselves up after defeat . . .*

The best leaders are apt to be found among those executives who have a strong component of unorthodoxy in their characters. Instead of resisting innovation, they symbolize it—and companies cannot grow without innovation.

Great leaders almost always exude *self-confidence*. They are never petty. They are never buck-passers. They pick themselves up after defeat—the way Howard Clark of American Express picked himself up after the salad oil swindle. Under Howard's indomitable leadership, the price of American Express shares increased fourteen-fold.

Great leaders are always fanatically committed to their jobs. They do not suffer from the crippling need to be universally loved. They have the guts to make unpopular decisions—including the guts to fire non-performers. Gladstone once said that a great Prime Minister must be a good butcher.

I saw the head chef at the Hotel Majestic fire a pastry cook because the poor devil could not get his brioches to rise straight. This ruthlessness made all the other chefs feel that they were working in the best kitchen in the world.

Some men are good at leading the multitude—whether it be the labor force in their company, or the voting population in their country. But these same men are often miserable leaders of a small group.

Good leaders are *decisive*. They grasp nettles. Some of them are very odd characters. Lloyd George was sexually chaotic. General Grant, who won the Civil War, drank like a fish. On November 26, 1863, the *New York Herald* quoted Lincoln as saying: I wish some of you would tell me the brand of whiskey that Grant drinks. I would like to send a barrel of it to my other generals.

Winston Churchill was another hardened drinker. He was capricious and petulant. He was grossly inconsiderate of his staff. He was a colossal egotist. Yet his Chief of Staff wrote of him:

> I shall always look back on the years I worked with him as some of the most difficult and trying ones in my life. For all that I thank God that I was given the opportunity of working alongside of such a man, and of having my eyes opened to the fact that occasionally such supermen exist on this earth.

I do not believe that *fear* is a tool used by good leaders. People do their best work in a happy atmosphere. Ferment and innovation depend on *joie de vivre*. I am indebted to Charlie Brower of BBDO for his amendment to the 13th chapter of St. Paul's first Epistle to the Corinthians: A man who spendeth his life gathering gold for the United States Treasury and has no fun, is a sounding ass and a tinkling idiot.

The great leaders I have known have been curiously *complicated* men. Howard Johnson, the former President of MIT, has described it as a visceral form of spiritual energy which provides the element of *mystery* in leadership. I have seen this mysterious energy in Marvin Bower of McKinsey. Ted Moscoso of Puerto Rico, and Henry Alexander of Morgan Guaranty.

The most effective leader is the one who satisfies the psychological needs of his followers. For example, it is one thing to be a good leader of Americans, who are raised in a tradition of democracy and have a high need for independence. But the American brand of democratic leadership doesn't work so well in Europe, where executives have a psychological need for more *autocratic* leadership. That is one of many reasons why it is wise for American agencies to appoint locals to lead their foreign subsidiaries.

Great leaders are always fanatically committed to their jobs. They do not suffer from the crippling need to be universally loved.

It does an agency no good when its leader never shares his leadership functions with his lieutenants. The more centers of leadership you create, the stronger your agency will become.

There is an art in being a good *follower.* On the night before a major battle, the first Duke of Marlborough was reconnoitering the terrain. He and his staff were on horseback. Marlborough dropped his glove. Cadogan, his chief of staff, dismounted, picked up the glove and handed it to Marlborough. The other officers thought this remarkably civil of Cadogan. Later that evening, Marlborough issued his final order: "Cadogan, put a battery of guns where I dropped my glove."

"I have already done so," replied Cadogan. He had read Marlborough's mind, and anticipated his order. Cadogan was the kind of follower who makes leadership easy. I have known men whom *nobody* could lead.

Most of the great leaders I know have the ability to inspire people with their *speeches.* If you cannot write inspiring speeches yourself, use ghost-writers — but use *good* ones. Roosevelt used the poet Archibald MacLeish, the playwright Robert Sherwood and Judge Rosenmann. That is why he was more inspiring than any of the Presidents we have had since, with the exception of John F. Kennedy, who also used outstanding ghost-writers.

Very few chief executives are good on their feet. Whoever writes the speeches, the CEO delivers them atrociously. Competence, however, can be learned. All major politicians hire experts to teach them the art of delivery.

The man who said the wisest things about leadership was Field Marshal Montgomery:

> The leader must have infectious optimism, and the determination to persevere in the face of difficulties. He must also radiate confidence, even when he himself is not too certain of the outcome.
>
> The final test of a leader is the feeling you have when you leave his presence after a conference. Have you a feeling of uplift and confidence?

JOHN F. WELCH, JR.
1935 –

It is both ironic and an embodiment of the American dream that the son of a train conductor would one day be chairman of a company that built locomotives, among many other products. But it is to his mother that Welch gives the credit for molding his character. "Whenever I got out of line, she'd whack me one. But always positive. Always uplifting. Always constructive. Control your own destiny—she always had that idea." The high school altar boy eventually did his own share of whacking when he took over as CEO of General Electric (GE) in 1981. He was quickly dubbed "Neutron Jack" by *Newsweek* magazine as he eliminated or divested one third of the company's work force (170,000 jobs) over the next five years. In 1984 he was even labeled a heretic for selling the housewares division, which included traditional GE products such as irons, toasters, clocks, and coffee makers.

The "crazy Irishman" was definitely not endearing himself to the employees, but he was supremely confident in his reengineering strategy. It was based on a simple and direct philosophy: Every GE business unit had to be one or two in their respective industry, or they were gone. In other words, you either adapted to what he correctly anticipated as "a rapidly changing hightech global market," or you were vaporized. At the same time that GE was flooding the unemployment office, Welch heavily invested in the remaining workforce, because he understood that the employees' "enthusiasm is your most valuable asset."

To create a fluid organization that put a premium on spirited teamwork, Welch and company built their own management school. It was so successful that *Fortune* magazine labeled it "the Harvard of Corporate America," and other companies literally stole their textbooks. Welch succinctly stated his goal for the company's school, "The number one thing we're trying to achieve is to create and nourish a high-performing team. That's what leadership is. It isn't someone on a horse commanding the troops. It's the ability to succeed through other people's successes." Welch elaborates on his blueprint for effective leadership and his vision for GE in *Lessons for Success*.

Lessons for Success
John F. Welch, Jr.

When I try to summarize what I've learned since 1981, one of the big lessons is that change has no constituency. People like the status quo. They like the way it was. When you start changing things, the good old days look better and better.

You've got to be prepared for massive resistance.

Incremental change doesn't work very well in the type of transformation GE has gone through. If your change isn't big enough, revolutionary enough, the bureaucracy can beat you. Look at Winston Churchill and Franklin Roosevelt: They said, *This is what it's going to be.* And then they did it. Big, bold changes, forcefully articulated. When you get leaders who confuse popularity with leadership, who just nibble away at things, nothing changes. I think that's true in countries and in companies.

Another big lesson: You've got to be hard to be soft. You have to demonstrate the ability to make the hard, tough decisions—closing plants, divesting, delayering—if you want to have any credibility when you try to promote soft values. We reduced employment and cut the bureaucracy and picked up some unpleasant nicknames, but when we spoke of soft values—things like candor, fairness, facing reality—people listened.

If you've got a fat organization, soft values won't get you very far. Pushing speed and simplicity, or a program like Work-Out, is just plain not doable in a big bureaucracy. Before you can get into stuff like that, you've first got to do the hard structural work. Take out the layers. Pull up the weeds. Scrape off the rust.

People like the status quo. They like the way it was. *When you start changing things, the good old days look better and better.*

Every organization needs values, but a lean organization needs them even more. When you strip away the support systems of staffs and layers, people have to change their habits and expectations, or else the stress will just overwhelm them. We're all working harder and faster. But unless we're also having more fun, the transformation doesn't work. Values are what enable people to guide themselves through that kind of change.

To create change, I believe in the Crotonville/Work-Out concept: Direct, personal, two-way communication is what seems to make the difference. Exposing people—without the protection of title or position—to ideas from everywhere. Judging ideas on their merits.

You've got to be out in front of crowds, repeating yourself over and over again, never changing your message no matter how much it bores you.

You need an overarching message, something big but simple and understandable. Whatever it is—*we're going to be No. 1 or No. 2, or fix/close/sell, or boundarylessness*—every idea you present must be something you could get across easily at a cocktail party with strangers. If only aficionados of your industry can understand what you're saying, you've blown it.

Another takeaway for me: Simplicity applies to measurements, too. Too often we measure everything and understand nothing. The three most important things you need to measure in a business are customer satisfaction, employee satisfaction, and cash flow. If you're growing customer satisfaction, your global market share is sure to grow, too. Employee satisfaction gets you productivity, quality, pride, and creativity. And cash flow is the pulse—the key vital sign of a company.

Another thing I've learned is the value of stretching the organization, by setting the bar higher than people think they can go. The standard of performance we use is: *to be as good as the best in the world.* Invariably people find the way to get there, or most of the way. They dream and reach and search. the trick is not to punish those who fall short. If they improve, you reward them—even if they haven't reached the goal. But unless you set the bar high enough, you'll never find out what people can do.

I've made my share of mistakes—plenty of them—but my biggest mistake by far was not moving faster. Pulling off an old Band-Aid one hair at a time hurts a lot more than a sudden yank. Of course you want to avoid breaking things or stretching the organization too far—but generally, human nature holds you back. You want to be liked, to be thought of as reasonable. So you don't move as fast as you should. Besides hurting more, it costs you competitiveness.

Everything should have been done in half the time. When you're running an institution like this you're always scared at first. You're afraid you'll break it. People don't think about leaders this way, but it's true. Everyone who's running something goes home at night and wrestles with the same fear: *Am I going to be the one who blows this place up?* In retrospect, I was too cautious and too timid. I wanted too many constituencies on board.

Timidity causes mistakes. We didn't buy a food company in the early 1980s because I didn't have the courage of my conviction. We thought about it, we discussed it at Crotonville, and it was the right idea. I was afraid GE wasn't ready for a move like that. Another thing we should have done is eliminate the sectors right away. Then we could have given the sector heads—who were our best people—big jobs running businesses. We should have invented Work-Out five years earlier. I wish we'd understood boundarylessness better, sooner. I wish we'd understood all along how much leverage you can get from the flow of ideas among all the business units.

Now that we've got that leverage, I wonder how we ever lived without it. The enormous advantage we have today is that we can run GE as a laboratory for ideas. We've found mechanisms to share best practices in a way that's trusting and open. When our people go to a Xerox, say, or their people come here, the exchange is good—but in these "fly-bys" the takeaways are largely conceptual, and we both have difficulty getting too far below the surface. But when every GE business sends two people to Louisville for a year to study the Quick Response program in our own appliance business, the ideas take on intensity and depth. The people who go to Louisville aren't tourists. When they go back to their businesses to talk about Quick Response they're zealots, because they're owners of that idea. They've been on the team that made it work.

All those opportunities were out there, but we didn't see them until we got rid of the staffs, the layers, and the hierarchies. Then they became obvious. If I'd moved more quickly in the beginning, we'd have noticed those opportunities sooner, and we'd be farther ahead than we are today.

The only way I see to get more productivity is by getting people involved and excited about their jobs. You can't afford to have anyone walk through a gate of a factory, or into an office, who's not giving 120%. I don't mean running and sweating, but working smarter. It's a matter of understanding the customer's needs instead of just making something and putting it into a box. It's a matter of seeing the importance of your role in the total process.

The point of Work-Out is to give people better jobs. When people see that their ideas count, their dignity is raised. Instead of feeling numb, like robots, they feel important. They *are* important.

You've got to be hard to be soft. You have to demonstrate the ability to make the hard, tough decisions — closing plants, divesting, delayering — if you want to have any credibility when you try to promote soft values.

I would argue that a satisfied work force is a productive work force. Back when jobs were plentiful and there was no foreign competition, people were satisfied just to hang around. Now people come to work with a different agenda: They want to win against the competition, because they know that the competition is the enemy and that customers are their only source of job security. They don't like weak managers, because they know that the weak managers of the 1970s and 1980s cost millions of people their jobs.

With Work-Out and boundarylessness, we're trying to differentiate GE competitively by raising as much intellectual and creative capital from our work force as we possibly can. That's a lot tougher than raising financial capital, which a strong company can find in any market in the world.

Trust is enormously powerful in a corporation. People won't do their best unless they believe they'll be treated fairly — that there's no cronyism and everybody has a real shot.

The only way I know to create that kind of trust is by laying out your values and then walking the talk. You've got to do what you say you'll do, consistently, over time.

It doesn't mean everybody has to agree. I have a great relationship with Bill Bywater, president of the International Union of Electronic Workers. I would trust him with my wallet, but he knows I'll fight him to the death in certain areas, and vice versa.

He wants to have a neutrality agreement in GE's non-union plants. He wants to recruit more members for the union.

I'll say, "No way! We can give people everything you can, and more."

He knows where I stand. I know where he stands. We don't always agree—but we trust each other.

That's what boundarylessness is: An open, trusting, sharing of ideas. A willingness to listen, debate, and then take the best ideas and get on with it.

I've made my share of mistakes—plenty of them—but my biggest mistake by far was not moving faster. Pulling off an old Band-Aid one hair at a time hurts a lot more than a sudden yank.

If this company is to achieve its goals, we've all got to become boundaryless. Boundaries are crazy. The union is just another boundary, and you have to reach across the same way you want to reach across the boundaries separating you from your customers and your suppliers and your colleagues overseas.

We're not that far along with boundarylessness yet. It's a big, big idea, but I don't think it has enough fur on it yet. We've got to keep repeating it, letting everybody know all the time that when they're doing things right, it's boundaryless. It's going to take a couple of more years to get people to the point where the idea of boundarylessness just becomes natural.

Who knows exactly when I'll retire? You go when it's the right time to go. You pray to God you don't stay too long.

I keep asking myself, *Are you dealing with new things? When you find yourself regenerating? Are you in a new environment, do you come up with a fundamentally different approach?* That's the test. When you flunk, you leave.

Three or four times a year, I hop on a plane and visit something like seven countries in fifteen days. People say to me, *Are you nutty?*

No, I'm not nutty. I'm trying to regenerate.

The CEO succession here is still a long way off, but I think about it every day. Obviously, anybody who gets this job must have a vision for the company and be capable of rallying people behind it. He or she has got to be very comfortable in a global environment, dealing with world leaders. Be comfortable dealing with people at all levels of the company. Have a boundaryless attitude toward every constituency—race, gender, everything. Have the very highest standards of integrity. Believe in the gut that people are the key to everything, and that change is not something you fear—it's something you relish. Anyone who is too inwardly focused, who doesn't cherish customers, who isn't open to change, isn't going to make it.

Finally, whoever gets the job will have to have what I call an "edge"—an insatiable passion for winning and growing.

In the end, I think it will be a combination of that edge and those values that will determine who gets this job.

I think any company that's trying to play in the 1990s has got to find a way to engage the mind of every single employee. Whether we make our way successfully down this road is something only time will tell—but I'm sure this is the right road.

If you're not thinking all the time about making every person more valuable, you don't have a chance. What's the alternative? Wasted minds? Uninvolved people? A labor force that's angry or bored? That doesn't make sense!

If you've got a better way, show me. I'd love to know what it is.

OWEN D. YOUNG
1874 – 1962

In 1911 the Sherman Anti-trust Act was used to bring suit against General Electric (GE). In 1913 the newly elected U.S. President Wilson promised further investigations into the practices of big business. In that same year GE hired Young, a very reputable lawyer, to help prevent against and protect the company from government inquiries. On arrival, he was overwhelmed because as he said, "Electricity was then a new art and the notion that great machines could move without belts or other visible ties opened my eyes and mouth with wonder." It didn't take long to learn the business and Young was elected chairman of GE in 1922. Young was the first to reinvent and reengineer GE, and he did it 70 years before the two words became an integral part of the businessperson's vocabulary. He was hailed as a new kind of manager—a scientific one.

To the public the new chairman pledged "either a better product at the old price or the same product at a lower price." To the employees he emphatically promised, "We must aim to make the earning power of human beings so large as to supply them not only with a living wage, but a cultural wage. . . ." In other words, the company's wealth would be shared, so that everyone could have the opportunity to develop their intellect and enjoy life more. Young had known poverty growing up on a farm and wished it on no one. The GE shareholders, in contrast, found such talk upsetting and smacking of idealistic inefficiency. However, Young, like Henry Ford, understood that well-treated employees would ultimately be far more productive.

Productivity was also increased through Young's scientific methods of management, which replaced the old "rule o' thumb." In revolutionizing the company's practices, he believed that any stubbornness encountered was not the fault of the man, but "the facts he has accepted." He decisively dispelled with irreverent facts and used poignant information to optimize return on capital, labor, and output. *Interpreting the Weather Signs of Business* exemplifies Young's scientific approach to management and leadership. Also, he was a foremost expert on the concept of "business cycles," a term that did not officially enter the English language until 1919.

Interpreting the Weather Signs
of Business

Owen D. Young

Business, taking it very broadly, is not unlike a Jacquard loom. If the pattern card be right and the yarn be right and the machine be in order, then we may be reasonably sure that the product will be what we intended it to be. That is, our plans will work out.

A well-ordered business seems to weave its profits just as though it were an automatic loom. But it only seems to do that. Actually, there is nothing automatic about business, for business is only a phase of the affair of supplying the wants of human beings. It has more to do with human beings than it has with materials. And human beings are not automatons. In the mass we act and react over long periods to certain forces. We do not entirely know what these forces are. If we did know them we should hardly be able better to plan our lives—for we are not glaciers living through the ages. It would not help us to know that the year 2000 is going to be one of plenty—for none of us will be here. We cannot eat the meals of yesterday or of tomorrow; we have to eat as of today. Even the largest corporation, although it may tentatively plan through, perhaps, five years, must really live from year to year. A few individuals may live from year to year, but most must live from month to month, and many from week to week, more than a few from day to day.

Business, since it serves people, must live with them from day to day, and hence its plans cannot be impersonal. Which is as it should be, for if we were to permit statistics and the cold logic of economists to act without the disturbing factor of the human being, then life could not be worth while. For the art of living would be substituted the drudgery of living.

All of which is not merely a philosophic comment born out of a contemplation of the scheme of things in general, but it is rather a warming-up before attacking the daily bread-and-butter side of the business cycle.

The term "business cycle" is formidable. Many comprehend it as clearly as they do the Einstein theory—they admit it might be important, if true. Others find more in it than at present there is to be found. They erect a vast structure of learning on a small foundation and, of course, the walls will not stay put. It is not helpful to get the business cycle out of perspective. It is not a tangible thing, like a big truck going down the road. We cannot hitch our sleds to it. But can we, as individuals, use the cycle to keep our own affairs going smoothly—to keep our factories and our shops going along and our men at work, to keep our bank accounts sturdy, to keep our income above our outgo, and, in general, to carry on with reasonable surety? In other words, can we find and use information so that at midyear we can do more than hope for the kind of dinner we should like to have at Christmas?

None of us is without interest in the general state of prosperity. We hope that a share may come to us. But our most exuberant enthusiasm centers around our own particular prosperity. We live as individuals in a nation—not as a nation in which we are individuals. A man who does his own job well is probably doing as much as the man who is adjusting the affairs of the universe. If we all took to managing the universe there would be no universe to manage.

What we principally want is some method of guiding our own business affairs, whether they run into thousands or into millions of dollars a year, so that we may take advantage of the maximum number of opportunities and make the minimum number of errors.

A control to be worth anything must be positive as well as negative. Is it possible for each individual in business to establish for himself a control which will be something more than a mere hobbling—that will help him to go swiftly and surely? I think it is. Being slow and sure usually gets around to being just slow. First of all, let us find out what the business cycle is.

It is not helpful to get the business cycle out of perspective. It is not a tangible thing, like a big truck going down the road. We cannot hitch our sleds to it.

The business cycle is the movement of business over any given period. Like a stream, it finds its way between and around obstacles. It is influenced by many different forces acting and counteracting, but its coarse is ever onward. The principal influencing forces are political, economic, and psychological. The strength of the respective influences varies. Or take it in another way. The cycle is the rope in a terrific tug of war—now the rope goes this way, now that. It rests when the pulls are exactly equal. On the team called "politics" we find domestic and international relations, tariffs, budgets, and all kinds of smaller fry. Under "economics" are finance, gold movements, credits, discounts, security markets, and many others. Under "psychology" are the relations between employer and employee, confidence of investors, want of confidence, the exhilaration of the incoming tide of prosperity, the lassitude and even despair of the ebb-tide of depression. If one thinks of all of these forces as individuals pulling on a rope, sometimes on one side, and sometimes on another, and then thinks of the rope as resting for an instant, then moving and changing its course, one has the picture of how and why business resolves itself into a curve or cycle. In the report of the Subcommittee on Business Cycles and Unemployment we defined the cycle thus:

"The committee uses the term 'business cycle' to describe the series of changes in business conditions which are characterized by an upward movement toward a boom, followed by a downward movement into depression.

"But most business men know that the term 'business cycle' is too simple to describe accurately the complexity of the problems that are involved. In reality, the name covers a long series of influences in which a more or less unknown part is played by the individual establishment, by the industry of which it is a part, by conditions in other industries, and by credit conditions and policies."

There can be no doubt of the existence of the cycle, and also there can be no doubt that it has both major and minor swings. In the long swings of the last two centuries fundamental improvements in the technique and development of new regions, plus, perhaps, changes in gold production, seem to have counted for more than changes in rainfall. If you will throw out from the chart the influence of the great wars, earthquakes, floods, and other disturbances, you will see that the long swings of the cycle are irresistibly economic. They are the resultants of the great contending forces of brute nature and human intelligence. The rainfall, the sunshine, the crops, the number of mouths to be fed, the hungers, the thirsts, and the satisfactions of peoples, all these are the contending forces which come to an equilibrium that we call the economic law. This is impersonal and it is beyond the control of human beings.

Not only is it uncontrollable, but also it is unpredictable. Men's individual lives, loves, hates, exhilarations, and depressions live too little a while greatly to influence the tremendous sweep of economic laws. It is only the sum of these through generations which affect the law. Even great governmental disturbances have only a little effect. But if these forces are irresistible, why talk about them when we cannot contend against them?

Fortunately, we have no need to fight them and we shall not have that need unless some discovery of medicine permits us all to live as long as elephants.

For these long swings are of the ages. We do not know they are going on. We live in the short swings of the cycle. These are largely man-made, and, if we are wise enough, they can be largely man-corrected. The little ups and downs—and they are by comparison to the big ones, prosperity and depression—are but the chartings of our hits and misses. It would seem by the score that we have mostly been shooting with our eyes shut. There is nothing irresistible about this cycle. It is just a record of how persistently we misinform ourselves or fail to inform ourselves.

How is one going to inform oneself? What is information? The business of no single concern, no matter how large it may be, seems more than trivial when taken in connection with national statistics of business and it is quite true that the ordinary individual in business can, of himself, do very little toward controlling the whole business movement, but he can do something for himself through interpreting them to his own affairs. Each individual has his own little business cycle. This is the cycle he is most interested in and it is one which he must work out for himself. It is the one in which he can be most useful.

By no means is every business good in "prosperity" or bad in "depression." The individual business has to be controlled on its own data and cannot proceed on general forecast. Sailors have learned to use the weather reports. They read the signals and then do whatever seems best under the circumstances. The storms which are predicted do not always turn up on schedule and a few turn up which are not scheduled. The reports are not 100% accurate. Nevertheless, no sailor thinks of disregarding them. He uses them. They do not use him. And that is the point in business statistics.

We are never helpless before business conditions. The cycle is a combination of two curves — the great major, economic swing, and the minor, human fluctuation. The big swing is absolutely impersonal; the little swing is absolutely personal.

Through many years past business has been going up and down. We have come to expect that a crisis will be followed by a depression, a depression by a revival, the revival by prosperity, and prosperity by a new crisis. . . .

Nearly every one in business reaches the conclusion in a rising market that he is a clever buyer, and nearly everybody reaches this conclusion at about the same moment — which usually happens to be about the day before the crash.

The large corporation, which can control every process from the raw material to the consumer, is in a better position to regulate its affairs according to its judgment of business than is the manufacturer or retailer who must buy from others.

But almost the same effect could be gained by a chain of independent units if all were to follow an identical policy based on reasonably accurate research. This is already being done in a way by collective buying in a good many industries and in more than a few lines of retailing.

The point is this. We are never helpless before business conditions. The cycle is a combination of two curves—the great major, economic swing, and the minor, human fluctuation. The big swing is absolutely impersonal; the little swing is absolutely personal. As a community of business men we can learn in time to control the little swing, but, in the meantime, it is easily possible for the individual to control his own affairs to such a degree as to avoid being caught in the violent movements of business.

RICHARD W. SEARS
1863 – 1914

For many turn-of-the-century Midwest farmers, the only two books they ever read were the Bible and the Sears catalog. Of course, the catalog was at times a little more racy, as the audacious Sears would occasionally advertise items like the Heidelberg Belt—it was electrified and an alleged cure for impotency, among other ailments. The mail order merchant possessed natural literary talents that were critical to his success. He maximized them in embellishing the descriptions of his merchandise presented in the catalog. Those who knew him said, "he could sell a breath of air." But Sears was quick to point out that the descriptions were never misleading, for he believed, "Honesty is the best policy. I know. I've tried it both ways." He worked hard to cultivate trust by providing "Free Trial Offers" and "Money Back Guarantees," and then sticking to his promises, no questions asked. Although such claims are common today, he was one of the first to make and uphold them.

As business flourished, Sears hired Alva Curtis Roebuck, and after several metamorphoses, Sears, Roebuck and Company was founded in 1893. However, chaos reigned in a company with no organizational chart, let alone no cohesive management nor growth strategy. Sears compensated with his enthusiastic and contagious personality, working 12- to 14-hour days, sometimes seven days a week. Unfortunately, it wasn't long before the amicable Roebuck burned out and resigned in 1895, selling his stock for $25,000 (to be worth millions in a few short years). Sears would then take on two new partners, one being Julius Rosenwald, a management and control systems genius.

Sears welcomed Rosenwald and his skills because he perceived that there were few successful one-man organizations. In *The Men Behind the Guns of Business,* Sears also points to the critical importance of all subordinates. They must be trusted and given latitude to operate using their own methods. And although his leadership style may have appeared loose, especially compared to that of Rosenwald, he firmly demanded that his employees "make good" and "prove their right to remain part of the organization."

The Men Behind the Guns of Business
Richard W. Sears

A few notable successes have been made in the industrial world through what is known as the "one man organization." But I believe that in the great majority of cases it is the men you choose as subordinates who make your success.

Select your men carefully and at the right time—then give them a free rein within certain well defined limits. This attitude toward employees I believe underlies the success of a large number of big businesses.

Many a hundred-dollar man remains a fifteen-dollar subordinate because he is not given any latitude and is not allowed to develop. The head of a concern may have an employee off in one corner of the office who is in reality his superior in ability if he were only allowed to show it—if he were only given carte blanche to take the initiative.

It is far better to select an employee when young and start him at $10 a week, educate and develop him, than to transplant a man from some other business and put him into a position over the heads of old employees.

Let your employees grow up with you. Having selected an employee, give him a chance and a thorough trial and ascertain what he can do and just what his limits are. In this way only can be determined whether he is a fit employee or not. Give this employee a wide latitude and discretion over little things and observe the results over a considerable period of time.

Many a hundred-dollar man remains a fifteen-dollar subordinate because he is not given any latitude and is not allowed to develop.

Men learn only by the mistakes they make. An employer should expect and should encourage his men to take the initiative and make mistakes. Only in this way can they gain experience. This method of handling employees may be expensive in its early stages, but it is the only proper schooling for a position.

No man can learn to be a "crack shot" unless he wastes some ammunition. The employer should stand the expense of the experiments made by a new man who shows ability; it will pay in the long run. If mistakes continue and positive results do not come the man must go. But, on the other hand, if after a trial of this kind a man's caliber is determined, then the time for promotion and increase of salary is at hand.

No man can learn to be a "crack shot" unless he wastes some ammunition. The employer should stand the expense of the experiments made by a new man who shows ability; it will pay in the long run.

The great advantage of this method is that it inspires in the employee confidence in himself, without which he can make no success for himself or for his firm. It cultivates the

quality of initiative, which means business creation and profits for the firm.

The surest way to gain the unswerving loyalty of
employees is to show them from the start that they will be
allowed to make the most of themselves. A man wants to stay
with the firm with which he can reach his greatest efficiency.
And where these relations exist, the employee never leaves
to seek a better place if he is the right kind. Occasionally a
firm may have a man who will reach his limit; he only has a
certain capacity and certain restricted capabilities. When he
reaches this stage he will remain stationary.

The head of a concern often talks to his men about the
methods they use. Yet methods are minor considerations. It

---

*The surest way to gain the unswerving loyalty
of employees is to show them from the start
that they will be allowed to make the most of
themselves. A man wants to stay with the firm
with which he can reach his greatest efficiency.*

---

is the sum total—the actual results—that we want in business I do not care what method a man uses in any department of a business so long as he "makes good."

The matter of success should be put up to the pride of
the individual. He should be made to understand that his
development depends upon himself and the quality of his
work. If a salesman can show an increase of three per cent
in the sales of his territory or department in a given period
he has proved his right to remain a part of a business organization regardless of his methods for achieving these
results.

Following out this same idea, I believe that too many
instructions to employees are often fatal. Don't be too specific; such an attitude makes a man into a machine. When

sending a man on a certain duty it is never best to say, "do exactly this," or "don't do that." The proper course is to say "go and look into this matter to the best of your ability."

The employee, if he is the right kind, will then, as a matter of course, do his best. Following out this policy, our firm has never had any specific rules for employees, but has made the business and personal conduct of each individual a matter for each to look after.

We never use verbal praise with employees, nor reprimands. We often tell a man that he is working too hard or that he is underpaid; but in this case we add that he is being paid the limit that his position is worth and that he will be advanced as soon as an opening offers itself, if he is capable. The raise in salary or the promotion always comes to the individual without asking. Not that it would not be very proper for the employee to ask for a raise, but, basing our attitude toward employees upon these principles, we soon discover whether a man is doing more than he is paid for and reward him because it pays us as a matter of business.

Too many instructions to employees are often fatal. Don't be too specific; such an attitude makes a man into a machine.

It is the man who, in the position that he holds temporarily, does more than is expected of him, that gets the increase in salary or the higher position. Anything like special rewards, presents or bonuses are wholly out of place in a system of handling employees such as this. Men working on this basis would consider anything of the kind an insult. It would imply that they were not doing their best—it would be in the nature of a bribe. The giving of prizes for special effort, which is considered so effective in enthusing men in some organizations, would fail to have the desired effect in an organization where every man is given free reign.

This method of handling subordinates accomplishes all the usual results of the most highly developed system of choosing, training and retaining employees. It tries them out thoroughly—it finds the right man for the right place, and the right place for the right man. It enthuses the worker and inspires in him loyalty to the firm.

MARY KAY ASH

Don't be fooled by the pink car with the Mary Kay logo. Behind this cute prize for top saleswomen is a tough leader who readily admits "Recognition was as vital to me as money." She now has both. Ash attributes her success to her mother's simple mantra, "You can do it," that was constantly reinforced over her formative years. Unfortunately, one month before Mary Kay Cosmetics was to open in 1963, her husband had a fatal heart attack, and all seemed lost. Both Ash's accountant and lawyer advised her to liquidate and cut losses, but as she says, "no matter what anyone thought, I just couldn't give up my dream."

Ash went on to build a unique sales force of women, in which the saleswoman purchases her own inventory and then sells it to her customers. This atypical method prevents any kind of draw on future sales; therefore, it keeps her sales representatives out of debt and keeps herself solvent. The sales philosophy preached to this devoted army of women, according to Ash, is based on a "low-key educational approach. We don't sell—we teach." Otherwise known as "polite persuasion." If the customer shows interest, the sales representative is fully prepared to quickly "close" the sale. The cosmetics they demonstrate are always on hand for immediate purchase because Ash understands that when consumers want something, they want it now. And you don't want to give them a second chance to think about it.

The low-key approach to sales is part of a larger business philosophy that embodies Ash's maternal outlook. It includes generous incentives for employees (like the car) and an open-door policy. Of course, once an open-door policy is implemented, the key to its success lies in how the employees are treated after they walk across the threshold. In *The Art of Listening* Ash explains the importance of giving the employee your undivided attention. So listen up.

The Art of Listening
Mary Kay Ash

All through school we're taught to read, write, and speak — we're never taught to listen. But while listening may be the most undervalued of all the communication skills, good people managers are likely to listen more than they speak. Perhaps that's why God gave us two ears and only one mouth.

Some of the most successful people managers are also the best listeners. I remember one manager in particular. He had been hired by a large corporation to assume the role of sales manager. But he knew absolutely nothing about the specifics of the business. When salespeople would go to him for answers, there wasn't anything he could tell them — because he didn't know anything! Nonetheless, this man *really* knew how to listen. So no matter what they would ask him, he'd answer, "What do *you* think you ought to do?" They'd come up with the solution; he'd agree; and they'd leave satisfied. They thought he was fantastic.

He taught me this valuable listening technique, and I've been applying it ever since. Recently one of our consultants came to me to discuss her marital problems. She asked my advice as to whether she should divorce her husband. Since I didn't even know the man, and hardly knew her, there was no way I could give her advice. All I did was listen, nod my head, and ask, "What do *you* think you ought to do?" I asked her that several times, and each time she went on to tell me what she thought she should do. The next day I received a beautiful bouquet of flowers with a lovely note thanking me for my terrific advice. Then about a year later she wrote to tell me that her marriage was wonderful—and again my advice was credited!

Many of the problems I hear don't require me to offer solutions. I solve most of them by just listening and letting the grieving party do the talking. If I listen long enough, the person will generally come up with an adequate solution.

Several years ago a friend of mine purchased a small manufacturing company at a bargain price. The previous owner said, "I'm glad to get rid of it. My employees have become very militant, and they just don't appreciate all I've done for them over the years. They're going to vote for a union any day now, and I don't want to deal with those union people."

After he became the owner, my friend conducted an open meeting with his total staff. "I want you all to be happy," he told them. "Tell me what I can do to make that happen." As it turned out, he only had to provide a few minor conveniences: modern bathroom fixtures, larger mirrors in the locker rooms, and vending machines for the recreation area. These were the only things they wanted. As a result the union was never voted in, and today everyone is content. All they really wanted was someone to listen to them.

Listening is an art. And the first tenet of the skill is that undivided attention to the other party. When someone enters my office to speak with me, I don't allow anything to distract my attention. If I'm talking to someone in a crowded room, I try to make that person feel as though we're the only ones present. I shut out everything else.

I look directly at the person. Even if a gorilla were to walk into the room, I probably wouldn't notice it. I remember how offended I once was when I was having lunch with my sales manager, and every time a pretty waitress walked by, his eyes would follow her across the room. I felt insulted and kept thinking to myself, "That waitress's legs are more important to him than what I have to say. He's not listening to me. He doesn't care about me!" You've got to pay attention in order to hear what the other person is saying. Without discipline and concentration, our minds wander.

People can also be distracted by their own petty prejudices. For instance, a person may use profanity or some expression that you don't like. Or perhaps you are irritated by a certain accent. I know Southerners who can't stand a New York accent, and I've met New Yorkers who feel the same way about a southern drawl. Consequently they allow something this insignificant to distract from the value of another person's thoughts.

Everyone has seen jokesters who get together to exchange stories. No sooner does one tell a joke than the other person matches him. Neither one listens to the other, because they're both too busy getting their next joke ready. At some point each of us has failed to listen because he was restlessly awaiting a turn to speak.

Often people feel uneasy whenever there's a pause in the conversation. They feel compelled to rush in and start talking. Perhaps if they would remain quiet, the other person might clarify or provide additional information. Sometimes it's good for both parties to keep quiet for a few moments — to think. A conversation interrupted by silence can be a welcome relief. In fact, nonstop conversation may be an indication that something is seriously wrong.

Many managers make the mistake of creating a boss–employee relationship between themselves and their people — like student to teacher. However, while it is true that a teacher generally stands at the head of the class and does most of the talking, a good teacher also knows how to listen attentively. So does a good manager. To play an authoritarian role with a subordinate establishes a we-they adversary relationship. Effective communication breaks down, and nobody listens!

MARVIN BOWER
1903 –

Bower has been called "the legendary spiritual leader" of McKinsey & Co., a world-renown management consulting firm. It was founded in 1926 by James O. McKinsey, who later left his own company to head Marshall Field & Co. Bower, a Harvard-trained lawyer, joined the consulting firm in 1933, and held the prestigious managing director position from 1950 to 1967. According to Bower, when he got his start in the 1930s, "management consulting wasn't even called that. It was called management engineering." Undoubtedly, clients did not appreciate being compared to a machine that is tinkered with by engineers. Bower, however, placed a premium on satisfying the customer, and with his law degree he also brought a code of ethics to the fledgling consulting industry. A former employee best described Bower's influence: "He led that firm according to a set of values, and it was the principle of using values to help shape and guide an organization that was probably the most important thing I took away."

Bower believed that "success in managing a business is determined largely by how effectively, resolutely, and consistently top management makes simple concepts work." The standards Bower set have remained part of the firm's culture, or cult of success. Many former McKinsey employees have risen to prominence over the years, including Louis Gerstner (who became Chairman and CEO of IBM), Harvey Golub (Chairman and CEO of American Express), Robert Haas (Chairman and CEO of Levi Strauss), and Michael H. Jordan (Chairman and CEO of Westinghouse Electric), among many others. However, the fact that these were McKinsey men did not and does not necessarily guarantee success for the various companies they joined. As Bower critically noted, it takes more than a one-man show to manage a large company, and in addition, he warned that "The will to manage is not synonymous with the will to succeed." In *Leadership*, Bower deciphers the qualities that make a successful leader, as opposed to those that simply make a willful manager.

Leadership
Marvin Bower

T he best means of activating people, of course, is leadership. Leadership skill is needed in some depth by every company that aims to achieve maximum success.

Fortunately, the nature of business leadership and the tools required for developing it in depth are such that this need can more easily be met in a system-managed company. Such a company can be more successful with a given amount of leadership skill; and where the will to manage is present, a management system tends almost automatically to foster the development of that skill.

Extent of Need: Since only a minor competitive advantage can enable a company to gain substantial success, business strategy need not be designed to achieve a towering competitive position like that of General Motors. Such competitive superiority is neither necessary nor common. Moreover, even GM built its present share-of-market from an initial position of slight competitive advantage which it compounded through systematized management.

The elements of business success are numerous, and many companies can be successful without leadership skill in great depth. But it is wise to aim high in developing leadership skill, since the more a company possesses, the greater its success is likely to be.

Although leadership is desirable at all levels in a company, it is most important in the chief executive and those reporting to him. In any company the number of key leaders required is not very great, and in a large company the proportion can be small indeed.

Nature of Business Leadership: When we think of "leadership" in the abstract, we are inclined to think of statesmen like a Lincoln or a Churchill—someone who can arouse or inspire men to rise to great achievements by perceiving their capacities and motivations, articulating the goals to be achieved, and inspiring the efforts and sacrifices needed to achieve them. In this sense, leadership seems somehow mystical—and unattainable for the ordinary person.

But I believe that *business* leadership—the only kind with which we are dealing here—does not require vastly superior or unusual qualities, especially in a system-managed company. Given a chief executive with the will to manage, most system-managed companies can attract a reasonable proportion of high-caliber people and from them develop the leaders they need for success. It doesn't quite come about automatically, but it is fairly likely to happen if the system is followed.

I have two reasons for believing this. First, a system-managed business is not really dependent on personal leadership of an inspirational nature, desirable though such leadership always is. The various system components provide people in the business with guidelines for action. The individual's economic and emotional self-interest will cause him to follow these guidelines without a high order of inspired leadership. Since he knows what to do, self-government under the system will encourage him to do it. And the interactions of system components will further stimulate his performance.

Second, the requirements of business leadership are less demanding than those of great political leadership. The statesman must arouse people to do the unusual; the business leader need only stimulate them to do well in the task of earning their livelihood. Not that business may not demand sacrifice: I know one 47-year-old executive of a large company who has moved his family 28 times. But business sacrifices usually involve a larger and more perceptible element of self-interest than civic sacrifices. In fact, truly inspirational statesmanship moves citizens to put aside their self-interest. Business leadership, though it does appeal to people's higher motives, seldom has to meet such a challenge.

Next, a look at the qualities that business leaders need shows that men with those qualities are likely to be found in a system-managed company.

Every basic analysis of leadership emphasizes the importance of integrity. As Pearl S. Buck, the only American woman thus far to win the Nobel Prize for Literature, has said: "Integrity is honesty carried through the fibres of the being and the whole mind, into thought as well as action so that the person is complete in honesty. That kind of integrity I put above all else as an essential of leadership." People won't follow a person they don't trust. But integrity is widely scattered in the population.

A business leader must have a good but not necessarily brilliant mind; reasonable degrees of imagination, initiative, and sustained drive; considerable achievement motivation; and some ability to understand the position and point of view of the other fellow. Again, these basic qualities are widely scattered in the population.

Thus, countless individuals possess all of the qualities required for effective business leadership. Yet, they lead poorly, if at all, because they don't know how to go about it. As executives with authority, they settle for orders and discipline. They fail to create constructive job attitudes. They lose for their companies the great potential advantages of self-direction and self-control.

Forces Favoring the Development of Business Leaders: Three primary forces at work in our society favor the development of leadership skill in U.S. business today:

1. *A free society:* Anyone in the United States can aspire to any level of business leadership for which he is fitted by his personal capabilities and ambition, just as he can aspire to leadership in government or any other field. Hence, a policy of advancement on the basis of performance is really useful in encouraging people to perform well and become leaders as well as managers.

2. *Universal education:* Our generally accepted *requirement* for a high minimum level of education and the *opportunity* to get a graduate education that our society affords to any capable and ambitious person develop leadership skills for business as well as other fields.

3. *The free enterprise system:* The competitive profit-and-loss system is a great help to the leader at any level in a company. Fortunately, in the United States at least, most people still regard profit as the one measure of business success that is best for employees, stockholders, and citizens generally. Hence, business leadership is fostered simply by getting everyone in the company to recognize that long-term profit is the best single measure of company success and the most useful guide to decision making and action. In fact, the profit-and-loss system not only helps develop leadership skill but reduces the *need* for that skill by providing guidelines for self-direction and self-control.

Yet it is surprising how often business executives fail to make full use of this wonderful management and leadership tool. Many, for example, prefer to use volume, size, or prestige as measures of success. Many others simply fail to make effective use of the profit measure. It is a powerful and effective management and leadership instrument, and it is available to every business leader.

In addition to these general forces favoring the development of business leadership skill in the United States, a *system-managed* company has two additional advantages. A system of management (1) reduces the *need* for leadership and (2) provides specific assistance in *learning* leadership and making it effective in action.

How System Reduces the Need for Leadership: In discussing leadership, Semon Knudsen of GM said that a leader "is a man with a mission." In a system-managed company the mission is clear because objectives and strategy are definite elements of management. Not only the top managers but executives at all levels have strategic plans before them. The mission does not depend on a single individual, because the system approach keeps many minds focused on the company's objectives and goals for increasing volume, share-of-market, and profits, and for maintaining continuity of effective management.

A business leader must have a good but not necessarily brilliant mind [and] reasonable degrees of imagination, initiative, and sustained drive . . .

The same is true of the other managing processes. With all of the guidelines provided by the system, people know what to do and can get on with the job. The need for orders, penalties, and advice is minimized, and the company moves closer to the self-government end of the activating spectrum.

A system-managed business carries on a continuous hunt for talent and a continuous program for developing and motivating that talent. The better the talent, the less external activating it needs. With guidelines set by the system, self-direction and self-control are purposeful and productive.

Finally, by interaction the various managing processes that make up the system tend to support each other, thus reducing the need for leadership activation. For example, if the philosophy calls for decisions based on facts, managers at any level feel free to change their plans and programs as conditions change and new facts are disclosed. With established policies and clearly delegated authority, they can make decisions without waiting for either instructions or leadership from higher up.

In deciding to systematize the business, the executive makes two commitments to himself: first, to maintain the will to manage; second, to devote much of his time to building, maintaining, articulating, and supporting the system and to making it effective in action.

Thus, action under one managing process interacts with actions under other processes within the system to strengthen all the actions and processes involved. Moreover, people lean more heavily on the *system* and less heavily on personal instructions, attitudes, and power. Once the system is established and understood by the people in the company, therefore, a system-managed company is actually easier to manage.

How the System Helps Develop Leadership Skill: Even though a system-managed company requires less leadership skill to achieve success, the system nevertheless helps to develop that skill. This is simply because the leader in a system-managed company knows better what to do to *be* a leader.

There is nothing mystical about the leadership process in a system-managed company. The leader at any level merely takes the steps necessary to build, articulate, support, and operate the system. These steps, in *themselves*, constitute adequate leadership for company success. Beyond this, whatever the leader accomplishes through brilliance in strategy, risk-taking, administration, or stimulation of people will be limited only by his own capabilities and ambitions. The system will give leverage to any brilliance he may possess. For a given input of ideas and actions, it will make him more productive. In short, it will increase his chances of becoming a Carnegie, Ford, Firestone, Sloan, or Watson.

In summary, then, here's how the system approach provides guidance and leverage for business leadership:

1. *The decision to systematize:* A decision by the head of any company, division, or department to systematize the business is in itself an act of leadership. Yet it is an easy, specific step to take — a concrete way of making the will to manage effective in achieving company success.

   In deciding to systematize the business, the executive makes two commitments to himself: first, to maintain the will to manage; second, to devote much of his time to building, maintaining, articulating, and supporting the system and to making it effective in action. This means that he will have less time for day-to-day operational decision making. He will have to keep out of the details. He will be forced into a leadership posture.

2. *Company philosophy:* Crystallizing or shaping a company philosophy to control "the way we do things around here" is also an act of leadership, because it involves establishing a fact-founded approach to decision making and developing a greater sense of competitive urgency.

3. *Strategic and management planning:* Leadership by ideas that build volume and share-of-market can be supplied by requiring that concrete strategies and management plans are developed to provide specific answers to these questions: What kind of business should we be in? Why should customers buy our products or services? What problems need to be solved? What opportunities can we capitalize on?

   Ideas are one of the few ways to gain a real competitive advantage, but the top-management executive need not furnish the ideas himself. He can stimulate the production of ideas from others by requiring them to develop alternative objectives and strategies and by insisting that they tackle any problems arising from shifts in external forces at work.

4. *Action guidelines:* Building the system requires the establishment of many action guidelines: a plan of organization, policies, standards, procedures, management plans, and information for managing. Certainly these guidelines are concrete ways of providing leadership. As they become known and used, they facilitate self-government.

5. *Personnel leadership:* The head of any organizational unit can provide important leadership by leading the talent hunt for high-caliber people. Then he can see to it that plans and programs are prepared for developing and motivating these people to become supervisors and executives qualified for advancement.

High-caliber people who know the company's philosophy, who are qualified as executives, and who have been trained in the company's system can give any company a competitive advantage that is hard to duplicate. So, by devoting substantial time to this system component, the top executives provide leadership.

6. *System articulation:* As the system becomes established, it must be communicated—to executives and supervisors at a minimum, but preferably to everyone. The leader cannot do less than discuss the system orally with key executives to be sure they understand all the components and how they interact on one other. If it is to guide people, a system must be known and understood by the people to be guided—the more of them the better. Hence, the leader should put all the components of the system into writing—perhaps in the form of a pamphlet presenting the over-all system and its components, emphasizing their relative importance, and clearly describing their interaction.

But a general pronouncement is only the beginning of articulation. After that, every management communication, whether oral or written, should tie the specific action into the system. No orders, advice, discipline, reward, or other activating or motivating action should be taken unless it is tied clearly into the system. "Let's do this. Here is how it fits into the system and interacts with other components."

Ideas are one of the few ways to gain a real competitive advantage, but the top-management executive need not furnish the ideas himself.

Once established, a system will not be useful or even hold together unless it is consciously used and believed in. The leader must constantly reiterate, in all his written and oral communications, what the system is, how it works, and why it helps to do the managing job. The will to manage through a system requires the will to build an effective system and the determination to articulate it constantly.

7. *System support:* The best way to kill a management system is to violate it. The second best way is to ignore it. So the leader must support the system by following it himself and by inspiring and requiring others to do likewise.

Support and articulation go hand in hand. By following the system himself and explaining to others what is accomplished by doing so, the leader sets an example and so communicates in the most powerful way possible. And by training his subordinates to take the same approach, he can build a momentum for managing that both stimulates leadership and minimizes the need for leadership.

A superb expression of the value of the system approach to managing is found in a statement made at the 1965 meeting of General Motors stockholders by John F. Gordon, on the eve of his forthcoming retirement as president: "It has been GM's people — the individual and collective contributions of thousands of men and women down through the years — who have been responsible for the Corporation's consistently outstanding performance.

"Let me make it clear that I am not contending that General Motors men and women are inherently superior people. Individually, they probably cover as broad a range of capabilities as you will find in most large companies.

"It is what happens when you put them together that makes the difference. It is the potency of the mixture rather than the strength of its ingredients that is most important. General Motors is a very potent mixture of many different ingredients . . . its basic organization takes this wide diversity of elements fully into consideration. Its decentralized operations and responsibilities with centralized policies and coordinated control make it possible to balance . . . things like individual initiative and freedom of action on the one hand with guidance and restraint on the other.

The best way to kill a management system is to violate it. The second best way is to ignore it.

"Working in such an organization, people not only act individually but react positively upon one another. Each person can and usually does increase the effectiveness of those with whom he works as well as his own effectiveness — and it makes their total performance considerably greater than the sum of their separate acts.

"Unexceptional men and women turned in exceptional performance for many reasons: for personal recognition, for monetary reward, for advancement and for personal satisfaction; also because of the urge to excel and to compete successfully, out of loyalty to the Corporation and to the people they work with — and for every possible combination of these and other motives."

150

8. *Constructive job attitudes:* Part of the down-the-line communication and training job is to give everyone a belief in the worthwhileness of the company's contribution to society, a sense of belonging and participation, and — at least at the supervisory level and up — an understanding of their contributions to the total enterprise. This is an intangible act of leadership, but again the system provides substantial assistance.

9. *Opportunities and problems:* An effective system of management will disclose opportunities that can be seized and problems that should be solved. If the system fails to produce the action indicated, the leader will have to step in. Especially should he see that personnel problems are dealt with promptly, fairly, and firmly.

10. *Dealing with extremes:* When the system functions poorly, as at times it will, the leader must be ready to act himself, choosing the activators and motivators most appropriate for the occasion. The system will still give leverage to his actions.

   And even when the system is functioning well — as it should be most of the time — the executive can add vision, zeal, inspiration, exhortation, or brilliance in any form or degree. If in so doing he does not interfere too much with the system, he will add to his company's success. But leadership in a system-managed company seldom requires such unusual abilities.

As you put down this book, I hope that your will to manage is strong. I hope, too, that you have come to share my conviction that a management system provides the best means for making that will to manage effective — the best way for your company to expand its volume and share-of-market, increase its long-term profits, and provide for continuity of effective management. Translated into action, that will and that conviction can bring substantial benefits to any enterprise. And enormous benefits for the nation will flow from the improvements in many enterprises.

T. BOONE PICKENS
1928 –

Pickens has been called "a corporate raider, a greenmailer, a communist, even a piranha." This is the man who claims he was so shy that in the fourth grade he had to have a schoolmate read his homework out loud when he was chosen by the teacher. At some point in the ensuing years he obviously became a competitive extrovert who refused to lose at anything. After studying geology at Oklahoma State University, Pickens' first job was with Phillips Petroleum in 1951 as an oil-well–site geologist. It was not long before he became disillusioned with the company's bureaucracy and subsequently quit at the age of 26.

With a wife, two young children, a third on the way, and his back against the wall, Pickens was looking for a deal. He lived out of his station wagon as he drove around Texas, prospecting choice land to drill and raising the financing to do it. In 1956, with two partners and $2,500, Pickens founded the company that would become Mesa Petroleum and evolve into the largest independently owned oil and gas company in the United States. The up-and-coming Pickens was soon rubbing shoulders with America's elite CEOs, whom he saw as only interested in furthering their own personal gains and not those of the stockholder or America in general. He believed, "most corporations are misappropriating your money. It is legal under the system; every day this respectable crime is perpetrated. . . ." As Pickens targeted what he viewed as being soft or mismanaged companies, he realized "we could out think, out work, and out fox the big boys, and that would beat all the money in the world."

Pickens gambled big, investing millions of dollars in what he thought were poorly managed companies as he attempted to gain control, and then force change on corporate America. However, behind his gambling was meticulous financial analysis; Pickens knew how to discover an undervalued company as well as an oil field. This dynamic paradox of both the freewheeling and the disciplined pervades his management philosophy. In *Leadership,* Pickens develops his dichotomous ideas that include leading with loose reins while employing an iron grip.

Leadership
T. Boone Pickens

A lot has been written in the last few years about management: theory X and theory Y, grids and objectives. Lately there has even been a book telling managers how to do it all in a miracle visit of one minute, like a holy man conferring a blessing on the workplace. Other books tell us how to dress, arrange our office furniture, even what to order for lunch. Frankly, I think most of this is a waste of time.

There are three kinds of managements. Some see changes coming well in advance and may even accelerate the process. Some see changes coming just in time to adjust before it's too late. Some never see changes coming, so they don't adjust. The last group gets run over by change, and it almost always comprises the arrogant, iron-headed managements who have had it their way for years and, by God, they are going to keep it their way. Good-bye to the management that can't adjust.

A management style is an amalgamation of the best of other people you have known and respected, and eventually you develop your own style. The Boone Pickens management style started back in the oil fields of the Panhandle, Gulf of Mexico, and Canada and progressed through a long series of financial dealings.

A wise woman, Grace Hopper, now retired, was the best known female admiral in the U.S. Navy. She expressed my management philosophy succinctly when she said, "You don't manage people, you manage things. You *lead* people." She was right.

I never consciously manage anybody. I try to lead people.

Leadership is hard to define. You know when you're around it and when you see it. I've experienced many good leaders, from my old high school coach to Ronald Reagan to some of the young people who work at Mesa today. I've watched them inspire and galvanize others. I know that the important part of being a leader is what goes on inside your own mind—what you do to yourself, not what you do to others.

Leadership is the quality that transforms good intentions into positive action; it turns a group of individuals into a team.

Part of leadership is taking risks and building confidence in yourself. You have to serve many apprenticeships throughout your life. Show me somebody who won't serve an apprenticeship, and I'll show you somebody who won't go very far. If you take up golf, you're going to serve an apprenticeship learning to play; you're going to serve an apprenticeship when you break in with a new group of people. Those who lack confidence will seldom serve an apprenticeship; they're afraid they'll fail. But a few people take it in stride and move on.

In corporate America, those who lack confidence surround themselves with people who continually stroke their egos. If my style were to jerk people around, you can bet your life that it would be practiced throughout the organization. At Mesa, people who are good, strong players find their apprenticeships to be surprisingly short. You can move up quickly, for there is always room at the top.

Leadership is the quality that transforms good intentions into positive action; it turns a group of individuals into a team. I learned early, in business as well as politics, that people love a leader. They like decisive action.

You lead by example. You don't run over your personnel, but you don't pump them up with false praise, either.

We work hard at Mesa—long hours, intense analysis. When House and Senate conferees agreed on a compromise for the new tax bill on Saturday, August 16, 1986, five of our men were in the office early the next morning to see how it would affect us. We worked most of that Sunday—and I wasn't the one who called the meeting. On any weekend, there are always cars in the garage while their owners take care of business that won't wait until Monday. It goes with the territory, and the rewards are proportionate—both financially and in terms of professional satisfaction. If you aren't a worker, you won't make it with me.

You can do some things to set up an organization so that leadership will flourish on all levels.

Concentrate on the goals, not the size of the organization. You can't measure a place by size unless it's a football stadium.

At Mesa, we work short-handed. That way people have a greater opportunity to advance and less time for office politics. If you are worrying about keeping your head above water, you're not going to spend a lot of time trying to figure out how to do in a colleague. I want people to be challenged and to have the opportunity to advance.

It's unusual to find a large corporation that's efficient. I know about economies of scale and all the other advantages that are supposed to come with size. But when you get an inside look, it's easy to see how inefficient big business really is. Most corporate bureaucracies have more people than they have work. Large corporations were great at setting up massive assembly lines, but terrible at modifying those same lines to fit changing conditions. Insulated from the real world, most executives don't even notice what is happening.

There are few visionaries at the top of our major corporations. "America has a pioneering spirit, a spirit of innovation we have to beat," a Japanese official said in 1939, recognizing the real strength of our brand of capitalism. Not many years later, inertia had replaced innovation in corporate America, something that became painfully clear once the foreign companies were competing on our turf.

The automobile industry is a perfect example of an industry paralyzed by bureaucratic inertia. The Japanese and Germans concentrated on building a better automobile while the U.S. automakers added a little trim and rested on their laurels. Then, when the rest of the auto world caught up, Detroit ran to Washington for bailouts and protection. All their preoccupation with bigness got them was vulnerability.

At Mesa, our goal is to have fewer people managing more assets; profits are a much better indicator of business acumen than size. I decided a long time ago to hire the best people, pay them well, get the best equipment, provide the best working conditions, and let size take care of itself. I have the best people I have ever had; it took years to put this group together, but it was worth it.

Forget about age, which means giving the young people a chance. I have a bias toward youth, but I also think that youth is a state of mind. I am interested in whether a person can do the job. Mesa personnel know this well, and it is a great boost for morale. The average age at Mesa is thirty-six years old. (The joke is that if I would retire it would drop to thirty-one.)

Young people are a little rash sometimes, but they often make up for it by generating good ideas. I choose employees for their intelligence, attitude, and enthusiasm. I'm convinced that you can be old at thirty or young at seventy—it's all up to you.

Years ago, a CEO of a major company asked me how I included my young people. My answer was: "Just invite them in; it's easy."

Keep things informal. Talking is the natural way to do business. Writing is great for keeping records and pinning down details, but talk generates ideas. Great things come from our luncheon meetings, which consist of a sandwich, a cup of soup, and a good idea or two. No martinis.

Concentrate on the goals, not the size of the organization. You can't measure a place by size unless it's a football stadium.

Communication is crucial—not the formal stuff but frequent conversation among the people who make the decisions. The dialogue should take place regardless of where you are. I talk to David Batchelder and Paul Cain at least twice a day no matter where we are. When Bea and I went to Africa, I was supposed to be incommunicado for two weeks, but I was on the phone to David after just three days from Maun, Botswana.

People know that they can talk to me, no matter how busy I am. My accessibility keeps me up to speed on our projects, and when it's time to make a decision I'm ready, with no need for lengthy presentations.

With good communication, there are no surprises. I hate surprises. I feel as though I'm not on top of things if I get surprised.

You don't have to rise through four levels before you make it at Mesa. David Batchelder said he couldn't believe the meetings he was in soon after he joined Mesa; he was only twenty-eight at the time. When we're involved in a big deal, there's so much going on that almost anyone can step up and say, "I can do that."

When people disagree with me, they do it openly, respectfully, but directly in front of the others. You've got to remove any fear of disagreeing with the CEO. It forces everyone down the line to use the same technique. You either speak up if you don't like it or forever hold your peace.

When I started PEI in 1956, one of the first things I did was to put each day's correspondence on a clipboard for anyone in the company to read if he or she wanted to take the time. As our business grew, it became impractical; but the message was clear: I want everybody informed; that way we don't have office rumors and speculation.

There are many ways to avoid mistakes, but the best way to sidestep the disasters is to be available. You don't have to make every decision, but you should always be accessible. If your people are smart they will keep you informed, and if you're informed, you're a part of the decision. With that in place, it's easy for you to back your people and it eliminates second-guessing.

Play by the rules. Every year, I speak on about twenty campuses to ten thousand or more students. I'm interested in their ideas, and they're interested in the range of experience I bring to them. More than anything else, I emphasize that they don't need to cheat, or even bend their principles, to succeed in business. I tell them that pursuing a career is no different from playing golf or tennis. It's no fun to win by breaking the rules, and they can beat the competition and still stick with everything they believe in. As simple as it sounds, students really seem to appreciate hearing that advice. Maybe no other businessman tells them that they can win without cheating.

The oil business is rife with opportunities to bend the rules, but that is short-sighted. We plan on being around for the duration, and even though we might be tempted to take a short cut, it could ruin the good reputation that we're determined to build and keep. Playing by the rules applies to life within the company, too. I'm disturbed by what I've seen in the last several years, with people being asked to take "early retirement" in their fifties while the CEO stays on past the mandatory retirement age of sixty-five. Are any of us so valuable to an organization that we should be exempt from the rules?

On hiring and firing: What I am always looking for is people who can do a job better than I can. When I find them, they are damn sure going to get that job. I never load myself so that people under me aren't challenged. Years ago, a man I was interviewing for a vice presidential post said, "The position doesn't have a good job description. I'm not sure I'll be challenged." I told him, "You won't ever have to worry about having plenty to do at Mesa."

When someone tips his hand and gives you an insight to his character, good or bad, don't forget it. When I look back over the people who have worked for me, it's surprising how close my initial evaluation was to my final one. A good manager will follow his instincts.

Some people are not comfortable in a fast-moving operation. They want more time to think or maybe procrastinate. It won't work here. You have to think fast and not let the decisions stack up.

Of course you make hiring mistakes, and people sometimes have to be fired. I'll live with a bad situation just long enough to know there's no other choice. The rest, believe it or not, is easy. People know when they aren't doing the job, and the kindest thing to do is to release them.

There are three things I will fire someone for on the spot: drinking on the job, stealing, and carrying on an interoffice relationship, all of which are very damaging to morale, not to mention the work habits of those involved.

Some people are not comfortable in a fast-moving operation. They want more time to think or maybe procrastinate. It won't work here. You have to think fast and not let the decisions stack up. My advice to our people is: if you aren't happy, then you should leave. I can't imagine going through life in a job that I didn't like. The wear and tear year after year on me and my family would be unbearable. I would go back to field geology rather than serve my time in an unhappy situation, no matter what they paid me.

Keep fit. Physical fitness is an essential part of the best-run companies, for it has economic as well as spiritual and psychological benefits. Its popularity will continue to grow over the years.

In 1979, we built a first-class athletic facility equipped as well as any commercial health center. A fitness center is a great asset for any company that cares about its employees and wants to stay competitive.

As early as the 1960s, Mesa paid for employee memberships at the Amarillo YMCA, but I wasn't a regular participant. I never had a weight problem because I did things in moderation. The gene mix was also to my advantage. My father has done very little exercise in the last twenty-five years, and he's still going strong at eighty-eight. But I gradually got out of shape, which is easy to do in your late thirties or early forties.

It wasn't long after I married Bea, in 1972, that a friend introduced me to racquetball, a new game that was sweeping the country. I began working myself back into shape. I jogged and took up racquetball seriously. Today, I may be the best fifty-eight-year-old racquetball player in America (there aren't many players my age).

I discovered that all those things you hear about being in shape were true. I felt better. My stamina improved and so did my powers of concentration. I was getting a lot more done each day and still had energy to burn.

About three quarters of Mesa's employees participate in the fitness program. It's like having an ongoing research project in your backyard. We've been keeping statistics since we opened the center, and the results are spectacular. The Fitness Center saves Mesa more than $200,000 in insurance claims annually. We know that employees who exercise regularly average $173 in medical bills a year, whereas it costs $434 for inactive employees. Exercisers average 27 hours of sick leave per year; non-exercisers, 44 hours.

You can quantify the insurance savings and even the sick time, but there are also many intangibles. For one thing, I am a regular participant at the Fitness Center, and this is good for overall morale. In 1985, Mesa was named the Most Physically Fit Company in America, winning the National Fitness Classic in Houston. Once again, we were out in front of the pack. But when you're a little guy in a big game, you'd better be out front or you'll get run over. I continually promote this theme.

Corporations were never set up to meet all the needs of their employees or management — they were set up to make money. That is their primary objective and it should also be the objective of management.

"A small band of fit people" can do most anything. As one of our people said, "We are like the French Resistance."

Make sure that as many people as possible have a personal stake in the company. Some 95 percent of Mesa's employees own stock in the company.

As I look at corporate America today, it's clear that one of the basic problems is the separation of ownership and control. Executives and employees who have a financial stake in the company tend to think and act like stockholders. The typical CEO of a large corporation owns very little stock, yet he has absolute control over assets worth billions of dollars. As a result, the goal of the professional manager is like that of a bureaucrat. The emphasis is on bigger budgets and expanding empires, not on serving the interests of owners.

Early on, I set up stock options and a profit-sharing plan for Mesa's employees. In 1984, *Money* magazine listed Mesa's benefits among the ten best plans in the nation, ahead of all the other oil companies. *Forbes* listed Mesa at the top in net income per employee in 1985 and 1986.

Not everyone can or should be an entrepreneur; most people work effectively for another person, or a corporation. Security is a reasonable and proper concern for most people, and working for a corporation is probably better than working for the government.

The desire for security, which led so many people to the corporate life, also developed a corporate culture that more closely resembled a government agency than a business operation. In the last two years, corporate bureaucracies have been shaken to the core. They have finally realized that they have to get competitive, and that means cutting out several layers of management. This will be good for all the employees because for the first time they'll see what decisiveness is all about.

Additional pressure is coming from the entrepreneurial movement that is sweeping the country. The young people moving up are becoming adamantly opposed to large organizations that they could get lost in.

Corporations were never set up to meet all the needs of their employees or management—they were set up to make money. That is their primary objective and it should also be the objective of management. Good managers make money for stockholders, serving both employees and consumers in the process.

Finally, enjoy it. We may work hard, but there are no stomachaches. We laugh a lot. If we screw up, then we all screwed up. We move quickly, which often creates an advantage.

It's like racquetball, when you move in and cut off a shot. Your opponent thinks you're going to let the ball go to the wall, so he thinks he has a second to regroup. You may not be set up, or your feet may not be exactly right; you might not be best at an overhead shot, but the fact that you took the shot right then may ruin your opponent's timing. It works the same way in business.

Some companies operate on a two-, five-, or ten-year plan. At Mesa, we're a different company every two years.

Once committed, we don't appoint committees and have more studies and discussions; we don't have beautiful slide presentations. We decide what we want to do and then do it.

People sometimes get too serious about business. Business isn't life itself: life is tragic, but business is not. There are no disasters in business that you can't avoid—if you see them coming and make the adjustments. If you understand markets, you can do as well in a down market as you can in an up market. Business, like racquetball, is fun.

PART IV

THE ESSENTIALS OF GOOD MANAGEMENT

ALFRED P. SLOAN, JR.
1875 – 1966

In 1923 Sloan was elected president of a company that was compared to "an orchestra without a conductor." According to Sloan, it was "management by crony, with the divisions operating on a horse-trading basis." The company was General Motors (GM), and it was controlled by the powerful du Pont family, who had semigraciously removed Sloan's predecessor—William C. Durant, GM's founder. It was actually Durant who brought—or rather bought—Sloan for the company. After Sloan graduated from MIT in 1895 with a degree in electrical engineering, he joined the Hyatt Roller Bearing Company of Newark, New Jersey, which was making billiard balls at the time. He soon became a partner with a $5,000 investment and moved the company into ball bearings for automobiles. In 1916 Durant entered the picture and bought the company and Sloan for $13.5 million.

After taking over GM's operations, Sloan fully implemented his ingenious plan of "decentralization with co-ordinated control" to eliminate duplicated efforts and senseless waste, otherwise known as horse-trading. His organizational blueprint, he said, was modeled partly after the Constitution of the United States. The two most important and most tangible factors leading to the success of Sloan's management concept were opportunity and motivation. Greater opportunity to move up the corporate ladder was provided by the decentralization, and motivation was achieved by introducing incentive compensation plans based on production and cost reduction.

After 30 years of heading GM, Sloan wrote a book, *My Years with General Motors,* that was an instant best-seller and became a manifesto for management practices. Although written and ready for print 10 years prior to the actual publication in 1963, Sloan refused to publish until every person critically addressed in the book was deceased. It was an extension of his business philosophy, which included "A manager does not criticize subordinates in public." The following selection was written in 1924, after Sloan had been president for only one year, but his sophisticated principles of management are already clearly defined.

The Most Important Thing I Ever Learned about Management
Alfred P. Sloan, Jr.

Every executive has to recognize sooner or later that he himself cannot do everything that needs to be done. Until he recognizes this, he is only an individual, with an individual's power, but after he recognizes it, he becomes, for the first time, an executive, with control of multiple powers. This necessary conversion happened to me while I was assisting John Hyatt to perfect his mechanisms for making billiard balls, some of the patents for which are still in his name and some in mine. A job like that, involving intensive study, could be performed as an individual.

Then automobiles suddenly loomed on the horizon. The fundamental motions of making billiard balls out of ivory for sport alone, we saw, could be adapted to making roller bearings out of steel for the much wider uses of general commerce.

Revolving bearings were not at all a matter of course then as they are now. It was at first assumed that the automobile would have a simple greased axle like the wagon out of which the first designs developed, but this assumption soon passed away, because of the increased speed of the automobile. It was easy to sell roller bearings to the pioneer automobile manufacturers.

I could do most of the selling personally, by closing long-term contracts. Here, again, I could get accomplishment as an individual, and on going back to the shop, could even help with the plant layout.

But there the individual capacity stopped. Neither Hyatt nor I could personally make all the product. If we wanted things done right, we had to depend upon other individuals, and arouse their individual initiative, at the same time getting united effort.

Up to that time I was an engineer, a designer, or a salesman—not a manager. Even an embryo manager must have learned how to arouse the individual initiative of the men working with him.

Naturally, the change in attitude of mind could not take place overnight. We floundered more or less, after the fashion of a boy thrown into the water to swim. But after a while we thoroughly grasped the principle that the work must be done by other men. Granted that, we had to find a way to arouse their initiative.

That is still the most important thing I have ever learned about management—to make men think and act with individual zeal and initiative, yet cooperating with each other.

That principle was equally important in the next bigger unit which came under my control, and in the next and the next. I found the principle important in all activities, whether in production, engineering, buying, or sales, even when the unit consists of only a few persons. In fact, this management principle is, perhaps, the one link connecting all our diverse units, large or small.

In my opinion, the organization of which I am now president would be impossible without the principle of individual initiative.

When General Motors was formed it was a holding company, owning the stock or controlling the stock of the various units. It now owns outright the assets of these companies, and has become an operating company as well as a holding company. The company became a consolidation. But there is one thing which we have never consolidated. We have consolidated the cash assets of a great many plants and former independent companies into one pool for financial management, but we have never consolidated the various units of personnel. We have left each personnel unit to develop its own corps spirit and initiative. Our Cadillac unit today is not so much a matter of plant or equipment or even design and patents, as it is a matter of men. We could destroy

---

Even an embryo manager must have learned how to arouse the individual initiative of the men working with him.

---

the buildings of the Cadillac plant, and yet we would have the Cadillac car intact in the Cadillac organization, for they are used to making the car, skilled in the team-work of assembling it, and are held together by an enthusiastic belief in the supremacy of their product. They have been left free to develop it by their own initiative so that they feel it is theirs. Likewise with the Buick or any other of our cars. Each unit is a part of the General Motors Corporation, but the relation between them is not consolidation but coordination. They are like regiments of an army or companies of a regiment, all have their common aim, but each group of men must keep its identity and initiative.

In that way we get the most done. Each unit has a definite part to play in the entire program. In fact, each of our units now has to make a product aimed at a particular group of consumers, the groups being graded according to certain strategic price classes of the product, ranging from below $1,000 to above $3,000. None of our products now competes with any other within one price class. Each unit has its own clearly defined part well coordinated with the others, so our men are willing to move in coordination with each other, without losing their individual initiative in carrying out their own functions.

We were confronted very definitely with a choice between two attitudes toward our men. We had to choose between two types of organization, the consolidated or the coordinated.

In one type of organization policies and methods are determined at the top and orders are issued down.

The other type of management comes from the bottom up and arouses individual initiative.

We chose the coordinated type, the one which would apply even to our small businesses. For the sake of efficiency we deliberately preferred to be a collection of small- or moderate-sized units, well coordinated, rather than one large consolidated business.

Thus we avoid many of the mistakes of large businesses, and take advantage of the good points of small businesses.

Whether the units are separate corporations with presidents of their own or are not incorporated separately, the general manager of each plant has complete authority. Whether his title is president or general manager, the head of each division is absolutely responsible for its actions, its success or failure.

Even when we make recommendations from the general corporation's office, the head of a division is at liberty to accept or reject—and once in a while he rejects.

At first many of our men believed that this was too good to be true. Some feared that although we meant it, we could not carry it out. They began tentatively unleashing their brains and making important decisions, but they kept one eye on the general corporation office, expecting at any moment to receive a veto of their decisions, or an order that would conflict with their decisions.

No such thing happened. We do not issue orders. I have never issued an order since I have been the operating head of this corporation.

The presidency carries the power to issue orders, but I never use it, and do not intend to use it. Orders arise in a different way, which I will explain.

When our managers saw that I did not promulgate orders or vetos, they began to make decisions with more confidence. Having ascertained that their plans are in accord with general policies, they put their decisions immediately into action. They began to think and act with more freedom and more effectiveness.

Many times there were strong temptations to step in and do things the quick way, following my own opinion, but we used patience. If, at any time, I or any of our other officials from the general office had stepped in with a sudden order, it would have halted our progress. Men would have had their fears confirmed. They would not only stop short, but fall back. They would have left decisions altogether to us. And the work would have been too heavy for any one man or few men.

So, it was necessary to choose absolutely our habits. We could have no middle ground. We could not follow one policy some of the time, and another policy the rest of the time. We could not follow one policy in the main with exceptions to it once in a while.

We do not issue orders. I have never issued an order since I have been the operating head of this corporation.

We must be absolutely authoritative or else depend upon the initiative of our men.

So complete is their authority that we do not even force them to use inside of their own units the type of organization that we find so valuable, although we recommend it.

We try to extend this same principle of independence and initiative down into the organization as far as possible. We even get initiative from our machine operatives and laborers.

With initiative aroused, we need team-work. It is easy to get both initiative and team-work at the same time, even among workmen. Workmen in some of our plants are paid in groups, according to their production. Two hundred and forty-seven men in one group have each day's pay determined by the number of finished motors that pass the last man in the group. Anything that any one can do to help production comes back to them all in the pay envelope. We put no limit on earnings, and the men put no limit on production.

Those men show initiative. They also show team-work. If a man can help his neighbor, or break in a green hand to be a profit producer more quickly, he does so, with the approval and aid of his fellow workers. The production of that group has gone up several hundred per cent in two years.

We believe in profit sharing in other ways, too. We take the first step toward a common ground with our men, from the "management side," without waiting for the worker to make the first step from his "side."

We have a savings and investment plan designed for labor; a bonus plan for salaried employees and executives; and a managers' profit-sharing plan for managers of big units.

The third of these plans was explained to stockholders of the corporation in the letter in which the following extracts explain why initiative by individuals is important to the success of the business as a whole:

"There are approximately 70 managerial positions upon the occupants of which the corporation must rely for the successful management of its business. From practical experience and observation your directors believe that the men occupying these positions can secure a better, broader and more sympathetic understanding of the stockholders' interests, and, therefore, of the interests of the corporation as a whole, if they can be attracted into partnership with the stockholders through becoming substantial stockholders themselves.

"In a great structure such as the General Motors Corporation, where our problems and our operations are so diversified, where capital must be employed and plants operated in the best interests of the corporation as a whole, as against any separate part or division, and where new capital supplied should be injected where it will accomplish the greatest good, it is important to find, develop, and retain men to occupy important managerial positions who are capable of assuming great authority and the responsibilities that make these positions important. Not only is it necessary that these managers be capable of handling efficiently the immediate problems of their respective positions and divisions, but it is essential that they view broadly and understand the policies necessary to coordinate the various ramifications of this vast business and thus secure proper return to the stockholders on upwards of $500,000,000 of capital employed."

Great numbers of our men have thus had aroused their personal initiative on the financial side. Simultaneously there springs up initiative in their work. Initiative, developed in any way, develops in other phases of life also, and affects every activity of the man.

Initiative must be accompanied with correct principles. Take our buying problems. Naturally, among so many units we had some buyers whose principles of buying were indeterminate or wobbly. This condition reflected itself in loss. We needed initiative and correct principles. But I could not promulgate any principle as a decree, no matter, how correct it was. I cannot go to a purchasing agent and tell him what to do in one case, because I cannot possibly find the time to tell him what to do in all cases. Nor do I know his job.

For a year we studied for a solution and got it by accident.

We formed a committee on purchasing, with 10 members. Five of these members are the purchasing agents of five principal units that manufacture cars. These units represent 60% of all our purchasing.

We supplemented these 10 permanent memberships with two revolving memberships.

All our units other than our car-making plants fall into two groups: those which make accessories such as bearings and starters; and those which manufacture things that do not sell outside the corporation, such as castings and glass.

These two revolving memberships in the purchasing committee are assigned to these two groups, one to each group, but never to the same man for two successive meetings.

This committee gets together at regular intervals to exchange information and vote on policies.

Thus, we secured a workable committee of 10 men, plus personal contact with every buyer in turn.

Revolving members are not very useful to the purchasing committee in deciding policies, because they are not on it long enough, but the committee is of very great use to the revolving member by giving him a bigger view. It is a good way to develop men and to discover them after they are developed.

It is this committee which determines purchasing policies, not the president or operating head.

Policies should be performed by the men who make them. . . . A group of men who have invented a policy together understand the policy.

Part of the job of a president is to develop business policies among the members of our various business units. That sounds like too big a job for one man. It is too big. If I started the job, I could not handle it. Anyone who tried to handle it would soon be in an asylum or a sanitarium. And it is not necessary to handle it as an individual. Certainly, I do not know enough to become an individual instructor of policies.

Where do policies come from, if they are to be useful in the business? Out of the business itself. And that is where our policies come from. They must come from the men who are in daily contact with problems. They must handle activities of whatever sort, whether production, sales, service, or finance. Policies are not correct which do not fit such conditions. Our policies come from the bottom.

Everything possible in the organization starts from the bottom. That is where it must and will be carried out, and it is carried out better and sooner if it starts there.

Policies should be performed by the men who make them. The one man who understands a mechanism better than anyone else is the man who invented it. A group of men who have invented a policy together understand the policy.

Another thing that we have worked out is a method for using staff experts or consultants in such a way as to develop initiative, rather than suppress it.

We have an advisory staff attached to the general corporation, to serve all the units. The advisory staff has a production adviser, an advertising adviser, a sales adviser, a buying adviser, and so on. But they make it a policy never to dictate to anybody.

One of the revolving members of the purchasing committee, for instance, is a member of the corporation advisory staff. He is chosen from its purchasing section.

According to the intelligence, initiative, and practical grasp with which he serves them, they appreciate his advice when he gives any. He is their agent not the agent or adviser of the corporation or its president. There is a vast difference in attitude, and a vast difference in usefulness.

Because all our buyers cooperate formally in settling policies, they are quite willing to cooperate informally every day in action. They exchange with each other their latest prices. They contribute ideas, using the advisory member as a volunteer clearinghouse.

Now it is apparent why purchasing methods seldom come up to me. They are settled where they should be settled by the men who can act upon them then and thereafter.

We do the same thing with sales policies, service policies, and advertising, and are continually extending the same idea to other functions. Significant occurrences rise just so far as they will be of use to the sort of men among whom the incidents arose. Then the knowledge travels horizontally to other men or units, and permeates down again.

This method of determining decisions is a far different thing from issuing decisions from above, formulated by one man's mind. Even if one man could formulate correct decisions for an organization like ours, he could not get them received sympathetically or acted upon immediately with the necessary understanding and zeal. But no one man could formulate correct decisions for an organization like ours. The job of the president is not to formulate all the decisions in the organization, but to provide channels for letting decisions arise out of a day's work.

Our men are learning business from each other. Our buyers are learning purchasing. For instance, the fundamental principles of inventory control cannot be too often studied or too intelligently applied. Our ratio of stock on hand to production is constantly going down, without interfering with continuity of manufacture. The saving of interest on investment is considerable, but a far more important consideration is the reduced risk of loss of capital tied up in inventory if prices for material go down. A month's supply could be entirely used up without loss, where three months' or four months' supply would project unused into any period of depression, unable to be moved even at lower prices.

Our buyers are learning to buy for the needs of production, rather than to buy for a speculative profit—another fundamental principle. Then they are learning from each other bits of current knowledge which are of current advantage, such as the lowest prices, and which firms give the best deliveries, and where they may dispose of factory waste.

Every exceptional case is weeded out from the routine and passed up high enough so that it can be passed back to all those who can make use of it. It becomes their common property.

Of all business activities, 99% are routine. They do not require management attention except in the aggregate. Only the one exception in a hundred cases need come to a manager's attention.

The entire 100% can be handled by managing the 1% of exceptions. Deciding the symptomatic cases, the exceptional cases which emerge above routine, keeps routine flowing in its channels, and, at the same time, allows for progress.

We get that 1% of exceptions managed as closely as possible to the men from whom they arise. That makes work possible for the man above.

My office force is very small. That means that we do not do much routine work with details. They never get up to us. I work fairly hard, but it is on exceptions or construction, not on routine or petty details.

Of all business activities, 99% are routine. They do not require management attention except in the aggregate.

It means also—and this is more important than any effect on me personally—that I do not bother the other men below me with a continual stream of questions about details, and requests for reports. The only report we ask from all our units is one page a month.

This page summarizes essentials, however, such as the inventory on hand, the turnover or ratio of materials in process to a year's finished goods and sales.

Each month's page contains actual figures for the month just closed and estimates for each of the four following months. In writing the figures, each manager has to plan the big essentials of operation and profit and tell us his plans.

Each manager's past estimates are compared with his subsequent estimates and his present accomplishment to form what is called an accuracy report. Our men are becoming more and more accurate in their estimates of the future.

The same advantages of individual initiative that apply to our big units apply to our small ones, too.

Our men sometimes find a dealer with only three or four salesmen who yet work at cross purposes against one another rather than with one another for mutual success. Surely, three or four men are not too many for a dealer to keep in line, if the old-fashioned method of keeping men active by domination will work at all.

The truth is that the method of domination almost never works so well, even with a few men, as the method of arousing individual initiative. One of the ways in which our dealers increase their business is by getting the sort of team-work which takes the lid off individual initiative. They get results in the same way that we do in much larger units.

In a meeting of our principal managers, which took place some months ago, this problem was placed before them: "Have we, a combined corporation, been putting out a complete line, logical, and non-duplicating?" The answer was "no," and the remedy was to cut out all duplications of price fields.

That called for each manager to strike out some of his products. Naturally, they did not like to abandon habits and individual pride. But they got together. They selected the best make and styles to fit pocket-books ranging below $1,000, between $1,000 and $2,000, and above $2,000, and abandoned all duplicating products. Then they did the same thing with all the other price classes. The result was that each part of the line thus simplified increased in volume and decreased in cost and price.

Each man is making the best product in its class, and is making or selling the class of product that he can handle best.

As we made more and more progress, our men became more and more confident of their own ability, and more and more effective in production, sales, and profit.

In January, 1921, we stood with a disorganized collection of units. Today we have a team. Our team first got into fair stride about January of 1923. Results followed.

During the first six months of 1923 sales went up. We were able to reduce prices and still make a good profit. The low prices broadened our market, which is a good investment for future stability and economy. Engineers at our plants and at our laboratory in Dayton designed improvements with the cooperation of our plant men who quickly put the improvements into production.

These improvements so stimulated sales that before the beginning of 1924 one of our plants had practically sold a year's production in advance, though the construction department assured us that they would have a new plant going in time to take care of additional orders.

JOHN L. MCCAFFREY

The harvesting reaper was invented in 1831 by Cyrus McCormick, who subsequently founded the McCormick Harvesting Machine Company and revolutionized the farming industry. In 1902 J. P. Morgan formed his farm machine trust, International Harvester, by combining McCormick's company with Deering Harvester Company and three smaller firms. By 1909 it was the fourth largest corporation in America, and in that same year McCaffrey joined the company as a warehouse clerk. McCaffrey, who was characterized as "Clever, persistent, and blessed with a sly Irish wit," quickly moved into sales, and very successfully converted farmers from their loving horses to gas-powered machines.

The McCormick family, who had maintained control of the company through the Morgan years and thereafter, witnessed the end of their reign when the board of directors named McCaffrey CEO in 1951. Of McCaffrey's tenure, it was said that tallness ruled the day. He apparently promoted "towering men [like himself] who could crack jokes, crush hands, and intimidate anybody with their sheer presence alone." International Harvester also became a "salesman's company" with a breezy management style. The research and development group was even subjected to the whim of the sales force, who wanted to give the customer every possible gadget. These whims often led to unjustified expenses. The one major criticism that plagued McCaffrey was his lack of attention to financial and other operational details, and in due course, numbers would prove more important than tallness.

By 1953 McCaffrey was faced with growing labor disputes, serious competition from John Deere, and the end of the postwar boom. These complicated times undoubtedly inspired McCaffrey's candor and humor in writing *What Corporation Presidents Think about at Night*. It was a speech originally given to businesspeople who had just completed the University of Chicago's two-year Executive Program. Few of them slept soundly that night.

What Corporation Presidents Think about at Night
John L. McCaffrey

The mechanics of running a business are really not very complicated, when you get down to essentials. You have to make some stuff and sell it to somebody for more than it cost you. That's about all there is to it, except for a few million details. I saw a play recently in which one of the characters summed up the fundamental problem of business pretty well. He said he'd been trying for two years to think of something that would cost a dime, sell for a dollar—and be habit-forming.

So it isn't hard to run a business, from the standpoint of business operations. And a President doesn't usually worry too much about the things that most people expect to bother him. For example, he seldom lies awake very long thinking about finances or lawsuits or sales or production or engineering or accounting problems. He is pretty well able to take care of those during regular business hours.

Furthermore, when he approaches such problems the President can bring to bear on them all the energy and the trained judgment and past experience of his whole organization. He has a lot of help with problems of that kind.

There are other problems, however, that he has to sweat and struggle with, largely by himself. They are the problems he thinks about at night. They all arise out of one simple fact. I can sum up this situation in one sentence:

The biggest trouble with industry is that it is full of human beings.

The longer you are a President, the more firmly that fact will be riveted in your mind. That is why you will lose sleep. That is why your hair will first turn gray, then get thin, and then fall out altogether, unless you are lucky.

You will learn to your sorrow that, while a drill press never sulks and a drop hammer never gets jealous of other drop hammers, the same cannot be said for people. You will learn that a turret lathe may run one part for ten years without affecting its ability or its willingness to be switched at any time to another part. But men are not that way. They develop habits and likes and dislikes.

You will learn that you have with people the same general problems of preventive maintenance, premature obsolescence, or complete operational failure that you have with machines. Only they are much harder to solve.

You will discover that problems change rapidly, techniques change rapidly, products can be transformed in a period of months; but, unfortunately, people change slowly if at all. And you cannot rearrange or retool the human organization of your business with the same ease and frequency as you rearrange or retool the plant.

You will learn to your sorrow that, while a drill press never sulks and a drop hammer never gets jealous of other drop hammers, the same cannot be said for people.

We have constructed in this country an economic system which is marvelously complicated. In the last forty years or so, this system has developed from what the football coaches call in their trade a one-platoon system to something that approximates a thirty- or forty-platoon system in industry.

All this is because we have applied to its uttermost limits the principle of the division of labor which was first described by the classical economists. We have come from the age when a product was made in its entirety by one craftsman, performing all operations, to the present age where nearly every small operation on every part of every

---

You will discover that problems change rapidly, techniques change rapidly, products can be transformed in a period of months; but, unfortunately, people change slowly if at all.

---

product is performed by different men. We have reached a form of production so specialized that frequently the machine does all the work and the man merely nurses and feeds it, as in the case of the boltmaker or the automatic screw machine. The division of labor has gone so far, here in America, as it affects the factory worker, that labor has been atomized rather than just divided.

The sociologists and psychologists, as well as the practical operating men in industry, have recognized some of the problems this extreme specialization creates. There is the problem of loss of versatility. There is the problem of loss of pride in personal accomplishment and skill. There is the problem of boredom from repetitive operations, and many others, as they affect the worker at the machine or on the assembly line.

The thing I want to point out to you is this: We are only now beginning to understand that the effects of this atomizing of labor are not limited to production employees. As management, too, has become extremely specialized, these same problems have spread over into the management group, and even into the executive group. The specialization of manage-

183

ment at all levels, including the executive, has lagged somewhat behind the specialization of equipment and employees,
but it is following exactly the same course, and giving rise to
the same problems.

A GOOD OLD-FASHIONED JACKKNIFE

The President of a modern company often seems to me like
the ringmaster of a thirty-ring circus. We sit at our desks all
day, while around us whiz and gyrate a vast number of special activities, some of which we only dimly understand. And
for each of these activities there is a specialist.

We have engineers of assorted kinds. We have lawyers of
many breeds, from patents to admiralty. We have market
analysts and sales engineers and industrial-relations experts
and credit men and research metallurgists and time-study
engineers. We have accountants and economists and statisti-
cians, purchasing agents and traffic men and chemists.

All of them, no doubt, are good to have. All seem to be
necessary. All are useful on frequent occasions. But it has
reached the point where the greatest task of the President is
to understand enough of all these specialties so that when a
problem comes up he can assign the right team of experts to
work on it. We have a lot of people like Ed Wynn's famous
painter who only painted boats and not horses, and when a
customer insisted that he do a picture of his horse, the
painter said: "Well, all right. But it's gonna look like a boat."

The President is like a man confronted by an enormous
tool bench, who only hopes that he can pick the right screw
driver for a particular special job. There must be others like
me, who sometimes wish for a good old-fashioned jackknife,
with twelve blades and a corkscrew, that could handle
almost any job in passable fashion.

Because business has wanted these specialists, the colleges and universities have produced them by the thousands.

If we need a good cost accountant, one is available. If we want an industrial psychologist, he can be had. If a man is needed to estimate a market potential with the latest scientific methods, he will be on tap.

And that's fine, as far as it goes, but it still doesn't let the President sleep at night. The President has no great problem in finding men to run a section or a department, where one line of work is followed. But he tosses plenty over the problem of finding executives who have wider knowledge, more general savvy, and enough background of the right kind to run a whole group of things.

The President of a modern company often seems to me like the ringmaster of a thirty-ring circus. We sit at our desks all day, while around us whiz and gyrate a vast number of special activities, some of which we only dimly understand.

What are the plus and minus factors in specialization, as it applies to management men? On the plus side, the great advantage is that by limiting his work to a relatively small area, the man becomes a genuine expert in that area. Many detailed improvements are possible as a result. By specializing from the start, in education and in work, he greatly reduces the time and expense which his employer would otherwise have to devote to his training. By coming as a ready-made specialist he is more useful at an earlier time, and this tends to give him a larger income at a younger age than the average man. That's an attraction to him, and is one of the reasons why he specializes.

What are the disadvantages? The great disadvantage, of course, is that specialization produces a man with limited knowledge and limited interests and experience, except in rare instances. The world of the specialist is a narrow one and it tends to produce narrow human beings. The specialist usually does not see overall effects on the business. And so he tends to judge good and evil, right and wrong, by the sole standard of his own specialty.

We have all seen the credit man whose big interest in life is not the making of good sales under variable conditions, but simply the ratio of past-due paper, and the possibility that at some future time, on a particular deal, he might be criticized.

We have seen the time-study man who clings so firmly to what he regards as a principle that he just doesn't care whether it meets ordinary human standards of fairness, or whether his actions shut down a 3,000-man plant.

We have seen the salesman who expects complicated machines to be redesigned in a week whenever one of his customers has a whim, and who bitterly blames engineering if it doesn't happen that way. Or the engineer who knows what is good for the customer, even if the customer doesn't like it. Or the manufacturing man who can't see why we won't pour more millions into his plant, even though the product is already losing money.

We have seen the industrial-relations man for whom life begins and ends with a legalistic interpretation of the union contract, and who never looks past the grievance committee, gathered around his desk, to catch a glimpse of the human individuals who work in his plant.

MIDDLE-MANAGEMENT MORALE

This narrowness of view, this judgment of all events by the peculiar standards of his own specialty, is the curse of the specialist from the standpoint of top-management consideration for advancement. Except in unusual cases, it tends to put a road block ahead of him after he reaches a certain level.

This presents a problem to the President in building his top organization. Because of the trend of the times, he finds that he has more and more specialists and fewer and fewer general executives just below the top level. Some of these specialists he simply cannot promote. And even with the others, if he does promote them, he has to ask them to make a sudden and radical change in the thinking and acting habits of a lifetime.

This may or may not present a problem to the specialist himself. In most cases I believe it does. There are men, of course, who, after achieving reasonable eminence in their specialty, ask nothing more of life. But among men of real ability, specialists or no, we usually find ambition to advance. And in such cases, specialization can produce a considerable degree of frustration.

So we have a two-horned problem. There are many specialists whom the President simply cannot promote. And because they are not promoted there is a natural tendency for the mature specialist to become somewhat sour.

There is another fact about the specialist which is a problem to him and therefore to the organization. It arises from the very fact that he knows more about his specialty than his superiors or anyone else in the business. This situation frequently arises: a problem comes up related to his special field. He produces a solution which is entirely satisfactory from the standpoint of good practice in his specialty. But then the higher management won't buy it. They do something else instead.

This can happen either because the specialist has failed to explain and sell his solution adequately, or because he did not take into account other factors of the problem which might lie outside his special field. To put it bluntly, such a situation can occur either because top management knows more than he does or because it knows less. In either case, the result for him is the same. His advice has been disregarded and his judgment overruled. That will seldom make him happy.

HIGH-PRICED OFFICE BOYS

In this area probably lies a good part of the cause for a new note which has begun to creep into some of the studies of corporate management—the beginning of concern about the morale of what is called "middle management," which includes nearly all the specialists and is largely composed of them.

The man in the middle of the management pyramid, however, neither makes the decisions nor carries them out. . . . He often feels, and he frequently says, that he is just a high-priced office boy.

The top men operate high, wide, and handsome. The decisions are theirs, so their attitudes are usually good. In spite of frequently expressed concern about attitudes of foremen and other first-line management men, it is a fact that the first-line men have specific duties and responsibilities, and they are at the point where things happen. In spite of their normal griping, they have the relief of taking personal part in action.

The man in the middle of the management pyramid, however, neither makes the decisions nor carries them out. He finds it easy to feel that his judgment is neither sought nor honored, that his training and experience are ignored, and that he does not participate to any real degree in the management of the corporation. He often feels, and he frequently says, that he is just a high-priced office boy.

Now, those are some of the reasons why many a President lies awake at night. How can he maintain the interest of and get full advantage from the specialists who are too specialized to be promoted? On the one hand, the company absolutely requires the skills of the specialists in order to carry on its complicated operations. On the other hand, he has to get future top management from somewhere. And that somewhere has to be largely within the existing company, if he is to have any management morale at all.

SHEEP WITH GOAT'S BLOOD

The problems are easy to describe. But the ground becomes uncertain and the atmosphere cloudy when someone raises the simple question: What will we do about it?

One answer that has been offered is to start with the educational processes that take place before the man goes to work. Recently we have seen, as an example, some attempts made by engineering and other technical schools to give a larger part in their courses to the liberal-arts subjects, to try to produce an educated man as well as a trained engineer or doctor or what not. I think that is a hopeful trend.

We have also seen in recent months a number of speeches by corporation officials, pointing out the necessity for rounded education and underlining the importance of the liberal-arts college for the future, not only for the future of business but also of this country. The nation, like the corporation, suffers from this problem of too much specialization.

Unhappily, it appears that we company Presidents are not practicing what we preach in this regard. True, some of us have been giving money to support liberal-arts colleges, but we have not been offering jobs to such graduates.

Fortune Magazine [in April 1953] recounted some of the actual experiences of educational institutions with business recruiters who came to the campus looking for talent. At Yale University, for example, in 1950, only 18 out of 66 corporation talent scouts were willing to talk to arts college graduates. In 1951 it was 15 out of 91. And in 1952 it was 16 out of 117. At Johns Hopkins University this year only 16 out of 200 scouts had any interest in the liberal-arts man as compared with the engineer, the chemist, or other specialists.

So we are obviously not making progress in that field and will have to change our approach before we do. These graduates are bright young men with a natural desire to eat. They see what is happening. And however much we may cry about overspecialization, we'll get more and more of it so long as our hiring policies are not in tune with top management's thinking and talking.

Another answer which has been proposed is to catch the specialist after he is in industry but while he is still young enough to respond and try to give him a wider training, a broader outlook—to take him away from his tree and show him the forest.

This has sometimes been attempted by means of coaching, as it is called. Coaching consists basically of selecting promising young men and moving them around through different functions of a business, letting them stay long enough in each to get a real feel of it. Its advantage is that it teaches through experience and not just through precept.

One of the difficulties, however, is that it soon becomes obvious to everyone that certain people are on the coaching list while others are not. You create a sheep-and-goat division among your younger men and the goats don't like it a bit. Mistakes are also made, of course, and sometimes a sheep turns out to have goat's blood in him.

BACK TO COLLEGE

Still another answer to the same problem has been the training of executives at a university. The theory is something like this. The employer says: "Here's a younger man who has a record of accomplishment up to now. There may be something wrong with him that we don't yet know, but, as matters stand, he looks as if he had the possibility for future development. Maybe he has. Maybe he hasn't. Training can't hurt and it may help a lot. So we'll give him the training, give him the chance to grow, and then wait and see what happens."

My personal view happens to be that this is the most promising of the approaches to the problem and that results so far have justified it in the case of my own company.

By one means or another, we need to produce a type of business executive who, after carefully learning that all balls are round, will not be completely flabbergasted the first time he meets one that has a square side. And he will meet them, for we live in a complicated world—a world that has spiritual and moral problems even greater than its economic and technical problems. If the kind of business system we now have is to survive, it must be staffed by men who can deal with problems of both kinds.

Businessmen today and in the visible tomorrows will need to know how to earn a profit and why it is good for everyone that a profit should be earned. That's obvious. They also need to know how to get along with, and direct the efforts of, other human beings, both individuals and groups. And, finally, every businessman needs to know enough about the society in which he lives and operates so that he can follow its changes intelligently, adjusting himself and his enterprise to changing conditions, and making sure that his business serves its most useful purpose for society.

Those are some of the problems you will think about at night, when you are President. I sincerely hope you will find better answers—and get more sleep—than I have.

LEE IACOCCA
1924 –

In April of 1964, Iacocca made the covers of both *Time* and *Newsweek;* the son of Italian immigrants was now a proud father himself—of the revered Ford Mustang. His celebrity status eventually carried him to the presidency of the company in 1970, but the ascension was not without a great deal of politicking and "tribal warfare," in a monarchy ruled by Henry Ford, II. Passed over for the job several times, Iacocca had finally and successfully sold himself to the man he later characterized in his autobiography as a Machiavellian drunkard. Constant bickering with Henry, II, was not the only drawback to the new and highly visible position; the "Manson Family" put Iacocca on their hit list of business executives.

Iacocca's success was partly because he never left behind the image of the working-class neighborhood where he grew up in Allentown, Pennsylvania. America perceived him as a regular guy who told it like it was, and he naturally evolved into a great pitchman for his company. As Iacocca said, "You don't succeed for very long by kicking people around. You've got to know how to talk to them, plain and simple." In 1978 Iacocca himself was given a good kicking when Ford fired him. Fortunately, he was able to pick himself up and was immediately tapped for the presidency at Chrysler. Once at the helm of the nearly bankrupt company, he used plain language with the union to gain concessions and reduce overhead. He simply told them, "I've got a shotgun at your head. I've got thousands of jobs available at seventeen dollars an hour. I've got none at twenty. So you better come to your senses."

One of his other primary tasks (in addition to establishing a rapport with the union) was to obtain $1.2 billion in loan guarantees from the U.S. government to bail out Chrysler, which he did. The company's financial woes were ironically turned around by the antithesis of the Mustang; it was the minivan that came to the rescue. Undoubtedly, Iacocca's deft salesmanship and tough management style were put to the test, and eventually put into words in his best selling book *Talking Straight,* from which the following excerpt is taken.

More on Good Management
Lee Iacocca

Whenever the subject of management comes up, everybody—and I mean everybody, right down to the janitor—seems to have some mystical approach to it. By now there have been about as many books written on management as there have been on diets—and, I might add, with about the same measure of success. There's probably even a grapefruit management book in the works somewhere.

How good are all those diet books? Well, none of them delivers unless you remember to do one thing: Don't eat so much. It's still the only way to lose weight. In the end, if you don't follow through on a few simple principles, what good is reading all those books?

The same is true of management. I got so much reaction to the management tips in my last book that I went back and reread them to see why all these testimonials were crossing my desk. All I'd done was toss out a few broad concepts— my quarterly review system, my firm belief in communications—and yet people were writing from all over the world to tell me they had turned their hardware store or their Good Humor route into a stunning success. I said to myself: I'd better try to figure out what my theory of management is. So here's my contribution to the never-ending debate.

If you make believe that ten guys in pin-striped suits are back in a kindergarten class playing with building blocks, you'll get a rough picture of what life in a corporation is like. Grown men in a meeting will do anything—absolutely anything—to avoid being shown up. If someone doesn't know the facts about a subject, he'll ad-lib, just like a kid. Instead of saying "I'll have to get that for you, boss; I don't have the answer right at hand," he'll try to fake it. He's scared that if he confesses he doesn't know, the boss will think he's not as sharp as the other little kids in class and maybe he'll miss nap time. As a result, he'll embarrass himself and babble like an idiot.

Only the boss can set a tone that lets people feel comfortable enough to say those magic words "I don't know." Followed by: "But I'll find out." Business, after all, is nothing more than a bunch of human relationships. It's one guy comparing notes with another: "Here's what I'm doing. What are you doing? Is there some way I can help you—and you can help me?"

Whenever I talk about this subject, I feel like a five-year-old myself. People are always saying to me: "But there's got to be something mysterious. There must be a formula." There really isn't. Start with good people, lay out the rules, communicate with your employees, motivate them, and reward them if they perform. If you do all those things effectively, you can't miss.

If you make believe that ten guys in pin-striped suits are back in a kindergarten class playing with building blocks, you'll get a rough picture of what life in a corporation is like.

There are two broad management subjects that business people will argue about until long after I'm dead. One is the role of the staff (or planners) versus the line guys (or doers).

The other subject is consensus management versus arbitrary one-man rule.

First things first. Staff, to reduce it to its simplest terms, is what supports the boss. I don't mean who brings the coffee, but who furnishes the information that helps the boss make decisions. The important question that every manager has to answer for himself or herself is: How much staff do I need to run my organization? In some businesses, often one good secretary will do. At Ford, either because of the family's mentality or the Harvard Business School mentality, you had to plan and analyze down to the last gnat's hair. Before you made a move, you had to examine every alternative and research every factor to be sure you didn't make a mistake. That was the ultimate sin. Ford is so chock-full of staffs that it even has a super staff—the Corporate Strategy and Analysis Staff—which oversees all the other staffs!

I don't care how successful Ford or anyone else might be with that approach; it's not the kind of environment that gives big business a good name. After a while, such companies have a hard time attracting young, entrepreneurial people, because there's just no room for guts management and instinct when you're loaded down with a lot of second-guessing.

My problem at Chrysler is exactly the opposite. I have a ridiculously small staff. My line guys are so aggressive that they may make multimillion-dollar mistakes before I've had one alternative to look at. Frankly, I'm so lean on staff that it sometimes scares me. That's why I've recently installed a few staff people, most notably Tom Denomme, who's listed on the chart as my vice-president of corporate strategy.

His real title should be Devil's Advocate. He tosses out an idea a minute, some of them a bit off the wall, in order to keep me in constant turmoil. It can get crazy sometimes, but I like it that way because I don't have—or want—a purchasing staff, a marketing staff, an engineering staff, and a manufacturing staff to ride herd on the operating guys who are doing all the work.

My feeling is that if I'm going to err, I'd always err on the side of leanness, because the decision making is faster. Of course, if you get too lean, you'll wind up making momentous decisions with no more information than what the weather is like outside. But you don't need a bloody bureaucracy to make sure everybody's ass (especially the boss's) is covered in case of a screw-up.

When it comes time to make decisions, you shouldn't get too old over them. Sure, they won't all be perfect. In fact, some of them will be duds. Learn from them, but don't stop trying. The introverts of the world, the non-risktakers, are probably that way because they got burned young. Maybe they made the wrong move in a marbles tournament or a game of checkers and now they're never going to take a risk again. That's no way to live—and it's certainly no way to make a profit.

The big fuss about consensus management is another issue that boils down to a lot of noise about not much. The consensus advocates are great admirers of the Japanese management style. Consensus is what Japan is famous for. Well, I know the Japanese fairly well: They still remember Douglas MacArthur with respect and they still bow down to the Emperor. In my dealings with them, they talk a lot about consensus, but there's always one guy behind the scenes who ends up making the tough decisions.

It doesn't make sense to me to think that Mr. Toyoda or Mr. Morita of Sony sits around in committee meetings and says, "We've got to get everybody in this organization, from the janitor up, to agree with this move." The Japanese do believe in their workers' involvement early on and in feedback from employees. And they probably listen better than we do. But you can bet that when the chips are down, the yen stops at the top guy's desk, while we're wasting time trying to emulate something I don't think really exists.

Business structures are microcosms of other structures. There were no corporations in the fifteenth century. But there were families. There were city governments, provinces, armies. There was the Church. All of them had, for lack of a better word, a pecking order.

The big fuss about consensus management is another issue that boils down to a lot of noise about not much. . . . they talk a lot about consensus, but there's always one guy behind the scenes who ends up making the tough decisions.

Why? Because that's the only way you can steer clear of anarchy. Otherwise, you'll have somebody come in one morning and tell you: "Yesterday I got tired of painting red convertibles, so today I switched to all baby-blues on my own." You'll never get anything done right that way.

What's to admire about consensus management anyway? By its very nature, it's slow. It can never be daring. There can never be real accountability—or flexibility. About the only plus that I've been able to figure out is that consensus management means a consistency of direction and objectives. But so much consistency can become faceless, and that's a problem too. In any event, I don't think it can work in this country. The fun of business for entrepreneurs, big or small, lies in our free enterprise system, not in the greatest agreement by the greatest number.

Another thing that a lot of management experts advocate importing from the Far East is that the boss should be one of the boys. Democratic as that philosophy may sound, I don't think it's very practical. If the boss lets his hair down too much, he ends up like Rodney Dangerfield. No respect.

And yet, the boss can't be aloof either. A lot of the guys in the Fortune 500 seem to feel it's beneath their station even to talk to their own work force. Someone who's got 200,000 people working for him and who makes a million dollars a year begins to believe his position and his power make him infallible. He forgets to listen. He gets caught up in the clack of all the yes men around him.

My style, I hope, falls somewhere between those extremes. For example, I go to the National Automobile Dealers Association convention every year. In fact I haven't missed one in thirty years. Why? Because my presence tells the dealers in the best way possible that I think they're a vital part of the company. My being with them for a few days is the most effective investment I can make, and so I'm there religiously. I shake hands with the dealers and try to tell them how much I appreciate all their efforts.

By the way, that goes for everybody on the team. Once in a while you've got to show them you care. I have a minimum of four press conferences; I even care for the reporters (how about that!). I have formal management meetings with our top five hundred people four times a year. I visit our top bankers twice a year. You cannot call on these people only when you're in a jam. Handling crises is a hell of a lot easier if you've already got some rapport with the people who can help you solve them.

At Chrysler we've initiated an idea that works quite well. Every Monday, the top operating people have a meeting to go over basic operations. Before they discuss any business, they bring in someone from a lower level who has been named the winner of the week for his or her performance, and offer their congratulations for a job well done. Word gets around, and other people start thinking, *I'd like to be invited too.* They see that it's real recognition, right from the top.

Delegation versus the one-man band is another hot topic in management circles these days. The Harvard Business School says "Delegate," so people dutifully do it. But all too many of them never bother to get involved afterwards with the people they delegated to. This is where Reagan ran into trouble in the Iran crisis. The other extreme, of course, is the strong-willed leader who never lets go of anything, who has to be in on every decision. For instance, Donald Trump, the real estate tycoon, signs every check in his organization. Every check. He's a fanatic about knowing where each and every penny is going. Obviously, that style works for him, but in a big organization it sure can slow things down.

In the end, you've got to take a little of each approach. Alone with yourself, you have to look in the mirror and analyze your strengths and weaknesses. The stuff you're good at you can hang on to, but the stuff you're lousy at, you delegate. Then you try to learn from the person you delegated to.

As for me, I delegate plenty, but I still have a hard time keeping my hands off the marketing and design areas of the business. I want to be there, because I like them. And so I drive the people in those departments nuts. I've just got to stop carrying on this way!

If I've got a fault, it's probably that I manage hands-on too much. You shouldn't get so antsy that your people don't even have time to find out where the bathroom is.

Let's say you've done a good job delegating. Even if the people to whom you've assigned responsibilities are top-notch, you must let them know that you remember what you gave them and that you're keeping track, for everyone's sake.

Charlie Beacham at Ford was a great delegator. And by and large he picked terrific people. If I ever questioned some of his choices, he'd snap back, "Well, I picked you. What the hell are you complaining about?" But after he delegated, he used to drive his people crazy. He didn't need to know every last fact, but when he'd drop into your office, sit on your desk, and say, "How are you doing? I haven't seen you in three months, but your truck sales stink," you'd snap to attention pretty quick.

I used to label that "management by nagging." A lot of business people might say, "Boy, I wouldn't want someone like that over me." But Charlie had such an engaging personality that he could get away with it. When he walked out, even though he'd just shoved a spear into you, you were still happy that he'd come to see you.

I learned that technique from him, and so I've always managed hands-on. If you ask my crew, they'll probably tell you that I'm a pretty good nagger in my own right. If I've got a fault, it's probably that I manage hands-on too much. You shouldn't get so antsy that your people don't even have time to find out where the bathroom is.

It's also very important to be flexible. I don't want to quote you the old cliché "Management's an art, not a science," but dammit if it isn't the truth. Some heads of companies maintain that they have a system and they don't care who they stick into it. They'll say, "Let's put No. 1573-8 in that slot," as if they're assigning a prisoner to a cell. I don't see how you can manage that way. You have to adapt to personalities or you're finished.

By the time people get to a company, they're pretty well molded. Time and again, I've tried to change people who are over twenty-one, and I don't think I've succeeded with a single one. Over the years, I've been stuck with people who had some rotten work habits, and so I thought I'd pump some energy into them. Although I'm a pretty good salesman and can often be very persuasive, they wouldn't budge. Not one inch. Why? Their parents and their grade school teachers got to them before I did.

Charlie Beacham was right on the mark when he told me: "Don't try to change anyone. Use your energies on something better. You might win over one in a hundred, but you'll take such a long time finding him that you'll go crazy trying."

What does that mean? You have to take people with all their warts. And then, to make the system work, you have to discipline them a little bit. You have to say, "Okay, I don't care how you grew up or what you are — here's the way we're going to run this ball club. And here are the plays. If you don't like them, it's going to show. By that time, you won't have to get off the team — I'll throw you off."

Once you've laid down the rules, you have to sit back and trust your people, even though you won't know for a while if they'll come through on the battlefield. You can never be sure with live ammunition if the lieutenant is going to take you up the hill or turn around and run like a scared rabbit. . . .

ANDREW S. GROVE
1936 –

Grove lives by the motto "Only the paranoid survive." Few can blame the pessimistic outlook when his early life is considered. He was born Andras Grof in Budapest, and "was forced into labor on the Russian front during World War Two." When the Soviets invaded Hungary during the popular uprising of 1956, Grove departed for America to study a subject that left little room for emotion: science. Eventually he was awarded a PhD in chemical engineering from the University of California, Berkeley. Grove was working as an assistant director at Fairchild Camera and Instrument with Robert Noyce and Gordon Moore when the latter two decided to leave in 1968 and start their own company, Intel. Grove followed their lead and joined Intel. It was a good game of follow the leader, as he became president of Intel in 1979 and then CEO in 1987.

During his tenure, Grove has built Intel into a microchip Goliath; their chips are in 80 percent of the world's PCs. It was accomplished through technological breakthroughs, relentless aggression, legal maneuvering (i.e., patents), and a cold, analytical management philosophy. However, it has been noted that Grove's style is double-edged. "Andy's analytical approach is his tremendous strength—and at times a weakness. Not everything with human beings is done with the accuracy of electrons." To compensate, Grove reportedly sits in an open cubicle at the office, like everyone else, to break down any perceived barriers. He also encourages "constructive confrontation," which provides a questioning atmosphere with no fear of being fired.

Grove forever contemplates management techniques and has written books as well as numerous articles on the subject. In terms of managing oneself, he makes a unique point, "you have to accept that no matter where you work, you are not an employee; you are in a business with one employee—yourself. You are in competition with millions of similar businesses . . . capable of doing the same work that you can do and perhaps more eager." To successfully compete, Grove prescribes the exploitation and efficient use of what he considers the most critical resource available to everyone: time.

Your Most Precious Resource: Your Time
Andrew S. Grove

A great deal of a manager's work has to do with allocating resources: manpower, money and capital. But the single most important resource that we allocate from one moment to the next is our own time. How you handle your own time is, in my view, the single most important aspect of being a role model and leader.

A manager must keep many balls in the air at the same time and shift his energy and attention to activities that will most increase the output of his organization. In other words, he should move to the point where his *leverage* will be the greatest.

Much of my day is spent acquiring information. I read standard reports and memos but also get information ad hoc. I talk to people inside and outside the company, managers at other firms, financial analysts and members of the press. Customer complaints are, for instance, a very important source of information. This includes internal customers as well. The Intel training organization, which I serve as an instructor, is an internal customer of mine. To cut myself off from the casual complaints of people in that group would be a mistake because I would miss getting an evaluation of my performance as an internal "supplier."

I have to confess that the type of information most useful to me, and I suspect most useful to all managers, comes from quick, often casual conversational exchanges, many of them on the telephone. These usually reach a manager much faster than anything written down. And usually the more timely the information, the more valuable it is.

How you handle your own time is, in my view, the single most important aspect of being a role model and leader.

So why are written reports necessary at all? They obviously can't provide timely information. What they do is constitute an archive of data, help to validate ad hoc inputs and catch, in safety-net fashion, anything you may have missed. But reports also have another, totally different function. As they are formulated and written, the author is forced to be more precise than he might be orally. Hence their value stems from the discipline and the thinking the writer is forced to impose upon himself as he identifies and deals with trouble spots. Reports are more a *medium* of *self-discipline* than a way to convey information. *Writing* the report is important; reading it often is not.

There is an especially efficient way to get information, much neglected by most managers. That is to visit a particular place in the company and observe what's going on there.

I have to confess that the type of information most useful to me, and I suspect most useful to all managers, comes from quick, often casual conversational exchanges . . .

Think of what happens when somebody comes to see a manager in his office. A certain stop-and-start dynamic occurs when the visitor sits down, something socially dictated. While a two-minute kernel of information is exchanged, the meeting often takes a half-hour. But if a manager walks through an area and sees a person with whom he has a two-minute concern, he can simply stop, cover his subject and be on his way.

It's obvious that the quality of your decision-making depends on how well you comprehend the facts and issues in your business. This is why information-gathering is so important in a manager's life. Other activities—conveying information, making decisions and being a role model for your subordinates—are also governed by the *base of information* that you have. In short, information-gathering is the basis of all other managerial work, which is why I choose to spend so much of my day doing it.

You often do things at the office designed to influence events slightly, maybe making a phone call to an associate suggesting that a decision be made in a certain way, or sending a note or a memo that shows how you see a particular situation, or making a comment during an oral presentation. In

---

Information-gathering is the basis of all other managerial work, which is why I choose to spend so much of my day doing it.

---

such instances you may be advocating a preferred course of action, but you are not issuing an instruction or a command. Yet you're doing something stronger than merely conveying information. Let's call it "nudging" because through it you nudge an individual or a meeting in the direction you would like. This is an immensely important managerial activity in which we engage all the time, and it should be carefully distinguished from decision-making that results in firm, clear directives. For every decision we make, we probably nudge things a dozen times.

Finally, there is a subtle aspect of our work that we all must consider. While we move about, doing what we regard

---

Much has been said and written about a manager's need to be a leader. The fact is, no single managerial activity can be said to constitute leadership, and nothing leads as well as example.

---

as our jobs, we are role models for people in our organization—our subordinates, our peers and even our supervisors. Much has been said and written about a manager's need to be a leader. The fact is, no single managerial activity can be said to constitute leadership, and nothing leads as well as example. Values and behavioral norms are simply not transmitted easily by talk or memo, but are conveyed very effectively by doing and doing visibly.

Don't think for a moment that the way I've described leadership applies only to large operations. An insurance agent in a small office who continually talks with personal friends on the phone imparts a set of values about permissible conduct to everyone working for him. A lawyer who

---

When I look at my schedule, I don't see any obvious patterns. I deal with things in seemingly random fashion, and my day always ends when I'm tired, not when I am done. A manager's work is never done . . .

---

returns to his office after lunch a little drunk does the same. On the other hand, a supervisor in a company, large or small, who takes his work seriously exemplifies to his associates the most important managerial value of all.

On a typical working day, I participate in some 25 separate activities, mostly information-gathering and information-giving, but also decision-making and nudging. I spend two-thirds of my time in a meeting of one kind or another. Before you are horrified at how much time I spend in meetings answer one question: Which of the activities—information-gathering, information-giving, decision-making, nudging and being a role model—could I have performed outside a meeting? The answer is practically none.

When I look at my schedule, I don't see any obvious patterns. I deal with things in seemingly random fashion, and my day always ends when I'm tired, not when I am done. A manager's work is never done: There is always more to be done, more that should be done, always more that can be done. That is why choosing and performing activities with high leverage is the key to managerial effectiveness.

DAVID E. LILIENTHAL
1899 – 1981

The name is obscure compared to other giants of American industry; however, Lilienthal was one of the midcentury's most respected business intellects who made a remarkable transfer from government service to private enterprise. He graduated from Harvard Law School and practiced for eight years before Franklin D. Roosevelt (FDR) appointed him as one of three directors of the Tennessee Valley Authority (TVA) in 1933. From 1941 to 1946 he served as TVA's chairman. Lilienthal's contribution to the public sector continued from 1946 to 1950 while he served as the first chairman of the United States Atomic Energy Commission. Considered a borderline socialist, many were surprised when Lilienthal left the government and formed his own consulting business.

Lilienthal's mission was to use his experiences in FDR's New Deal to bring "business imagination, character, and creative financial judgement and experience" to underdeveloped countries to privately or publicly develop their economic bases. Consulting jobs took him to India, Italy, Colombia, Venezuela, Ghana, Nigeria, Morocco, and Iran, among other nations. Lilienthal truly wanted the people of these countries to have a better life, a desire that sprung from his own sobering experiences during the Great Depression. He witnessed poverty, saw entire communities destroyed by it, and wished it for no one. History clearly molded his business philosophy as he said, "It is important to understand history, to grasp the significance of the past, in order to get a concept of what lies ahead." Simply stated, learn from the past to create a vision of the future.

Lilienthal was concerned that business leaders generally lacked a broad vision of how past events shaped the future. He said, "So few of them [business leaders] have any use or patience with trying to begin with what has happened, so little understanding of the uses of perspective. It is for lack of this that so many businessmen have failed to establish themselves as more than temporary heads of important economic institutions, rather than as the creators of institutions and of ideas." Lilienthal was definitely a creator of both institutions and ideas, and he depicts the required skills in *Management: A Humanist Art.*

Management: A Humanist Art
David E. Lilienthal

The world's *needs* are many; they are prodigious. The technical means at hand to meet them are almost unlimited. There is no lack either, goodness knows, of the articulation of these goals, of eloquent concepts of great revolutionary change. No lack of phrase-makers, no lack of theorists and theories. No lack of institutes, conferences, foundations, research grants to scholars and students. Reports and surveys pour out until we are inundated.

But what about the do-ers, the managers, those who must translate these aspirations, these wants and demands, these unending reports into something tangible in men's lives? Their function, it seems to me, is not too well understood; even by the do-ers themselves.

I suggest to you that under the blowtorch of necessity the function of the do-er, the manager, must be far broader, more comprehensive and more sensitive to the human personality than anything we now know.

The managerial function—whether in private business or public affairs—is too often defined and practiced as solely that of administration—that is, of unifying and weaving together the separate skills and knowledge of technicians and professions. Only rarely is there recognition of dynamic management's chief art—providing the understanding and the inspiration by which men are moved to action. Management's primary skill, in my view, is human, not technical, and therefore the manager must be measured broadly in terms of human personality, the intangible qualities of leadership.

The manager-leader would combine in one personality the robust, realistic quality of the man of action with the insight of the artist, the religious leader, the poet, . . .

What is the heart of the broad managerial process? I might put it in these words: management requires a humanist outlook on life rather than merely mastery of technique. It is based on the capacity for understanding of individuals and their motivations, their fears, their hopes, what they love and what they hate, the ugly and the good side of human nature. It is an ability to move these individuals, to help them define their wants, to help them discover, step by step, how to achieve them.

The art of management in these terms is a high form of leadership, for it seeks to combine the act—the getting of something done—with the meaning behind that act. The manager-leader would combine in one personality the robust, realistic quality of the man of action with the insight of the artist, the religious leader, the poet, who explain man to himself, who inspire man to great deeds and incredible stamina. The man of action alone, nor the man of contemplation alone, will not be enough in the situations we now confront; these two qualities together are required to meet the world's need for leadership.

As we all see so clearly, the world is changing, and so, therefore, is management changing, more rapidly and more completely than we can fully realize. The manager who hasn't had a new idea in twenty, or even in ten years, who isn't able, by temperament, to jettison most of the ideas of what management leadership consisted of a decade ago, may be as much an anachronism as the prairie schooner or the crossbow in this risky world. Large-scale business, we know, has changed almost beyond recognition, becoming rapidly multi-national and world-wide. The change in government activities is equally rapid and startling, even to the joining with business in a venture in the heavens—Comsat—and soon deep under the sea as well. Europe is far along toward being an economic unit; Latin America begins to follow that example of economic unification. Eastern Asia, the richest of all regions in resources and most numerous in people, is on the way to changing the strategic balance of power and of influence, so that it will be almost unrecognizable in a decade or so.

In the face of such change upon change, managers and management concepts of even ten years ago are also changing. To seek to learn the essence, the basic essentials of the new management in a changing world is therefore an imperative. And these will not be found, I predict, by too great preoccupation with attractive and ingenious mathematical and systems analysis techniques. For the subject of management is man; the objective of management is the moving of man's mind and will and imagination.

It is worth reminding ourselves that management does not really exist. It is a word, an idea. Like science, like government, like engineering, management is an abstraction. But managers exist. And managers are not abstractions; they are men, they are human beings. Particular and special kinds of human beings. Individuals with a special function: to lead and move and bring out the latent capabilities—and dreams—of other human beings.

It is important that we describe and identify these human beings, these managers. This we can do only by recognizing the nature of the demands made upon them as leaders, the pressures they are subjected to by their task of leadership of other men. And consequently the kind of human resources the manager-leader must possess and draw upon, and how those resources, those human talents, make these leaders different from other leaders, leaders who are, let's say, superior poets, or ironworkers, or teachers. These manager-leaders we shall find are different from other men, because of their different, their distinctive function. But the basic fact is that though different, they still are men.

This I believe, and this my whole life's experience has taught me: the managerial life is the broadest, the most demanding, by all odds the most comprehensive and the most subtle of all human activities. And the most crucial. . . .

The objective of management is the moving of man's mind and will and imagination.

In calling for broad managerial leadership I am not asking that we wait for a new race of supermen, a new elite. No; rather I am convinced that there already exists an enormous resource of management, as I have defined it; however, it remains to be more fully tapped, to be nurtured, motivated, encouraged, indeed liberated. As one example, we need to draw into management, both in private enterprise and in public activities, young people of the kind who bring their enthusiasm, their dedication, their human skills of empathy and leadership to the Peace Corps—but this time not for an interlude of two years or so but as the basis for a career in business or in government. Such young people do exist. And yet all too few are drawn into enterprises that call upon these personal qualities.

It is of the nature of leadership that it reproduces and engenders itself over and over again. The leader must be able to recognize leadership potential in others, he must be able to help bring it forth, to enlarge the vision of other men so that their faith and excitement are aroused. But before he can accomplish this essential act of developing human capabilities, he must see clearly that this is the most crucial part

212

of his task. If he considers it incidental or secondary, then he will perform it in an incidental or secondary way. Only if he sees it as primary—if the concept of management which he holds has this as the chief element, whether in a village or a small town or in a great city or in a great company—will he go to the heart of the managerial life which is developing leadership in himself as well as in others. This is an act I have witnessed time and again, perhaps the most inspiring of all, more so than seeing a great dam rising in a mountain gorge, or a giant factory in operation: that of observing and participating in the liberation of human energies.

The essential mark of a successful new manager is that he understands the nature of his function—the kind of job he has, what it will demand of him, the broad range of personal response it must evoke from him, this job which is unlike any other in the world. He must, in short, know what he is. If he cannot interpret himself, then he cannot perform his most important function to others—that is, of interpreting to these others what is going on in their lives, how it could be changed—cannot, therefore, create this community of excitement which produces human results. This concept of the pioneering manager in the urgent and most consequential jobs of the world must be fully understood first by the managers themselves; for a limited technical concept, a concept of conventional management, of slide rule or operations analysis expertise, of old-fashioned stop watch "efficiency," will lead, I fear, to human failure.

THOMAS J. WATSON, JR.
1914 – 1993

Watson was a top salesman for IBM in the late 1930s, more of a result from being the boss's son than through hard work. Quite aware of this fact, he was obsessed with getting out of the company and escaping his father's realm. Watson also feared that his privileged upbringing would eventually lead to disaster, and he would be unable to follow in his father's footsteps. In fact, growing up he was known as terrible Tom; in preparatory school he tried marijuana; and he barely graduated from Brown University. World War II aided Watson's escape from IBM. "Finally" he said, "I felt in the position to do something that counted. My war was going to involve flying airplanes, the one thing I knew I was good at."

Watson was commissioned as a second lieutenant in the Air Force and quickly learned how to manage the men under his command. He realized "that I had the force of personality to get my ideas across to others." After the war he was prepared to work as a pilot for United Air Lines and then move into their management ranks. However, his commanding general said, "I always thought you'd go back and run the IBM company." It was then that Watson realized he should never sell himself or his abilities short. He was no longer an awkward young man; he was a confident leader ready to make his mark. Watson quickly rose through the ranks of IBM, became president in 1952, and succeeded his father as chairman in 1956.

Although his father had built a very respectable company, it was the younger Watson who guided it into the computer age and built a colossus. He has been called "the greatest capitalist in history" by *Fortune* magazine, but work was never his entire life. He continued to fly airplanes, sail, and travel the world, and, while in retirement, President Carter appointed him Ambassador to the Soviet Union in 1979. Watson pursued a balanced life, and in the following selection his struggle to maintain an honest perspective in the cult of IBM is clearly present. He provides a case study for both personal development and business retooling.

The Question of Organization
Thomas J. Watson, Jr.

W e tackled the question of organization in 1956. Until the mid-1950s the company was run essentially by one man, my father. If IBM had had an organization chart at that time, there would have been a fascinating number of lines—perhaps 30—running into his office. As a consequence, people were constantly waiting outside his door, sometimes for as long as a week or two, before they could see him. He saw the important ones, of course, but when I complained about people wasting time in his anteroom, he said, "Oh Tom, let them wait. They're well paid."

This chaotic style had worked exceedingly well since 1914, but it couldn't support the scale of operations many of us anticipated. After several months of study in 1956, we called the top 100 people or so to a three-day meeting in Williamsburg, Virginia, where we distributed responsibility for running the company. We installed a check-and-balance arrangement that later became famous as the IBM system of contention management, in which staff officials would challenge the views of operating men. No decision was final without a staff man's concurrence—and if he signed, his job was just as much at stake as the executive's who made the decision. When an executive and a staff man couldn't agree, the problem got kicked upstairs to senior management, which didn't suffer indecisiveness gladly.

I never varied from the managerial rule that the worst possible thing we could do would be to lie dead in the water with any problem. Solve it, solve it quickly, solve it right or wrong. If you solved it wrong, it would come back and slap you in the face and then you could solve it right. Lying dead in the water and doing nothing is a comfortable alternative because it is without immediate risk, but it is an absolutely fatal way to manage a business.

My way of doing business was never entirely scientific, but I think the emotional, dramatic kind of manager can hold his own with a scientific manager. I never hesitated to intervene if I saw the company getting bogged down.

---

*I never varied from the managerial rule that
the worst possible thing we could do would be to
lie dead in the water with any problem. Solve it,
solve it quickly, solve it right or wrong.*

For instance, we were having a dreadful time in the late 1950s moving the development people into transistors. The Japanese were already making cheap transistor radios by the millions, and we were putting our computers together with acres and acres of vacuum tubes. The transistor was obviously the wave of the future: It was faster than the tube, generated less heat, and had great potential for miniaturization. But our people had labored to master the tube. This new invention shocked them and they resisted it. Williams and I finally wrote a memo that said, after June 1, 1958, we will design no more machines for electronic tubes. Signed, Tom Watson, Jr. The development people were awfully mad. But I kept giving them transistor radios. I ordered 100 of them, and whenever an engineer told me transistors were undependable, I would pull a radio out of my bag and challenge him to wear it out.

I managed with a council of eight to ten executives, and I had a good deal more respect for the opinions of several of these people than for my own conclusions. I would dissolve this committee whenever it reached a point where I thought some people couldn't keep up as IBM grew. Then I would establish a new committee with a different name and most, but not all, the same people. By changing those committees I was able to keep them staffed with the hottest boys in town.

My most important contribution to IBM was my ability to pick strong and intelligent men and then hold the team together by persuasion, by apologies, by financial incentives, by speeches, by chatting with their wives by thoughtfulness when they were sick or involved in accidents, and by using every tool at my command to make that team think that I was a decent guy. I knew I couldn't match all of them intellectually, but I thought that if I used fully every capability that I had, I could stay even with them.

My younger brother, Dick, was the leader who made the company live up to the "international" part of the name our father gave it in 1924. Father organized the IBM World Trade Corp. as a wholly owned subsidiary in 1950, and Dick soon became chief executive. He spoke fluent French, learned Spanish and Italian, and traveled the world to develop businesses in 80 countries. By 1970, World Trade's net earnings matched those of the domestic company, at about $500 million each.

In IBM's domestic business I depended most heavily on Williams and Red LaMotte, to whom I turned on delicate issues of personnel. The most able operating man in IBM was Vin Learson, who eventually succeeded me as chief executive. Learson was an imposing figure, 6 feet 6 inches tall, and his mere presence in a room was enough to get people's attention. He came from a Boston Irish family and put himself through Harvard. For 20 years I gave him IBM's toughest assignments, such as selling off our time-clock company and rescuing a new line of mainframes that had gotten bogged down, and he did each task successfully.

My most important contribution to IBM was my ability to pick strong and intelligent men and then hold the team together by persuasion, by apologies, by financial incentives, by speeches, by chatting with their wives . . . , and by using every tool at my command to make that team think that I was a decent guy.

I never hesitated to promote someone I didn't like. The comfortable assistant—the nice guy you like to go on fishing trips with—is a great pitfall. Instead I looked for those sharp, scratchy, harsh, almost unpleasant guys who see and tell you about things as they really are. If you can get enough of them around you, and have patience enough to hear them out, there is no limit to where you can go.

With so much contention built in, why did IBM's management work? For one thing, with rare exceptions we promoted from within. Virtually every IBM executive started as a salesman. Because we were growing so fast, promotions came quickly. All of our senior executives, including me, knew what it felt like to be thrown into deep water not knowing if you could swim.

When the Williamsburg reorganization created dozens of slots for staff specialists in such areas as manufacturing, personnel, finance, and marketing, we "made" the expert simply by naming the man to the job. This method worked in the main because, as young and inexperienced as these executives might be, they had come up from the bottom. They knew what IBM stood for as well as they knew their own names.

IBM employees all had job security, dating back to the days when my father refused to fire people during the

Depression. Instead, he kept the factories running and made parts for the bins, which stood us in good stead when the Social Security Act passed and we landed the contract to supply the accounting equipment the government needed. If you proved ineffectual at a job, you were not put out on the street; you were reassigned to a level where you were known to perform well. In doing this we would sometimes strip a man of a fair amount of dignity, but we would then make a great effort to rebuild his self-respect.

To survive and succeed in a hot market, a company must be willing to change everything about itself except its basic beliefs. IBM operated for decades on a simple set of principles: Give the individual full consideration, spend a lot of time making customers happy, go the last mile to do a thing right. Everyone shared these values, but we never got around to codifying them until the early 1960s.

I never hesitated to promote someone I didn't like. . . . I looked for those sharp, scratchy, harsh, almost unpleasant guys who see and tell you about things as they really are.

You would be surprised how primitive our training methods were up until the late 1950s. We looked up to General Electric, which had an excellent school. We had our sales school and machine school, but nothing to teach a man how to be someone's boss. A branch manager would call a salesman in and say, "You're promoted to assistant manager. Be careful with people, don't swear, and wear a white shirt." Not until 1966 did we pass a rule that people could never manage unless they had been to management school.

When we started the program, we used cases straight from the Harvard Business School. I took the head of the program aside one day and said, in my usual undiplomatic way, that if we were really going to do something unique, we had to teach something unique.

He said, "Don't you want them educated to be good managers?"

"You don't understand," I said. "We are going to educate them in IBM management: communications, supreme sales and service efforts, frequent meetings, going to a guy's house if his wife is ill and seeing if you can help out, making post-death calls." You don't read that in anybody else's manual. Those were things we'd built up over the years, and new IBM managers have to know them in addition to technology.

For disgruntled workers we had the Open Door Policy, a practice tracing back to the early 1920s. Employees had to first take up their gripes with their managers. If they got no satisfaction, they could come to my office. I spent about one-fifth of my time on Open Door complaints or walking through plants, talking to salesmen, and chatting with customers. I asked what was right and, more important, what was wrong. You don't hear things that are bad about your company unless you ask. It is easy to hear good tidings, but you have to scratch to get the bad news.

My father strove to blur the distinction between white-collar and blue-collar workers. Not only did he pay well, but he eliminated piecework in the factories. For many years IBM's retirement package was identical for all employees, with pensions based solely on length of service, not salary or position. This philosophy stood my father in good stead during the period where there was a lot of labor unrest in America. Organizers were hitting pretty hard at the lush retirement plans some companies offered their executives. I don't think we were primarily driving to stay unorganized, but it had that effect.

In 1958 Jack Bricker, our manager of personnel, suggested that we shift all of our employees to salaries, eliminating the last difference between factory and office work. Although this move came off well, it was thought at first to be very risky. The joke went around that on the first day of hunting season no one would show up for work at our Rochester, Minnesota, plant.

I considered taking even more radical steps to increase our employees' commitment to IBM. When I talked to my wife at night, I would speak of various ways of sharing our success more broadly. Those at the top were doing fantastically well on stock options. This despite the fact that Williams and I stopped taking options in 1958, after Williams said, "We don't want to look like pigs." While IBM's workers were making high salaries, they weren't making the kind of capital gains that employees with options were.

You would be surprised how primitive our training methods were up until the late 1950s. . . .
We had our sales school and machine school,
but nothing to teach a man how to be someone's boss. A branch manager would call a salesman in and say, "You're promoted to assistant manager. Be careful with people, don't swear, and wear a white shirt."

I even asked myself whether our present system of corporate ownership is the system that will support the free American way long term. Though I never found a practical way to achieve it on a meaningful scale, I looked for ways to increase employee ownership of the business. Historically even the employee stock purchase plan has done little to encourage long-term investment by employees, because people sell when the stock rises. And the plan can create bad morale problems whenever the stock value is declining. We decided we could do the best for our employees by developing benefits such as major medical coverage and matching grants for charities and schools. Those we worked very hard on.

I disliked applying a double standard to managers and employees. A business is a sort of dictatorship. You have the antitrust laws that tell you what you can do, and you know you shouldn't be a thief. But the top man has wide discretion. He can give unfair bonuses, he can suggest policies that are not right, he can run airplanes to golf resorts. I never criticized my contemporaries publicly, but there are a lot of things that IBM did differently from other businesses during my watch. Maybe they didn't have my philosophies—or my markups, either.

I thought that the head of a business has responsibilities almost like the head of a country—without a supreme court and without the checks and balances, except for the checks and balances that the marketplace and the annual report impose on his operation. For that reason you cannot treat management differently from the employees. If a manager does something unethical, he should be fired just as surely as a factory worker.

A business is a sort of dictatorship. You have the antitrust laws that tell you what you can do, and you know you shouldn't be a thief. But the top man has wide discretion.

It took me a number of years to realize that a CEO has to spot-check decisions made by his subordinates. Early in my career some managers in one of our plants started a chain letter. The idea was that one manager would write to five other managers, and each of those would write to five more, who would each send some money back to the first guy and write to five more, and so on. Pretty soon they ran out of managers and got down into employees. It ended up that the employees felt pressure to join the chain letter and pay off the managers.

I got a letter of complaint about this and brought it to the attention of the boss of the division. I expected him to say, at a minimum, "We've got to fire a couple of guys. I'll handle it." Instead he simply said, "Well, it was a mistake." I couldn't persuade him to fire anybody. Now you could admire him for defending his team, but I think there is a time when integrity should take the rudder from team loyalty. He was in many ways a capable manager, but from then on I thought he had a blind spot, and it retarded his career.

If it had happened a few years later, I would have fired the managers involved myself. I did this in perhaps a dozen cases when managers broke rules of integrity. Each time I overruled a lot of people who argued that we should merely demote the man, or that the operation would fall apart without him. The company was invariably better off for the decision and the example, but the decisions were lonely.

SAM WALTON
1918 – 1992

Walton grew up in a poor farm community of rural Missouri, in the heart of the dustbowl of the depression years. Poverty taught him to respect the value of the dollar and to be a spendthrift. So, when it was announced by *Forbes* in 1985 that Walton was the richest man in America, he was incredulous when reporters descended on his home in Arkansas to catalog his riches and witness his luxurious lifestyle. They were severely disappointed by his modest living and the fact that he even drove a pickup truck. The press labeled him an eccentric hillbilly. Walton countered, "I just don't believe a big showy lifestyle is appropriate for anywhere, least of all here in Bentonville where folks work hard for their money and where we all know that everyone puts on their trousers one leg at a time."

Walton was able to escape his humble roots by attending the University of Missouri, and then going to work for J. C. Penney three days after graduation. He served in World War II, but afterward, instead of returning to his old job, he was determined to enter into business for himself. In 1945 he bought his first variety store, a Ben Franklin, with $5,000 of his own savings and a $20,000 loan from his father-in-law. Five years later he sold it and opened Walton's 5 & 10 in Bentonville, Arkansas. A second five-and-ten was opened in 1952, and with it he introduced a fairly new concept: self-service. This new concept was a big hit, for it allowed him to keep his payroll down and offer lower prices on merchandise. As he opened more stores, Walton started buying much of his stock directly from manufacturers, thus eliminating the middleman and permitting his stores to offer wider discounting. His affordable prices fueled his phenomenal success in rural communities.

It was not until 1962 that Walton officially opened his first store under the Wal-Mart name, and the company did not go public until 1970. In *Running a Successful Company: Ten Rules that Worked for Me,* Walton provides his basic formula for business. He semiapologetically prefaces them by saying that some of his rules involve simple common sense; but then again, using common sense and sticking to basic principles is something often overlooked.

Running a Successful Company: Ten Rules that Worked for Me
Sam Walton

Awhole lot has changed about the retailing business in the forty-seven years we've been in it—including some of my theories. We've changed our minds about some significant things along the way and adopted some new principles—particularly about the concept of partnership in a corporation. But most of the values and the rules and the techniques we've relied on have stayed the same the whole way. Some of them are such simple commonsense old favorites that they hardly seem worth mentioning.

This isn't the first time that I've been asked to come up with a list of rules for success, but it *is* the first time I've actually sat down and done it. I'm glad I did because it's been a revealing exercise for me. The truth is, David Glass is right. I do seem to have a couple of dozen things that I've singled out at one time or another as the "key" to the whole thing. One I don't even have on my list is "work hard." If you don't know that already, or you're not willing to do it, you probably won't be going far enough to need my list anyway. And another I didn't include on the list is the idea of building a team. If you want to build an enterprise of any size at all, it almost goes without saying that you absolutely must create a team of people who work together and give real meaning to that overused word "teamwork." To me, that's more the goal of the whole thing, rather than some way to get there.

I believe in always having goals, and always setting them high. I can certainly tell you that the folks at Wal-Mart have always had goals in front of them. In fact, we have sometimes built real scoreboards on the stage at Saturday morning meetings.

One more thing. If you're really looking for my advice here, trying to get something serious out of this exercise I put myself through, remember: these rules are not in any way intended to be the Ten Commandments of Business. They are some rules that worked for me. But I always prided myself on breaking everybody else's rules, and I always favored the mavericks who challenged my rules. I may have fought them all the way, but I respected them, and, in the end, I listened to them a lot more closely than I did the pack

---

Commit to your business. Believe in it more than anybody else. I think I overcame every single one of my personal shortcomings by the sheer passion I brought to my work.

---

who always agreed with everything I said. So pay special attention to Rule 10, and if you interpret it in the right spirit—as it applies to you—it could mean simply: Break All the Rules.

For what they're worth, here they are. Sam's Rules for Building a Business:

RULE 1: COMMIT to your business. Believe in it more than anybody else. I think I overcame every single one of my personal shortcomings by the sheer passion I brought to my work. I don't know if you're born with this kind of passion, or if you can learn it. But I do know you need it. If you love your work, you'll be out there every day trying to do it the best

226

you possibly can, and pretty soon everybody around will catch the passion from you—like a fever.

RULE 2: SHARE your profits with all your associates, and treat them as partners. In turn, they will treat you as a partner, and together you will all perform beyond your wildest expectations. Remain a corporation

---

Communicate everything you possibly can to your partners. . . . If you don't trust your associates to know what's going on, they'll know you don't really consider them partners.

---

and retain control if you like, but behave as a servant leader in a partnership. Encourage your associates to hold a stake in the company. Offer discounted stock, and grant them stock for their retirement. It's the single best thing we ever did.

RULE 3: MOTIVATE your partners. Money and ownership alone aren't enough. Constantly, day by day, think of new and more interesting ways to motivate and challenge your partners. Set high goals, encourage competition, and then keep score. Make bets with outrageous payoffs. If things get stale, cross-pollinate; have managers switch jobs with one another to stay challenged. Keep everybody guessing as to what your next trick is going to be. Don't become too predictable.

RULE 4: COMMUNICATE everything you possibly can to your partners. The more they know, the more they'll understand. The more they understand, the more they'll care. Once they care, there's no stopping them. If you don't trust your associates to know what's going on, they'll know you don't really consider them partners. Information is power, and the gain you get from empowering your associates more than offsets the risk of informing your competitors.

RULE 5: APPRECIATE everything your associates do for the business. A paycheck and a stock option will buy one kind of loyalty. But all of us like to be told how much somebody appreciates what we do for them. We like to hear it often, and especially when we have done something we're really proud of. Nothing else can quite substitute for a few well-chosen, well-timed, sincere words of praise. They're absolutely free—and worth a fortune.

RULE 6: CELEBRATE your successes. Find some humor in your failures. Don't take yourself so seriously. Loosen up, and everybody around you will loosen up. Have fun. Show enthusiasm—always. When all else fails, put on a costume and sing a silly song. Then make everybody else sing with you. Don't do

---

Control your expenses better than your competition. This is where you can always find the competitive advantage.

---

a hula on Wall Street. It's been done. Think up your own stunt. All of this is more important, and more fun, than you think, and it really fools the competition. "Why should we take those cornballs at Wal-Mart seriously?"

RULE 7: LISTEN to everyone in your company. And figure out ways to get them talking. The folks on the front lines—the ones who actually talk to the customer—are the only ones who really know what's going on out there. You'd better find out what they know. This really is what total quality is all about. To push responsibility down in your organization, and to force good ideas to bubble up within it, you *must* listen to what your associates are trying to tell you.

RULE 8: EXCEED your customers' expectations. If you do, they'll come back over and over. Give them what they want—and a little more. Let them know you appreciate them. Make good on all your mistakes, and don't make excuses—apologize. Stand behind

---

Swim upstream. Go the other way. Ignore the conventional wisdom.

---

everything you do. The two most important words I ever wrote were on that first Wal-Mart sign: "Satisfaction Guaranteed." They're still up there, and they have made all the difference.

RULE 9: CONTROL your expenses better than your competition. This is where you can always find the competitive advantage. For twenty-five years running— long before Wal-Mart was known as the nation's largest retailer—we ranked number one in our industry for the lowest ratio of expenses to sales. You can make a lot of different mistakes and still recover if you run an efficient operation. Or you can be brilliant and still go out of business if you're too inefficient.

RULE 10: SWIM upstream. Go the other way. Ignore the conventional wisdom. If everybody else is doing it one way, there's a good chance you can find your niche by going in exactly the opposite direction. But be prepared for a lot of folks to wave you down and tell you you're headed the wrong way. I guess in all my years, what I heard more often than anything was: a town of less than 50,000 population cannot support a discount store for very long.

Those are some pretty ordinary rules, some would say even simplistic. The hard part, the real challenge, is to constantly figure out ways to execute them. You can't just keep doing what works one time, because everything around you is always changing. To succeed, you have to stay out in front of that change.

PART V

SELLING SKILLS AND
CUSTOMER FOCUS

JOHN J. JOHNSON
1918 –

Johnson, the most powerful African-American businessperson, was born in rural Arkansas. His father was killed when he was a child, and he lived in poverty; yet, Johnson claims, "I was lucky. I was born into a strong family and reared in a strong community where every Black adult was charged with the responsibility of monitoring and supervising every Black child." His family moved to Chicago in 1933, and it wasn't long before Johnson secured his first job, which was with the National Youth Administration, an arm of President Roosevelt's New Deal. Even with this new prospect of rising out of poverty, Johnson realized that he was not in control of his destiny—that being on the bad side of just one white person could change his life.

An opportunity to seize control of his future arose when Johnson took a job with an African-American life insurance company and received some scholarship money to study at the University of Chicago. He took full advantage of the opportunity. Over the next few years he built a network of friends and business associates, and in 1942 he seized his destiny by founding the *Negro Digest* magazine. He did it with $500 he borrowed using his mother's furniture as collateral. Three years later he started *Ebony,* which would become the cornerstone of his empire. To succeed in publishing, he knew he had to reverse the prejudice against advertising in African-American magazines; white businesspeople were blind to African-American consumers and their purchasing power. Johnson emphatically argued "that Blacks were brand-conscious consumers who wanted to be treated like everyone else—not better, not worse."

Persistence eventually paid off, and Johnson was able to finance ventures in radio and television, book publishing, and cosmetics. He even purchased a controlling interest in Supreme Life Insurance, the company that had given him his first real opportunity. In retrospect, Johnson says the key to his success was dogged determination. "I refused to give up. I refused to take no for an answer, and I refused to let others take no for an answer." He had to sell himself and his ideas to a very biased audience, and in the process he became an absolute authority on *How to Sell Anybody Anything in Five Minutes or Less.*

How to Sell Anybody Anything in Five Minutes or Less
John J. Johnson

If I know enough about people, and if I have enough time, I can sell anybody anything.

Even if I don't have enough time, I can open the door to a future sale.

In my early days as a salesman, I usually asked clients and prospects for only five minutes. I've been known, in fact, to ask for only two minutes.

Sometimes you can't tell your story in five minutes, but if you ask for five minutes, people are more inclined to give you an appointment. If you get your foot in the door and tell a good story, they'll probably let you finish, even if it takes thirty minutes or an hour: If, on the other hand, there's no interest in what you're saying, a minute is enough.

It was my custom in the early days to ask for five minutes and to take fifteen or twenty minutes by creative ad-libbing. I would make my presentation in about five minutes, then stand up as if I intended to go. This usually relaxed the client, and I would say, "There's one more point I want to make."

Then, two or three minutes later, I would say, "I'm really going now, but I want to make sure you understand this point."

As I was going through the door with my briefcase, just before I pulled the door shut, I would pause, like TV detective Peter Falk, and say, "I just want to leave this final thought with you."

What made this five-minute drill effective was not the five minutes the client could see but the weeks and months of preparation that he couldn't see. For when the five-minute clock started ticking, I knew more about him—more about his interests, passions, hobbies, desires—than most members of his family.

Whether I had five or thirty-five minutes, I always based my presentation on three tried-and-tested rules:

1. Grab the client's attention in the first two or three seconds with a fact or an emotional statement that hits him where he lives or does business.
2. Find the vulnerable spot. Everybody has something that will make him or her move or say yes. It may have nothing in the world to do with his or her business life. It may be a dream or a hope or a commitment to a person or a thing. Selling is finding the vulnerable point and pushing the yes button.

   A remarkable example of this was reported by William Grayson, who discovered that a powerful advertising executive was a fan of Roy Campanella, the great Brooklyn Dodgers catcher. The executive and his son virtually lived in the old Ebbets Field and virtually worshipped the home-plate ground Campanella walked on.

You don't have to compromise your integrity to sell. You simply have to find and emphasize the things that unite you instead of the things that divide you.

Grayson, who lived down the street from Campanella, asked the baseball star to autograph one of his home-run balls to the boy. The ball carried not only Campanella's name but the date he hit the home run. By coincidence, the advertising executive and his son had been in Ebbets Field on the day Campanella hit the home run. That sold the account. Nothing—neither statistics nor pretty graphs nor hundreds of telephone calls—was as powerful as an unexpectedly powerful gift to a loved one.

3. Find and emphasize common ground. You and the client may disagree on many things. You may like Jesse Jackson and he or she may dislike Jesse Jackson. You're not there to talk about what divides you. You're there to emphasize the values, hopes, and aspirations that bind you together. Successful selling is a matter of finding common ground, no matter how narrow it might be, on which you and your client can stand together.

That's true in selling and life, especially in the area of race relations, where both Blacks and Whites must make a special effort to emphasize the things that unite them.

Does this mean that you have to sacrifice your integrity? Certainly not. I've been selling on the edge for forty-seven years, and I don't think I've had to compromise my integrity. I've stooped in some cases to conquer, but I don't apologize for that—the conquering, I mean.

You don't have to compromise your integrity to sell. You simply have to find and emphasize the things that unite you instead of the things that divide you.

By these different methods, by persistence and ingenuity and gall, I established narrow but solid common ground that gave me room to maneuver. Although I found and pushed a lot of yes buttons, the struggle for a fair share of the advertising dollar continued, and continues.

In advertising, as in politics, you're no better than your last schedule or your last election. No matter how many accounts you've broken, no matter how many elections you've won, you always start a new campaign at ground zero. And you're always faced with the task of going on cold and proving to a new audience how good you are.

The future chairman of Philip Morris and, according to B. C. Forbes, "one of America's master salesman," was expected to take over his father's antique dealership in London. However, Lyon found the family business too slow, so he sought his fortune in the relative wilderness of Canada, where he found more dazzling employment selling diamonds. His promising career in sales was briefly interrupted by War World I, during which he served under the Canadian flag in India and was wounded. After the war he discovered his greatest passion, tobacco, and accepted a position with the Tobacco Products Corporation. For the next 10 years he sold its wares all over the world. Finally, he began working for Philip Morris in 1929, and eventually became president in 1945 and then chairman in 1949.

In a harrowing first year as president, Lyon almost ruined the company for several reasons: Sales declined dramatically with the end of World War II; he then foolishly ordered the repackaging of stale, stockpiled cigarettes that had been returned; and he got into trouble with the Securities and Exchange Commission for not disclosing a weakened financial position when the company issued more stock. Lyon publicly admitted to being "a damn fool in trying to do everything, including many tasks I didn't know anything about." His belated candor was an extension of the motto hanging on his office wall that read, "There are a hundred thousand reasons for failure but not a single excuse."

The initial setbacks did little to slow down the flamboyant salesman, who authorized aggressive ad slogans encouraging smokers to make "The Switch That Takes The Fear Out of Smoking." He was always looking for an angle that suggested Philip Morris brands were more healthy than the others. Another example was the ad "King Dunhill Screens Out Irritants." Only, Dunhills had no filters back then! In the following selection, his enthusiasm not only for salesmanship, but also for cigarettes, is obvious. It is difficult to imagine Lyon surviving in today's smoke-free environment, where he would be forced from his office building and onto the streets just to light up his favorite brand.

Sell Yourself First
Alfred E. Lyon

"Remember, your customers don't buy your product. They buy you and they sell your product for you." That's what I've been telling my salesmen for 25 years, and it is still the best advice I know. I urge upon them: "Sell yourself first."

"If you've got a good, straight-forward look in your eye, if you make a nice appearance, and if you make a courteous approach, dealers will buy your cigarettes. We've spent millions of dollars telling people how good Philip Morris are, but if the dealers know that you are good too, they will go out of their way to help you."

The best way one of my "boys" can sell himself is to do that little extra-something for his dealers. Give the customer dividends which he didn't figure on, and you have a friend for life. There are thousands and thousands of dealers who carry Philip Morris products. I know many of them by their first names. This is no tribute to my memory, which is not phenomenal. This is because I've always made a practice of going out on the road to get acquainted with dealers. I've kept up this personal contact over the years and still remember a customer's birthday or a young son's graduation. My office door at 100 Park Avenue is always open. The dealers, small or large, from Paducah and Syracuse, drop in on me when visiting New York. I love it, and so do they.

How can a salesman give that extra value? Well, he can show a dealer how to push another (but non-competitive) product more successfully. For instance, I may suggest to a dealer—"Why don't we place Philip Morris next to these fountain pens. That will boost both Philip Morris and the pens." Sure enough! When a customer who comes in for Philip Morris spots the pens, he gets another idea. The result: another sale and everyone is happy.

Give the customer dividends which he didn't figure on, and you have a friend for life.

Our salesmen often suggest more attractive window displays for a dealer, new products to carry, how to improve generally the layout of the shop. Because they have been trained to be tactful (and sell themselves first), they are never resented. I honestly believe that Philip Morris salesmen are the best-liked and best-behaved in the entire cigarette industry. This is no accident: it is the whole foundation of our selling success. Twenty years ago the brown-packaged special blend was only a gleam in the eye of our company. Today, it is a firm No. 4 in the industry.

Recently, we did a favor for the hat makers of America. We got more than we bargained for in return. Over my signature a letter went to all Philip Morris employees. It opened: "It has come to our notice that the habit of going around hatless is becoming more and more prevalent. There are good reasons that you should always wear a hat. . . ." Then I enumerated such reasons as "good grooming," "gives an air of authority," "completes a person's dress." The letter wound up with a real sales clincher—". . . the man who makes and sells hats also smokes cigarettes."

Quicker than you can open a pack of Philip Morris, the President of the Hat Research Foundation of America reciprocated with his own letter to hundreds of hat stores and manufacturers. ". . . In an unsolicited letter to all Philip Morris employees, Mr. Lyon has expressed his personal interest in hats and his belief in the advantages of hat wearing. . . . I will welcome any effort you make to demonstrate to the Philip Morris Company our sincere appreciation of this action." Philip Morris and the hat men got more business, and everyone got much happier.

A good salesman is a good actor. He has to be in order to know what his "audience" wants, and when he wants it. If a dealer is in a bad mood, my salesman should use all his tact in trying to resolve the situation; if necessary, even stay away for a while. If he is in a good mood, my salesman must know enough not to over-press his advantage. A sensitive salesman (and "sensitive" here means intelligent) knows exactly where and how he stands with a customer at all times.

Many years ago I called upon a distributor in the midwest. The dealer was puttering around and blithely ignored me. I hung around for nearly 20 minutes, then started out.

A good salesman is a good actor. He has to be in order to know what his "audience" wants, and when he wants it.

Gruffly, the dealer yelled after me, "Is there something I can do for you?" I turned and smiled: "There *was* something you could do for me. You could be polite, but I don't believe you know how." The proprietor melted right then and there and apologized profusely. He told me he'd had a fight with his wife that morning and was upset. Most people are pleasant, and when you find a disagreeable one, there is usually a good reason behind it. This dealer and I are now the best of friends, and he's one of our best customers.

The right sales approach is very important. I remember well how I sold the initial order of Philip Morris to a large drug chain out West. Before 1933, when Philip Morris cigarettes first appeared on the American scene, Marlboro Cigarettes were the main source of our income. The chain had always been a big buyer of Marlboro, and I wanted them to properly promote our new Philip Morris brand. But they were a cut-rate chain, and I was afraid that the President of the chain would try to cut Philip Morris which would be fatal. So, I used the hard-to-get-approach. I dropped in one day, and we chatted about Marlboro, sports and the political situation. Casually, I lit a Philip Morris, dropping the opened package on his desk. I didn't say anything as I watched his eyes drop on the handsome package with anticipation. In a few moments, he was all questions wanting to know about this new cigarette. By the time I was ready to leave, he was planning fifty-carton displays on all his counters.

Devotion of any kind produces a zealousness in a person, a kind of fervency. This is what drives our salesmen.

By appearing to be indifferent, I made him come to me. He was so happy about "discovering" this new, attractively-packaged cigarette, that he never even thought of cutting the price. That's what I mean when I say a good salesman is a good actor, is sensitive to the customer's moods. You take your cue from the customer and throw him a line which suits his particular mood. Naturally, every customer throws out a different mood. An attentive salesman is always switching "lines" and reactions, but must, above all, always be honest.

We, at Philip Morris, are dedicated to the proposition that our cigarette is clearly the finest cigarette available. If our salesmen don't believe this, they have no right to be selling for us. Devotion of any kind produces a zealousness in a person, a kind of fervency. This is what drives our salesmen. This is what drove up our sales to $306 million in 1950, a good $50 million above the previous year. We want and expect our salesmen to "convert" people wherever they are—in a coffee shop, at a drug store, everywhere.

JULIUS FLEISCHMANN
1872 – 1925

When Fleischmann's Austrian father, Charles, immigrated to Cincinnati in 1868, he found the quality of American bread intolerable. The culprit was an unreliable yeast, so he immediately began developing a better packaged product and quickly became the industry leader. Later, under the guidance of Julius Fleischmann, the company diversified into vinegar, malt, feed, and margarine, and became recognized as a premier food conglomerate. The company's continued success was attributed to Fleischmann's personal belief that "The superlative executive is the one who has the backbone to cut costs and trim sail when business is good, and the company is making money." He never fell to the dangerous trait of self-satisfaction.

In 1929 the Fleischmann family sold the company and it became part of Standard Brands. Standard Brands eventually merged with Nabisco in 1981 to form Nabisco Brands, which was then purchased by R. J. Reynolds in 1985 to form RJR Nabisco, which was then purchased in a leveraged buyout by the brokerage house of Kohlberg Kravis Roberts (the subject of the renown book, *Barbarians at the Gate*). Whew!—if the Fleischmann's had known their company would become part of this colorful and tainted genealogy, perhaps they would have liquidated and returned to Austria long before 1929. But they did not. In fact, Julius Fleischmann remained in Cincinnati and was eventually elected mayor, a true testimony of his outstanding character and business acumen. Salesmanship and people skills are vital for a politician, and in *My Three Essentials of Management*, Fleischmann shares what he has learned.

My Three Essentials of Management
Julius Fleischmann

T est any business that is not progressing as it should and you will find either: (1) that it puts the immediate dollar of profit into the limelight; (2) that it scatters its energies by going into temporary side-lines that seem to offer an extra profit; or (3) that it is hide-bound—it will not change a policy to meet a new condition.

Any one of these three violations of sound business policy is enough to hold back any business, whether it is manufacturing, wholesaling, retailing, or personal service.

Service, in its broadest sense, and concentration of effort are, in my opinion, two policies which are necessarily fundamental to any business which hopes to grow in size and stability. There is another one that might be called a superpolicy, which is essential to the growing business. It is that all policies must be flexible and expedient.

To show how these policies are followed in our organization, it is necessary to tell something of what we do and how we are organized.

Of our sales volume 90% consists of compressed yeast used for various purposes, the three most important of which are, for baking, for health, and in dry form for cattle and live stock. The other 10% is made up of sales of other products which are closely related to the manufacture of compressed yeast—malt extract and vinegar.

Compressed yeast is sold in two forms: the small packages which the grocer sells for a few cents to the housewife, and the same product which is sold in packages of large bulk to the baker. Yeast is a highly perishable product, and even though kept under the best possible conditions will change in strength when stored. This has a vital bearing on distribution.

To the baker it is of paramount importance that the yeast he uses in making bread be of uniform strength every day, otherwise his bread will suffer in quality. We early found that to insure this uniformity of strength—that is, to make sure that our customers always get fresh yeast—we had to control our distribution.

Old Ben Franklin's maxim, "If you would have a thing well done, do it yourself," seems to fit our marketing problems exactly, so we followed his advice. This necessity for controlling the distribution of our product automatically eliminated distribution through any form of commission agents or wholesale houses, and forced us to build a selling and distributing organization of our own.

This is handled by 23 district offices, each under the control of a local district manager. The district offices have direct supervision over 960 agencies and subagencies. Every day from these agencies and subagencies, delivery cars owned by us and driven by men who are directly on our payroll and are employed solely by us deliver yeast to more than 30,000 bakers and 225,000 grocers. Every day our agents get by express from our nearest plant their day's requirements of yeast. In that way we make sure that the customer will get strictly fresh yeast of uniform strength.

The job of making these daily express shipments to our 960 agencies presents a real traffic problem. It is handled by our traffic department, which has ramifications in every corner of the country. Local traffic managers are stationed at strategic points throughout the country. Their sole job is to see that deliveries are made promptly.

The point is that the mere matter of prompt delivery is one of the biggest parts of our service policy. It is primarily service that we are selling, rather than merchandise, for if the service failed, shortly no one would buy the merchandise. There can be no such thing as too much real service in business.

A story which is intended to show that service can be carried to extremes, has to do with a merchant who delivered a spool of thread with a five-ton truck. Admittedly, the picture of a tiny spool riding all alone in state in a big truck is rather funny; but the service rendered appears to me to be not at all ridiculous.

I can picture a housewife and her seamstress-by-the-day, sitting idle in a littered sewing room waiting for that spool of thread and unable to proceed with the all-important job of sewing until it gets there. If the truck was the only conveyance available, it was entirely proper to use it. Although the story does not tell who that merchant was, I'll venture the guess that he is a mighty successful one. Very likely the next time the truck went to that same address it carried a grand piano and a dining room suite.

It is primarily service that we are selling, rather than merchandise, for if the service failed, shortly no one would buy the merchandise.

Such service is an every-day affair with us. Frequently, in the middle of the night some baker will telephone one of our agents that he needs yeast and that agent will, as a matter of course, get dressed and deliver it. It matters nothing whether the baker is large or small. We have sent yeast into snow-bound villages by dog-sled. At a cost of several hundred dollars we have often delivered yeast by airplane to cities cut off from the world by floods or earthquakes, so that the inhabitants could have their one indispensable item of food—bread. Our men have often been the very first to get into stricken communities.

While these are spectacular instances of service, they are entirely analogous to the five-ton truck and the spool of thread. When emergencies like this are handled, the profit on that sale goes into red ink. But in the long run the service that we have given in such cases has brought us big profits in satisfied customers, whose continued patronage is the reason for the stability of our business.

When this business was started more than 50 years ago, it was doubtless run as a purely commercial or trading proposition. The basis of all business in those days was simple. It could be stated something like this: "I have these goods; you have a use for them. I'll trade my goods for as much of your money as I can separate you from." No one, hardly, had conceived of business as a service. Markets were thought of as rigid. There were few bakers—some bought yeast and some made it. Most bread was baked at home by women who made their own yeast, just as they made their own soap.

At some time in the history of our business, I am not sure just when, someone got the dazzling vision that the market for yeast is not rigid—that it could, in fact, be expanded. The first thought was that we should urge the convenience of buying yeast instead of making it. Still we were in the position of hammering at the doors of our largest prospective customers, the bakers, and trying to get them to substitute our yeast for what they were using.

In 1912 we first realized that the development of our business depended on the development of the baking industry, and that if we were to increase the consumption of yeast in the bakeries, we first had to increase the bakers' output by increasing the consumption of bread. Therefore, the weight of our first campaign was to "Eat More Bread." We saw that we should first help the bakers to sell more bread and that our sales of yeast would automatically increase. We realized that as our customers profited we should profit.

Running through our policy of serving is another policy—concentration of effort. It is a phase of that policy broadly known as "simplification."

Because we sell directly to bakers and grocers, we are constantly tempted to sell other articles that all our customers buy—lines out of harmony with our production and sales policies. That is a temptation, I imagine, to which most business men are subject and to which many of them succumb. At first thought, it seems so logical to utilize an existing sales force in selling other products to a large list of retailers who are already accustomed to buy from us. Seldom, however, does it pay. The slight reduction in selling cost would be more than offset by increased manufacturing and management costs that always come when efforts are scattered rather than concentrated.

We do, however, sell certain products which are closely affiliated with the manufacture of yeast and which are also used in the manufacture of bread. One of these is malt extract. The malt from our own malting plant is used both in the manufacture of yeast and in this malt extract. The sale of this product also dovetails with the general selling organization, and because it is used by the baker to whom we also sell our yeast, we are able to handle it without any change in our selling organization.

Another of these products, which is not, however, so closely related to the baking industry, is vinegar. The alcohol which we get as a by-product of yeast manufacture is converted into vinegar and is sold mostly to packers for preserving their products.

Just as we keep all phases of selling in our hands, we also, for protection, keep as much as is practical of our manufacturing under our control. We buy no semifinished materials. We own all plants in which all processes are performed, and we even own grain elevators in the West. We could own the farms on which the grain is raised, for we use the production of a great many thousand acres. We could also own sugar plantations, steamship lines, paper mills, and box-making plants, for our production enables us to use the output. But we do not go into those businesses. In my opinion, the tendency to make everything that one uses is short-sighted and foolish for most concerns.

To be successful yeast manufacturers takes all of our time, thought, and effort. We do not know how to operate ships. We are not paper manufacturers and we know little about making boxes. If we tried to get the profit that exists in each of these lines we might find that our inattention to the yeast business was cutting down the profit on our yeast production. I believe that if those concerns that make, for instance, their own containers—and there are lots which do—had accurate cost figures, they would find that they were not profiting from the activity. We keep reminding ourselves that we are yeast manufacturers solely—not farmers, nor papermakers, nor anything else.

So far as operating sugar plantations and grain farms is concerned, there is another restraining influence in the danger of local crop failures. If we owned farms, that might cripple us. As it is, a crop failure affects us but slightly—we can, if necessary, buy anywhere.

Expediency is a sort of superpolicy. By that I do not mean that policies should be designed to make the best possible showing for today—to grab the dollar which is closest at hand. Any business must have a plan for the future and its methods must always keep a jump or so ahead of the needs of the growing business, but it is a mistake, I feel, to consider a policy sacred. Tradition has held many a business back, and it is the old business that has been strongly founded that often suffers most from hampering tradition. In this concern, we never think of yesterday except as experience.

Some time ago, one of my principal associates, a man who held an important post and who had devoted upwards of 30 years to building this business, retired from active service. At the time, he explained his action by saying that he was retiring, not because he was worn out, but because he recognized that a new order of management along new lines was necessary. He felt the business was getting so big that it was necessary to delegate authority, and his training was such that he feared that he could not learn the new way. He was truly a big man, and so he was able to sense the evolution that any business goes through when it grows.

This evolution in a business must be guided. To be most effective, changes in method must come at just the right time. To make changes too soon—before the business is ready for them—is nearly as bad as to make them too late.

One of our executives not long ago felt somewhat hurt when we installed a new method which he had proposed 10 years before. As I explained to him, the plan he had devised showed keen and progressive thinking, but he was 10 years too soon with it. In my capacity as a professional conservative, I had to hold him back until the business was ready for the new method.

As I see the job of any chief executive, he must be ready within a single hour to play the part of conservative, progressive, and even radical. The instance I have just related is one when I wore the mask of the conservative.

As a radical I once unhesitatingly abandoned a $750,000 plant and built a new one, because the old one was not efficient. New methods and machinery had been developed that we could not afford to be without. The results in lower manufacturing costs fully warranted the step that to some seemed rank extravagance.

There is somewhat of good in the attitudes of the conservative, the progressive, and the radical in business. The conservative's function is to see to it that the sound ideas of the radical and the progressive are not put into use too soon. In a successful business, progressive ideas must necessarily prevail. The radical ideas of today will be the progressive ideas of tomorrow. There is only one thing more dangerous to a business than to give the radical and progressive business ideas full play, and that is to have too much conservatism without the push of the progressive behind it.

Everyone knows the brand name Coca-Cola, the soft drink invented in 1886 by Dr. J. S. Pemberton, a concocter of patent medicines from Atlanta. It is the soft drink that conquered the globe during World War II, when it was rationed at home so the boys overseas could have it. The soldiers in turn exposed both friend and foe to the drink (even the empty bottles were used for everything from emergency electrical insulators to glass bombs dropped on the enemy's airfields in hope of puncturing tires). However, few knew the enigmatic man behind this mastery of patriotism and commercialism, the impenetrable Robert Woodruff, who presided over the Coca-Cola empire for 60 years.

One factor that was crucial to building Woodruff's hardened exterior was his father, who secretly had him fired from a variety of jobs he held as a young man in order to "teach him a lesson in hard knocks." Naturally, when Woodruff found out, it created a rift between father and son; however, in 1919, when his father devised a scheme to buy Coca-Cola, he chose to participate (as did his hunting buddy Ty Cobb, who incidentally made a fortune from Coca-Cola stock). Woodruff became a dedicated shareholder and employee, and ascended to the presidency at the age of 33. Coca-Cola became his deity, and the employees his congregation. He preached to them, "I can never divorce myself, my affections, my life from Coca-Cola, and neither can any of the rest of you." And most of them did not. Well, there was that marketing blunder in 1985 when the company introduced their new formula. Luckily, Woodruff died two months before it was put on the market.

Along with Woodruff's intense personality came an uncanny ability to evaluate people, and as one colleague said, "He can take a man's measure so rapidly that the man does not realize he is being observed." This quality undoubtedly contributed to his phenomenal success early on as a salesman for the company. In *You in a Career of Selling* he emphatically states that it is the salesperson who maintains "the dynamics of the American dream," and he explains why and how it is done.

You in a Career of Selling
Robert W. Woodruff

Philosophers tell us that the gift without the giver is bare. In a very real sense, this axiom applies to what we call selling. No act of salesmanship is soundly successful unless something of the salesman goes with it. His personal integrity, his belief in himself and his product must be an essential part of each sales agreement, if the company selling and the customer buying are mutually to benefit. The mere act of completing an exchange of goods or a product for an agreed price does not necessarily constitute a successful sale, no matter how much the profit may be, for the real salesman must sell something of himself with each sale.

It is necessary, too, for him to be a believing man, believing in himself and his product. Nor is this all. The salesman needs also to believe that what he sells will help the business of the merchant or company buying it. He cannot really separate himself from his product, even after he has sold it and delivery has been effected. He cannot escape this if he wishes. Since he cannot, the wise salesman accepts this reality as opportunity, as a door to a successful selling career.

The more cynical image of American selling is the so-called fast-buck operator, or the theatrical stereotype of Willy Loman in the stage play, *Death of a Salesman,* or that of the girl-chasing "drummer" of another generation. We will leave the sophisticates with their empty cynicism.

The real salesman must sell something of himself with each sale.

The truth is, the nation properly has an affection for the "drummer" of by-gone years. He is a well-loved legend, a part of our national folklore. He deserves more than passing attention, because his contribution was substantial. If he was picturesque, it was because the obstacles he had to surmount were unusual, requiring not merely enterprise, imagination, and intelligence, but a pair of good legs, a strong back, and a stomach able to digest what could be bought at remote "general" stores. The sales custom in those days was to visit every general store in a state. They could be reached sometimes by an "accommodation" train, which accommodated by stopping at every flag stop. More often than not, however, the out-of-the-way towns could be reached only by horse and buggy. The salesman usually could manage breakfast and dinner (or supper as it then was known) at a county-seat hotel or boarding house. Lunch was had at some general store—most of these stores kept a bowl or so for the use of drummers, and many a sale has been made over a handful of crackers and a bowl of canned tomatoes or sardines and cheese. Old-timers have fond memories of how good Cove oysters tasted, eaten out of the can with a spoon. These salesmen were a part of our economic growing up. They earned the place they have in our hearts.

No one disputes, for example, that it was the distribution of goods from the first machines and handicrafts of the young Republic that stimulated the phenomenal economic growth of the new nation. Some of the biographies of Alexander Hamilton note that he urged the first Congress to consider how Great Britain had spread "her factories and agents over the four quarters of the globe." "Consider," Hamilton said, "Britain's huge and varied pile of manufacturers." He planned to draw skilled labor, tools, and machines from Britain, in order to expand the commerce of the Union formed by adoption of the Constitution—and he planned, too, for "agents," for salesmen.

No historian has truly told the story of the salesman in the rapid development and productive growth of our country. The soldier, the statesman, the pioneer, the Indian fighter have all had their biographers. The salesman played an equally important role. He moved goods along the rivers and the trails. The men who went to the frontier with goods to exchange for furs, the traders who opened trading posts deep in the wilderness—all these were a part of the necessary movement and distribution of consumer goods and products. "Selling" was then, as now, the motive power in our prosperity and growth. All through our history, the large majority of our salesmen have been hard-working, competent, knowledgeable men who have made an invaluable, essential contribution. The stereotypes of stage and fiction remain what they have always been: the exceptions.

We tend to think of the Industrial Revolution in terms of vast new machines, of automation, of mass production and assembly. But nothing happens until a salesman books an order. And distribution does not continue unless the product and the man who sold it produce a profit for the man who bought it. Selling is more than a sale.

In the latter half of the Twentieth Century, selling has become complex and specialized. Economic changes have demanded specialization in many endeavors and the salesman, too, must now have special knowledge and the ability to use it. The old drummer has almost disappeared; instead, we can think of salesmen as ranging the world to sell their goods. All the industrial nations now send their salesmen to far places, and the competition for world markets is more demanding than even the economists could believe a decade ago. Indeed, not until near the beginning of the 1960's did our own economists speak so insistently that they finally made themselves heard: "As a nation, we must sell and export more than we have ever done," they said.

So, in a time of increasing economic competition, the nation is calling on its salesmen. This is nothing new to salesmen. Whenever they travel alone, they represent the country. Sometimes, when they are sent out in groups to represent industry or our government, they are called "trade delegations" or "national sale forces"; but they are just plain salesmen, after all—and that is why you are being told this, why it is being emphasized, so that you can recognize and understand the dignity and the importance that can go with selling. There can be pride and many kinds of satisfaction for you, as well as profit, if you decide to go into a career of selling.

The vast broadening of the scope of selling is not merely in the international field. It permeates our domestic growth as well. For example, all kinds of service jobs are increasing and the service industries are continually discovering new ways to sell their services. They remind us of the variety of our selling, just as the expanding range of retail items underscore its magnitude. Think, for instance, in the range of our selling, of the myriad small items in our dime stores over the country and then compare these small things with the new computers and electronic marvels sold to universities, businesses, and research organizations.

A young man or woman seriously considering selling as a career must, first of all, have a genuine interest in other people, their problems, their aspirations and needs.

We can better realize the whole drama of selling if we think of the thousands of sales clerks in the huge department stores and the smaller retail shops; of grocery clerks and drug salesmen; of insurance salesmen out selling protection of life and property; of men from newspapers and agencies selling the influence and power of advertising; of men whose job it is to sell automobiles, supplies of all kinds, hardware, soft goods, cosmetics, beverages, heavy machinery, tools—the story is unending. But what we plainly see, here and everywhere around us, is that selling is tied irrevocably into our world of business and into our daily living.

Besides all that we are accustomed to, and have come to expect from selling, there will be the new demands of a changing world, the demands of an expanding economy, and this will mean more responsibilities for salesmen and sales managers. At the beginning of the 1960's, salesmen could be said to be helping to create and maintain employment for almost sixty-eight million people. The future will make even greater demands on salesmen, asking that they assist in creating even more jobs. This significant part in the whole national economy is a part of the rewards in the profession of selling, and a part of the satisfaction for the person who will give himself or herself to it.

Now let us consider some assets that a good salesman must have. A young man or woman seriously considering selling as a career must, first of all, have a genuine interest in other people, their problems, their aspirations and needs. It may not be commonly recognized, but it is the salesman, more than any other person, who sees one particularly intimate side of men and women. It is the salesman who meets the true desires, and also glimpses some of the motivations, of mankind; for what man buys not only shows what he wants at the moment, but it can indicate an incentive that may tell the kind of man he is. He may have a compelling incentive for status—the old-timer spoke of it as a desire to feel important—and he may buy accordingly, sometimes acquiring things for show rather than use. He may be dominated by a desire for bodily comforts, for exaggerated security, for pleasure, romance, an urge to keep up with the Joneses, selfishness, greed—all these emotions are encountered, and must be recognized, by the salesman. But recognition is not enough, the wise and successful salesman must know how to use—and when to ignore and discard—such motivations. Only a person who is sensitive to the problems, and the character, and the needs—beyond any buying needs—of other people can become a truly great salesman.

There are many shelves of books written on the art and science of selling. There are pages of procedures and techniques. It may be possible to reduce them to three rules that seem elemental. They involve three closely related areas of knowledge.

One is so obvious it seems needless to say it. Yet, too many young salesmen neglect it. This rule is to learn all he can about the product or the service he is selling. He should be able to discuss it with confidence and enthusiasm. He knows all about his product. He likes to talk about it. He believes in it. He gives it something of himself.

A second is that the salesman must know and study himself. His personality must be genuine. It cannot be contrived or artificial. The greatest salesmen have all been able to project themselves—it is called selling one's self. A teacher or a sales manager can offer instruction in this, but, finally, it can be done only by the man himself. Only he knows if he really believes in his product and if he can sincerely and happily associate himself with it, believing in it and believing, too, that it will fill the needs of the man or company who is buying it.

A third rule follows naturally out of the previous one. The salesman must study customers, or buyers, as thoroughly as he studies himself. He needs to learn the objectives of each, the personality and motivations of each. He should know what sort of man it is he deals with, whether or not he goes to church, what he reads, what his recreations are, and what others think about him. He should know, too, something about the man's business and his business needs. Will the product be of use and value to him? Will it bring him a profit and help him stay in business? Will he welcome the salesman when he comes back? Unless these questions can be answered favorably, the salesman had better pass up that sale. No sale is a success unless the buyer finds out later that he has bought a good product, and that the salesman is genuinely interested in him and his enterprise. One might say, in the best sense, that a salesman and a customer are two people, each of whom needs what the other has to offer.

Selling has its rules. It also has its philosophy. The art of selling can be narrow or broad. Like any other activity, it can be limited by indifference, either in personality or performance, and by lack of imagination. Either limitation is fatal. The person who selects selling as a career must come to his job with a valid image of it. He must see in it an opportunity for service and a challenge in the imperative job of maintaining the dynamics of the American dream: a free society and a free economy, concerned with the needs of free men everywhere.

No sale is a success unless the buyer finds out later that he has bought a good product, and that the salesman is genuinely interested in him and his enterprise.

There is a deep and abiding philosophy in selling. Those who come to it without this understanding will not be too happy or successful. As with most things in secular life, selling involves the material and the philosophic. One flies across the continent, looking down on the exciting, changing panorama that is America. Or, one drives the far-reaching networks of highways, looking at the changing landscape of city, country, forest, and farm. One sees, for example, the vast fields of wheat and corn in the Midwest, and the mind says: "Someone sold the miraculous machines that will come to harvest, to thresh, and to sack the grain. Someone will sell a portion of it for flour or meal. Bread will be baked and salesmen will sell it. Cereals will be manufactured, packaged, and someone must sell it. Some of the grain will become feed for poultry and livestock, and salesmen will sell the fowls and the animals."

The long freight train roars by—and men dig ore and salesmen sell it somewhere to steel-makers. Rails are made and salesmen sell them. Engines, machines, tools, girders for bridges are produced and salesmen travel over the country selling them. In all the cities, buildings rise on land that is bought and sold, and salesmen sell the steel in the buildings, the stone and the trim. Salesmen sell the brick, the cement, the workmen's tools, the glass windows, the air conditioning, the heating. Always and forever, in industry and commerce, there is, and must be, the salesman.

The salesman is usually a resilient man, perhaps because he must be. He frequently encounters the word "no." He is no stranger to resistance.

A salesman—wherever he is, wherever he goes—can always say to himself that one of his profession has been there, that salesmen have a part in the lives of individuals, of cities, and nations. The best salesman is he who sees and feels these things. If he can bring a philosophy to it, if he can say to himself that he and others in his profession are filling the needs of the present and future, that the thousands of men and women who sell make specific contributions that meet needs, large and small, insignificant, imperative—if he can realize all this, he will have more success and a happier, more rewarding life.

These conclusions serve, of course, to bolster the basic rules about knowing one's self, the customer, and the relationship between the two.

The salesman is usually a resilient man, perhaps because he must be. He frequently encounters the word "no." He is no stranger to resistance. Competitive life is not soft and he learns to retreat—without quitting—and to come back with a new approach. The history of American business includes the stories of many men who have been in sales and who have become heads of companies or occupied prominent places in management. This almost certainly comes about because in the give and take of selling, in learning to meet and compete with disappointment and negative forces, salesmen acquire a great deal of knowledge about human nature and what is required to make a company's products acceptable, and a company itself a success.

It is difficult not to slip into platitudes in discussing the attributes and the facets of personality that go to make up a good salesman and sound sales practices. One must speak of integrity, of giving of one's self, of being a friend, of practicing, even in the face of severe competition, the tenets of the Golden Rule. We can comfort ourselves that the eternal verities can be called platitudes, if one wishes to be cynical; but be that as it may, the salesman whose career moves from success to success will be the one who is not afraid to live by the oldest of rules, who learns the meaning of true humility, who works hard, who deals honestly, is dependable, and believes that his job is one of service and meaning. All these qualities are involved in what we call good human relations. They are the intangibles of successful selling.

Some years ago *Forbes* magazine published "A Capsule Course in Human Relations." It was this:

1. The five most important words in the language are:
   I AM PROUD OF YOU.
2. The four most important words in the language are:
   WHAT IS YOUR OPINION?
3. The three most important words in the language are:
   IF YOU PLEASE.
4. The two most important words in the language are:
   THANK YOU.
5. The least important word in the language is:
   I.

MILTON S. FLORSHEIM

"Florsheim is a good soul, but he never lets anyone walk all over him, either." This corny but poignant statement might have been used at one time to describe the modest shoe salesman turned shoe mogul. In 1892 Florsheim had had enough of lugging a sample trunk all over the countryside and decided to start his own manufacturing company for men's shoes. In order to sell them, he established a second corporation to set up and finance independently owned outlets. The stores' sizes and sales volumes varied greatly from one location to the next, but early on Florsheim made the decision to offer the same wholesale price to anyone and everyone, regardless of the quantity ordered. Florsheim explained, "The one-price policy is absolute. The small man's dollar looks just as good to me as the large man's."

As these outlets were established, advertising played a critical role in the company's growth; however, Florsheim found that he was "not able to quote any figures from our business which prove directly advertising pays." It was more intuitive than scientific, and in complete contrast to today's careful measurement of advertising's impact on sales. To describe the importance of advertising, Florsheim preferred to use an allegory instead, "I like to compare business to a house. Advertising and selling are the heating plant. A man can let his furnace go without fresh fuel if he wants to. For a while there is enough heat left in the coal, and enough steam in the coils, to keep the house warm. And then the family begins to get cold!"

In *Planning for the Business You Are Going to Have*, Florsheim offers several more poignant metaphors for advertising and customer relations, as he contemplates the need to balance short-term and long-term goals. Ultimately, he concludes that a solid business is built "through the thousand daily acts, for better or worse, of the management. . . ." In a brief side note, Florsheim finally chose 1929 to start selling women's shoes. Of course, the Great Depression followed and the company's net income fell from $3 million in 1929 to $717,000 in 1931. Fortunately, ever focused on the customer, Florsheim's business would flourish once again.

Planning for the Business You Are Going to Have
Milton S. Florsheim

I had been on the road as a traveling salesman, selling other makes of shoes, and the policies and principles acquired while on the road were carried with me into our business. Our company was organized in 1893. We soon found success. Our business was profitable; and our volume grew with each succeeding year.

Apparently, we were making progress.

In the course of time, we found that the business was not as substantial as we had thought. We weren't selling shoes, but selling "price." Our customers were not loyal. They did not care for quality. They did not demand our goods. They only demanded "price." If we were forced through competition to reduce our price, we had to skimp the shoes to retain our customers. If the quality was poor, we were always blamed. When we did succeed in obtaining a price that permitted making a real good shoe, we received no credit for it.

"How," I asked myself, "can we keep our customers and build a permanent business?"

I knew we could do so for a short time by selling "price." But I was far more concerned about the future. On the road I met salesmen who represented houses with well-known brands. They were graciously received by the trade because they were known to stand for something—quality, style, comfort, or whatever it might be. Suffice it to say that this brought home to me, all the more forcibly, that our policy was wrong.

We started our business to make a good shoe. What chance is there of doing so when outsiders dictate price — what future is there for our company?

That was our line of thought.

Our problem was to create a demand for our product because it was ours. So we made a "right-about-face" in our policy. While it is true that we lost one-half of our business during the subsequent year, we have never since let a shoe go out of our factory without our name and brand.

Our thought was that if we made a bad product, we meant to stand by it and take the blame and repair the loss. If we made a good product, we wanted credit for it.

Briefly, then, this was the initial and vital step in building our business for its future prosperity. There were many other problems that were gradually developed. Our chief problem was to create the lasting demand for our goods. We had to impress the public with the knowledge that we manufactured a real good shoe.

So the manufacturing policy which we developed, consistent with the fundamental idea of permanence, was to make the best shoe possible for the money, continually seeking to improve our quality and, incidentally, always being satisfied with a small margin of profit per unit.

That policy, we were confident, would in the long run give our customers faith in our shoes. This faith was essential! And since this central thought, the embodiment of our business policy, untiringly employing every means to improve our product, was in the customer's interest, we sought to let him know by giving our idea publicity. This led to advertising.

At first, we had very little money to devote to advertising. We took a small amount of space and placed advertisements in publications which we felt would reach the largest variety and greatest number of people.

Our advertising was not for the purpose of getting in a "crush" of orders—mark that! Rather, we meant to use it to tell a story—to create an impression. We tried to say to the public over and over again:

"The Florsheim shoe is a good shoe! The Florsheim shoe is a good shoe!"

... we always insisted that our business be conducted in such a way in every contact as to minimize the number and ill-effect of enemies.

That was our thought—to associate the name of the maker with quality. Good shoes, with consistent advertising, gradually created a constantly growing demand and paved the way for future business. Again we were trying to look ahead. We felt that our advertising was incidental. Whether it appeared in magazines or newspapers or what not, it was only one means to the end, however important in itself. Our policy, no matter what business conditions existed, was to repeat the message in all possible ways.

So the foundation on which this business is built, when carefully analyzed, is very simple: to give the best product possible for the money and then tell the public we are doing so through our advertisements.

As a salesman, I came to realize keenly the value of sales good-will. For our future safety, I knew we could not afford to have many "knockers." And policies in every department were built up with the purpose of avoiding them. Every business will make some enemies, perhaps. But we always insisted that our business be conducted in such a way in every contact as to minimize the number and ill-effect of enemies.

For example, the merchant to whom we refused to sell any more goods because his business was unprofitable to him, left us without any quarreling or difference about the money due us. We said:

"Take as long as you need to close up your account and make new arrangements."

He was, it is true, a little slow and it took him a long time to pay, but eventually, every penny was paid, and what is all-important, he remained our friend. We feel sure that even though our business relationship terminated, he had only a good word to say of us and our product. At best, "sharp-shooting" collection methods are costly. We expect payment for everything due, but often it is money well spent to "charge off" a disputed difference.

Whether it be a question of sales, returned goods, or collections, a customer's friendship is far more vital and necessary than getting his dollar today. This policy is repaid many fold in future dollars.

Many difficulties affecting the future of the business can arise within as well as without. The loyalty of employees, coordination between departments, assuring good-will and efficient service, is necessary for the prosperous future.

Whether it be a question of sales, returned goods, or collections, a customer's friendship is far more vital and necessary than getting his dollar today.

Throughout our organization, we endeavor to have a mutual interchange of ideas between the various departments. It is just as necessary for a credit man to be thoroughly conversant with the general sales policies and sales improvements, as it is for the sales manager to be familiar with the credit situation. It is with this thought in mind that we have daily joint meetings of our credit and sales departments, spending from 10 minutes to an hour in discussing various problems and difficulties that are encountered from day to day.

Not only does this broaden the viewpoint of the various individuals connected with our company, but it also gives them an insight into the activities of departments which might ordinarily be considered outside of their sphere.

There is an extremely close natural relationship between credits and sales, one is entirely dependent upon the other. A knowledge of all the different elements that enter into an account must be given careful attention before a decision can be intelligently arrived at. The daily meetings encourage the interchange of vital information.

Consistent with this, our factory foremen and superintendents meet with our sales department each morning. These meetings are not held for the mere purpose of criticism, but with the thought of giving mutual constructive suggestions. Nothing is more essential than this coordination of departments. Yet in some organizations it is utterly overlooked; one department is pulling one way and another is pulling in another direction. The continued improvements that we demand—the improvements in our products, in sales policy, methods, promotional activities, and so on, can be readily accomplished only when there is the closest cooperation between the employees. Everyone must pull together—there must be team-work rather than individual striking out along lines suggested by private initiative without due consideration of the business in its entirety. Yet in every way possible, we try to keep the avenues of promotion open so that proper initiative and ability need not be balked anywhere by unnecessary obstacles.

These things are important. They are also widely recognized.

But there is one thing which is often unfortunately overlooked by the business executive. I refer to the man in authority who abuses that authority, acts arbitrarily, snarls unpleasantly at associates, and speaks to subordinates in a humiliating manner as if they were mentally inferior. No influence so speedily enfeebles an organization and renders unlikely a lasting success, as to have such a person in a pivotal position.

It is easy for executives to accomplish their purpose by speaking to employees pleasantly instead of ordering them crossly. A kindly word rather than a brutal fist obtains the same results without creating antagonism, disrespect, and disintegration of the organization. And we insist on the kindly word. We know that this business, any business, cannot thrive, its future cannot be assured, under the burden of men whose tongues spread bitterness and disloyalty among employees. While immediate success might be attained by such driving methods, the future will stand on a precipice ready to totter and fall upon provocation.

"Plan for the future now"—that, in short, is the thought carried into any and every project contemplated. Nothing is so vital. Foresight alone can carry the business through the privations of hard times, as well as through the prosperity— and occasional temptations—of good times.

Policies or principles in a business are, of course, not necessarily inflexible. They must be varied, depending on the nature of the enterprise and the times. But our experience has taught me the utmost respect for the man who boldly stands by his principles and policy, notwithstanding hardships or poor times. He is the one who ultimately succeeds, always provided that the policies he stands by are sound and based on the background of experience.

You can carry the idea I have described into nearly every business activity. Here is a case. At present we have plans for a new factory, increasing our output from 25% to 30%. It will not only necessitate many changes in our present organization to maintain a correct balance, but we will also have to have an additional force of employees. One method of getting that force would be to wait until the building is completed, then advertise for help and obtain as many people as might be suitable for our purpose.

We are going about it differently.

Our plans for this new building are only being completed; but already we have obtained a short term lease on a building in which we have established a small shoe factory.

A kindly word rather than a brutal fist obtains the same results without creating antagonism, disrespect, and disintegration of the organization.

Presently, a number of people will be employed, who will learn to manufacture our shoes. When our new factory is finished, we will have a trained nucleus upon which we can rely to build the remaining necessary organization for our new factory.

You can find opportunities to plan ahead like that, regardless of where you turn. No business makes its future by a few gloriously successful strokes. It builds through the thousand daily acts, for better or worse, of the management and of everyone in the organization.

THOMAS J. WATSON
1874 – 1956

Watson's first job was selling pianos, organs, and sewing machines from the back of a wagon to farm families in upstate New York. Although many of his customers were poor, the more he traveled as a salesman, the more he saw of well-to-do businessmen, which led to an ever greater desire to succeed. As he once explained to his sons, "My ambition grew in stages." Watson's first break came as a salesman for the National Cash Register Company under the tutelage of John Henry Patterson, who is considered the father of modern salesmanship. However, Watson, a selling genius in his own right, was eventually forced out by the egotistical Patterson.

Watson joined the Computing-Tabulating-Recording Company (CTR) in 1915, which at the time specialized in punch card machines, recording census data, and handling payrolls, among other tasks. He eventually gained complete control of the company and changed the name to International Business Machines (IBM), envisioning the day it would be a global operation. Watson ran the company until 1952, when he handed it over to his son, Thomas, Jr.

The success of IBM relied more on Watson's ability to forge and lead a well-trained, devoted sales force than it did on technological leadership. The enduring loyalty of his salesmen sprung from Watson's own dedication to them: He refused to lay off anyone during the Great Depression; those who served in World War II remained on partial salary; and IBM's commissions were always the best in the industry. To further enthusiasm, employees were *requested* to memorize such slogans as "Make Things Happen," "Ever Onward," "Beat Your Best," and the simple but famous "Think" that was hung throughout the office buildings. In the following selection, "Sell with Sincerity," he illustrates how thinking, among other characteristics, can make for a better salesman.

Sell with Sincerity
Thomas J. Watson

I started on my first selling job during the panic of 1893, as a salesman for National Cash Registers, in Buffalo. Although I pounded the pavements for ten days without making a sale, this total lack of success was not due to the hard times. Other salesmen were selling two or three cash registers a week.

When my employer, Mr. Range, asked me how I was getting along I told him that in ten days I hadn't been able to find anybody who wanted to buy a cash register.

"Well," said Mr. Range, "that is what I hired you for—to find them. You just haven't gone far enough. Keep going. If at five o'clock you have not found anyone, go on until six or until the stores close at nine if necessary. There is somebody in your territory who will buy a cash register if you are willing to go far enough to find him. It does not require a genius to find people who need these machines. Walking and talking are all that is necessary. Most of us can talk but some of us are a little shy on walking. Keep going long enough and you will find enough people who will say 'yes' to make you a success in this business."

What Mr. Range said to me over a half century ago is still the best basic advice for a salesman, *"Pack your todays with*

269

effort—extra effort! Your tomorrows will take care of themselves. They will also take good care of you and your family."

There was much more that I learned from Mr. Range which was to help me all through the years in my own selling and, later, as sales manager, when I was helping others to sell. It was he who taught me to use that important word "why?" in selling.

I was baffled, as are many beginning salesmen, when a man I was calling on would say flatly, "No, I don't want to buy a cash register."

I learned from Mr. Range that I could keep the door wide open to a possible sale by smiling and agreeing, "I know you don't. That's why I came to see you. I knew if you wanted one you would come down to the office and pick one out. What I've come for is to find out why you don't want one."

---

the "yes but" is one of the most frequent killers of sales. . . . argument creeps in, and this serves no good purpose in selling. It takes two people to make an argument, and the salesman should never be one of them.

It is worth any salesman's thinking time to figure out ways to work a "why" into interviews. By the very sincerity of listening to a prospect's reasons for not buying you bring the sales call to its most perfect form—two men talking with each other in a friendly, relaxed way.

While the "why" offers a good chance to build a sale, the "yes but" is one of the most frequent killers of sales. Those two words, I firmly believe, should be banished from the vocabulary of every salesman. With the first "yes but", argument creeps in, and this serves no good purpose in selling. It takes two people to make an argument, and the salesman should never be one of them.

In looking back and analyzing your selling interviews, it is a good idea to be on the lookout for traces of an argumentative tone in what you have said. Spend time figuring out ways to get over your sales points forcibly while keeping in an attitude of agreement with your prospect. It is easy to say, for instance, "You are perfectly right on that score, and I am wondering if you have thought of this angle, too." With this you lead the discussion to the points you want to make.

Selling is a skill, and, like all skills, it must be learned through study and practice. All it takes to get better is to work at it. The rules for success in selling are the same rules for success in any line of work. They are summed up by George Washington Carver in these simple words: "Start where you are. Work with what you have. Make something of it. Never be satisfied."

Starting where you are means starting today to go forward. It means refusing to call it a day until you have put in some extra effort toward making a success of yourself. It means losing your contentment with being "as good as the average." It means getting up from your desk and putting on your hat and taking the shortest route to a prospect's office. It means going on until there isn't a chance of seeing one more prospect.

To "work with what you have" calls for self-study. It is not a matter of comparing yourself with others and wishing you had "this man's art and that man's scope." It is a matter of developing your own particular talents within the framework of your own individuality. All of us can change ourselves for the better, but this never comes about through imitation. Within himself every man has more to work with than he ever uses to its full capacity. It is by searching yourself that you find the power you aren't using. When you begin using it, you "make something of it."

Take up the challenge, "Never be satisfied," and watch your power to sell increase. When your company sets quotas, set yourself a still bigger quota. Always assume they have set their estimates of the business in your district too

271

low. They certainly will not take you to task for proving them wrong in this particular! The greatest satisfaction you get out of a selling career is never to be satisfied, and to do something about it.

The salesman who thinks in big figures, and then puts high-powered perseverance into his day-by-day work always makes his goal. This happens just as surely when he is given a so-called "tough territory" as in one that looks more promising.

One of the best salesmen I ever met in my life worked provincial territory, and he always had a big record. When he was asked how he did it, he said, "When I get into a town I unhitch!"

He meant, of course, that when he reached a town he stayed there until he finished the job, until he had talked to every possible prospect. If a salesman will start out every day with the idea of finishing the day's job before he leaves, nothing can stop him.

Loyalty to his company and to his product are a must for a salesman. This never takes the form of knocking a competitor's product, of course.

One element of loyalty is the acceptance of the prices your company sets for its products or services. Salesmen frequently try to justify their lack of success by the alibi that "the price is too high." Unless a salesman absolutely believes in the fairness of his company's price structure, he works against severe odds. Nobody can do a real selling job on anything unless he sincerely believes it is worth the money.

Joining a company is an act that calls for absolute loyalty in big matters and little ones. No firm is perfect, of course. What strikes you as a fault may be real, or apparent, but in no case should it be the subject of discussion on the outside as long as you are employed by that firm. If you feel that something should be done about it, go to the proper authorities within the company. Seal your lips to discussion of it in any other place.

People sometimes take it upon themselves to point out to an employee the things that are wrong with the way his company operates, or with its services or products. Loyalty demands that you never join in such criticism, and that you make clear that your stand is with your company, not against it.

When your company sets quotas, set yourself a still bigger quota. Always assume they have set their estimates of the business in your district too low.

A good many years ago when I was riding in a club car of the Erie Railroad, I heard two other travelers voicing a long list of complaints about the railroad's service to one of its employees.

The loyalty this young man had for his company was immediately apparent in the way he handled the situation. Without being quarrelsome, he stood his ground against the barbs of criticism. Later, when he and I were alone, I gave him my card and asked him to come in to see me. I saw in his loyalty a jewel of great price which would make him an asset to our company, or any company.

When I hired that young man I was hiring the future treasurer of I. B. M. He has served in that capacity for a good many years.

For a salesman, the state of absolute loyalty to his company and his product is basic for success. It puts into his selling that deep-seated sincerity which wins the prospect's respect and leads to sales.

Every step upward in any salesman's progress is one that he must build for himself. Training courses, books and articles on salesmanship can serve an excellent purpose as eye-openers and thought-provokers. But in the final analysis, each salesman must think his own way to success.

We place a great deal of emphasis on that word "think" at I. B. M. A great many comments have been made about the

THINK signs which are to be seen on our desks and walls, on notebooks and scratch pads in I. B. M. offices and factories all over the world. Every year we fill more than a hundred thousand requests for the THINK slogan, which are printed not only in English, but in French, Italian, Spanish and Chinese as well. They serve to remind people of a fact that is too often forgotten — that to *think* is the most important verb in any language and in any occupation. This is particularly true about sales work.

It might be good exercise for any salesman who is troubled by his lack of success to take a piece of paper and print on it the word "worry." Then draw a heavy line through the "worry" and write a much bigger "think" above it. This simple visualization expresses an important truth about thinking: when you think, you cannot worry. Because the two mental processes are direct opposites, thinking never fails to cancel out worrying.

The knowledge you gain from reading, listening, discussing and observing cannot be put to work without thinking. All of us have known men who are storehouses of facts and information but are not successful. Goods in any storehouse are useless until somebody takes them out and put them to the use they were meant for. That applies to what man stores away in his brain, too. Use is what makes any information valuable, and use can come only through thinking.

All the THINK signs in the world cannot make any man think. But they serve the useful purpose of reminding people to think. We all need to be reminded if we want to be successful in our work and our lives.

What I said when I wrote the first THINK slogan on a blackboard at a sales meeting in 1911 is just as true today:

"The trouble with every one of us is that we do not think enough. We don't get paid for working with our feet. We get paid for working with our heads. Thought has been the father of every advance since time began. Knowledge is the result of thought and thought is the keynote of success in our business. Any man on the selling force today can make $2 where he now makes $1 if he would but think along the right lines."

Keeping one's thoughts traveling along the right lines takes constant vigilance. It is not the kind of thinking that leads a salesman to neglect the prospect who says "no" but might say "yes" on future calls.

My manager used to say, "There are only two classes of people who never change: fools and dead people." That is fairly true. Keep track of those people who say "no" because next week, next month or next year they are going to say "yes" to somebody who is selling your kind of product. Selling is a building proposition. It is building the "no" man up into a live prospect, and then changing him into a customer.

Every salesman has to learn to take "no's" in his daily stride. As my manager used to say, "Just think what would happen if every prospect already knew all about our machines and was ready to buy. There would be no jobs for any of us because they would write in and buy the machines by mail."

Selling on a commission basis is often the best starting point for a career in sales work. Here the relationship between sustained effort and reward is clearly drawn. There is no prop in the way of a drawing account. What a man gets stems directly from what he gives. It is the best possible way to learn to make every day count.

Goods in any storehouse are useless until somebody takes them out and put them to the use they were meant for. That applies to what man stores away in his brain, too.

When you sell on commission you own your own business. It is "You, Incorporated," and like every business it must be systematized. You must have a complete and reliable record of your time and costs. This should take the form of a daily written tabulation of your hours and how you spend them.

Give yourself a challenge at the beginning of each day to better your efficiency record in the matter of productive time—the time you spend talking to prospects. Do you find yourself spending, say, three hours a day in the actual business of selling—which is interviews? Is that enough during the regular eight-hour business day when prospects are available? How can you plan your day to get in more calls? Were those inefficiencies and time unnecessarily lost.

Any salesman will find that such a written record will reveal much that he does not realize in the way of inefficiencies and time unnecessarily lost.

Don't try to build a personality to fit some preconceived idea you may have of what a salesman ought to be. Just get into an office or store or home and try to sell with sincerity.

Such records are of no value, of course, unless a man analyzes them, thinks about them, does something about bettering them right now—today. Now is the most valuable time any of us will ever have, yet most of us fall far too short of taking full advantage of it. The man who succeeds best in substituting "now" for "later" in his thinking succeeds best selling.

If your own supervision is at fault, you are likely to shy away from the supervision of others. It is usually true that when a salesman resents turning in reports to his field manager or his sales manager, he is not proud of the job he has been doing. If such a check-up irks, it is time to check up on yourself.

My own interpretation of supervision is cooperation, the sharing of knowledge and experience all along the line. If you keep an open mind about learning everything you possibly can about selling your product and your company, you will welcome every bit of supervision offered.

Selling is an occupation you cannot go into half-heartedly and hope to find success. The men who fail at selling are apt to be those who are "trying" it for a few weeks or months while perhaps looking for another job.

There can be nothing tentative about your decision to become a salesman. The only way to go into selling and make it pay is to put everything you have into it, without any reservations.

Some products are so complex that they require a long training period before the first call can be made. In this case the company usually pays you while learning, and is highly selective about the men chosen to enter its training course.

Other products are simple enough to be mastered quickly. These are the products most often sold on a commission basis.

Whether you are selling a complicated, or a comparatively simple, product, your first step is to concentrate on learning all you can about it and the company back of it.

When you are equipped with this information, start out to make as many calls a day as you can possibly fit in. Do not worry because you don't have the earmarks of a "natural born salesman." Don't try to build a personality to fit some preconceived idea you may have of what a salesman ought to be. Just get into an office or store or home and try to sell with sincerity.

That is all there really is to selling—talking with sincerity about a product or service you believe in. The whole proposition is so simple that most men do not see the point. They complicate it by such words as "the science of salesmanship" and lose sight of how natural and basic a process it is. According to the old verse,

"The centipede was happy quite
　　Until a toad in fun
Said 'Pray, which leg goes after which?'
　　That worked her mind to such a pitch
She lay distracted in the ditch
　　Considering how to run."

There is no need for a salesman to ponder whether to start forward with his left foot or his right. All he has to do is to get going and keep going—toward the place where the prospect is.

PART VI

MAINTAINING INDIVIDUALITY IN THE CORPORATE WORLD

J. IRWIN MILLER
1909 –

Miller, who transformed the family's struggling Cummins Engine Company into the largest diesel engine maker in the world, was characterized as "a philosopher disguised as a businessman." He attended Yale, was a Rhodes Scholar, studied Plato, enjoyed playing Bach on his Stradivarius, and taught Sunday school at church. Miller also donated an astounding 30 percent of his family's income to charity. Why so much? His answer: To "change things for the better. Else why are you taking up space?"

When the scholarly Miller finished school, he had no background for business, and had little confidence in his ability to run Cummins among other family operations he inherited. He feared failing the family's capitalist tradition that dated back to his great grandfather, who founded the Irwin Union Bank and Trust Company in 1871. Miller was able to put his situation in perspective. "You can't copy what they did. What you copy is their spirit." Their spirits successfully motivated him to turn Cummins around and build it into a *Fortune* 500 company that took on the engine divisions of companies like General Motors and Mack Trucks. Cummins even began selling engines to its competitors. The irony was not lost on Miller who observed, "We're in the business of selling engines to engine makers, which is surely not the smartest way to make a living."

In building his business, Miller never forgot the many ethical issues he became familiar with during his classical education. Ethical conduct became his company's centerpiece, not an "expense" to be reduced. For Miller, ethics was the "only way you survive . . . hold your customers . . . have good labor relations, which means good productivity. . . ." In *The Dilemma of the Corporation Man* he contemplates a related topic: the spiritual welfare of the employee within the corporate machine.

The Dilemma of the Corporation Man
J. Irwin Miller

T here is much talk today that the organization is the enemy of the individual, and that while all organizations are enemies of sorts, the archenemy is undoubtedly the Business Organization. It produces "the man in the gray flannel suit"—this fellow who is a registered Republican and a member of the Chamber of Commerce, who believes in lower taxes and stronger defenses, opposes "giveaway" foreign aid, and is the husband of the Corporation Wife. The charge is that the Organization Man has lost his individuality and has become no more than a cog, indistinguishable from other cogs, in a machine composed not of metal parts but of linked and intermeshed human beings.

There is a great deal of truth to the charge. We know that it is not the whole truth, and that even within the fearfully demanding, complex, high-speed large business organization, many men find attraction and challenge. But I choose to ignore the blessings of the organization and instead to concentrate upon its genuine threat to the individual, trying to describe some of the manifestations of this threat, and finally to make a few suggestions as to how the threat may be successfully opposed.

Let me make a side comment on smaller businesses and the professions before looking at the lot of people in the big organization. How do individuals who are free of the big organization flourish outside of this powerful, compressive force? It is quite true that they may not dress or act like the Organization Man, or share his peculiar ambitions. But they do dress and look all too much like each other, and their houses are indistinguishable from one another, all being compounded out of *Houses Beautiful* and the *Ladies' Home Journal.* They are to be found every Monday noon dozing through a Rotary Club program that warns about the threat to the American way of life. They are all vigorous free enterprisers, who sponsor, if they are realtors, bills to fix real-estate commissions; if they are bankers, bills to set ceilings on savings interest; if they are dairymen, bills to prevent selling milk below a liberally calculated "cost." While the Organization Men are alike in fearing their boss and in conforming in order to achieve the same promotion, the entrepreneurs are also conformed by a common fear that someone is going to take something away from them. All this is true of the labor leader, who is not able to indulge in any public criticism of his own organization. It may be true even of the college professor, who also has his uniform pattern of dress, of liberal politics, and of standardized nonconformity.

Is this a special sickness of our own day that other ages of men have successfully resisted? I think not. The problem of the individual versus the organization is a very old problem that man has had little luck in solving. The problem is new today only in its manifestations.

THE LAST FREE MAN

Man apparently feels he has to organize. We have all had in our elementary courses in economics the story that the last independent man was the early New England farmer, who grew or made everything he needed; and we were told that to achieve better standards man had to organize into larger and more complex groups, all of which is truly described in the economics textbooks. Man does have to organize, and in so doing he has to expose himself to the demands of the organization.

While the Organization Men are alike in fearing their boss and in conforming in order to achieve the same promotion, the entrepreneurs are also conformed by a common fear that someone is going to take something away from them.

Perhaps for the greater number of human beings this conforming to the organization is no great worry, for the organization has its comforts for the mind and the spirit, just as it has for the body. Because of the organization we are no longer compelled to walk if we don't want to. The organization transports us. And for our minds the organization supplies acceptable opinions on politics, on business, on labor, on marriage, on religion. We do not have to think for ourselves if we do not wish, and most of the time this is a comfort. And while it is fashionable to view this situation with alarm, the truth is most of the time we love it.

There appear to me to be several reasons why we alternate between love and hate of the organization. First of all, I seriously doubt that there is any one of us who is really ever entirely sure that he belongs. The intense desire to be accepted by the group is so strong in all of us that it generates doubt that we are wholly accepted and wholly approved. It makes us uncritically eager to conform to the society with which we desire to identify ourselves, and it makes us violently critical of the "off-beat" member; by driving him out, we hope to thrust ourselves more surely into the center of the group.

THE SCARED AND OVEREAGER

This desire is expressed within the business organization in the standard forms of griping around the Coke machine and the standard forms of bootlicking in the boss's office and around the conference table. It is a sort of tyranny imposed by ourselves on ourselves, and it arises basically out of fear. This fear also has another manifestation. If we are a boss or a supervisor, it causes us to demand in the area within our control an excessive and unreasonable amount of agreement,

---

There appear to me to be several reasons why we alternate between love and hate of the organization. First of all, I seriously doubt that there is any one of us who is really ever entirely sure that he belongs.

---

and I think it is against this particular type of conformity and pressure that we find the most obvious resistance and complaint. It is true, more often than the business manager likes to think, that the more doubtful he is about the wisdom of a course of action, the more insistent he is that his associates openly and repeatedly agree that the policy is the absolutely correct one. Out of his fear the subordinate is overeager to conform to the group. Out of his fear the boss is overeager that the group conform to him.

My point so far is not that business organizations are generally composed of spineless and contemptible human beings: it is another kind of point—namely, that each one of us in different times fits this picture and shares these same sharp fears concerning himself and the opinions of men, and exhibits in varying degrees these same essentially cowardly responses. When we do, we are quite ashamed of ourselves and we proceed then to damn the very organization whose favor and approval we desire above everything else. And so in our anger we now identify the organization, not as our god, but as our enemy. Someone has said that there is no such thing as sand, there are only grains of sand. The organization, in addition to the many other good, bad, useful, and dangerous things it may be, is also a collection of internally isolated human beings, each, from time to time, consciously or unconsciously fearful that he doesn't belong to the collection in some important sense.

Let us for the moment turn from the individual as he reacts to the organization and examine the monster, to see whether we can identify any representative types of problems that exist within the organization itself rather than within the individual. In my opinion most of these problems in business today may quite probably arise because the most important new situation is the interdependence of very large numbers of persons who are at the same time far removed from each other by organization structure. Because of this fact many a businessman's problems sometimes seem to him to be simply past his solving.

INSIDE THE PRESIDENT'S HEAD

To illustrate, let us suppose we can see inside the head of the president of a large manufacturing organization. His company employs 20,000 persons and operates half a dozen plants. It distributes its products in every state and in many foreign countries, and — most frightening of all — it has competitors.

Now let us suppose that these competitors are extremely vigorous, and that our president knows that to maintain his share of the market and to make earnings which will please his directors, he must accomplish the following very quickly:

design and perfect a brand-new and more advanced line of products; tool up these products in such a way as to permit higher quality and lower costs than his competitors; purchase new machinery; arrange major additional long-term financing. At the same time his corporation's labor contract is up for negotiation, and this must be rewritten in such a way as to obtain good employee response and yet make no more concessions than do his competitors. Sales coverage of all customers has to be intensified, and sales costs reduced. Every one of these objectives must be accomplished simultaneously, and ahead of similar efforts on the part of his competitors — or the future of the company is in great danger. Every head of a corporation lives every day with the awareness that it is quite possible to go broke. At the same time he lives with the awareness that he cannot personally accomplish a single one of these vital objectives. The actual work will have to be accomplished by numerous individuals, some actually unknown to him, most of them many layers removed from his direct influence in the organization. It is because of this that a president becomes frantic.

Feeling that every one of these goals must be accomplished in the way he conceives them, and at the same time feeling that other people down the line do not fully share either his understanding of the company's need or his own sense of urgency, realizing that he cannot personally supervise all whose work is necessary to the achievement of the program, he becomes dogmatic. He issues orders. He says things are jolly well going to be done this way and no other. He says the company's negotiators are not to give in on the union's demand for premium pay or the union shop. He says every salesman must make so many calls each day. He says you can't add a single person to this office, which has already got too many people in it. And he pounds the table every time he says these things. For he feels that this great, vast, and ponderous organization is his enemy and that inside its faceless exterior all his plans, his programs, his timetables will be diluted, slowed down, and ultimately defeated. Successes seem to him to have come only in rare instances, and to have been of a temporary and ephemeral nature. He thinks of himself as being in a race that has no finish line. And his real antagonist is neither the customer, nor his bankers, nor the union. His real antagonist is the organization.

THE BIG SPECKLED BIRD

Let us turn our attention to another fellow in this act an executive from the ranks known as "middle management." He is several positions removed from our unhappy president. In fact he may never have seen him, being in charge of one of the distant plants that the president has not yet got around to visiting. But we must not make the mistake of supposing our man is a man with little responsibility. As a matter of fact, he is running a plant employing a thousand persons, which is bigger than the founder of the company ever ran throughout his whole business career. This plant, in addition, is the major employer in its small community. Now let us assume that our middle-management executive is bargaining for his first labor contract.

And let us suppose that every other plant in town has for years had a union-shop contract. Our middle-management executive knows that if he grants a union-shop contract, the rest of his negotiations may not be too difficult, but that refusal to grant such a contract may not only involve him in a strike, it may earn him the lasting hostility of the community. From the head office he receives a wire that says, "No union shop. Period. All our other plants have successfully negotiated contracts without it, and you are not going to negotiate one with it." When, therefore, he obediently refuses the union shop, the bargaining committee says, "How come? Are you antilabor? If you were to conduct an election, you would have an almost unanimous vote in favor of it. Are you afraid to ask the men how they feel about it?" If our middle-management executive replies, "Boys, I know you're right, but the big speckled bird up in the head office says, 'No,'" the committee can have only one reply, and that is, "Then what is the use bargaining with you? You aren't allowed to do any negotiating. The only way we'll get anywhere with this company is to strike," which they do. The head of the corporation, when he learns of this and sees that no success is made in settling the strike, begins to wonder whether Bill, the manager in the plant, is really executive material or not.

WHY BILL IS ON MILK

Or Bill may be required to tool up a product that has been designed at the company's research center. One part in the product may be so designed that an extraordinary amount of scrap results. Bill's crew finds out that a small change in the design would eliminate this problem: but the word from on high is, "You fellows have got to stop making changes. Get this model into production before we lose all our business to our competitors." So if Bill tells his people, "You make it like it is because the big shot says so," his boys know that Bill is not really running the plant. If, on the other hand, he accepts full responsibility himself for the head-office decision, then his boys put him down as stupid. And when his costs soar, the head office wonders for the second time if Bill is management material. By this time Bill who is now on a milk diet, is beginning to wonder the same thing.

The special problem of the middle management man is this: On the one hand, he is required to discharge what in the past have been considered very great responsibilities. On the other hand, the need to conform to the broad programs of the whole organization, which are established without the possibility of his direct participation, deprives him of the power of determination and decision that his own people expect him to have and forces him at times to carry out policies and programs he may passionately believe to be wrong, at least in their local application. So the organization also becomes his special enemy, and appears always to be able to deprive him of genuine accomplishment. This arouses his fears and induces in him a conformity which at times he despises and yet from which there is no escape, at least on terms he is willing to contemplate.

"NEVER MIND WHAT YOU THINK"

We have pictured two broad kinds of problems: the first arising from an individual's consuming desire to "belong" and his surrender of individuality to the organization in the hope of gaining his desires; the second arising from the way the organization manages to defeat both the individual who runs it and the individual who works within it.

If I stop here without some qualifications, I will be guilty both of oversimplification and of exaggeration. These are not the only problems that can be said to face the individual in the business organization, but I do feel that they are examples of the kinds of problems which are encountered, and that useful solutions to these problems have some valid, general application. And while I admit that the aspect presented by the organization to the individual is not nearly so uniformly dismal as I have implied, nevertheless the problems are like the theme in a symphony, which sometimes dominates the music, at other times goes unnoticed in a minor part, later appears in altered aspect, and never quite disappears. Our Organization Man may be more conscious of these conditions and problems at some times than at others, but for him they can never be wholly absent from his mind and spirit. He has to learn how to handle them, rather than resent them, or indulge in the vain hope that he may somehow, someday, be rid of them. The spectacle of the businessman who chooses the world of tension, frustration, confusion, compromise, and crisis for his life's work and then complains because he has to grapple with tension, frustration, confusion, compromise, and crisis is more pathetic than tragic.

... the organization also becomes [the middle manager's] special enemy, and appears always to be able to deprive him of genuine accomplishment.

How shall we advise him to go about handling his problems? Since we have shown that at least some of our examples are probably natural characteristics of the large organization, a man is going to have better luck modifying his own approach to the organization than he is trying to remake the monster itself. My first suggestion is a fairly obvious one. The man in the business organization who is determined to master the special problems of the organization must neither embrace the organization uncritically nor despise it categorically. Instead, he must try to understand it, which of course is easier said than done. How do you go about understanding such a thing? You begin, as in most things, by using your mind, and you determine early in your organization life not to listen to the cynical advice: "Give the boss what he wants. Never mind what *you* think." The corporation Man has got to have the courage to reject this basically adolescent notion, and the good sense, as well, to reject that other attitude: "We'll take care of our own department, let the damn engineers solve their own problems." The wise man will try to understand the part that his department or group is playing, and the requirements laid on him individually, if his actions are to be consistent with the main purpose of the institution. Those who are in positions of business management realize how rare is the member of the organization deep in the ranks who succeeds in keeping the purpose and aim of the institution uppermost in his mind.

Of course even if he does succeed, all his problems are not yet ended, for while his actions and his plans and his decisions may be of an astonishing quality, this very quality, this habit of appearing to aim at goals beyond those of his associates, may earn him the active dislike and resentment of those around him, including his own boss—unless he knows and understands how these people with whom he associates feel and operate.

MEN DON'T CRY

This may be a silly-sounding statement, but bear with me while I try to make it more respectable. We are born as persons who are capable of tears, of anger, of great joy, of passionate love, of rending sorrow, but the Anglo-Saxon tradition in which we and our fellows are raised compresses these feelings and squeezes out their power. It is beaten deep into every boy: men don't cry; gentlemen don't get angry; be civilized about love; excessive enthusiasm is unsophisticated; uncritical admiration is childlike. All of this is summed up in the phrase of our day. "Don't get shook up."

Men who are true to the type will probably have read their last poem when they leave college. There will be no creation of art that will move them to tears. There will be no shocking condition in the world or tragic event that can cause consuming anger in them or raise genuine righteous indignation. Their marriages will be mild and convenient. Their capacity to feel will be slowly extinguished and only the appetites will remain. How, then, will they understand those with whom they live and work? If they have no feelings left of their own, how can they enter into and share and comprehend those of others? And, if they do not, how can they hope to walk through life without giving grievous offense?

Somewhat more important to the man in the organization than a knowledge of double-entry bookkeeping, or of the ins and outs of corporate politics, is the cultivation of a capacity to feel. Does it seem odd that painting and poetry and music and suffering and great causes and dedication to religion are essential to the making of an effective Organization Man? Well, they are, for without them he is a half-man, half happy, half bored, half effective, killing the time of which at the end he learns there was so very little.

Finally, in dealing with the corporation he must cultivate courage. I mean the courage to take a right stand and to draw a right line, and, what is more important, to accept the consequences of so doing. It may mean the willingness to change a job or to lose a job. It means the kind of courage to speak the truth as you see it, to your customer if

---

Somewhat more important to the man in the organization than a knowledge of double-entry bookkeeping, or of the ins and outs of corporate politics, is the cultivation of a capacity to feel.

---

you are a salesman, to your boss, to your union if you are a negotiator. And it means the courage to do all this when you have families to support, children to educate, debts to pay, pension reserves to lose—and at a time when you have reached the age at which prospective employers consider you no longer young. These may sound like very prosaic remedies—to think, to feel, to be brave. They are in all the copybooks. But they are perhaps man's only weapons, and the persons who employed them well are also in all the history books. Those of us who take up these weapons and grow strong and skilled in their use may find the organization altering surprisingly before our eyes. The organization will no longer appear as the enemy of the individual but, instead, a most effective means to the individual's fulfillment.

J. PAUL GETTY
1892 – 1976

Getty has been characterized as one of the most contradictory business geniuses ever. He was a master oil man who excelled during the Great Depression and pioneered the drilling of oil in the Middle East in the 1950s; however, his personal life was total chaos as he took lovers across the world, married new wives before he divorced prior ones, and estranged his children in the process. His origins were much more humble, growing up a typical child in the Midwest. His father was an insurance lawyer who happened to be collecting on a debt in Oklahoma when the state's first oil was being drilled. The elder Getty immediately recognized the opportunity this burgeoning industry presented, and subsequently became one of the original oil wildcatters in Oklahoma and California. Young Paul quickly followed and made his first million in 1916 at the age of 24.

It was the stock market crash of 1929, when the price of a barrel of oil was almost halved, that gave Getty his first opportunity through speculative buying. He seized a second great opportunity in 1949, when he acquired rights to drill in the Middle East. Eight years later he was named the richest man in America by *Fortune* magazine. Getty won few friends along the way, but he took the criticism in stride, declaring, "The businessman who moves counter to the tide of prevailing opinion must expect to be obstructed, derided and damned." In more flamboyant language to match his character, he also unequivocally stated, "There is mighty little room in business for either the man who wants his subordinates to be bootlickers or the man who is willing to do the licking."

Getty, the cutthroat businessman, but again, of contradictory qualities, believed that man is completely civilized only if he truly loves art. This cultivation of art not only led to his founding of the renowned J. Paul Getty Museum (an excellent tax shelter as well), but also to his own need to be creative. Getty wrote several books and numerous articles on the conduct of business and life. The following selection is an excerpt from his book, *How to Be Rich*. Using both a sharpened wit and blunt language, Getty provides insight into how to work within the corporate framework with dignity and respect.

The Art of Individuality
J. Paul Getty

T he successful executive—
the leader, the innovator—is the exceptional man. He is *not* a
conformist, except in his adherence to his own ideals and
beliefs.

A young business executive I met once might well serve
as the prototype for the entire breed of case-hardened conformist "organization men" one finds in ever-increasing numbers in the business world today. His clothes, manners,
speech, attitudes—and ideas—were all studied stereotypes.
It was obvious that he believed conformity was essential for
success in his career, but he complained that he wasn't getting
ahead fast enough and asked me if I could offer any advice.

"How can I achieve success and wealth in business?" he
asked earnestly. "How can I make a million dollars?"

"I can't give you any sure-fire formulas," I replied, "but
I'm certain of one thing. You'll go much further if you stop
trying to look and act and think like everyone else on Madi-
son Avenue or Wacker Drive or Wilshire Boulevard. Try
being a *non*conformist for a change. Be an individualist—and
an individual. You'll be amazed at how much faster you'll
'get ahead.' "

I rather doubt if what I said made much impression on
the young man. I fear he was far too dedicated a disciple of
that curious present-day hyperorthodoxy, the Cult of Con-

formity, to heed my heretical counsel. I'm sure he will spend the rest of his life aping and parroting the things he believes, or has been led to believe, are "right" and safe. He'll conform to petty, arbitrary codes and conventions, desperately trying to prove himself stable and reliable—but he will only demonstrate that he is unimaginative, unenterprising and mediocre. The success and wealth for which men such as this yearn will always elude them. They will remain minor executives, shuffled and shunted from one corporate pigeonhole to another, throughout their entire business careers.

I pretend to be neither sage nor savant. Nor would I care to set myself up as an arbiter of anyone's mores or beliefs. But I do think that I know something about business and the business world. In my opinion, no one can possibly achieve any real and lasting success or "get rich" in business by being a conformist. A businessman who wants to be successful cannot afford to imitate others or to squeeze his thoughts and actions into trite and shopworn molds. He must be very much of an individualist who can think and act independently. He must be an original, imaginative, resourceful and entirely self-reliant entrepreneur. If I may be permitted the analogy, he must be a creative artist rather than merely an artisan of business.

The successful businessman's nonconformity is most generally—and most obviously—evident in the manner and methods of his business operations and activities. These will be unorthodox in the sense that they are radically unlike those of his hidebound, less imaginative—and less successful—associates or competitors. Often, his innate impatience with the futility of superficial conventions and dogma of all kinds will manifest itself in varying degrees of personal eccentricity.

Everyone knows about the late John D. Rockefeller, Sr.'s idiosyncratic habit of handing out shiny new dimes wherever he went. Howard Hughes is noted for his penchant for wearing tennis sneakers and open-throated shirts. Bernard Baruch held his most important business conferences on park benches. These are only three among the many multimillionaires who made their fortunes by giving their individualism free rein and who never worried if their nonconformity showed in their private lives.

Now, I would hardly suggest that adoption of some slightly eccentric habit of dress or manner is in itself sufficient to catapult a man to the top of a corporate management pyramid or make him rich overnight. I do, however, steadfastly maintain that few—if any—people who insist on squeezing themselves into stereotyped molds will ever get very far on the road to success.

I find it disheartening that so many young businessmen today conform blindly and rigidly to patterns they believe some nebulous majority has decreed are prerequisites for approval by society and for success in business. In this, they fall prey to a fundamental fallacy: the notion that the majority is automatically and invariably right. Such is hardly the case. The majority is by no means omniscient just because it is the majority. In fact, I've found that the line which divides majority opinion from mass hysteria is often so fine as to be virtually invisible. This holds as true in business as it does in any other aspect of human activity. That the majority of businessmen thinks this or that, does not necessarily guarantee the validity of its opinions. The majority often has a tendency to plod slowly or to mill around helplessly. The nonconformist businessman who follows his own counsel, ignoring the cries of the pack, often reaps fantastic rewards. There are classic examples galore—some of the most dramatic ones dating from the Depression.

The Rockefellers began building Rockefeller Center, the largest privately-owned business and entertainment complex in the United States—and possibly the entire world—in 1931, during the depths of the Depression. Most American businessmen considered the project an insane one. They conformed to the prevailing opinion which held that the nation's economy was in ruins and prophesied that the giant skyscrapers would remain untenanted shells for decades. "Rockefeller Center will be the world's biggest White Elephant," they predicted. "The Rockefellers are throwing their money down a bottomless drain." Nonetheless, the Rockefellers went ahead with their plans and built the great Center. They reaped large profits from the project—and proved that they were right, and that the majority was dead wrong.

Conrad Hilton started buying and building hotels when most other hoteliers were eagerly scanning all available horizons for prospective buyers on whom they could unload their properties. There is certainly no need to go into details about nonconformist Conrad Hilton's phenomenal success.

I, myself, began buying stocks during the Depression, when shares were selling at bargain-basement prices and "everyone" believed they would fall even lower.

The conformists were selling out, dumping their stocks on the market for whatever they would bring. Their one thought was to "salvage" what they could before the ultimate economic catastrophe so freely predicted by "the majority" took place.

Nevertheless, I continued to buy stocks. The results? Many shares I bought during the 1930s are now worth a hundred—and more—times what I paid for them. One particular issue in which I purchased sizable blocks has netted me no less than 4500% profit through the years.

No, I'm not boasting nor claiming that I was endowed with any unique powers of economic clairvoyance. There were other businessmen and investors who did the same— and profited accordingly. But we were the exceptions, the nonconformists who refused to be carried along by the wave of dismal pessimism then the vogue with the majority.

The truly successful businessman is essentially a dissenter, a rebel who is seldom if ever satisfied with the *status quo*. He creates his success and wealth by constantly seeking—and often finding—new and better ways to do and make things.

The list of those who have achieved great success by refusing to accept and follow established patterns is a long one. It spans two centuries of American history and runs the alphabetical gamut from John Jacob Astor to Adolph Zukor.

These men relied on those four qualities already enumerated: their own imagination, originality, individualism and initiative. They made good—while the rock-ribbed conformists remained by the wayside.

The conformists simply do not realize that only the least able and efficient among them derive any benefit from the dubious blessings of conformism. The best men are inevitably dragged down to the insipid levels at which the second-raters—the prigs, pedants, precisians and procrastinators—set the pace. The craze for conformity is having its effect on our entire civilization—and, the way I see it, the effect is far from a salubrious one. It isn't a very long step from a conformist society to a regimented society. Although it would take longer to create an Orwellian nightmare through voluntary surrender of individuality—and thus of independence—than through totalitarian edict, the results would be very much the same. In some respects, a society in which the members reach a universal level in which they are anonymous drones by choice is even more frightening than one in which they are forced to be so against their will. When human beings relinquish their individuality and identity of their own volition, they are also relinquishing their claim to being human.

In business, the mystique of conformity is sapping the dynamic individualism that is the most priceless quality an executive or businessman can possibly possess. It has produced the lifeless, cardboard-cutout figure of the organization man who tries vainly to hide his fears, lack of confidence and incompetence behind the stylized façades of conformity.

The conformist is not born. He is made. I believe the brainwashing process begins in the schools and colleges. Many teachers and professors seem hell-bent on imbuing their students with a desire to achieve "security" above all—and at all costs. Beyond this, high school and university curricula are frequently designed to turn out nothing but "specialists" with circumscribed knowledge and interests. The theory seems to be that accountants should only be accountants, traffic managers should only be traffic managers, and so on *ad nauseam.* There doesn't appear to be much effort made to produce young men who have a grasp of the over-all business picture and who will assume the responsibilities of leadership. Countless otherwise intelligent young men leave the universities where they have received over-specialized educations and then disappear into the administrative rabbit warrens of overorganized corporations.

To be sure, there are many other pressures that force the young man of today to be a conformist. He is bombarded from all sides by arguments that he must tailor himself, literally and figuratively, to fit the current clean-cut image, which means that he must be just like everyone else. He does not understand that the arguments are those of the almost-weres and never-will-bes who want him as company to share the misery of their frustrations and failures. Heaven help the man who dares to be different in thought or action. Any deviation from the mediocre norm, he is told, will brand him a Bohemian or a Bolshevik, a crank or a crackpot—a man who is unpredictable and thus unreliable.

The conformist is not born. He is made. I believe the brainwashing process begins in the schools and colleges. Many teachers and professors seem hell-bent on imbuing their students with a desire to achieve "security" above all—and at all costs.

This, of course, is sheer nonsense. Any man who allows his individuality to assert itself constructively will soon rise to the top. He will be the man who is most likely to succeed. But the brainwashing continues throughout many a man's career. The women in his life frequently do their part to keep him in his conformist's straight jacket. Mothers, fiancées and wives are particularly prone to be arch-conservatives who consider a weekly paycheck a bird in hand to be guarded, cherished and protected—and never mind what valuable *rara avis* may be nesting in the nearby bushes. Wives have a habit of raising harrowing spectres to deter a husband who might wish to risk his safe, secure job and seek fulfillment and wealth via imaginative and enterprising action. "You've got a good future with the Totter and Plod Company," they wail. "Don't risk it by doing anything rash. Remember all the bills and payments we have to meet—and we simply *must* get a new car this year!"

Consequently, the full-flowering conformist organization man takes the 8:36 train every weekday morning and hopes that in a few years he'll be moved far enough up the ladder so that he can ride the 9:03 with the middle-bracket executives. The businessman conformist is the Caspar Milquetoast of the present era. His future is not very bright. His conformist's rut will grow ever deeper until, at last, it becomes the grave for the hopes, ambitions and chances he might have once had for achieving wealth and success. The confirmed organization man spends his business career bogged down in a morass of procedural rules, multi-copy memoranda and endless committee meetings in which he and men who are his carbon copies come up with hackneyed answers to whatever problems are placed before them. He worries and frets about things that are trivial and superficial—even unto wearing what someone tells him is the "proper" garb for an executive in his salary bracket and to buying his split-level house in what some canny realtor convinces him is an "executives' subdivision."

Such a man defeats his own purpose. He [the organization man] remains a second-string player on what he somewhat sophomorically likes to call "the team" instead of becoming the captain or star player. He misses the limitless opportunities which today present themselves to the imaginative individualist. But he really doesn't care. "I want security," he declares. "I want to know that my job is safe and that I'll get my regular raises in salary, vacations with pay and a good pension when I retire." This, unhappily, seems to sum up too many young men's ambitions. It is a confession of weakness and cowardice.

There is a dearth of young executives who are willing to stick their necks out, to assert themselves and fight for what they think is right and best even if they have to pound on the corporation president's desk to make their point.

True, an executive who crosses swords with his superiors may sometimes risk his job in the process, but a firm that will fire a man merely because he has the courage of his convictions is not one for which a really good executive would care to work in the first place. And, if he is a good executive, he will quickly get a better job in the event he *is* fired—you may be sure of that. You can also be sure that the conformist who never dares vary from the norm will stay in the lower—or at best middle—echelons in any firm for which he works. He will not reach the top or get rich by merely seeking to second-guess his superiors. The man who will win success is the man who is markedly different from the others around him. He has new ideas and can visualize fresh approaches to problems. He has the ability—and the will—to think and act on his own, not caring if he is damned or derided by "the majority" for his nonconformist ideas and actions.

The men who will make their marks in commerce, industry and finance are the ones with freewheeling imaginations and strong, highly individualistic personalities. Such men may not care whether their hair is crewcut or in a pompadour, and they may prefer chess to golf—but they will see and seize the opportunities around them. Their minds unfettered by the stultifying mystiques of organization-man conformity, they will be the ones to devise new concepts by means of which production and sales may be increased. They will develop new products and cut costs—to increase profits and build their own fortunes. These economic free-thinkers are the individuals who create new businesses and revitalize and expand old ones. They rely on their own judgment rather than on surveys, studies and committee meetings. They refer to no manuals of procedural rules, for they know that every business situation is different from the next and that no thousand volumes could ever contain enough rules to cover all contingencies.

The nonconformist . . . can wear a green toga instead of a gray-flannel suit [and] drink yak's milk rather than martinis . . . and none of it will make the slightest difference.

The successful businessman is no narrow specialist. He knows and understands all aspects of his business. He can spot a production bottleneck as quickly as he can an accounting error, rectify a weakness in a sales campaign as easily as a flaw in personnel procurement methods. The successful businessman is a leader—who solicits opinion and advice from his subordinates, but makes the final decisions, gives the orders and assumes the responsibility for whatever happens. I've said it before, and I say it again: There is a fantastic demand for such men in business today—both as top executives and as owners and operators of their own businesses. There is ample room for them in all categories of business endeavor.

The resourceful and aggressive man who wants to get rich will find the field wide open, provided he is willing to heed and act upon his imagination, relying on his own abilities and judgment rather than conforming to patterns and practices established by others.

The nonconformist—the leader and originator—has an excellent chance to make his fortune in the business world. He can wear a green toga instead of a gray-flannel suit, drink yak's milk rather than martinis, drive a Kibitka instead of a Cadillac and vote the straight Vegetarian Ticket—and none of it will make the slightest difference. Ability and achievement are *bona fides* no one dares question, no matter how unconventional the man who presents them.

WILLARD F. ROCKWELL, JR.

Back in 1919 Rockwell's father started a modest truck axle firm. Fifty years later Rockwell-Standard was making aerospace equipment for NASA's Apollo program, a result of their merger with North American Aviation. It was the younger Rockwell who successfully guided the company into the space age after becoming president in 1963. The reason the automotive parts maker merged with the country's largest space contractor was to create synergy, or as a Rockwell executive explained, "Those scientific longhairs throw away ideas every day that should be useful to us. We're going to get out there and go through their wastebaskets." The company's pervasive enthusiasm for cutting-edge modernization stemmed from Rockwell's dedication to investing in research and development. He said, "If we don't obsolete most of our own products ourselves at least every five years, our competition will do it for us."

It was Rockwell's high-flying vision of the future that distinguished him from his ultraconservative father. However, the elder Rockwell had planned well for his own son's future by encouraging him to study both engineering and accounting at Penn State University. He said to his son, "It's the safest training you can get. When business is good, the bosses want engineers. When it's bad, engineers are the first people they fire, but then they begin looking for accountants to figure out what's wrong." Another quality that made Rockwell successful was his emphasis on human relations and personnel development. For example, in their merger with North American, his first commandment was to "absorb people with care." Unfortunately, the new company found it necessary to lay off thousands within several years (a result of that accounting learned in college).

Merger casualties aside, over the years Rockwell initiated a college recruiting program, introduced a variety of progressive training practices, and "persistently pushed young people into positions of responsibility." His commitment to investing in the employee's development is obvious in *The Hat of the Student;* however, Rockwell also clearly points out that success depends greatly on self-improvement and independent thinking.

The Hat of the Student
Willard F. Rockwell, Jr.

Build the man as well as the manager. In my view, the manager who makes it to the top in the seventies and eighties will not be a super-specialist; he will not be the manager with exposure to and expertise in one limited area of the business, and information gaps in other areas that are like great empty barns with the wind whistling through them. He will be a cultured and well-rounded individual.

Knowledge enriches knowledge, and the more the variety, the greater the enrichment. A financial manager, for example, may hammer away endlessly at the financial aspects of the business. Assuming he is endowed with ample intelligence and that the necessary specialized training is provided, he may become a so-called financial wizard in time. But wizard or not, he will be limited both as a manager and as a person if his education is confined to financial aspects exclusively. He will be limited in working with and dealing with people. He will be limited in relating financial considerations to other aspects of the business such as marketing, research, and manufacturing. He will be limited in projecting the desired corporate image. He will be limited in generating the warmth and rapport that are so essential to the development of trust relationships at high levels and the consummation of important business deals.

That is not to say no important place in business will exist for the specialized manager. He will always be needed. But the top man of the future, in my view, will be the specialist plus. His abilities will grow like a mushroom, not like a bean sprout.

The broadening process I have in mind will not just happen. It can occur only by design. A manager must plan his cultural development as thoughtfully as he plans his work schedule and his profit goals.

I think it's a healthful experience, too, for the executive to ask himself from time to time, honestly and searchingly, "Is the manager functioning at the expense of the man?"

The erosion of the man can be sinister and deadly. I have seen it happen. I can call one man in particular to mind, ambitious, talented, imaginative. He worked long hard hours. He took course after course, steeping himself in systems lore and little else. He never paused long enough to consider how narrow and limited his focus was. And his superior was not sufficiently perceptive, or lacked the proper interest, to point this out to him. In time his talent faded. His imagination dried up. All that remained was the ambition. But it was too late. He had boxed himself into the super-specialist's airtight container. He wound up frustrated and disenchanted, but none the wiser.

Do you have adequate time for random soul searching, mental excursions of self-renewal not directly related to the job?

The head of a large chemical company told me recently, "I regard it as a danger signal if a manager is too busy to think beyond his everyday problems."

A manager I know prides himself on being always in the mainstream of activity. And I mean *always*. He triggers projects. He gets in on the detailed planning stages. He watches personally over each phase like an old mother hen. This executive is project oriented to the point that he is becoming mentally muscle bound. He finds it difficult adjusting his sights to unrelated activities. In truth, he is insecure. He's fearful of getting out of the mainstream and not being missed.

The effects of his outlook are corrosive. It narrows his perspective, undermines his faith in subordinates. It creates an underlying suspiciousness of nature that is difficult to pinpoint but impossible not to sense.

On the other hand, I have been told, a manager has to be realistic. And this is true. The sad fact is that in some organizations you had best stay rooted to the scene of major activity if you do not wish to be squeezed out. Here the disease is not individual but corporate, and it is the fault of the man at the top.

I know of one organization that is a hotbed of political upheaval. The manager too long away from the shop drops down notches on the structural power jack. One executive in this company is a personal friend of mine. He came back recently from a three-month assignment in Europe.

"I left as a key executive and returned feeling like a fifth wheel," he told me. "My place in the political hierarchy had neatly and mysteriously shifted. I had found the European experience broadening and educational. But I decided to take the fruits of my knowledge elsewhere. I found another job."

Smart manager. I think this is another question every executive might well pose to himself from time to time: "Is the climate in my company conducive to cultural enrichment, self-renewal, the broadening of the man as well as the manager?"

It is up to the president to generate and sustain such an atmosphere. If he is lax in fulfilling this responsibility, the alternatives bargained for may be empire building and political patronage.

YOU CAN'T MANUFACTURE THE WILL TO LEARN

It is my suspicion that a situation I can call to mind is not uncommon in U. S. business. The company in question is a medium-size manufacturer of industrial products. For years—until about two years ago—it had a costly and involved system in operation that was loosely referred to as the "management development program."

Actually, the term was a misnomer. The system was fraught with an unbelievable hodgepodge of motivational gimmickry. A prodigious variety of techniques had been structured, most of them designed to impel in managers and supervisors the will to learn, to grow, to advance.

The goal was praiseworthy. But the system had cost a fortune to establish and even more to administer. In my view, it was a vast and colossal waste for the simple reason that true motivation cannot stem from without. It must originate inside the man.

In this case, for each motivational gimmick there was a failure alibi to match. The alibis were concocted, I suspect, more to justify the program than to explain the individual shortcomings inherent in it.

In any event, extensive and complex analyses were made — with the help of attitudinal consultants — in an effort to determine, for example, what caused Smith to walk when he was expected to run. ("His motivational drive is not money, but the desire for increased status." Ergo more experiments.) Or why Johnson was reluctant to respond to the opportunity of a proposed transfer to New York. (It never occurred to the experts that he was comfortably ensconced in a home-grown groove and perfectly content with the status quo.) Or explain Wilson's refusal to take the training required to advance him from research chemist to an administrative post in the lab. (Perhaps he was just a scientist at heart and had no further ambitions.)

Another favorite explanation for "motivational resistance" was age. ("Benson's too old a dog to learn new tricks, and he knows it.")

This, I contend, is the sheerest of nonsense. As Louis Cassels writes in *Nation's Business:* "Modern research has exploded the notion that learning capacity dwindles rapidly as a person ages. It shows that adults can learn effectively at all ages. But it also shows that adults learn in their own way—and this way differs significantly from the way in which children learn."

Some companies attempt to apply children's techniques of motivation to an adult audience, and I don't think it can be done successfully. In any case, this company's program eventually died of its own ineptitude. What much of the motivational gimmickry boils down to, I am convinced, is little more than a series of fads devised by self-styled experts. And I do not mean to imply by this that there is not much good work being done by some of the nation's employee development professionals and attitudinal consultants. My only point is a simple one. The manager who refuses to motivate himself cannot be motivated by others.

A good manager who cares about his people can help to awaken or stimulate the desire to learn. But he cannot *create* it. You cannot force knowledge down people's throats. You can require men to sit through sessions designed to improve their decision-making technique, or help them understand better how to cope with problems, or how to tackle tricky human relations situations. But the only one who will truly benefit from the instruction is the man who would have volunteered for the course, and probably taken it on his own time and at his own expense.

Some companies attempt to apply children's techniques of motivation to an adult audience . . .

This does not mean to say that industry should not underwrite education. I am all for this, and to the maximum degree possible. But I believe the manager's responsibility is to make the knowledge available to his subordinates, to sharpen awareness, to inspire if he can and, from that point, expect the prospect to take the initiative on his own. For that is the way that people learn.

B. C. FORBES
1880 – 1954

One of 10 children born to a tailor in Scotland, the future builder of a publishing empire found it necessary to enter the workforce at the age of 14. Forbes knew then that he wanted to write, so he applied for a seven-year apprenticeship as a compositor. Unfortunately, he misinterpreted the word to mean one who writes compositions; the job involved, of course, the grueling work of typesetting that which had already been written. Later, after a second disappointment involving a broken romance, Forbes began a roundabout journey that would eventually bring him to America. "I shook the dust of Scotland off my feet, and sailed for the remotest corner of the world I could think of, South Africa, then in the close of the Boer War, where I figured I could find enough excitement to assuage my black, black woe." After spending two years in South Africa, he came to America in 1904.

Through various connections, Forbes acquired a job as a newspaper reporter. His aggressive style subsequently found an admirer in William Randolph Hearst, who lured him away from his modest position with the *Journal of Commerce and Commercial Bulletin*. Forbes' work at Hearst's *New York American* brought him further recognition for "putting flesh and blood on the dry bones of business news." Forbes decided to launch his own magazine in 1917, which he was going to call "Doers and Doings." Friends convinced him otherwise; they believed his name was an excellent marketing tool in and of itself, thus *Forbes*.

The new business magazine embodied his aggressive style. For example, in the first edition he courageously attacked the old robber baron Jay Gould for "his narrowness of vision, his unreasoning jealousy, his chronic suspicion, etc." Forbes never allowed himself to become complacent. He feared falling into a routine or a rut, because "Ruts, when worn deep enough, become graves." Part of avoiding a routine involves constant stimulation of the mind, which he discusses *In Budgeting Your Days, Allow Time for Thinking*. Forbes also leads us to believe that the next time an employee appears to be catnapping, perhaps he or she really isn't—perhaps.

In Budgeting Your Days, Allow Time for Thinking

B. C. Forbes

Do you plan your day?

If so, do you allow in your program adequate time for thinking?

"When do busy business men think?" is the interesting question asked by a man who does take time to think.

Well, when do they do their thinking? Or do they indulge in any great amount of thinking?

The answers, I believe, should run something like this:

A great many men in business, perhaps the majority, provide no time in their schedules for quiet, undisturbed thinking.

A good many arrange their life so that they can spend one or two quiet evenings a week, when they read and take time for more or less reflection.

A great many other busy men are driven along by the force of events day by day and week by week, and are content to give quick decisions all day long on any matter whatsoever which the day's events bring up.

When Frank A. Vanderlip was president of the largest bank in America his whole day at the bank was taken up by appointment after appointment, meeting after meeting. I asked him once, "When do you find time to think?" He replied: "As you can well imagine, I certainly can't get the time here in the bank to do any real thinking. I have to do it all at home."

Harriman, the railroad wizard, once declared that he liked to drop in unannounced and find one of his executives with his feet on his desk, apparently doing nothing. Harriman assumed that the man was taking time to think.

But isn't it true that nine executives of every ten would hesitate, would be almost ashamed, to be seen sitting at a desk apparently completely idle? Has it not become fashionable to appear busy every moment of the day?

During the last spasm of acute business depression in this country a very large enterprise became financially crippled and the bankers had to take hold. There was urgent necessity for evolving a reorganization plan. The bankers were supposed to put their minds to work and to offer suggestions or a program at a later meeting.

At this later meeting a youngish bank president, after listening to the rather vague talk of his elders, got up and outlined a complete plan. He first presented a clear picture of the exact status of every phase of the corporation's position, and then recommended how each matter should be handled. His plan was received with cordial approval.

. . . isn't it true that nine executives of every ten would hesitate, would be almost ashamed, to be seen sitting at a desk apparently completely idle? Has it not become fashionable to appear busy every moment of the day?

Leaving the meeting, one of the older bankers told the younger man that he would be willing to give a million dollars to be able to analyze so clearly such a complicated problem and to work out so thorough and businesslike a solution.

How was the younger banker able to do it? Because he devotes five evenings every week, not simply to idle reading, but to serious reading and to intense thought and study. This whole reorganization plan was evolved by him at his home during long evenings of severe application.

Daniel Guggenheim, head of the famous smelting family, once said to me: "The man who works twelve months a year works only six months a year." He meant that any man carrying tremendous responsibilities must take time for recreating his body and brain.

Do we always keep in mind the simple, basic fact that all success springs from thinking? Not only success but everything else first comes into being as a thought in some man's mind. The Woolworth Building for years was nothing more than a thought, an idea, in the mind of Frank W. Woolworth. The billion-dollar Steel Corporation first was a thought in the mind of one individual, generally understood to have been Charles M. Schwab. The Egyptian sphinx was once nothing but a thought.

If we can only get it firmly into our heads, and will eternally keep it at the forefront of our mind, that thinking is the material of which success is made, will it not influence us so to plan our days and our weeks that we shall set aside more time for calm, sustained thinking?

Greenewalt's big break on his way to becoming Du Pont's president came in 1926 when he married the boss's daughter, Margaretta du Pont. The plan to woo her had germinated several years earlier when he was working the graveyard shift, watching vats of stirring chemicals and playing his clarinet to pass the time. Actually, truth be known, they were childhood friends. Greenewalt's real break came in the late 1930s when the MIT chemist brought nylon from the test tube to mass production. This synthetic material became a huge moneymaker for Du Pont. His second highly visible success was realized during World War II when he headed Du Pont's participation in the top-secret Manhattan Project—the building of the A-bomb. At the University of Chicago Greenewalt witnessed the first controlled atomic reaction, and was convinced that neither he nor the city would survive the experiment. He did, of course, and three years after the war Greenewalt was elected president of the company.

Greenewalt was a unique and dichotomous leader. A colleague described him as having "energy, charm, a chain-reacting mind, and some seeming contradictions. He has the cold precision of a trained scientist. . . . Just as quickly, he can become as gregarious as a travelling salesman." The cold precision was a necessity in order to focus on problems and make decisions in an extremely complex business. He was also the type of leader who could leave problems at the office. Greenewalt's favorite hobby (for which he was also famous) was of all things the study and photography of hummingbirds. Amazingly, his mind was able to witness a nuclear reaction one minute, and then write an article on ornithology for the *Audubon* nature magazine the next.

This humanistic approach to life and business contributed to Greenewalt's great capacity for being a leader. He understood that all people were not created equal in terms of their skill sets. The key, therefore, was to "bring into play the full potential of all men, whatever their station." Within the confines of the corporation, the employee's potential is not always easily realized, and Greenewalt addresses this issue among others in *The Uncommon Man.*

Freedom, Individuality, and Conformity
Crawford H. Greenewalt

To the extent that it can be said to exist, conformity is not, of course, a characteristic peculiar to business, nor is it uniquely the province of the large group. It may be found in some degree in all organizations of whatever nature or size. I am inclined to think that, man for man, the large business unit represents greater opportunities for individuality and requires less in the way of conformity than other institutions—in the government service, say, or in the academic world, or in the military.

I would judge, too, that "conformity" is at least as likely, perhaps more likely, to be present in small groups as large. Adjustment to a given behavior pattern is, after all, just as obligatory in a group of ten as in a group of a thousand, with the important difference that deviations attract far more attention. It is proverbial that small towns will discipline a dissenter far more drastically than the big city would take the trouble to do. By the same token I venture that conformity is more likely to be found in a small, closely held firm with a dozen employees than in the giant corporation, if only because the range of tolerance in a group of 100,000 people must necessarily be wider than in one numbering ten or twelve.

Nevertheless, it seems to be the large business unit which attracts notice in this regard and the belief seems widely prevalent that there is a pattern to which the manners, dress, and political views of each candidate for advancement must conform. The general impression has some rather bizarre twists; someone once asked me seriously if it were not true that the Buick had been selected as the official hierarchical automobile because its many grades of size and elegance could be assigned in accordance with rank! Some popular magazines have been airing the curious conviction that the wives of business executives are screened critically as part of the criteria for promotion. A number of novels, movies, and TV shows have sounded the same theme.

I cannot speak for corporations generally, nor for any, specifically, save our own. As for our Company, I will say that such notions are sheer nonsense and I will venture as a guess that the same can be said for most. The superficial symbols like the Gray Flannel Suit—I don't own one, by the way—actually mean little. Among my most valued associates, taste in dress covers a pretty broad pattern. The same goes for personal habits, enthusiasms, and, I may say, for automobiles. I could not list off-hand the kinds of cars my principal associates drive. One, I know, drives an Opel, as he never fails to proclaim its virtues; another passes me occasionally in a topless Corvette in which he wears a baseball cap. Perhaps one even has a Buick, grade and model unknown.

As for wives, I can report that, among my closest coworkers, there are, of course, a number whose ladies I have known well for many years. We live in a small town and I remember some when they were on roller skates. There are a number whose wives I know well enough to exchange a "How do you do, Mrs. Smith," "How do you do, Mr. Greenewalt," and there are a number whose marital partners, I regret to say, I have never met at all.

Emphasis on the irrelevant factors of habit and custom and on the various fictional characteristics obscure the truth, and the truth offers sufficient challenge without inconsequential distractions. The alert and well-managed organiza-

316

tion will be fully aware of the dangers associated with individual submersion. Progress will be made in direct proportion to the intellectual freedom of action given all the men on the team. There is nothing inherent in large organizations which closes the door to high individual performance, but the larger the organization, the more assiduously it must work at the job of keeping its channels of encouragement and recognition open and flowing.

Men as well as children can lose their way in crowds. Men in organizations can be obscured, frustrated, or overlooked; injustices may be done, indignities suffered, promise suddenly turned to indifference. It is the better part of leadership to see that it doesn't happen, that no individual is hidden behind his neighbor and his potential dissipated.

Not only the organization, but society itself suffers when people are allowed to sacrifice identity in the damp laundry of mediocrity.

Organizations are in trouble when success causes them to be so enraptured with their accomplishments that they are moved, like Narcissus, to fashion everything in their own image. I would venture the assumption that each of us, whatever our vocation, has at some time passed through an unhappy period caused by the boss' insisting that we "do it his way" instead of letting us use the methods which fall most easily to our hand.

Great emphasis is placed on training today, particularly in that nebulous area called executive development, but too much codification in training procedures often results in perpetuating facsimiles and freezing rigid patterns of thought. Thorough training is obviously a necessity, but it must always be remembered that organizations do not make men—men make organizations. It is what they bring with them in the way of character and adaptability and fresh ideas

317

that enrich the organizational bloodstream and insure corporate longevity.

Not only the organization, but society itself suffers when people are allowed to sacrifice identity in the damp laundry of mediocrity. Competent leadership will minimize these hazards, although, people being people, perfection in this area comes hard. There are, unfortunately, few valid standards of direct comparison among human beings, and the functions and opportunities of individuals working within an organization will obviously differ with their capacities and special competence. Contributions to the joint effort will vary in kind as they vary in importance. Creative imagination will be expressed in varying ways and in varying proportion. Some contribute in brilliant flashes of form; others through their steadiness, persistence, or the gruelling and often overlooked grind of hard routine work. The important thing to the organization is that each individual be given the opportunity to exploit his talents to the fullest and in the way best suited to his personality.

Only in this way will the organization sift its more able people to the top, and although much can be said for the high general average, it is with men of first rank that the organization as well as society itself must selfishly be most concerned. The role of the common man has been widened and improved, and it operates in a great variety of useful ways; the role of the truly uncommon man in this or in any age is unique. A special word concerning his status is in order:

All human accomplishments are important in varying degree, but the achievements of a limited few have been very great indeed. This is to be expected, for in any field of endeavor, some will lead and some will follow; some will succeed conspicuously, some moderately, others not at all. While all contribute to the common good, the few at the top of their respective fields contribute in an extraordinary degree, since great individual success is never attained without bringing a measure of that success to many others.

Individual accomplishment marks the beginning of a chain reaction extending its influences far and wide; it is a catalyst which awakens desire in others and crystallizes effort which might otherwise lie dormant.

Henry Ford's genius for mass production created wonders in terms of employment, profit, and enjoyment for millions of people. The impact of Albert Einstein upon scientists and laymen alike the world over has been profound; Kreisler's extraordinary mastery of the violin has brought enjoyment to millions.

Try as we will, we can create no synthetic genius, no composite leader. Men are *not* interchangeable parts like so many pinion gears or carburetors; genius, as John Adams said, is bestowed "imperiously" by nature upon an individual. And behind every advance of the human race is a germ of creation growing in the mind of some lone individual, an individual whose dreams waken him in the night while others lie contentedly asleep. It is he who is the indispensable man.

Organizations are in trouble when success causes them to be so enraptured with their accomplishments that they are moved, like Narcissus, to fashion everything in their own image.

With all our technical advances, dreams are not yet machine made and cannot be produced by crash programs. They cannot be stockpiled, prefabricated, or improvised. They remain one of the most characteristic symptoms of human aspiration and one of the activities which is most exclusively the province of the individual.

By dreams, of course, we mean creative genius, and the task in science, in business, in education, and in every other phase of human activity is to develop and preserve within our institutions this priceless human quality. Unless we can do so, the problem we will bequeath to our successors will be a dismal legacy indeed.

J. P. Morgan wanted a new partner to help manage his international operations, and his top candidate was Perkins, a vice president of New York Life at the time. When Morgan extended a generous offer, Perkins declined, one of few who said no to the Wall Street icon. He explained, "I have never been in this world merely to make money. I early learned that any man who starts out simply to make money never gets very far, for he will ruin his health, or sacrifice his friends. . . ." After rethinking his decision, he accepted the job two months later, providing he be permitted to hold his position at New York Life. Morgan quickly acquiesced, with his eye on the insurance company's huge pool of funds that were ripe for investing.

Perkins' conflict of interest in doubling as a partner with Morgan and as an officer with an insurance company was painfully obvious and quickly assailed. A competitive banker accusingly said, "He gave the impression of considering himself above the law; legal restrictions, he seemed to be saying, only applied to people who were dishonest, which he was not." Although not convicted of any crimes in a subsequent criminal investigation, the somewhat hurt Perkins was forced to resign from New York Life, where he had begun his career as an office boy. He found comfort in recalling what his father had once told him: a change of vocation "is almost equal to a vacation." Morgan paid him handsomely, too.

Although Perkins felt rejuvenated in his new vocation, it quickly became obvious he would need all his energy and more working as Morgan's right-hand man. He defended the company against Roosevelt's trust-busting attacks; he brilliantly formed the International Harvester Company, a farm equipment trust; and while negotiating a deal in Russia, he narrowly escaped with his life aboard a chartered steamboat during the violent uprising of 1905. Perkins came to embody Morgan's belief in creating trusts in the name of efficiency and public good. Morgan himself burned or otherwise destroyed most of his personal papers, so special note must be made of Perkins' ideas about the individual within the framework of corporate America, which he relates in *The Modern Corporation*.

The Modern Corporation
George W. Perkins

We have heard many warnings that because of the great corporation we have been robbing the oncoming generation of its opportunities. Nothing is more absurd. The larger the corporation, the more certain is the office boy to ultimately reach a foremost place if he is made of the right stuff, if he keeps everlastingly at it, and if he is determined to become master of each position he occupies.

In the earlier days, the individual in business, as a rule, left his business to his children—the firm to its relations. Whether or not they were competent did not determine the succession. But the giant corporation cannot act in this way. Its management must have efficiency—above and beyond all else it must have the highest order of ability; and nothing has been more noticeable in the management of corporations in the last few years than that "influence," so called, as an element in selecting men for responsible posts, has been rapidly on the wane. Everything is giving way and must give way to the one supreme test of fitness.

And is it not possible that the accumulating of large fortunes in the future may be curtailed to a large extent through the very workings of these corporations? Are there not many advantages in having corporations in which there are a large number of positions carrying with them very handsome annual salaries, in place of firms with comparatively few partners — the annual profits of each one of whom were often so large that they amassed fortunes in a few years? A position carrying a salary so large as to represent the interest on a handsome fortune can be permanently filled only by a man of real ability, so that in case a man who is occupying such a position dies, it must, in turn, be filled with another man of the same order while the fortune might be, and most likely would be, passed on regardless of the heir's ability. Therefore, the more positions of responsibility, of trust and of honor, that carry large salaries, the more goals we have for young men whose equipment for life consists of integrity, health, ability, and energy.

The larger the corporation, the more certain is the office boy to ultimately reach a foremost place if he is made of the right stuff, if he keeps everlastingly at it, and if he is determined to become master of each position he occupies.

Furthermore, the great corporation has been of benefit to the public in being able to standardize its wares, so that they have become more uniformly good. Wages are unquestionably higher and labor is more steadily employed; for, in a given line of trade, handled to a considerable extent by a corporation, there are practically no failures; while, under the old methods of bitter, relentless warfare, failures were frequent, and failure meant paralysis for labor as well as for capital.

The great corporation is unquestionably making general business conditions sounder. It is making business steadier; for one reason, because firms inevitably change and dissolve, while a corporation may go on indefinitely. It is making business steadier, for another and more potent reason — because it is able to survey the field much better than could a large number of firms and individuals and, therefore, vastly better able to measure the demand for its output and, if properly managed, to prevent the accumulation of large stocks of goods that are not needed—a condition which often arose under the old methods when many firms were in ruthless competition with one another in the same line of business, oftentimes producing serious financial difficulties for one and all.

Broadly and generally speaking, the corporation as we know it to-day, as we see it working and feel its results, is in a formative state. In many cases actual and desperately serious situations caused it to be put together hurriedly. In many cases serious mistakes have been made in the forms of organization, in the methods of management, and in the ends that have been sought. In some instances the necessity for corporations has grown faster than has the ability of men to manage them. Yes, mistakes have been many and serious. But the corporation is with us; it is a condition, not a theory, and there are but two courses open to us—to kill it or to keep it. If you would kill it you must kill the cause, or the thing will come back to plague you. The principal causes are steam and electricity.

Could anything be more dangerous to the public welfare than steam and electricity themselves? Then why not prohibit their use and, so far as possible, abolish them? Has anyone ever suggested this? No. Why? Because their benefits were too apparent, and so we have bent our energies towards regulating and controlling them—by using all that is good in them and carefully protecting ourselves from all that is injurious. If we are not willing to exterminate the cause of corporations we can never permanently exterminate the corporation itself. There is, then, but one thing left to do, viz., to regulate and control them; to treat them as we have treated steam and electricity; to use the best that is in them and to protect ourselves from the worst that is in them.

A large percentage of the mistakes of corporate management have occurred because managers have failed to realize that they were not in business as individuals, but were working for other people, their stockholders, whom they were in honor bound to honestly and faithfully serve; further, that they owed a duty to the general public and could, in the long run, best serve themselves and their stockholders by recognizing that duty and respecting it.

Then, too, many of our corporations, being of comparatively recent origin, have, at the outset, been managed by men who were previously in business, in some form or another, for themselves; and it has been very difficult for such men to change their point of view—to cease from looking at questions from the sole standpoint of personal gain and personal advantage, and to take the broader view of looking at them from the standpoint of the community of interest principle.

It is by no means clear that the danger-point in the development of corporations is found in the giant corporation. Indeed, it is more likely to be found in the corporation of lesser size; because the latter does not attract the eye of the public sufficiently to have its managers impressed with the fact that they are semi-private servants—responsible not only to their stockholders but to the public as well. It is easier and more natural for a giant corporation to adopt a policy of publicity with the public and of fair-dealing with its associates in the same trade, because such a course, from the broad, far-reaching view of the great corporation, becomes the wisest, most successful course. Then, again, the relation of the giant corporation to its labor is an entirely different relation from that of the small corporation or the firm to its labor; the officers and trustees of a giant corporation instinctively lose sight of the interest of any one individual because such interest at best is infinitesimal compared with the whole. This places the officers and trustees of the giant corporation in a position where they can look on all labor questions without bias and without any personal axe to grind—solely from the broadest possible standpoint of what is fair and right between the public's capital, which they represent, and the public's labor, which they employ. In short, they assume on all such matters the attitude of the real trustee, the impartial judge, the intelligent, well-posted, and fair arbitrator.

The great semi-public business corporations of the country, whether they be insurance, railroad, or industrial, have in our day become not only vast business enterprises but great trusteeships; and there would be far less attacking of corporations if this truth were more fully realized and respected. The larger the corporation becomes, the greater become its responsibilities to the entire community. Moreover, the larger the number of stockholders, the more it assumes the nature of an institution for savings.

... the corporation is with us; it is a condition, not a theory, and there are but two courses open to us — to kill it or to keep it.

It is not sufficient in corporate management to do the best one can from day to day. Corporate responsibility extends beyond to-day. It is the foresight, the planning ahead, the putting the house in order for the storms of the future, that are the true measure of the best and highest stewardship as well as of the highest order of managerial ability.

The corporations of the future must be those that are semi-public servants, serving the public, with ownership widespread among the public, and with labor so fairly and equitably treated that it will look upon its corporation as its friend and protector rather than as an ever-present enemy, above all believing in it so thoroughly that it will invest its savings in the corporation's securities and become working partners in the business. It would have been impossible, in the day of the ox-team, for people in every State of this Union to be partners in any one business; and yet to-day we have at least one giant corporation made up of partners resident not only in every one of our States, but in almost every country in the world, and reinforced by thousands of its own employees having become stockholders themselves. . . .

So much for corporations. Now, may I detain you a moment longer while I say a word to the young men who are here today.

Success does not come by chance. It is an opportunity that has been lassoed and organized.

How hopeless would your condition be if the world were perfect—if there were nothing left for you to do to improve conditions—if those who had gone before had finished the job. Really, can you imagine a condition more discouraging, more hopeless to an oncoming generation? Happily, this is not your situation. Our corporations have made mistakes. Many of these have been pointed out. Things have been done wrongly. Many of these wrongs are now being corrected. But in those mistakes, in that mis-management, lies the opportunity of the man of today and of the young man of tomorrow. Your task will be to search out and eliminate the bad in all that has preceded you—retaining the good, preserving and adding to it for the benefit of yourselves and of those who follow you.

Let us, then, take the best that we find, cut out the worst that we find, improve, develop, make more useful and beneficial.

In this great country of ours there stands out preeminently the inventive genius, the masterful ability, the resourcefulness, the courage, the optimism of America's business men. At no period in the world's development have there been in any given country at any one time so many men of from 20 to 30 years of age, standing ready to embrace so many opportunities and to move on to such splendid achievements, as we have in our United States today. It cannot be possible that these young men will be pessimists—that they will miss the legion of opportunities that are theirs!

I wonder if many of you realize how fortunate in one respect alone you are as compared with the young men in many other countries. You are not obliged to spend a number of the most impressionable years of your lives in compulsory military service, learning to obey orders which have no relation to the realities of life and its actual successes. Those precious years in this country are given to you to observe, to learn, and to prepare for the practical work of the world. Your individuality is not hampered or circumscribed by your being moulded into a machine in your early manhood. You are free to make of yourself what you will. What would the young men of Europe give for their opportunities if some magic wand could give them one currency, one language, one government, one people, from London to Moscow!

Success does not come by chance. It is an opportunity that has been lassoed and organized. I doubt if a man ever met with success, worthy to be called success, who was not an optimist—who did not believe in something heart and soul, and who did not play fair. And remember that when you set about a task which you really want to accomplish, the work involved is not drudgery—it is the most invigorating sort of play.

Do not lose your red blood; whatever you are, wherever or however you are situated, keep your heart warm and your humanity at par. Push forward; be of good cheer. Believe in our people, in our methods, in our country, in your neighbor and in yourself; and remember, if you are going into business, that, after all is said and done—after your fortune is made, however great it may be—in the small hours of the night, in your heart of hearts, the thing you are really going to enjoy, take satisfaction in and be proud of—the thing that will carry you over the rough places—that will keep your heart strong and your brain clear, will be the thought of what you have done to help others—what you have left to a world that has offered so much to you.

PART VII

GUNSLINGERS AND THE
ENTREPRENEURIAL SPIRIT

HENRY FORD
1863 – 1947

The first American car was built in 1893. Two years later Ford was driving his own model on the streets of Detroit; however, it was considered more of a nuisance than a marvel, as it made noise, scared the horses, attracted unruly crowds, and brought the ire of the police on Ford. At the time, Ford was a chief engineer for Thomas Edison's Light Company. Edison, who believed electrical power was the fuel of the future, scoffed at the combustion engine and discouraged Ford's work. Regardless, Ford left Edison in 1899 to pursue his dreams, and founded the Ford Motor Company in 1903.

Ford's fundamental business decision to make "a car for the great multitude" drove his success. It led to the development of the economical Model T in 1908 and to the conveyor belt assembly line in 1913. Within a few years of building this revolutionary factory, the Ford Motor Company was producing half of the cars in the world. Intertwined with the concept of assembly line production was Ford's philosophy on leadership: "Industry is management, and management is leadership, and leadership is perfect when it so simplifies operations that orders are not necessary." This rigid, factory-oriented mentality led to Ford's famous quote, "a customer can have any color of car they want as long as it is black." In addition, it was not until 1927 that Ford bothered to introduce a new car model to replace the outdated Model T.

Ford's narrow outlook caused some to believe that he was a simple mechanic caught in an ever complex world; others thought he was a complex man with a single-minded will. Regardless, he was a man without a formal education who, in *What I Learned about Business*, provides some very insightful theories on conducting a successful business. Ford analyzes preconceived notions about finance, labor, manufacturing, sales, and service, and contemplates "the natural process" by which money *should* be made.

What I Learned about Business
Henry Ford

My "gasoline buggy" was the first and for a long time the only automobile in Detroit. It was considered to be something of a nuisance, for it made a racket and it scared horses. Also it blocked traffic. For if I stopped my machine anywhere in town a crowd was around it before I could start up again. If I left it alone even for a minute some inquisitive person always tried to run it. Finally, I had to carry a chain and chain it to a lamp post whenever I left it anywhere. And then there was trouble with the police. I do not know quite why, for my impression is that there were no speed-limit laws in those days. Anyway, I had to get a special permit from the mayor and thus for a time enjoyed the distinction of being the only licensed chauffeur in America. I ran that machine about one thousand miles through 1895 and 1896 and then sold it to Charles Ainsley of Detroit for two hundred dollars. That was my first sale. I had built the car not to sell but only to experiment with. I wanted to start another car. Ainsley wanted to buy. I could use the money and we had no trouble in agreeing upon a price.

It was not at all my idea to make cars in any such petty fashion. I was looking ahead to production, but before that could come I had to have something to produce. It does not pay to hurry. I started a second car in 1896; it was much like the first but a little lighter. It also had the belt drive which I did not give up until some time later; the belts were all right excepting in hot weather. That is why I later adopted gears. I learned a great deal from that car. Others in this country and abroad were building cars by that time, and in 1895 I heard that a Benz car from Germany was on exhibition in Macy's store in New York. I travelled down to look at it but it had no features that seemed worth while. It also had the belt drive, but it was much heavier than my car. I was working for lightness; the foreign makers have never seemed to appreciate what light weight means. I built three cars in all in my home shop and all of them ran for years in Detroit. I still have the first car; I bought it back a few years later from a man to whom Mr. Ainsley had sold it. I paid one hundred dollars for it.

During all this time I kept my position with the electric company and gradually advanced to chief engineer at a salary of one hundred and twenty-five dollars a month. But my gas-engine experiments were no more popular with the president of the company than my first mechanical leanings were with my father. It was not that my employer objected to experiments—only to experiments with a gas engine. I can still hear him say:

"Electricity, yes, that's the coming thing. But gas—no."

He had ample grounds for his skepticism—to use the mildest terms. Practically no one had the remotest notion of the future of the internal combustion engine, while we were just on the edge of the great electrical development. As with every comparatively new idea, electricity was expected to do much more than we even now have any indication that it can do. I did not see the use of experimenting with electricity for my purposes. A road car could not run on a trolley even if trolley wires had been less expensive; no storage battery was in sight of a weight that was practical. An electrical car had of necessity to be limited in radius and to contain a large amount of motive machinery in proportion to the power exerted. That is not to say that I held or now hold electricity cheaply; we have not yet begun to use electricity. But it has its place, and the internal combustion engine has its place. Neither can substitute for the other—which is exceedingly fortunate.

There was no "demand" for automobiles— there never is for a new article. . . . At first the "horseless carriage" was considered merely a freak notion and many wise people explained with particularity why it could never be more than a toy. No man of money even thought of it as a commercial possibility.

I have the dynamo that I first had charge of at the Detroit Edison Company. When I started our Canadian plant I bought it from an office building to which it had been sold by the electric company, had it revamped a little, and for several years it gave excellent service in the Canadian plant. When we had to build a new power plant, owing to the increase in business, I had the old motor taken out to my museum—a room out at Dearborn that holds a great number of my mechanical treasures.

The Edison Company offered me the general superintendency of the company but only on condition that I would give up my gas engine and devote myself to something really useful. I had to choose between my job and my automobile. I chose the automobile, or rather I gave up the job—there was really nothing in the way of a choice. For already I knew that the car was bound to be a success. I quit my job on August 15, 1899, and went into the automobile business.

It might be thought something of a step, for I had no personal funds. What money was left over from living was all used in experimenting. But my wife agreed that the automobile could not be given up—that we had to make or break. There was no "demand" for automobiles—there never is for a new article. They were accepted in much the fashion as was more recently the airplane. At first the "horseless carriage" was considered merely a freak notion and many wise people explained with particularity why it could never be more than a toy. No man of money even thought of it as a commercial possibility. I cannot imagine why each new means of transportation meets with such opposition. There are even those to-day who shake their heads and talk about the luxury of the automobile and only grudgingly admit that perhaps the motor truck is of some use. But in the beginning there was hardly any one who sensed that the automobile could be a large factor in industry. The most optimistic hoped only for a development akin to that of the bicycle. When it was found that an automobile really could go and several makers started to put out cars, the immediate query was as to which would go fastest. It was a curious but natural development—that racing idea. I never thought anything of racing, but the public refused to consider the automobile in any light other than as a fast toy. Therefore later we had to race. The industry was held back by this initial racing slant, for the attention of the makers was diverted to making fast rather than good cars. It was a business for speculators.

I tried to find out what business really was and whether it needed to be quite so selfish a scramble for money as it seemed to be . . .

A group of men of speculative turn of mind organized, as soon as I left the electric company, the Detroit Automobile Company to exploit my car. I was the chief engineer and held a small amount of the stock. For three years we continued making cars more or less on the model of my first car. We sold very few of them; I could get no support at all toward making better cars to be sold to the public at large. The whole thought was to make to order and to get the largest price possible for each car. The main idea seemed to be to get the money. And being without authority other than my engineering position gave me, I found that the new company was not a vehicle for realizing my ideas but merely a money-making concern—that did not make much money. In March, 1902, I resigned, determined never again to put myself under orders. The Detroit Automobile Company later became the Cadillac Company under the ownership of the Lelands, who came in subsequently.

I rented a shop—a one-story brick shed—at 81 Park Place to continue my experiments and to find out what business really was. I thought that it must be something different from what it had proved to be in my first adventure.

The year from 1902 until the formation of the Ford Motor Company was practically one of investigation. In my little one-room brick shop I worked on the development of a four-cylinder motor and on the outside I tried to find out what business really was and whether it needed to be quite so selfish a scramble for money as it seemed to be from my first short experience. From the period of the first car, which I have described, until the formation of my present company I built in all about twenty-five cars, of which nineteen or twenty were built with the Detroit Automobile Company. The automobile had passed from the initial stage where the fact that it could run at all was enough, to the stage where it had to show speed. Alexander Winton of Cleveland, the founder of the Winton car, was then the track champion of the country and willing to meet all comers. I designed a two-cylinder enclosed engine of a more compact type than I had before used, fitted it into a skeleton chassis, found that I could make speed, and arranged a race with Winton. We met on the Grosse Point track at Detroit. I beat him. That was my first race, and it brought advertising of the only kind that people cared to read.

The public thought nothing of a car unless it made speed—unless it beat other racing cars. My ambition to build the fastest car in the world led me to plan a four-cylinder motor. But of that more later.

The most surprising feature of business as it was conducted was the large attention given to finance and the small attention to service. That seemed to me to be reversing the natural process which is that the money should come as the result of work and not before the work. The second feature was the general indifference to better methods of manufacture as long as whatever was done got by and took the money. In other words, an article apparently was not built with reference to how greatly it could serve the public but with reference solely to how much money could be had for it—and that without any particular care whether the customer was satisfied. To sell him was enough. A dissatisfied customer was regarded not as a man whose trust had been violated, but either as a nuisance or as a possible source of more money in fixing up the work which ought to have been done correctly in the first place. For instance, in automobiles there was not much concern as to what happened to the car once it had been sold. How much gasoline it used per mile was of no great moment; how much service it actually gave did not matter; and if it broke down and had to have parts replaced, then that was just hard luck for the owner. It was considered good business to sell parts at the highest possible price on the theory that, since the man had already bought the car, he simply had to have the part and would be willing to pay for it.

The automobile business was not on what I would call an honest basis, to say nothing of being, from a manufacturing standpoint, on a scientific basis, but it was no worse than business in general. That was the period, it may be remembered, in which many corporations were being floated and financed. The bankers, who before then had confined themselves to the railroads, got into industry. My idea was then and still is that if a man did his work well, the price he would get for that work, the profits and all financial matters, would care for themselves and that a business ought to start small and build itself up and out of its earnings. If there are no earnings then that is a signal to the owner that he is wasting his time and does not belong in that business. I have never

---

The most surprising feature of business as it was conducted was the large attention given to finance and the small attention to service. That seemed to me to be reversing the natural process which is that the money should come as the result of work and not before the work.

---

found it necessary to change those ideas, but I discovered that this simple formula of doing good work and getting paid for it was supposed to be slow for modern business. The plan at that time most in favour was to start off with the largest possible capitalization and then sell all the stock and all the bonds that could be sold. Whatever money happened to be left over after all the stock and bond-selling expenses and promoters, charges and all that, went grudgingly into the foundation of the business. A good business was not one that did good work and earned a fair profit. A good business was one that would give the opportunity for the floating of a large amount of stocks and bonds at high prices. It was the stocks and bonds, not the work, that mattered. I could not see how a new business or an old business could be expected to be able to charge into its product a great big bond interest and then sell the product at a fair price. I have never been able to see that.

I have never been able to understand on what theory the original investment of money can be charged against a business. Those men in business who call themselves financiers say that money is "worth" 6 per cent. or 5 per cent. or some other per cent., and that if a business has one hundred thousand dollars invested in it, the man who made the investment is entitled to charge an interest payment on the money, because, if instead of putting that money into the business he had put it into a savings bank or into certain securities, he could have a certain fixed return. Therefore they say that a proper charge against the operating expenses of a business is the interest on this money. This idea is at the root of many business failures and most service failures. Money is not worth a particular amount. As money it is not worth anything, for it will do nothing of itself. The only use of money is to buy tools to work with or the product of tools. Therefore money is worth what it will help you to produce or buy and no more. If a man thinks that his money will earn 5 per cent. or 6 per cent. he ought to place it where he can get that return, but money placed in a business is not a charge on the business—or, rather, should not be. It ceases to be money and becomes, or should become, an engine of production, and it is therefore worth what it produces—and not a fixed sum according to some scale that has no bearing upon the particular business in which the money has been placed. Any return should come after it has produced, not before.

Business men believed that you could do anything by "financing" it. If it did not go through on the first financing then the idea was to "refinance." The process of "refinancing" was simply the game of sending good money after bad.

Money is not worth a particular amount. As money it is not worth anything, for it will do nothing of itself. The only use of money is to buy tools to work with or the product of tools. Therefore money is worth what it will help you to produce or buy and no more.

In the majority of cases the need of refinancing arises from bad management, and the effect of refinancing is simply to pay the poor managers to keep up their bad management a little longer. It is merely a postponement of the day of judgment. This makeshift of refinancing is a device of speculative financiers. Their money is no good to them unless they can connect it up with a place where real work is being done, and that they cannot do unless, somehow, that place is poorly managed. Thus, the speculative financiers delude themselves that they are putting their money out to use. They are not; they are putting it out to waste.

I determined absolutely that never would I join a company in which finance came before the work or in which bankers or financiers had a part. And further that, if there

---

In the majority of cases the need of refinancing arises from bad management, and the effect of refinancing is simply to pay the poor managers to keep up their bad management a little longer.

---

were no way to get started in the kind of business that I thought could be managed in the interest of the public, then I simply would not get started at all. For my own short experience, together with what I saw going on around me, was quite enough proof that business as a mere money-making game was not worth giving much thought to and was distinctly no place for a man who wanted to accomplish anything. Also it did not seem to me to be the way to make money. I have yet to have it demonstrated that it is the way. For the only foundation of real business is service.

A manufacturer is not through with his customer when a sale is completed. He has then only started with his customer. In the case of an automobile the sale of the machine is only something in the nature of an introduction. If the machine does not give service, then it is better for the manufacturer if he never had the introduction, for he will have the worst of all advertisements—a dissatisfied customer. There was something more than a tendency in the early days of the automobile to regard the selling of a machine as the real accomplishment and that thereafter it did not matter what happened to the buyer. That is the shortsighted salesman-on-commission attitude. If a salesman is paid only for what he sells, it is not to be expected that he is going to exert any great effort on a customer out of whom no more commission is to be made. And it is right on this point that we later made the largest selling argument for the Ford. The price and the quality of the car would undoubtedly have made a market, and a large market. We went beyond that. A man who bought one of our cars was in my opinion entitled to continuous use of that car, and therefore if he had a breakdown of any kind it was our duty to see that his machine was put into shape again at the earliest possible moment. In the success of the Ford car the early provision of service was an outstanding element. Most of the expensive cars of that period were ill provided with service stations. If your car broke down you had to depend on the local repair man—when you were entitled to depend upon the manufacturer. If the local repair man were a forehanded sort of a person, keeping on hand a good stock of parts (although on many of the cars the parts were not interchangeable), the owner was lucky. But if the repair man were a shiftless person, with an inadequate knowledge of automobiles and an inordinate desire to make a good thing out of every car that came into his place for repairs, then even a slight breakdown meant weeks of laying up and a whopping big repair bill that had to be paid before the car could be taken away. The repair men were for a time the largest menace to the automobile industry. Even as late as 1910 and 1911 the owner of an automobile was regarded as essentially a rich man whose money ought to be taken away from him. We met that situation squarely and at the very beginning. We would not have our distribution blocked by stupid, greedy men.

That is getting some years ahead of the story, but it is control by finance that breaks up service because it looks to the immediate dollar. If the first consideration is to earn a certain amount of money, then, unless by some stroke of luck matters are going especially well and there is a surplus over for service so that the operating men may have a chance, future business has to be sacrificed for the dollar of to-day.

. . . the only foundation of real business is service. . . . A manufacturer is not through with his customer when a sale is completed. He has then only started with his customer.

And also I noticed a tendency among many men in business to feel that their lot was hard—they worked against a day when they might retire and live on an income—get out of the strife. Life to them was a battle to be ended as soon as possible. That was another point I could not understand, for as I reasoned, life is not a battle except with our own tendency to sag with the downpull of "getting settled." If to petrify is success, all one has to do is to humour the lazy side of the mind; but if to grow is success, then one must wake up anew every morning and keep awake all day. I saw great businesses become but the ghost of a name because someone thought they could be managed just as they were always managed, and though the management may have been most excellent in its day, its excellence consisted in its alertness to its day, and not in slavish following of its yesterdays. Life, as I see it, is not a location, but a journey. Even the man who most feels himself "settled" is not settled—he is probably sagging back. Everything is in flux, and was meant to be. Life flows. We may live at the same number of the street, but it is never the same man who lives there.

And out of the delusion that life is a battle that may be lost by a false move grows, I have noticed, a great love for regularity. Men fall into the half-alive habit. Seldom does the cobbler take up with the new-fangled way of soling shoes, and seldom does the artisan willingly take up with new methods in his trade. Habit conduces to a certain inertia, and any disturbance of it affects the mind like trouble. It will be recalled that when a study was made of shop methods, so that the workmen might be taught to produce with less useless motion and fatigue, it was most opposed by the workmen themselves. Though they suspected that it was simply a game to get more out of them, what most irked them was that it interfered with the well-worn grooves in which they had become accustomed to move. Business men go down with their businesses because they like the old way so well they cannot bring themselves to change. One sees them all about—men who do not know that yesterday is past, and who woke up this morning with their last year's ideas. It could almost be written down as a formula that when a man begins to think that he has at last found his method he had better begin a most searching examination of himself to see whether some part of his brain has not gone to sleep. There is a subtle danger in a man thinking that he is "fixed" for life. It indicates that the next jolt of the wheel of progress is going to fling him off.

There is also the great fear of being thought a fool. So many men are afraid of being considered fools. I grant that public opinion is a powerful police influence for those who need it. Perhaps it is true that the majority of men need the restraint of public opinion. Public opinion may keep a man better than he would otherwise be—if not better morally, at least better as far as his social desirability is concerned. But it is not a bad thing to be a fool for righteousness' sake. The best of it is that such fools usually live long enough to prove that they were not fools—or the work they have begun lives long enough to prove they were not foolish.

The money influence—the pressing to make a profit on an "investment"—and its consequent neglect of or skimping of work and hence of service showed itself to me in many ways. It seemed to be at the bottom of most troubles. It was the cause of low wages—for without well-directed work high wages cannot be paid. And if the whole attention is not given to the work it cannot be well directed. Most men want to be free to work; under the system in use they could not be free to work. During my first experience I was not free—I could not give full play to my ideas. Everything had to be planned to make money; the last consideration was the work. And the most curious part of it all was the insistence that it was the money and not the work that counted. It did not seem to strike any one as illogical that money should be put ahead of work—even though everyone had to admit that the profit had to come from the work. The desire seemed to be to find a short cut to money and to pass over the obvious short cut—which is through the work.

Business men go down with their businesses because they like the old way so well they cannot bring themselves to change.

Take competition; I found that competition was supposed to be a menace and that a good manager circumvented his competitors by getting a monopoly through artificial means. The idea was that there were only a certain number of people who could buy and that it was necessary to get their trade ahead of someone else. Some will remember that later many of the automobile manufacturers entered into an association under the Selden Patent just so that it might be legally possible to control the price and the output of automobiles. They had the same idea that so many trades unions have—the ridiculous notion that more profit can be had doing less work than more. The plan, I believe, is a very antiquated one. I could not see then and am still unable to see that there is not always enough for the man who does his work; time spent in fighting competition is wasted; it had better be spent in doing the work. There are always enough people ready and anxious to buy, provided you supply what they want and at the proper price—and this applies to personal services as well as to goods.

During this time of reflection I was far from idle. We were going ahead with a four-cylinder motor and the building of a pair of big racing cars. I had plenty of time, for I never left my business. I do not believe a man can ever leave his business. He ought to think of it by day and dream of it by night. It is nice to plan to do one's work in office hours, to take up the work in the morning, to drop it in the evening—and not have a care until the next morning. It is perfectly possible to do that if one is so constituted as to be willing through all of his life to accept direction, to be an employee, possibly a responsible employee, but not a director or manager of anything. A manual labourer must have a limit on his hours, otherwise he will wear himself out. If he intends to remain always a manual labourer, then he should forget about his work when the whistle blows, but if he intends to go forward and do anything, the whistle is only a signal to start thinking over the day's work in order to discover how it might be done better.

The man who has the largest capacity for work and thought is the man who is bound to succeed. I cannot pretend to say, because I do not know, whether the man who works always, who never leaves his business, who is absolutely intent upon getting ahead, and who therefore does get ahead—is happier than the man who keeps office hours, both

---

I do not believe a man can ever leave his business. He ought to think of it by day and dream of it by night.

---

for his brain and his hands. It is not necessary for any one to decide the question. A ten-horsepower engine will not pull as much as a twenty. The man who keeps brain office hours limits his horsepower. If he is satisfied to pull only the load that he has, well and good, that is his affair—but he must not complain if another who has increased his horsepower pulls more than he does. Leisure and work bring different results. If a man wants leisure and gets it—then he has no cause to complain. But he cannot have both leisure and the results of work.

Concretely, what I most realized about business in that year—and I have been learning more each year without finding it necessary to change my first conclusions—is this:

(1) That finance is given a place ahead of work and therefore tends to kill the work and destroy the fundamental of service.

(2) That thinking first of money instead of work brings on fear of failure and this fear blocks every avenue of business—it makes a man afraid of competition, of changing his methods, or of doing anything which might change his condition.

(3) That the way is clear for any one who thinks first of service—of doing the work in the best possible way.

ESTÉE LAUDER

Born Josephine Esther Mentzer in Corona, Queens, Estée Lauder created for herself an ageless legend by completely disconnecting herself from her past. In applying her personal makeover, she claimed Vienna as her birthplace, never disclosed her birth date, and concealed her Hungarian-born parents from the public. Entry into the world of cosmetics was facilitated by her uncle, a chemist who made everything from facial creams and fragrances to lice killer, embalming fluid, and freckle remover. Mentzer became briefly sidetracked when she married Joseph Lauter (note the *t*) in 1930, and they opened a luncheonette together. Before long, she returned to cosmetics, and in 1937 Esther Lauter formally became Estée Lauder, completing the transformation of herself as a product.

It was not until 1947 that the Estée Lauder company was formally founded. Lauder was abrasive, demanding, and tyrannical as she competed with Elizabeth Arden, Helena Rubinstein, and Charles Revson of Revlon in a cutthroat industry. Along the way she befriended Princess Grace of Monaco, former First Lady Nancy Reagan, the Duke and Duchess of Windsor, among others, to promote herself and her company. She was even known to stalk fanatically the royal, rich, and famous in her pursuit of elite social status.

Although obsessed with the rich and their luxuries, Lauder was a hardworking salesperson, who for years schlepped around the country by train and bus, ate in cheap cafeterias, and slept on friends' couches to save money to put back into the business. Lauder came to her sales presentations "swinging like Sugar Ray Robinson," and women were mesmerized by her performance and her physical touch when applying face creams. Lauder always preached, "Touch your customer and you're halfway there." In *What I Didn't Learn from Business Schools or Books,* she avoids offering the reader "glittering generalities" about business and cuts straight to her own unique and honest truths, sometimes militaristic, sometimes ugly, and sometimes pure beauty.

What I Didn't Learn from Business Schools or Books

Estée Lauder

The schools and the books make it all seem so cut and dried. If you do this, you get this. Well, that's wrong. Just as a mother comes to know and work with her toddler, an executive comes to know the special vagaries and unique sensibilities of her business and of her own inner voice that tells the truth—if she listens hard enough. It's a delicate business, business is, and I never yet met anyone who learned her business from a book or school, just as I never met a mother who raised a wonderful child from a book. Each business person must find a style, that voice that grows clearer and louder with each success and failure. Observing your own and your competitor's successes and failures makes your inner business voice more sure and vivid.

These were, for example, some of my own observations: "Business is slow, business is dead," said the Wall Street wizards. So how do you grow in a slow, dead market? we asked ourselves. Simple. You take a share away from someone else by coming up with a better product. Aramis. Clinique. Night Repair. *New* concepts. Better products.

We observed, very carefully, the marketing of competitors. One major advertisement thrust ran a photograph of a handsome man holding a bunch of daisies; it was Revlon's Chaz man selling men's fragrance to men. Chaz did poorly. Why? Men like to smell good, but they don't like to think of themselves as prancing around with daisies in hand. Our fragrance advertisements would have to be less ethereal, more manly.

All around, during the acquisition binges of the 1970s, we saw business firms becoming conglomerates. There was pressure to do the same. The Lauder inner voices said no, stick to what you know best and don't change it lightly. Today, the same firms are spinning off the subsidiaries because they weakened instead of strengthened the original product.

The voice grows stronger with each success, each observed failure. All one has to do is listen—and watch.

Business is a magnificent obsession. I've never been bored a day in my life, partly because as a true business addict it's never been enough to have steady work; I had to love what I was doing. Love your career or else find another. Measure your success in dollars not degrees. Respect your product.

Am I offering you glittering generalities just as the books and schools do? No. There's not much difference between businesses, and certain basics apply to every business even if the products lie at different ends of the spectrum. Soup, glue, or beauty can all be packaged in jars, tubes, and bottles and vended like any other commodity. The big difference lies in the *vendor*—you, not the items to be vended. Even excellent glues, soups, and beauty products can die in the marketplace if the vendor isn't passionate and clever. Develop your style.

Our unique style has come from years of trial and error. Truths have emerged that work for us. Let me share them with you.

LAUDERISMS

- *When you're angry, never put it in writing.* I learned that rule a long time ago. If you write it down, you can never take it back. The recipient has your furious letter to rankle him for the rest of his life. It's like carving your anger in stone. That makes implacable enemies. If you tell him face to face, eventually you'll both cool off. You can then always smooth things over, and the relationship is not lost forever.

- *You get more bees with honey.* Remember this. Even if your anger is justified, don't ever sever relationships, especially business relationships. Being pleasant even when you don't feel like it is best for business in the long run. For example, I was never comfortable pulling out of a store even if they treated us poorly. If I had a disagreement with an owner or a manager and decided to leave,

---

Business is a magnificent obsession. I've never been bored a day in my life, partly because as a true business addict it's never been enough to have steady work; I had to love what I was doing.

---

do you think that the word in the industry would have it that *I* decided to pull out? It would not. Rumors would spread that my products were inferior or not selling, even if that was not the truth. The manager would make it known that I was asked to leave. Unpleasant business. You get more bees with honey.

- *Keep your own image straight in your mind.* From the beginning, I knew I wanted to sell the top-of-the-line, finest-quality products through the best outlets rather than through drugstores and discount stores. And so we have. We don't do dungarees, we don't do tablecloths. We do the best skin products available today, the best makeup and fragrance products. If I were to sell our cosmetics at discount stores, our sales would pick up for a brief time, and then decline dramatically. We are not a budget market, and we know it. The woman who buys the best (not always the most expensive, by the way) is reassured by finding the best where she expects it to be. Our credibility would be harmed if we cheapened our image.

- *Keep an eye on the competition.* It can't hurt. This doesn't mean copying them, as I've made clear. Being interested in other people's ideas for the purpose of saying, "We can do it better," is not copying. Innovation doesn't mean inventing the wheel each time; innovation can mean a whole new way of looking at old things. We have, for example, a room set aside for competitive products. We study these products closely; it would be foolish to wear blinders.

There is always one person on top who must be the final authority. . . . at the office, the name of the game is Lauder, imperial as that may sound. Running a business is rarely a matter of group vote.

We use defensive means also. Shredders. We never keep memos. Leonard, for one, hates memos. He likes handwritten notes because he feels, as I do, that memos get copied or filed and end up, too often, in unfriendly hands. Handwritten notes are just from me to thee and generally get tossed out in the wastebasket when they've been read.

- *Divide and rule.* In the beginning, I felt that our great strength lay in the fact that I was a woman telling other women how to make themselves beautiful, as opposed to Revson telling women that he, as a man, knew what would make women desirable to men. After a while, I became convinced that strength had less to do with being a female or a male executive than with being an executive at heart. One had to be sure of herself—or at least act as if she was. An executive had to subscribe to

350

the divide and rule theory. For me, that meant that I could divide authority and responsibility among the best staff I could find; but if they didn't produce, it was time to rule. I must admit I'm not terribly democratic in my business, and neither is my son Leonard. There is always one person on top who must be the final authority. That doesn't mean I don't have friends among my staff—I certainly do. Still, at the office, the name of the game is Lauder, imperial as that may sound. Running a business is rarely a matter of group vote.

- *Learn to say no.* Along with divide and rule comes saying no. Saying yes all the time stems from a childish desire to please and be loved all the time. Executives must say no to inferior products and ideas, no to those who seem to be making a mistake. Sometimes this is difficult and even the most intractable of executives, like me, can be swayed.

  A brand-new line was ready to be born. Advisers told me that studies and polls and questionnaires had determined that Premier would be a great new name for a line of cosmetics. I hated it. Premier? That meant a "beginning" to me rather than "first," which was what my advisers had in mind. Still, everyone persuaded me in eloquent argument that Premier would, one day, be as famous as Clinique. Have you bought anything named Premier lately? Of course you haven't. The line died instantly.

- *Trust your instincts.* I've discovered that pondering "facts" and other people's judgments usually leads me down the wrong path. My first reaction is almost invariably the right one. My body, my mind, my heart, tell me yes or no, and I've learned to act on my visceral reaction. Our brains are really tiny computers that register millions of impressions, every day, and store them away for future use. When it's time to compile the impressions, we do so instinctively—and that's called common sense. Common sense, instinct—trust that part of yourself, whatever you call it.

- *Act tough.* I'm interested in the word "tough." I hear it said frequently that entrepreneurs and executives should be tough. ARE WOMEN TOUGH ENOUGH TO SUCCEED? blare headlines from a dozen magazines. Toughness, let me tell you, is not dependent on being crude or cruel. You can be feminine and tough. I love my femininity—as much as I rely on my toughness.

  What others call tough, I call persistent. If you know you're correct, you must be firm and not bow to pressure. Too often women are taught as little girls that sweetness is more valuable than persistence or stubbornness. Little boys, on the other hand, are taught to win. Persistence and being tough make for success. I can't count the number of little plaques that Ronald has given out that read, IT CAN BE DONE. I agree. Anything can be done if you're certain it's right and you stay firm.

  I have some weaknesses in the "toughness" arena. Although I deal with customers and my own staff by being feminine and assertive at the same time, I still feel bereft when someone leaves. I try to hide that side, but I can never bear to be abandoned even if I know it's because I might have been too demanding. For the most part, no one knows that. Up until now anyway. For most women, for me anyway, a half-boudoir, half-boardroom image is the image that works best, and neither is stronger than the other.

- *Acknowledge your mistakes.* We all make mistakes. What we don't all do is acknowledge them. I've always found that it's best to cut your losses rather than to stick to a sinking ship. One of my big mistakes was artificial eyelashes. I always hated them, but I jumped on the bandwagon when every other company came out with them. They always looked false, never stayed on, just weren't pretty. We withdrew from the lash market almost as soon as we entered it. Instead, I instructed my chemists to come up with a fabulous mascara. They did.

Another mistake was trying to reach the teenage market. Teen cleanser, teen this, teen that. Teens simply were not our image, even though teens can surely benefit from our products.

Act tough. . . . Toughness, . . . is not dependent on being crude or cruel. You can be feminine and tough. I love my femininity — as much as I rely on my toughness. What others call tough, I call persistent.

A mistake I did not make was involving myself in hormone hoopla. Hormones on the skin can be dangerous business. My uncle taught me that many years ago. Because they are absorbed, they can have side effects that may not show up immediately, they can drastically alter the balance of natural estrogens and progesterones, and they can stimulate the growth of facial hair. Hormones do produce a temporary swelling of the skin, which smooths out wrinkles, but the effect is not worth the risk.

You're allowed to make a mistake. Once.

- *Write things down.* Your mother probably told you this. She's right. I do have a retentive memory, but I still forget something if it's not written down somewhere. Sometimes I awake in the middle of the night to jot down an inspiration, and I can't even read my handwriting in the morning. It comes back.
- *Hire the best people.* You can be the director of the company but you can't be there to direct all the time. You have to hire surrogate bosses, responsible, thinking people who are able to move fast, take risks, and make judgments that would be similar to yours. This is vital. Hire people who think as you do and treat them well. In our business, they are top priority.

E. W. Scripps
1854 – 1926

Scripps built a media empire that included daily newspapers in 15 states, the United Press Associations, and the United Feature Syndicate, among many other enterprises. Like Hearst and Greeley, he gave his readers what they wanted, poignant subject material and editorial flair. To accomplish these goals, Scripps clearly knew the type of editors he wanted. "I get me boys, bright boys, from the classes that read my papers; I give them the editorship and the management, with a part interest in the property. . . ." In addition, he wryly said, "in a year or so, as soon as the profits begin to come in, they become conservative and I have to boot them back into their class. . . ."

Truthfully, Scripps managed his editors with loose reins, but when he did provide advice, it was generally written in stone and "as to-the-point as a police warrant." Poison pen letters were necessary because he spent very little time in the offices of his enterprises, preferring to work from his ranch outside San Diego or his yacht. One reason for this was that he was simply difficult to get along with—and he knew that. Another reason was to avoid the corruptive nature of wealth and fellow millionaires. "I'm a rich man, and that's dangerous, you know. But it isn't just the money that's the risk; it's the living around with other rich men. They get to thinking all alike, and their money not only talks, their money does their thinking too." By remaining isolated, he was able to keep his money, business, and life in the proper perspective.

Ethics were everything to Scripps, and when he left his empire to his son Robert, he also left this message: "I would prefer that you should succeed in being in all things a gentleman, according to the real meaning of the word. . . . Being a gentleman you cannot fail to devote your whole mind and energy to the service of the plain people. . . ." In *Some Outlandish Rules for Making Money* the fighter for social justice paradoxically chooses to serve Mammon over God, but it is not so cut and dry. With his own unique code of ethics, Scripps depicts how he created a productive synergy between social and business concerns.

Some Outlandish Rules
for Making Money
E. W. Scripps

In Detroit I had some experiences as a reporter that made a deep impression on my mind. I often observed there the great suffering caused the mothers, wives, sisters and daughters of the city by publication of the misdeeds of their menfolk. When I took over the Cleveland *Press*, it was with the resolve that I would always keep in view the womenfolks, and that, so far as possible in carrying out my thoroughgoing system of journalism, I would avoid making any woman cry. Everything else being equal as between any two items, or any two ways of writing an item, I would prefer the item that would not hurt women, or the way of preparing it that would hurt them least.

I recall a trying experience of this sort. A woman came to me for the suppression of a perfectly legitimate piece of news, and one that I could not consistently leave out of the paper. Her husband had been guilty of some offense, and had been arrested. She told me the other papers were going to suppress the item. She said her attorney had told her that if publicity could be prevented, the judge who was trying the case had promised great leniency. He had even held out hopes that there might be no prosecution at all. The man was very well-known, and mouth-to-mouth gossip had made the event notorious or was sure to make it so.

I told the woman that the notoriety would be increased rather than diminished by the suppression of the story by the newspapers. I added I felt I had no right to conspire with a corrupt judge and prosecuting attorney to prevent the punishment of a man who had committed a crime. I was aware that my publication of the item was going to cause a great many women to weep, and was going to make certain the conviction and punishment of the criminal. Later the lawyer came to see me. Another person brought a verbal message from the judge. Other women appeared, and there was a great flow of tears. But, the item was printed. No sooner did I see it in the forms than I took my hat and left the office and went off for a long walk into the country, pondering deeply. That evening I almost resolved to abandon journalism.

When a man is fully prepared to take any risk
or pay any penalty in order to accomplish some
one thing, it rarely occurs to him that a man
has to take any risk or pay any penalty.

But I was a willful, headstrong, and determined young man. It was not in me to conceive failure. I would have what I wanted, and would get what I wanted in the way that I wanted it. I was engaged in founding a newspaper. My whole mind and will were concentrated on this one thing. There was only one thing worth while avoiding, and that was failure. Had there been 999 chances out of 1,000 of losing my life by proceeding along the course that I had determined on, and only one chance for living and hence succeeding, I think I would not have hesitated.

I must confess something more. I believe if it had been necessary for me to break every statute of the state of Ohio in order to accomplish the end I had in view, those laws would have been in great danger of being broken. When a man is fully prepared to take any risk or pay any penalty in order to accomplish some one thing, it rarely occurs to him that a man has to take any risk or pay any penalty. In those days I was never conscious of an effort to push my paper by choosing one side or another in any political issue or any other matter of public contention. I am sure that I did not make my great effort of propaganda for the full development of labor union- ism in Cleveland for the purpose of winning the good will and patronage of working-men. I was only chuck-full of opinions and ideas that were more the result of emotional activities than of reasoning. I had a newspaper under my own control, and I just turned myself loose on the public. . . .

In my actual running of the *Press*, I reverted to my boyhood scheme; I either sat on the fence and watched the other fel- lows work, or else I took my book and went off by myself to read and dream and plan or otherwise amuse myself.

It is true that I had a determination to make the *Press* a success. Aside from that I had no particular plan. I simply lived from day to day. Sometimes I worked hard. Always I was a hard thinker. Often I did not work hard at all, or was not conscious of working hard. I quickly fell into the habit of coming to the office late and leaving early. I forever sought

---

I hold very strongly that the world owes no human being a living, that society owes nothing to any individual member of itself. Only that human being who can support himself or her- self, . . . is entitled to a place in the world at all.

---

and found excuses for leaving the office and leaving my work for others to do. I always took along books to read, went into the country, and stopped at some rural hotel. I spent a good deal of time rowing and sailing on Lake Erie. Sometimes I would leave the office for weeks together. I doubt if, after the first few months, I averaged more than two or three hours a day in my editorial room. Sometimes I wrote in my hotel room. I wrote articles in a rowboat, drifting. But even the time given to this work was infinitesimally small. I used to say I carried my business under my hat and that it was when my hat was on, whether I was riding, driving, rowing or sailing, that I could do far more effective thinking than when sitting at a table, either in my office or at a hotel.

I knew my *Poor Richard* but I didn't agree with him. This resulted in my leaving many things undone—many things that I believe were better left undone. I have found by my life's experience that the big things accomplished in life, or the really important ones, are very few indeed. Doing a few important things that are right, and are right at the right time, and doing them thoroughly, is the important thing.

It is more blessed to pay wages than to accept them. At least, it is more profitable.

I know I very seldom gave any orders to my staff on the *Press*. More often I offered advice or suggestions. Recently I saw a copy of a letter written by R. F. Paine to some young man employed in our concern in which he said that, during the more than thirty years he had been in my service, he had not received more than six orders from me.

Although I have been personally responsible for the founding or purchase of not less than forty newspapers, I doubt if I have directly given a total of five hundred orders to all the men employed on these papers. My life's work has mainly consisted in selecting a few score of men, studying each, and then offering them opportunities and inspiring them, by my talks and letters, each to develop what was best in him to the highest extent.

I hold very strongly that the world owes no human being a living, that society owes nothing to any individual member

358

of itself. Only that human being who can support himself or herself, beginning at the age of adolescence is entitled to a place in the world at all.

This is nature's law. This is the law that governs all other living beings except humanity, and in the end it inevitably must govern humanity too. The individual man who lives contrary to nature perishes. Any society of men, whether it be a community of small numbers or of national proportions, must suffer the penalty of any and every infraction of natural law.

Never do anything yourself that you can get someone else to do for you.

The individual and the social body may—each and both of them, the one for a longer time than the other—violate nature's law for some time without suffering the death penalty, but the delay, the postponement, of the penalty is only that, only a delay or postponement.

Some other maxims that I have employed in my business, and which I commend to others interested in money-making, are:

1. Never spend as much money as you earn. The smaller your expenditures are in proportion to your earnings the sooner you will become rich.
2. It is more blessed to pay wages than to accept them. At least, it is more profitable.
3. Never do anything yourself that you can get someone else to do for you. The more things that someone else does for you the more time and energy you have to do those things which no one else can do for you.
4. Never do anything today that you can put off till tomorrow. There is always so much to do today that you should not waste your time and energy in doing anything today that can be put off till tomorrow.

Most things that you do not have to do today are not worth doing at all.

5. Always buy, never sell. If you've got enough horse sense to become rich you know that it is better to run only one risk than two risks. You also know that just as likely as not the other fellow is smarter than you are and that whether you buy or sell, in each case you run the risk of getting the worst of the bargain. By adopting my rule you will diminish by one-half your chances of loss.

6. Never do anything, if you can help it, that someone else is doing. Why compete with one person or many other persons in any occupation or line of business so long as it is possible for you to have a monopoly in some other field?

7. If circumstances compel you to pursue some occupation or to follow some line of business which is being pursued by some other person, then you do your work in some other way than that in which it is done by the other. There is always a good, better and best way. If you take the best way then the other fellow has no chance of competing with you.

8. Whatever you do once, whatever way you undertake to do a thing, don't do the same thing again or don't do the thing in the same way. If you know one way to do a thing you must know there is a better way to do the same thing.

9. If you're succeeding in anything you are doing, don't let anyone else know of your success, because if you do some other person will try to do the same thing and be your competitor.

10. When you become rich, as you will become rich if you follow my advice, don't let anyone know it. General knowledge of your wealth will only attract the taxgatherer, and other hungry people will try to get away from you something they want and something you want to keep.

11. One of the greatest assets any man can secure is a reputation for eccentricity. If you have a reputation of this kind you can do a lot of things. You can even do the things you want to do without attaching to yourself the enmity of others. Many an act which, if performed by an ordinary person, would arouse indignation, animosity and antagonism, can be performed by a man with a reputation for eccentricity

---

When you find many people applauding you for what you do, and a few condemning, you can be certain that you are on the wrong course because you're doing the things that fools approve of.

---

with no other result than that of exciting mirth and perhaps pity. It is better to have the good will than the bad will, even of a dog.

12. Never hate anybody. Hatred is a useless expenditure of mental and nervous energy. Revenge costs much of energy and gains nothing.

13. When you find many people applauding you for what you do, and a few condemning, you can be certain that you are on the wrong course because you're doing the things that fools approve of. When the crowd ridicules and scorns you, you can at least know one thing, that it is at least possible that you are acting wisely. It is one of the instincts of men to covet applause. The wise man regulates his conduct rather by reason than by instinct.

14. It is far more important to learn what not to do than what to do. You can learn this invaluable lesson in two ways, the first of which and most inspired is by your own mistakes. The second is by observing the mistakes of others. Any man that learns all the things

that he ought not to do cannot help doing the things he ought to do.

15. Posterity can never do anything for you. Therefore, you should invest nothing in posterity. Of course your heirs will quarrel over your estate, but that will be after you're dead and why should you trouble your mind over things which you will never know anything about?

16. A man can do anything he wants to do in this world, at least if he wants to do it badly enough. Therefore, I say that any of you who want to become rich can become rich if you live long enough.

17. After what I have said it goes without further saying that you should save money. But no man can save himself rich. He can only make himself rich. Savings are capital. It is only by doing things that one learns how to do things. It is only the capitalist who handles capital that learns how to handle capital profitably. The more capital you have the more skillful you become as a capitalist.

18. Fools say that money makes money. I say that money does not make money. It is only men who make money.

19. There are two cardinal sins in the economic world: one is giving something for nothing, and the other is getting something for nothing. And the greater sin of these is getting something for nothing, or trying to do so. I really doubt if anyone ever does get something for nothing.

   (Don't marry a rich wife. Women are what they are. At best they are hard enough to get along with. They are always trying to make a man do something that he doesn't want to do, and generally succeeding. When a woman is conscious of the fact that she has furnished all or any part of your capital, her influence over you will be so great as to be the worst handicap you can carry.)

20. If you're a prospective heir of your father or some other relative, you should also consider that a handicap. I would advise you to refuse to be an heir.

21. Despise not the day of small things, but rather respect the small things. It is far easier to make a profit on a very small capital invested in any business than it is to make the same proportion of profit off of a large capital. It is true that after you have learned how to make a profit on a business that shows small capital, successively, as your capital grows, you learn how to handle

---

The hardest labor of all labor performed by man is that of thinking.

---

it profitably. Then the time will come when the greater your capital becomes in this way the greater your proportion of profits on it should be. And, for an added reason, as your wealth and skill grow rapidly, your so-called necessary expenses grow much more slowly and in time cease to grow at all, so that beyond a certain limit all your income and added income becomes a surplus, constantly to be added to your capital.

22. It is far easier to make money than to spend it. As it becomes more and more difficult to spend money, you will spend less and less of it, and hence there will be more money to accumulate.

23. The hardest labor of all labor performed by man is that of thinking. If you have become rich, train your mind to hard thinking and hold it well in leash so that your thinking will all be with but one object in view, that of accumulating more wealth.

It is true that a man cannot serve both God and Mammon. If your only sin is to obtain wealth then you should devote all of your service to Mammon.

IGOR I. SIKORSKY
1889 – 1972

The Russian-born Sikorsky, a brilliant inventor and aircraft manufacturer, inherited an inquisitive nature from his father, who had a tendency to lecture to his young son about electricity, astronomy, and physics, rather than play ball. In 1903 Sikorsky entered Russia's Naval Academy, where he studied engineering and first dreamed of flying machines. This fantasy turned into reality in 1909, when according to Sikorsky, "not yet twenty years old, with a few ideas, no experience, some caution and, of course, with plenty of enthusiasm, I started the construction of my first flying machine." The result was a helicopter with a wooden frame and a 25-horsepower motor, which he successfully flew on his own. Soon he began designing airplanes for Russia, including bombers used in World War I. He did most of his own test flying. However, a more dramatic flight was necessary at the end of the war when he emigrated to the United States to escape the restrictive atmosphere of the Bolshevik revolution.

Sikorsky was unable to find work with a U.S. aeronautics firm and was forced to find solace in teaching the subject. It wasn't long before "the restlessness created by the magic supervisors called 'competition-ambition' " drove him to create the Sikorsky Aero Engineering Corporation in 1923. Later he would build airplanes for the U.S. war effort in World War II. Between his contributions to war machines and witnessing of events like the Bolshevik revolution, Sikorsky began to seriously question his role in the material progress of humanity. But he concluded, "The adventures of Tarzan look grand on screen, but, as a reality, such a life would quickly become quite intolerable." In other words, he understood that progress was desired and that the bad had to be taken with the good. Sikorsky's introspective nature is evident in *A Mysterious Faculty,* in which he grapples with a definition for intuition, or thinking outside of the box, and its relationship with success.

A Mysterious Faculty
Igor I. Sikorsky

Successful pioneering in art, science, engineering and in other branches of human activity usually includes one or both of the following factors: discovery and creation; the latter, in the technical field, may be called invention. As an example of the first we may mention the discovery of America by Columbus, or similar cases where the object or law existed in the material universe, but became known or explained to mankind as a result of the work of some individual. By creation, we may mean such work as a painting by Raphael or a Rachmaninoff symphony, or the steamship of Robert Fulton. According to extreme materialistic conceptions, such discoveries or creations may merely be the result of a cut and try process, repeated a sufficient number of times. The argument is familiar. . . .

Intuition appears to be some ability which permits an inventor, in a way not yet explained and possibly inexplainable, to "tune in" like a radio, and to learn, somehow, some facts or laws that are not yet known, or imagine and create a mechanism or part in correct accord with natural laws not yet discovered at the time of the invention. It may be said, therefore, that the work of a pioneer in science or technique often consists of finding a correct solution, or creating a working mechanism, based on laws that are not yet discovered.

I do not pretend to explain the nature of the process of intuitive discovery, but I can give a few examples of how it works. It may be in the form of a fact or information held in the memory for which there is no data or known foundation, but supported by a firm conviction that it is true. With reference to myself, I always had a belief, even as a small boy, that I would sometime build and fly large flying machines. Consciously, I did not pay much attention to this idea because for many years I considered it simply impossible, but subconsciously the conviction was always there. Intuition works even when one does not recognize it as such. In other cases, it works with a surprising speed and brilliance, when, in a moment, a solution of a difficult and complicated problem comes in with remarkable clarity, and so convincingly that no doubts are left as to its correctness. Quite often it is possible to select one out of a dozen sketches of proposed solutions and state positively that one is the best, when it is still not yet possible to say why. The reverse also happens once in a while, and it is possible to predict that certain solutions will not be satisfactory even when they appear to be correctly designed and calculated. . . .

Intuition works even when one does not recognize it as such.

The phenomenon of discovery of unknown facts by intuition, however, appears to be a reality, and while the background and the true nature of it can not be properly understood and explained, yet my personal feeling is that intuition represents not an overdevelopment of some of the existing faculties of apprehension and understanding, but rather an extremely primitive and barely noticeable beginning of a new faculty of a higher order, just as radio communication is not an improved or overdeveloped pony express, but is a totally new phenomena based on natural forces of a superior order. Intuition, if and when developed, would be superior to eyesight in a way in which this latter is superior to touching or smelling. As it is in the case of some other abilities, the new faculty is very differently pronounced in various individuals. It can be expanded and developed by training.

The idea of the connection between the intuitive abilities and the element of the fourth dimension can well be considered speculative and arbitrary. But every successful invention and discovery usually represents a work for the future; it is in fact the creation of the future. When Thomas Edison planned to flood this country with electric light, or when Henry Ford was contemplating putting it on wheels, they both succeeded because they were able to foresee correctly the future with its requirements and to arrange and direct their efforts accordingly.

VICTOR KIAM
1926 –

Kiam joined Lever Brothers as a management trainee after he graduated from Harvard Business School in 1951. For four years he found himself selling cosmetics to backcountry pharmacists, who had a habit of concocting cold medicines in their basements that "had the kick of low grade bourbon." He joined Playtex in 1955, and finding undergarments more interesting than dubious pharmacists, Kiam remained with the company long enough to become executive vice president. But then in 1968 he attended a conference that included a panel discussion on entrepreneurship. Kiam was so enthralled with the speakers that he quit Playtex that same year to pursue his own interests.

Kiam defines entrepreneurs as being people "who understand there is little difference between obstacle and opportunity, and are able to turn both to their advantage." He met both his biggest obstacle and greatest opportunity when he bought down-and-out Remington in 1978. Everyone who watched television back then must certainly remember his face and slogan, which was "I liked it so much [the electric shaver], I bought the company." As Kiam developed his entrepreneurial and management skills, he recognized that, "I couldn't always outthink or outplan my competitors. Who can? But I could sure as hell outwork them." However, making the commitment to being an entrepreneur requires more sacrifices than just time and sweat. Kiam warns that you must be prepared to accept a much lighter wallet in the beginning, and to lose friends, lovers, and even spouses. There is an upside, too, somewhere. For Kiam, it was his purchase of the New England Patriots in 1988.

Many critical factors contribute to the success of an entrepreneur, from product quality to customer service, but one of the most difficult to gauge is the entrepreneur himself. Who evaluates the entrepreneur's performance? The financial status of the company certainly says something. Kiam, however, prefers to use a different kind of balance sheet to evaluate his own performance, which he presents in A Useful Tool of Self-Examination.

A Useful Tool of Self-Examination
Victor Kiam

There is one element of accounting that I have found to be a useful tool of self-examination: the balance sheet. A balance sheet is a record, at some point in time, of the assets and liabilities of a company. At the Harvard Business School, we would study the balance sheets of various companies and try to determine their value. We also worked on profit and loss statements. A P&L is a company's scorecard. It reflects how the enterprise has utilized its assets and liabilities, and is tallied to cover the results of a specific period of time.

During the time corporations were sending representatives to Harvard to interview students as prospective employees, I wondered what I had to offer any of these companies. I decided to use a variation of the balance sheet to make an assessment of myself. I already had my P&L; that was represented by my grades. The balance sheet required some work.

I didn't bother to do a financial statement on myself; that would have been a disaster. Whenever a corporation draws up a balance sheet it can leave open a line for goodwill. This represents an intangible value. It could mean the value of a trademark or the company name. It could also be the difference between what a company has paid for an item and its net asset value. Since my financial worth was almost zero, I figured I had better measure my goodwill. But besides my assets, I also wanted to get a handle on my bad will, my intangible liabilities.

Taking out a notebook, I drew a line down the middle of a page. On one side I listed my pluses, everything that I thought a company would find attractive. Being single with freedom to travel, having a second language (French), and possessing a sound business-school background were among them. I also listed some personality characteristics that would not necessarily be a part of my business profile. I was the sort of chap who people took strong positions on. They either loved me or hated me. I wasn't sure if that was an asset or a liability, so I listed it in both columns. I had a slew of liabilities. I was shy. I was too disorganized. There were many others, but one stands out as the worst of the lot: I procrastinated. Given four days to complete a project at the Harvard Business School, I would wait until the third day to start it and then work like a bloody tiger to get it in on time. For example, we were required to have our weekly papers into the mailbox by nine o'clock Saturday night. Most of the time I would get it in just as the proctor was about to lock the box.

Confronting this negative attribute in black and white eventually helped me to overcome it. *I started making it a point to tackle distasteful jobs first.* I hate trivial details; I'm an activist, and nothing drives me crazier than having to go over and approve someone's expense report. But I have to do it in order to maintain a budget. Whenever that task was called for, it became the first thing I did. I would much rather have been studying orders or calling accounts, but I got the more loathsome expense reports out of the way before turning my attention to those things I enjoyed doing. That became my reward for doing a tiresome chore. In a short time, procrastination disappeared from my list of liabilities. Grappling with my other shortcomings in a like manner, I was able to at least get them under control.

I still continue to do a personal balance sheet, revising it every six months, and keeping track of my progress. It has become a private confessional. Since I am the only one who will ever see it, I can be painfully honest. Facing my negatives, I begin to get a more positive sense of myself. I realize that there is nothing on this list I can't overcome if I am just willing to make the effort.

Now it's your turn. Do a balance sheet of your own, and then find ways to turn your minuses into pluses. In the entrepreneurial game, that balance sheet is going to reflect your batting average. An upswing in assets should generate enthusiasm for further improvement. If the liabilities have crept ahead, you'll be able to identify these areas of chronic weakness and take the necessary steps to keep them in check.

This first chapter has served as something of a balance sheet. You should now have a pretty good idea whether or not you have what it takes to play the game. I hope I didn't dissuade you; that was not my intention. I just didn't want you to leap into the batter's box without knowing what to expect. Now that you've been told, I would be remiss if I didn't mention some of the rewards you'll receive for the sacrifices you've been asked to make.

You're going to find satisfaction in creating something out of nothing. You will gain a positive sense of self, derived from tackling a job others shy away from. A spotlight, powered by the respect of your peers and bosses, will seek you out. Of course, don't forget there are also financial rewards. In 1951 I joined Lever Brothers as a management trainee. Seventeen years later, barely past my fortieth birthday, I bought a piece of the Benrus Corporation. It didn't take long. Successful entrepreneurs are unique individuals. They are as prized as rare art. Once you've made your reputation, you're going to find it's a seller's market and you've got the goods.

It's not an easy life. Nothing worthwhile is ever easy. If David had slain a dwarf instead of a giant, who would have cared? Who would remember?

TOM MONAGHAN
1937 –

Monaghan, America's richest pizza maker, was placed in a Catholic orphanage as a child, and later attended the seminary with plans of becoming a priest. He was kicked out, however, and subsequently joined the Marines. After his discharge, he opened a pizza store in 1960 with $500, and his brother as a partner. The location was Ypsilanti, Michigan; the name was Domi Nick's Pizza. After several tough months, his brother quit the business, but for Monaghan making pizza was an obsession. It was also an art, from the feel of the dough to the cheesing technique. As he improved his artistic skills, his goal was 100 percent efficiency in the physical motion of making his masterpieces.

In 1965 Domi Nick's became Domino's, and 20 years later Monaghan was operating or had franchised 2,600 locations. With the introduction of home delivery guaranteed within 30 minutes from time of order, management of the stores had to be as simplified and efficient as the pizza making itself. Monaghan preached teamwork, and always looked to promote people who "have pizza sauce in their veins." In addition, as the number of franchises mushroomed, he was very careful in evaluating not only the pizza knowledge, but also the business character of those who applied for franchises, because he believed "winning in business is nothing unless you do it strictly by the rules."

Monaghan readily admits he has a pious side, dating from his youth, but he also admits to having a colorful alter ego with P. T. Barnum as one of his idols. Over the years he has initiated his own share of promotional stunts, some crazier than others. When it comes to generating ideas, from ad campaigns to strategic plans, Monaghan is famous for filling one yellow legal pad after another with extensive lists. He has literally boxed and stored thousands of note pads over the years, and has been confronted with the melancholy prospect of having to dispose of his archive of ideas. In *Goal Setting and Brainstorming* Monaghan analyzes the thinking process behind his compulsive note taking and describes how it reflects his own management style.

Goal Setting and Brainstorming
Tom Monaghan

I have no lofty theories about management. I take what Peter Drucker would call an empirical approach, and my only argument in its favor is to point to the results it has achieved in Domino's. But I believe my style would work just as well in any kind of corporation. The basic building block of management, for me, is goal setting. You must have a goal in order to know what direction to take. Whether you're managing a company, your own career, or a household, if you decide to just go through the motions and wait for something to turn up, you'll find your toes do it first.

Writing is the key to my system of goal setting; but goal setting sounds too ordinary to describe what I have in mind. What I'm doing is building exciting dreams. The goals must be exciting or people won't be motivated to strive for them. I carry a yellow legal pad with me everywhere I go. All my thoughts, my plans, my dreams, my analyses of problems— everything that comes into my mind, sometimes even a shopping list—are written down in my current pad. When that one is full, I start another; I sometimes have several pads going at once for different kinds of thoughts. I learned this method from my old friend Chuck Parsons, an Ann Arbor–based marketing consultant. Over the last twenty years I accumulated dozens of packing boxes full of these pads—I finally threw them away because they were taking up too much room, and I never look at them again once I'm finished writing, anyhow. The reason is that it's the process of writing that's important to me. It's the thinking that goes into writing, not the words that wind up on the paper, that makes the difference.

I set long-range goals, annual goals, monthly, weekly, and daily goals. The daily goals take the form of to-do lists. The long-range goals are dream sheets. But the other lists are specific and action-oriented. My goal list for 1980, for example, began with this entry: "500 units." To me, that meant we would have a total of 500 stores by the end of the year. This was a high goal at that point in our development, but it was attainable. The important thing about this goal, though, is that it was *specific*, it wasn't just "let's increase the number of units this year." It was *500 or bust!* If a goal is specific, it is easy to communicate it to others. This is important, because when you are dealing with a corporate goal, you have to *sell* it to the people who can help you achieve it: They have to understand exactly what the goal is, they must believe it can be done, and they must be convinced that it can be done by *them*.

Another important aspect of my goal setting is the time limit. A task is to be done by the end of the year, not just "in the near future." In 1979, my list for the coming year went on for four pages, 150 items, and covered not only business goals but physical goals—I wanted to get my weight down to 156 pounds, do 200 pushups in one session every other day, get my body fat and cholesterol level down, and finish a marathon. There also were personal items, including purchase of a third car and having a meeting with Ray Kroc. Most of these goals were achieved. I fell a bit short on some, including the big one: We didn't open our five hundredth store until the following year. But falling a bit short made me fight all the harder to attain that number.

When I talk of communicating my goal to other people and selling them on it—making them believe in their own ability to achieve—I'm not talking about hype. The process of building belief works on a strictly personal goal, too: when you tell someone else what your goal is, it gives you reinforcement, added incentive to accomplish it. I discovered this in 1962, when I quit smoking. I told everybody I knew, "This is it. I have smoked my last cigarette." That helped give me the strength to follow through. If you believe you're going to do something, and tell everybody else you're going to do it, their belief will be a backstop for yours.

Books have been important in development of my own style of management. I've selected useful techniques from a lot of them. But I emphasize *selected* because I find many things in books about management that would be poison for Domino's. The best book I've found on management philosophy was *In Search of Excellence* by Thomas J. Peters and Robert H. Waterman. But I didn't really learn much that was new to me from it. That book simply confirmed everything I instinctively believed. I was already living its precepts. I found as I was reading it that I knew the sense of what it was going to say next even before I read the words.

For example, *In Search of Excellence* talks about how companies need to have a "bias for action." I'm an action guy. I've always believed that the best plan is something you came up with through trying and failing. Failure shows you how to do something right. You can try, fail, and try again while someone else is still reading textbooks to try and learn how to do something, probably less effectively than if he'd bumped his nose on failure a few times. Failure strengthens you because it teaches you to look for the seed of benefit that every adversity contains. I believe my greatest strength is the ability I've developed to turn adversity into advantage. Every time I suffer a setback, I find myself thinking instinctively, How can I capitalize on this?

Excellent companies stay "close to the customer," according to Peters and Waterman. As far as I'm concerned, everything in Domino's begins with the customer. I learned this rule by making at least a million pizzas and delivering a lot of them. The customer is boss.

Getting "productivity through people" is another major point of *In Search of Excellence,* and it has always been one of my operating principles. I realized right at the beginning that I had to do things through other people, and I always tried to hire people who were smarter than I was. There've been some who've been paid higher salaries than I took, too. But that's always been fine with me if it helped Domino's move forward.

The book's identification and reinforcement of these and other management principles was helpful. I was delighted when Don Vlcek gave his entire staff a day off to read *In Search of Excellence*, because it echoes everything I've been preaching in Domino's.

There are some personal approaches in management that I don't think I could have learned from a book. My method of making decisions is one of them. I don't know that it would work for anyone else. But here, for whatever it's worth, is how I do it:

I sometimes compare my brainstorming on paper to the drilling of oil wells. The only way to strike oil is to drill a lot of wells.

I reach decisions by making lists on my yellow legal pads. Down one side of a page, I'll write all the reasons I can think of in favor of a given course of action. On the other side, I list every reason I can think of against it. Thinking of arguments for and against a decision is where my ability to dream comes in handy: I *imagine* the decision has been made. I see in my mind's eye how it affects people and the way they react. If it's a complicated issue, with many reasons for it and a lot of others against, I will break each point down into sub-lists and assign them a kind of point value so I can weigh them against each other.

Sometimes, as I learned from my experience with the proposal that we change our name to Pizza Dispatch, it's good to consider future situations, too. In that case, my list of the benefits of the name Pizza Dispatch were outweighed by the drawbacks of giving up Domino's. But I concentrated on the immediate situation. I didn't ask myself, Okay, five years from now, when we have more than two thousand stores and are in every state in the Union, what will the pros and cons be then? Had I done so, I would have made a better decision.

I also make lists as a way of brainstorming ideas with myself on paper. This is a written version of what I love to do verbally on the occasions when I can get on the same wavelength with another person. Doing it verbally is more fun because it's exciting to share the exploration of ideas. But the written approach is absorbing, too, and it can be extremely fruitful.

At the outset I'm often unable to see a good idea because there's a clutter of other things hiding it. There are roads through the clutter, though, and I have to go down them until I find the one that will take me up mentally above the clutter, to a point where I can see a good idea on the horizon. The roads are propositions that I think up, write down on my list, and follow one by one. A proposition might be stupid or obvious, but I take it anyway because I don't know where it will lead and what it might connect with. I say to myself, Why don't we do this? Well, I see that if we did that, it would allow us to do something else, and I just keep adding to it. If I don't go down those roads, I never get to the good idea, because there's a link, and I find the link by following something that may not work or is impossible.

I sometimes compare my brainstorming on paper to the drilling of oil wells. The only way to strike oil is to drill a lot of wells. My lists are wells, and every once in a while I hit a gusher. I'm working away, making lists, and all of a sudden something pops right out. I'll say, Hey, look at that!

Lots of times I'll be writing lists of things I want to do this year or next year, which I do just for the fun of it, and I'll find one item I want to think about some more. So I'll take a separate page, or sometimes even another pad, and start making lists of ideas about that particular thing. I expand on it, and who knows, maybe I'll find other things in *that* list that I want to expand on. It's like fishing. I never know what kind of idea I might catch.

Barnum wrote in his autobiography that his grandfather "would go farther, wait longer, work harder and contrive deeper, to carry out a practical joke, than for anything else under heaven." The older man was obviously a great influence on the young Barnum, who was known to fabricate and exaggerate just a little on his way to becoming America's greatest showman (and a multimillionaire to boot). Growing up on a farm in Connecticut, Barnum soon discovered handwork was not to his liking; he much preferred headwork and "laying plans for money-making." He found employment with the local merchants, where he learned the art of trading goods. Eventually he became proprietor of his own shop in New York City, and it was there that he realized his first opportunity as a showman.

Joice Heth, a black slave reputed to be 161 years old and to have been George Washington's nurse, was on display in Philadelphia. Barnum heard of her and was convinced she would be a hit in New York, so in 1835, he bought her for $1,000. She was indeed a success. But it was with the dwarf Tom Thumb, a bearded lady, and other "wonderful human curiosities," who could be viewed in his newly founded New York City museum, that Barnum made a name for himself in the 1840s. The coup de grâce was the Barnum circus that he formed in 1871, and billed as "The Greatest Show on Earth." Barnum just wanted to entertain an America he thought worked too hard and laughed too little.

Ironically, this showman who exploited human deformities also spent a great deal of energy contending with social issues of the time, such as fighting slavery and church corruption, and supporting women's rights and temperance. His integrity is clearly reflected in *The Art of Money-Getting,* a speech he delivered on more than 200 occasions. Barnum dedicates the first half of his speech to personal economy, moral principles, and the importance of physical health. In the second half, which is excerpted in the following selection, he presents 20 fundamental points for not only making money, but also for the more difficult task of keeping it.

The Art of Money-Getting
P. T. Barnum

Don't mistake your vocation. The safest plan, and the one most sure of success for the young man starting in life, is to select the vocation which is most congenial to his tastes. Parents and guardians are often quite too negligent in regard to this. It is very common for a father to say, for example: "I have five boys. I will make Billy a clergy-man; John a lawyer; Tom a doctor, and Dick a farmer." He then goes into town and looks about to see what he will do with Sammy.

He returns home and say, "Sammy, I see watch-making is a nice, genteel business; I think I will make you a gold-smith." He does this regardless of Sam's natural inclinations, or genius.

We are all, no doubt, born for a wise purpose. There is as much diversity in our brains as in our countenances. Some are born natural mechanics, while some have great aversion to machinery. Let a dozen boys of ten years get together and you will soon observe two or three are "whittling" out some ingenious device; working with locks or complicated machinery. When they were but five years old, their father could find no toy to please them like a puzzle. They are natural mechanics; but the other eight or nine boys have different aptitudes. I belong to the latter class; I never had the slightest love for

379

mechanism; on the contrary, I have a sort of abhorrence for complicated machinery. I never had ingenuity enough to whittle a cider tap so it would not leak. I never could make a pen that I could write with, or understand the principle of a steam engine. If a man was to take such a boy as I was and attempt to make a watchmaker of him, the boy might, after an apprenticeship of five or seven years, be able to take apart and put together a watch; but all through life he would be working uphill and seizing every excuse for leaving his work and idling away his time. Watch-making is repulsive to him. . . .

SELECT THE RIGHT LOCATION.

. . . When I was in London in 1858, I was passing down Holborn with an English friend and came to the "penny shows." They had immense cartoons outside, portraying the wonderful curiosities to be seen "all for a penny." Being a little in the "show line" myself, I said, "Let us go in here." We soon found ourselves in the presence of the illustrious showman, and he proved to be the sharpest man in that line I had ever met. He told us some extraordinary stories in reference to his bearded ladies, his albinos, and his armadillos, which we could hardly believe, but thought it "better to believe it than look after the proof." He finally begged to call our attention to some wax statuary, and showed us a lot of the dirtiest and filthiest wax figures imaginable. They looked as if they had not seen water since the Deluge.

"What is there so wonderful about your statuary?" I asked.

"I beg you not to speak so satirically," he replied. "Sir, these are not Madam Tussaud's wax figures, all covered with gilt and tinsel and imitation diamonds, and copies from engravings and photographs. Mine, sir, were taken from life. Whenever you look upon one of those figures, you may consider that you are looking upon the living individual."

Glancing casually at them, I saw one labelled "Henry VIII" and feeling a little curious upon seeing that it looked like Calvin Edson, the living skeleton, I said:

"Do you call that 'Henry the Eighth'?"

He replied, "Certainly, sir; it was taken from life at Hampton Court by special order of His Majesty, on such a day."

He would have given the hour of the day if I had insisted. I said, "Everybody knows that Henry VIII was a great, stout old king, and that figure is lean and lank. What do you say to that?"

"Why," he replied, "you would be lean and lank yourself, if you sat there as long as he has."

There was no resisting such arguments. I said to my English friend, "Let us go out; do not tell him who I am; I show the white feather; he beats me."

He followed us to the door, and seeing the rabble in the street he called out, "Ladies and gentlemen, I beg to draw your attention to the respectable character of my visitors," pointing to us as we walked away. I called upon him a couple of days afterward; told him who I was, and said:

"My friend, you are an excellent showman, but you have selected a bad location."

He replied, "That is true, sir; I feel that all my talents are thrown away; but what can I do?"

"You can go to America," I replied. "You can give full play to your faculties over there; you will find plenty of elbow room in America; I will engage you for two years; after that you will be able to go on your own account."

He accepted my offer and remained two years in my New York Museum. He then went to New Orleans and carried on a travelling show business during the summer. To-day he is worth sixty thousand dollars, simply because he selected the right vocation and also secured the proper location. The old proverb says, "Three removes are as bad as a fire," but when a man is in the fire, it matters but little how soon or how often he removes.

AVOID DEBT.

Young men starting in life should avoid running into debt. There is scarcely anything that drags a person down like debt. It is a slavish position to get in, yet we find many a young man hardly out of his "teens" running in debt. He meets a chum and says, "Look at this; I have got trusted for a new suit of clothes." He seems to look upon the clothes as so much given to him. Well, it frequently is so, but, if he succeeds in paying and then gets trusted again, he is adopting a habit which will keep him in poverty through life. Debt robs a man of his self-respect, and makes him almost despise himself. Grunting and groaning and working for what he has eaten up or worn out, and now when he is called upon to pay up, he has nothing to show for his money: this is properly termed "working for a dead horse." I do not speak of merchants buying and selling on credit, or of those who buy on credit in order to turn the purchase to a profit. The old Quaker said to his farmer son, "John, never get trusted; but if thee gets trusted for anything, let it be for manure, because that will help thee pay it back again."

But let money work for you, and you have the most devoted servant in the world.... There is nothing animate or inanimate that will work so faithfully as money when placed at interest, well secured. It works night and day, and in wet or dry weather.

Mr. Beecher advised young men to get in debt if they could to a small amount in the purchase of land in the country districts. "If a young man," he says, "will only get in debt for some land and then get married, these two things will

382

keep him straight, or nothing will." This may be safe to a limited extent, but getting in debt for what you eat and drink
and wear is to be avoided. Some families have a foolish habit
of getting credit at the stores, and thus frequently purchase
many things which might have been dispensed with.

It is all very well to say, "I have got trusted for sixty days,
and if I don't have the money, the creditor will think nothing
about it." There is no class of people in the world who have
such good memories as creditors. When the sixty days run
out, you will have to pay. If you do not pay, you will break
your promise and probably resort to a falsehood. You may
make some excuse or get in debt elsewhere to pay it, but that
only involves you the deeper. . . .

Money is in some respects like fire—it is a very excellent
servant but a terrible master. When you have it mastering
you, when interest is constantly piling up against you, it will
keep you down in the worst kind of slavery. But let money
work for you, and you have the most devoted servant in the
world. It is no "eye-servant." There is nothing animate or
inanimate that will work so faithfully as money when placed
at interest, well secured. It works night and day, and in wet
or dry weather.

I was born in the blue-law State of Connecticut, where
the old Puritans had laws so rigid that it was said they fined
a man for kissing his wife on Sunday. Yet these rich old Puritans would have thousands of dollars at interest, and on Saturday night would be worth a certain amount; on Sunday
they would go to church and perform all the duties of a
Christian. On waking up on Monday morning, they would
find themselves considerably richer than the Saturday night
previous, simply because their money placed at interest had
worked faithfully for them all Sunday, according to law!

Do not let it work against you; if you do, there is no
chance for success in life so far as money is concerned. John
Randolph, the eccentric Virginian, once exclaimed in Congress, "Mr. Speaker, I have discovered the philosopher's

stone: pay as you go." This is indeed nearer to the philosopher's stone than any alchemist has ever yet arrived.

PERSEVERE.

When a man is in the right path, he must persevere. I speak of this because there are some persons who are "born tired"; naturally lazy and possessing no self-reliance and no perseverance. . . .

It is this go-aheaditiveness, this determination not to let the "horrors" or the "blues" take possession of you, so as to make you relax your energies in the struggle for independence, which you must cultivate.

How many have almost reached the goal of their ambition, but losing faith in themselves have relaxed their energies, and the golden prize has been lost forever. . . .

Take two generals; both understand military tactics, both educated at West Point, if you please, both equally gifted; yet one, having this principle of perseverance, and the other lacking it, the former will succeed in his profession, while the latter will fail. One may hear the cry, "The enemy are coming, and they have got cannon!"

"Got cannon?" says the hesitating general.

"Yes."

"Then halt every man."

He wants time to reflect, his hesitation is his ruin. The enemy passes unmolested, or overwhelms him. The general of pluck, perseverance, and self-reliance goes into battle with a will, and amid the clash of arms, the booming of cannon, and the shrieks of the wounded and dying, you will see this man persevering, going on, cursing and slashing his way through with unwavering determination, and if you are near enough, you will hear him shout, "I will fight it out on this line if it takes all summer."

WHATEVER YOU DO, DO WITH ALL YOUR MIGHT.

Work at it, if necessary, early and late, in season and out of season, not leaving a stone unturned, and never deferring for a single hour that which can be done just as well *now*. The old proverb is full of truth and meaning, "Whatever is worth doing at all, is worth doing well." Many a man acquires a fortune by doing his business thoroughly, while his neighbor remains poor for life because he only half does it. Ambition, energy, industry, perseverance, are indispensable requisites for success in business.

Fortune always favors the brave, and never helps a man who does not help himself. It won't do to spend your time like Mr. Micawber, in waiting for something to "turn up." To such men one of two things usually "turns up": the poor-house or the jail; for idleness breeds bad habits, and clothes a man in rags. The poor spendthrift vagabond said to a rich man:

"I have discovered there is money enough in the world for all of us, if it was equally divided; this must be done, and we shall all be happy together."

"But," was the response, "if everybody was like you, it would be spent in two months, and what would you do then?"

"Oh! divide again; keep dividing, of course!"

I was recently reading in a London paper an account of a like philosophic pauper who was kicked out of a cheap boardinghouse because he could not pay his bill, but he had a roll of papers sticking out of his coat pocket, which, upon examination, proved to be his plan for paying off the national debt of England without the aid of a penny. People have got to do as Cromwell said: "not only trust in Providence, but keep the powder dry." Do your part of the work, or you cannot succeed. Mahomet, one night, while encamping in the desert, overheard one of his fatigued followers remark: "I will loose my camel, and trust it to God." "No, no, not so," said the prophet, "tie thy camel, and trust it to God!" Do all you can for yourselves, and then trust in

Providence, or luck, or whatever you please to call it, for the rest.

DEPEND UPON YOUR OWN PERSONAL EXERTIONS.

. . . I hold that every man should, like Cuvier, the French naturalist, thoroughly know his business. So proficient was he in the study of natural history, that you might bring to him the bone or even a section of a bone of an animal which he had never seen described, and reasoning from analogy, he would be able to draw a picture of the object from which the bone had been taken. On one occasion his students attempted to deceive him. They rolled one of their number in a cow skin and put him under the Professor's table as a new specimen. When the philosopher came into the room, some of the students asked him what animal it was. Suddenly the animal said, "I am the devil and I am going to eat you." It was but natural that Cuvier should desire to classify this creature, and examining it intently, he said,

"Divided hoof; graminivorous; it cannot be done!"

There is no such thing in the world as luck. There never was a man who could go out in the morning and find a purse of gold in the street to-day, and another to-morrow, and so on, day after day.

He knew that an animal with a split hoof must live upon grass and grain, or other kind of vegetation, and would not be inclined to eat flesh, dead or alive, so he considered himself perfectly safe. The possession of a perfect knowledge of your business is an absolute necessity in order to insure success.

Among the maxims of the elder Rothschild was one, an apparent paradox: "Be cautious and bold." This seems to be a contradiction in terms, but it is not, and there is great wisdom in the maxim. It is, in fact, a condensed statement of what I have already said. It is to say, "You must exercise your caution in laying your plans, but be bold in carrying them out." A man who is all caution, will never dare to take hold and be successful; and a man who is all boldness, is merely reckless, and must eventually fail. A man may go on "change" and make fifty or one hundred thousand dollars in speculating in stocks, at a single operation. But if he has simple boldness without caution, it is mere chance, and what he gains to-day he will lose to-morrow. You must have both the caution and the boldness, to insure success.

The Rothschilds have another maxim: "Never have anything to do with an unlucky man or place." That is to say, never have anything to do with a man or place which never succeeds, because, although a man may appear to be honest and intelligent, yet if he tries this or that thing and always fails, it is on account of some fault or infirmity that you may not be able to discover, but nevertheless which must exist.

There is no such thing in the world as luck. There never was a man who could go out in the morning and find a purse of gold in the street to-day, and another to-morrow, and so on, day after day. He may do so once in his life; but so far as mere luck is concerned, he is as liable to lose it as to find it. "Like causes produce like effects." If a man adopts the proper methods to be successful, "luck" will not prevent him. If he does not succeed, there are reasons for it, although perhaps he may not be able to see them.

USE THE BEST TOOLS.

Men in engaging employees should be careful to get the best. Understand, you cannot have too good tools to work with, and there is no tool you should be so particular about as living tools. If you get a good one, it is better to keep him, than keep changing. He learns something every day, and you are benefited by the experience he acquires. He is worth more to you this year than last, and he is the last man to part with, provided his habits are good and he continues faithful. If, as he gets more valuable, he demands an exorbitant increase of salary on the supposition that you can't do without him, let him go. Whenever I have such an employee, I always discharge him; first, to convince him that his place may be supplied, and second, because he is good for nothing if he thinks he is invaluable and cannot be spared. . . .

DON'T GET ABOVE YOUR BUSINESS.

Young men after they get through their business training, or apprenticeship, instead of pursuing their avocation and rising in their business, will often lie about doing nothing. They say, "I have learned my business, but I am not going to be a hireling; what is the object of learning my trade or profession, unless I establish myself?"

"Have you capital to start with?"

"No, but I am going to have it."

"How are you going to get it?"

"I will tell you confidentially; I have a wealthy old aunt, and she will die pretty soon; but if she does not, I expect to find some rich old man who will lend me a few thousands to give me a start. If I only get the money to start with, I will do well."

There is no greater mistake than when a young man believes he will succeed with borrowed money. Why? Because every man's experience coincides with that of Mr. Astor, who said it was more difficult for him to accumulate his first thousand dollars, than all the succeeding millions that made up his colossal fortune. Money is good for nothing unless you know the value of it by experience. Give a boy twenty thousand dollars and put him in business and the chances are that he will lose every dollar of it before he is a year older. Like buying a ticket in the lottery, and drawing a prize, it is "easy come, easy go." He does not know the value of it; nothing is worth anything, unless it costs effort. Without self-denial and economy,

---

Men in engaging employees should be careful to get the best. Understand, you cannot have too good tools to work with, and there is no tool you should be so particular about as living tools.

---

patience and perseverance, and commencing with capital which you have not earned, you are not sure to succeed in accumulating. Young men instead of "waiting for dead men's shoes" should be up and doing, for there is no class of persons who are so unaccommodating in regard to dying as these rich old people, and it is fortunate for the expectant heirs that it is so. Nine out of ten of the rich men of our country to-day, started out in life as poor boys, with determined wills, industry, perseverance, economy, and good habits. They went on gradually, made their own money and saved it; and this is the best way to acquire a fortune. Stephen Girard started life as a poor cabin boy; now he pays taxes on a million and a half dollars of income per year. John Jacob Astor was a poor farmer boy, and died worth twenty millions. Cornelius Vanderbilt began life rowing a boat from Staten Island to New York; now he presents our government with a steamship worth a million of dollars, and he is worth fifty millions.

"There is no royal road to learning," says the proverb, and I may say it is equally true there is no royal road to wealth. But I think there is a royal road to both. The road to learning is a royal one; the road that enables the student to expand his intellect and add every day to his stock of knowledge, until, in the pleasant process of intellectual growth, he is able to solve the most profound problems, to count the stars, to analyze every atom of the globe, and to measure the firmament—this is a regal highway, and it is the only road worth travelling.

So in regard to wealth. Go on in confidence, study the rules, and above all things, study human nature; for "the proper study of mankind is man," and you will find that while expanding the intellect and the muscles, your enlarged experience will enable you every day to accumulate more and more principal, which will increase itself by interest and otherwise, until you arrive at a state of independence. You will find, as a general thing, that the poor boys get rich and the rich boys get poor. For instance, a rich man at his decease, leaves a large estate to his family. His eldest sons, who have helped him earn his fortune, know by experience the value of money, and they take their inheritance and add to it. The separate portions of the young children are placed at interest, and the little fellows are patted on the head, and told a dozen times a day, "You are rich; you will never have to work, you can always have whatever you wish, for you were born with a golden spoon in your mouth." The young heir soon finds out what that means; he has the finest dresses and playthings; he is crammed with sugar candies and almost "killed with kindness," and he passes from school to school, petted and flattered. He becomes arrogant and self-conceited, abuses his teachers, and carries everything with a high hand. He knows nothing of the real value of money, having never earned any; but he knows all about the "golden spoon" business. At college, he invites his poor fellow-students to his room where he "wines and dines" them. He is cajoled and caressed, and called a glorious good fellow, because he is so lavish of his money. He gives his game suppers, drives his fast horses, invites his chums to fetes and parties, determined to have lots of "good times." He spends the night in frolics and debauchery, and leads off his companions with the familiar song, "We won't go home till morning." He gets them to join him in pulling down signs, taking gates from their hinges and throwing them into back yards and horse-ponds. If the police arrest them, he knocks them down, is taken to the lock-up, and joyfully foots the bills.

"Ah! my boys," he cries, "what is the use of being rich, if you can't enjoy yourself?"

He might more truly say, "if you can't make a fool of yourself"; but he is "fast," hates slow things, and don't [sic] "see it." Young men loaded down with other people's money are almost sure to lose all they inherit, and they acquire all sorts of bad habits which, in the majority of cases, ruin them in health, purse, and character. In this country, one generation follows another, and the poor of to-day are rich in the next generation, or the third. Their experience leads them on, and they become rich, and they leave vast riches to their young children. These children, having been reared in luxury, are inexperienced and get poor; and after long experience another generation comes on and gathers up riches again in turn. And thus "history repeats itself," and happy is he who by listening to the experience of others avoids the rocks and shoals on which so many have been wrecked.

Learn Something Useful.

Every man should make his son or daughter learn some trade or profession, so that in these days of changing fortunes — of being rich to-day and poor to-morrow — they may have something tangible to fall back upon. This provision might save many persons from misery, who by some unexpected turn of fortune have lost all their means.

Let Hope Predominate, But Be Not Too Visionary.

Many persons are always kept poor, because they are too visionary. Every project looks to them like certain success, and therefore they keep changing from one business to another, always in hot water, always "under the harrow." The plan of "counting the chickens before they are hatched" is an error of ancient date, but it does not seem to improve by age.

DO NOT SCATTER YOUR POWERS.

Engage in one kind of business only, and stick to it faithfully until you succeed, or until your experience shows that you should abandon it. A constant hammering on one nail will generally drive it home at last, so that it can be clinched. When a man's undivided attention is centered on one object, his mind will constantly be suggesting improvements of value, which would escape him if his brain was occupied by a dozen different subjects at once. Many a fortune has slipped through a man's fingers because he was engaging in too many occupations at a time. There is good sense in the old caution against having too many irons in the fire at once.

BE SYSTEMATIC.

Men should be systematic in their business. A person who does business by rule, having a time and place for everything, doing his work promptly, will accomplish twice as much and with half the trouble of him who does it carelessly and slipshod. By introducing system into all your transactions, doing one thing at a time, always meeting appointments with punctuality, you find leisure for pastime and recreation; whereas the man who only half does one thing, and then turns to something else and half does that, will have his business at loose ends, and will never know when his day's work is done, for it never will be done. Of course there is a limit to all these rules. We must try to preserve the happy medium, for there is such a thing as being too systematic. There are men and women, for instance, who put away things so carefully that they can never find them again. It is too much like the "red tape" formality at Washington, and Mr. Dickens' "Circumlocution Office"—all theory and no result.

When the Astor House was first started in New York City, it was undoubtedly the best hotel in the country. The proprietors had learned a good deal in Europe regarding hotels, and the landlords were proud of the rigid system which pervaded every department of their great establishment. When twelve o'clock at night had arrived and there were a number of guests around, one of the proprietors would say, "Touch that bell, John"; and in two minutes sixty servants with a water bucket in each hand, would present themselves in the hall. "This," said the landlord, addressing his guests, "is our fire bell; it will show you we are quite safe

---

Engage in one kind of business only, and stick to it faithfully until you succeed, or until your experience shows that you should abandon it.

---

here; we do everything systematically." This was before the Croton water was introduced into the city. But they sometimes carried their system too far. On one occasion when the hotel was thronged with guests, one of the waiters was suddenly indisposed, and although there were fifty waiters in the hotel, the landlord thought he must have his full complement, or his "system" would be interfered with. Just before dinner time he rushed down stairs and said, "There must be another waiter, I am one waiter short, what can I do?" He happened to see "Boots" the Irishman. "Pat," said he, "wash your hands and face; take that white apron and come into the dining-room in five minutes." Presently Pat appeared as required, and the proprietor said: "Now, Pat, you must stand behind these two chairs and wait on the gentlemen who will occupy them; did you ever act as a waiter?"

"I know all about it sure, but I never did it."

Like the Irish pilot, on one occasion when the captain, thinking he was considerably out of his course, asked, "Are you certain you understand what you are doing?"

Pat replied, "Sure and I knows every rock in the channel."

That moment "bang" thumped the vessel against a rock.

"Ah! be jabers, and that is one of 'em," continued the pilot. But to return to the dining-room. "Pat," said the landlord, "here we do everything systematically. You must first give the gentlemen each a plate of soup, and when they finish that, ask them what they will have next."

Pat replied, "Ah! an' I understand parfectly the vartues of shystem."

Very soon in came the guests. The plates of soup were placed before them. One of Pat's two gentlemen ate his soup, the other did not care for it. He said, "Waiter, take this plate away and bring me some fish." Pat looked at the untasted plate of soup, and remembering the injunctions of the landlord in regard to "system," replied.

"Not till ye have ate yer supe!"

Of course that was carrying "system" entirely too far.

READ THE NEWSPAPERS.

Always take a trustworthy newspaper and thus keep thoroughly posted in regard to the transactions of the world. He who is without a newspaper is cut off from his species. . . .

BEWARE OF "OUTSIDE OPERATIONS."

We sometimes see men who have obtained fortunes, suddenly become poor. In many cases this arises from intemperance, and often from gaming and other bad habits. Frequently it occurs because a man has been engaged in "outside operations" of some sort. When he gets rich in his legitimate business, he is told of a grand speculation where he can make a score of thousands. He is constantly flattered by his friends, who tell him that he is born lucky, that everything he touches turns into gold. Now if he forgets that his economical habits, his rectitude of conduct, and a personal attention to a business which he understood, caused his success in life, he will listen to the siren voices. He says:

"I will put in twenty thousand dollars. I have been lucky, and my good luck will soon bring me back sixty thousand dollars."

A few days elapse and it is discovered he must put in ten thousand dollars more; soon after he is told it is all right, but certain matters not foreseen require an advance of twenty thousand dollars more, which will bring him a rich harvest; but before the time comes around to realize, the bubble bursts, he loses all he is possessed of, and then he learns what he ought to have known at the first, that however successful a man may be in his own business, if he turns from that and engages in a business which he don't [sic] understand he is like Samson when shorn of his locks—his strength has departed, and he becomes like other men.

If a man has plenty of money, he ought to invest something in everything that appears to promise success and that will probably benefit mankind; but let the sums thus invested be moderate in amount, and never let a man foolishly jeopardize a fortune that he has earned in a legitimate way, by investing it in things in which he has had no experience. . . .

BE POLITE AND KIND TO YOUR CUSTOMERS.

Politeness and civility are the best capital ever invested in business. Large stores, gilt signs, flaming advertisements, will all prove unavailing if you or your employees treat your patrons abruptly. The truth is, the more kind and liberal a man is, the more generous will be the patronage bestowed upon him. "Like begets like." The man who gives the greatest amount of goods of a corresponding quality for the least sum (still reserving to himself a profit) will generally succeed best in the long run. This brings us to the golden rule, "As ye would that men should do to you, do ye also to them"; and they will do better by you than if you always treated them as if you wanted to get the most you could out of them for the least return. Men who drive sharp bargains with their customers, acting as if they never expected to see them again, will not be mistaken. They never will see them again as customers. People don't like to pay and get kicked also.

One of the ushers in my Museum once told me he intended to whip a man who was in the lecture room as soon as he came out.

"What for?" I required.

"Because he said I was no gentleman," replied the usher.

"Never mind," I replied, "he pays for that, and you will not convince him you are a gentleman by whipping him. I cannot afford to lose a customer. If you whip him, he will never visit the Museum again, and he will induce friends to go with him to other places of amusement instead of this, and thus, you see, I should be a serious loser."

"But he insulted me," muttered the usher.

"Exactly," I replied, "and if he owned the Museum, and you had paid him for the privilege of visiting it, and he had then insulted you, there might be some reason in your resenting it, but in this instance he is the man who pays, while we receive, and you must, therefore, put up with his bad manners."

My usher laughingly remarked, that this was undoubtedly the true policy, but he added that he should not object to an increase of salary if he was expected to be abused in order to promote my interests.

Be Charitable.

Of course men should be charitable, because it is a duty and a pleasure. But even as a matter of policy, if you possess no higher incentive, you will find that the liberal man will command patronage, while the sordid, uncharitable miser will be avoided. . . .

The best kind of charity is to help those who are willing to help themselves. Promiscuous almsgiving, without inquiring into the worthiness of the applicant, is bad in every sense. But to search out and quietly assist those who are struggling for themselves, is the kind that "scattereth and yet increaseth." But don't fall into the idea that some persons practise, of giving a prayer instead of a potatoe, and a benediction instead of bread, to the hungry. It is easier to make Christians with full stomachs than empty.

Don't Blab.

Some men have a foolish habit of telling their business secrets. If they make money they like to tell their neighbors how it was done. Nothing is gained by this, and ofttimes much is lost. Say nothing about your profits, your hopes, your expectations, your intentions. And this should apply to letters as well as to conversation. Goethe made Mephistopheles say: "Never write a letter nor destroy one." Business men must write letters, but they should be careful what they put in them. If you are losing money, be specially cautious and not tell of it, or you will lose your reputation.

Preserve Your Integrity.

It is more precious than diamonds or rubies. The old miser said to his sons: "Get money; get it honestly, if you can, but get money." This advice was not only atrociously wicked, but it was the very essence of stupidity. It was as much as to say, "If you find it difficult to obtain money honestly, you can easily get it dishonestly. Get it in that way." Poor fool, not to know that the most difficult thing in life is to make money dishonestly; not to know that our prisons are full of men who attempted to follow this advice; not to understand that no man can be dishonest without soon being found out, and that when his lack of principle is discovered, nearly every avenue to success is closed against him forever. The public very properly shun all whose integrity is doubted. No matter how polite and pleasant and accommodating a man may be, none of us dare to deal with him if we suspect "false weights and measures." Strict honesty not only lies at the foundation of all success in life financially, but in every other respect. Uncompromising integrity of character is invaluable. It secures to its possessor a peace and joy which cannot be attained without it—which no amount of money, or houses and lands can purchase. A man who is known to be strictly honest, may be ever so poor, but he has the purses of all the community at his disposal;—for all know that if he promises to return what he borrows, he will never disappoint them. As a mere matter of selfishness, therefore, if a man had no higher motive for being honest, all will find that the maxim of Dr. Franklin can never fail to be true, that "honesty is the best policy."

To get rich, is not always equivalent to being successful. "There are many rich poor men," while there are many others, honest and devout men and women, who have never possessed so much money as some rich persons squander in a week, but who are nevertheless really richer and happier than any man can ever be while he is a transgressor of the higher laws of his being.

The inordinate love of money, no doubt, may be and is "the root of all evil," but money itself, when properly used, is not only a "handy thing to have in the house," but affords the gratification of blessing our race by enabling its possessor to enlarge the scope of human happiness and human influence.

The desire for wealth is nearly universal, and none can say it is not laudable, provided the possessor of it accepts its responsibilities, and uses it as a friend to humanity.

The history of money-getting, which is commerce, is a history of civilization, and wherever trade has flourished most, there, too, have art and science produced the noblest fruits. In fact, as a general thing, money-getters are the benefactors of our race. To them, in a great measure, are we indebted for our institutions of learning and of art, our academies, colleges, and churches. It is no argument against the desire for, or the possession of wealth, to say that there are sometimes misers who hoard money only for the sake of hoarding, and who have no higher aspiration than to grasp everything which comes within their reach. As we have sometimes hypocrites in religion, and demagogues in politics, so there are occasionally misers among money-getters. These, however, are only exceptions to the general rule. But when, in this country, we find such a nuisance and stumbling block as a miser, we remember with gratitude that in America we have no laws of primogeniture, and that in the due course of nature the time will come when the hoarded dust will be scattered for the benefit of mankind. To all men and women, therefore, do I conscientiously say, make money honestly, and not otherwise, for Shakespeare has truly said, "He that wants money, means, and content, is without three good friends."

JOHN D. ROCKEFELLER
1839 – 1937

Rockefeller's father was to have said, "I cheat my boys every chance I get. I want to make 'em sharp." The business education Rockefeller received at home clearly sharpened his eye for deal making. Fortunately, his more pious mother provided a balance and instilled a few Christian values in the young man. Her influence served its purpose later in Rockefeller's life when he turned his interests to philanthropy and gave more than $500 million to charitable and public causes.

In 1859 Rockefeller began acquiring his astounding accumulation of wealth when he and a partner opened a commission house in Cleveland. By coincidence, oil was discovered in western Pennsylvania that same year. Crude oil and related products were soon bought and sold by Rockefeller's commission house. He quickly grasped the importance of oil refining, and in 1865 entered into the business himself. Rockefeller, with his brother William and two other partners, formally founded the Standard Oil Company of Ohio in 1870, and they began consolidating the industry. By the 1880s they controlled over 90 percent of the U.S. oil refinery business.

Rockefeller truly believed that duplication of effort was wasteful, and the consolidation of an industry into a "trust" would most benefit the public. Of course, not everyone agreed, and the company was declared in violation of the Sherman Anti-Trust Act by the Ohio Supreme Court in 1892. They reformed as Standard Oil of New Jersey, but after an extensive legal battle, the U.S. Supreme Court again found the organization to be in violation in 1911.

These legal battles contributed to the public's perception of Rockefeller as being a ruthless businessperson concerned solely with the accumulation of money. However, Rockefeller once told a reporter, "If I have no other achievement to my credit than the accumulation of wealth, then I have made a poor success of my life." It's an easy statement to make when you are a billionaire; however, his message becomes much more meaningful in *The American Business Man,* in which he emphasizes the importance of finding a fascinating occupation, maintaining a zest for work, and exercising some common sense.

The American Business Man
John D. Rockefeller

Y ou hear a good many people
of pessimistic disposition say much about greed in American
life. One would think to hear them talk that we were a race
of misers in this country. To lay too much stress upon the
reports of greed in the newspapers would be folly, since their
function is to report the unusual and even the abnormal.
When a man goes properly about his daily affairs, the public
prints say nothing; it is only when something extraordinary
happens to him that he is discussed. But because he is thus
brought into prominence occasionally, you surely would not
say that these occasions represented his normal life. It is by
no means for money alone that these active-minded men
labour—they are engaged in a fascinating occupation. The
zest of the work is maintained by something better than the
mere accumulation of money, and, as I think I have said elsewhere, the standards of business are high and are getting
better all the time.

I confess I have no sympathy with the idea so often
advanced that our basis of all judgments in this country is
founded on money. If this were true, we should be a nation
of money hoarders instead of spenders. Nor do I admit that
we are so small-minded a people as to be jealous of the success of others. It is the other way about: we are the most
extraordinarily ambitious, and the success of one man in any

walk of life spurs the others on. It does not sour them, and it is a libel even to suggest so great a meanness of spirit.

In reading the newspapers, where so much is taken for granted in considering things on a money standard, I think we need some of the sense of humour possessed by an Irish neighbour of mine, who built what we regarded as an extremely ugly house, which stood out in bright colours as we looked from our windows. My taste in architecture differed so widely from that affected by my Irish friend, that we planted out the view of his house by moving some large trees to the end of our property. Another neighbour who watched this work going on asked Mr. Foley why Mr. Rockefeller moved all these big trees and cut off the view between the houses. Foley, with the quick wit of his country, responded instantly: "It's invy, they can't stand looking at the ividence of me prosperity."

When a man's affairs are not going well, he hates to study the books and face the truth. From the first, the men who managed the Standard Oil Company kept their books intelligently as well as correctly. We knew how much we made and where we gained or lost. At least, we tried not to deceive ourselves.

In my early days men acted just as they do now, no doubt. When there was anything to be done for general trade betterment, almost every man had some good reason for believing that his case was a special one different from all the rest. For every foolish thing he did, or wanted to do, for every unbusiness-like plan he had, he always pleaded that it was necessary in his case. He was the one man who had to sell at less than cost, to disrupt all the business plans of others in his trade, because his individual position was so absolutely different from all the rest. It was often a heart-breaking undertaking to convince those men that the perfect occasion which would lead to the perfect opportunity would never come, even if they waited until the crack o' doom.

Commercial enterprises that are needed by the public will pay. Commercial enterprises that are not needed fail, and ought to fail.

Then, again, we had the type of man who really never knew all the facts about his own affairs. Many of the brightest kept their books in such a way that they did not actually know when they were making money on a certain operation and when they were losing. This unintelligent competition was a hard matter to contend with. Good old-fashioned common sense has always been a mighty rare commodity. When a man's affairs are not going well, he hates to study the books and face the truth. From the first, the men who managed the Standard Oil Company kept their books intelligently as well as correctly. We knew how much we made and where we gained or lost. At least, we tried not to deceive ourselves.

My ideas of business are no doubt old-fashioned, but the fundamental principles do not change from generation to generation, and sometimes I think that our quick-witted American business men, whose spirit and energy are so splendid, do not always sufficiently study the real underlying foundations of business management. I have spoken of the necessity of being frank and honest with oneself about one's own affairs: many people assume that they can get away from the truth by avoiding thinking about it, but the natural law is inevitable, and the sooner it is recognized, the better.

One hears a great deal about wages and why they must be maintained at a high level, by the railroads, for example. A labourer is worthy of his hire, no less, but no more, and in the long run he must contribute an equivalent for what he is paid.

If he does not do this, he is probably pauperized, and you at once throw out the balance of things. You can't hold up conditions artificially, and you can't change the underlying laws of trade. If you try, you must inevitably fail. All this may be trite and obvious, but it is remarkable how many men overlook what should be the obvious. These are facts we can't get away from—a business man must adapt himself to the natural conditions as they exist from month to month and year to year. Sometimes I feel that we Americans think we can find a short road to success, and it may appear that often this feat is accomplished; but real efficiency in work comes from knowing your facts and building upon that sure foundation.

DISINTERESTED SERVICE THE ROAD TO SUCCESS

If I were to give advice to a young man starting out in life, I should say to him: If you aim for a large, broad-gauged success, do not begin your business career, whether you sell your labour or are an independent producer, with the idea of getting from the world by hook or crook all you can. In the choice of your profession or your business employment, let your first thought be: Where can I fit in so that I may be most effective in the work of the world? Where can I lend a hand in a way most effectively to advance the general interests? Enter life in such a spirit, choose your vocation in that way, and you have taken the first step on the highest road to a large success.

It requires a better type of mind to seek out and to support or to create the new than to follow the worn paths of accepted success . . .

Investigation will show that the great fortunes which have been made in this country, and the same is probably true of other lands, have come to men who have performed great and far-reaching economic services—men who, with great faith in the future of their country, have done most for the development of its resources. The man will be most successful who confers the greatest service on the world. Commercial enterprises that are needed by the public will pay. Commercial enterprises that are not needed fail, and ought to fail.

On the other hand, the one thing which such a business philosopher would be most careful to avoid in his investments of time and effort or money, is the unnecessary duplication of existing industries. He would regard all money spent in increasing needless competition as wasted, and worse. The man who puts up a second factory when the factory in existence will supply the public demand adequately and cheaply is wasting the national wealth and destroying the national prosperity, taking the bread from the labourer and unnecessarily introducing heartache and misery into the world.

Probably the greatest single obstacle to the progress and happiness of the American people lies in the willingness of so many men to invest their time and money in multiplying competitive industries instead of opening up new fields, and putting their money into lines of industry and development that are needed. It requires a better type of mind to seek out and to support or to create the new than to follow the worn paths of accepted success; but here is the great chance in our still rapidly developing country. The penalty of a selfish attempt to make the world confer a living without contributing to the progress or happiness of mankind is generally a failure to the individual. The pity is that when he goes down he inflicts heartache and misery also on others who are in no way responsible.

PART VIII

PHILOSOPHY FROM WALL STREET

BERNARD M. BARUCH
1870 – 1965

President Wilson and his advisers labeled this Wall Street millionaire as "somewhat vain." His closest friend occasionally found it necessary to poke a hole in his balloon, and "let out a little gas." His vanity was described as "so artless that it often evoked wonder rather than scorn." And yet, Baruch's high self-appraisal was not without merit. Ralph Pulitzer's *New York World* wrote that Baruch was the "recognized leader in all great speculative movements on Wall Street." Others wrote that "The Stock Exchange contains no more spectacular character than Bernard M. Baruch. . . ." This was a man whose mother found him his first jobs, whose father dragged him from gambling tables, and who himself had foolishly sought his fortune in the Colorado gold mines. Only after he returned to New York did he make millions as a flamboyant trader on the New York Stock Exchange, and become a respectable adviser to U.S. presidents. He was even placed on a Nazi hit list for his government work in World War II.

Baruch believed his key to success "lay in the systematic efforts I made to subject myself to critical self-appraisal." Apparently he was not always vain, and to the contrary, he admitted to learning far more from his mistakes than his successes. As to self-appraisal, he further stated, "And as I came to know myself, I acquired a better understanding of other people," and Wall Street "became one long course of education in human nature."

Early in his Wall Street career, he learned to be wary of "tips" and insider information, discovering that "There is something about inside information which seems to paralyze a man's reasoning powers . . . he will disregard the most evident facts." Of course, it also depended on the source of the information. Baruch was a sociable, debonair man who made friends easily, and it wasn't long before he was running in the same circles as the Guggenheims and Rockefellers. And there was more than one occasion when these friends provided a profitable tip. Ultimately though, Baruch's advice was "to rely on one's own cold detached judgement of the economic facts," which is a major component in the investment philosophy he outlines in the following excerpt.

My Investment Philosophy
Bernard M. Baruch

I have heard attributed to Sir Ernest Cassell, who was the private banker to King Edward VI, a remark that I wish I had thought of first.

"When as a young and unknown man I started to be successful I was referred to as a gambler," Sir Ernest said. "My operations increased in scope and volume. Then I was known as a speculator. The sphere of my activities continued to expand and presently I was known as a banker. Actually I had been doing the same thing all the time."

That observation is particularly worth pondering by those who may think that there is such a thing as a sure investment. The elder J. P. Morgan could gag at the word "gamble" when I used it. Still, the truth is there is no investment which doesn't involve some risk and is not something of a gamble.

We all have to take chances in life. And mankind would be vastly poorer today if it had not been for men who were willing to take risks against the longest odds. In setting out to discover a new route to India, Columbus was taking a chance that few men of his time were willing to hazard. Again, in our own age when Henry Ford started to make the first Model T, he was embarking on one of the most gigantic speculations of all time.

Even if it could be done—and it cannot—we would be foolish to try to stamp out this willingness in man to buck seemingly hopeless odds. What we can try to do perhaps is to come to a better understanding of how to reduce the element of risk in whatever we undertake. Or put another way—and this applies to governmental affairs as well as money making—our problem is how to remain properly venturesome and experimental without making fools of ourselves.

As I already have pointed out, the true speculator is one who observes the future and acts before it occurs. Like a surgeon he must be able to search through a mass of complex and contradictory details to the significant facts. Then, still like the surgeon, he must be able to operate coldly, clearly, and skillfully on the basis of the facts before him.

The constant problem of the speculator or analyst is how to disentangle the cold, hard economic facts from the rather warm feelings of the people dealing with these facts.

What makes this task of fact finding so difficult is that in the stock market the facts of any situation come to us through a curtain of human emotions. What drives the prices of stocks up or down is not impersonal economic forces or changing events but the human reactions to these happenings. The constant problem of the speculator or analyst is how to disentangle the cold, hard economic facts from the rather warm feelings of the people dealing with these facts.

Few things are more difficult to do. The main obstacle lies in disentangling ourselves from our own emotions.

I have known men who could see through the motivations of others with the skill of a clairvoyant, only to prove blind to their own mistakes. . . .

Other people's mistakes, I have noticed, often make us only more eager to try to do the same thing. Perhaps it is because in the breast of every man there burns not only that divine spark of discontent but the urge to "beat the game" and show himself smarter than the other fellow. In any case, only after we have repeated these errors for ourselves does their instructive effect sink home.

Don't speculate unless you can make it a full-time job.

Being so skeptical about the usefulness of advice, I have been reluctant to lay down any "rules" or guidelines on how to invest or speculate wisely. Still, there are a number of things I have learned from my own experience which might be worth listing for those who are able to muster the necessary self-discipline:

1. Don't speculate unless you can make it a full-time job.
2. Beware of barbers, beauticians, waiters—of anyone—bringing gifts of "inside" information or "tips."
3. Before you buy a security, find out everything you can about the company, its management and competitors, its earnings and possibilities for growth.
4. Don't try to buy at the bottom and sell at the top. This can't be done—except by liars.
5. Learn how to take your losses quickly and cleanly. Don't expect to be right all the time. If you have made a mistake, cut your losses as quickly as possible.
6. Don't buy too many different securities. Better have only a few investments which can be watched.
7. Make a periodic reappraisal of all your investments to see whether changing developments have altered their prospects.
8. Study your tax position to know when you can sell to greatest advantage.
9. Always keep a good part of your capital in a cash reserve. Never invest all your funds.

411

10. Don't try to be a jack of all investments. Stick to the field you know best.

These "rules" mainly reflect two lessons that experience has taught me—that getting the facts of a situation before acting is of crucial importance, and that getting these facts is a continuous job which requires eternal vigilance. . . .

In no field is the old maxim more valid—that a little knowledge is a dangerous thing—than in investing.

In evaluating individual companies three main factors should be examined.

First, there are the real assets of a company, the cash it has on hand over its indebtedness and what its physical properties are worth.

I'd rather have good management and less money than poor managers with a lot of money. Poor managers can ruin even a good proposition.

Second, there is the franchise to do business that a company holds, which is another way of saying whether or not it makes something or performs a service that people want or must have.

I have often thought that perhaps the strongest force that starts an economy upward after it has hit bottom is the simple fact that all of us must somehow find a way to live. Even when we are sunk in the blackest despair, we have to work and eat and clothe ourselves; and this activity starts the economic wheels turning anew. It is not too difficult to determine the things people must have if they are to continue to live. Such fields usually open up investments which are likely to hold their value over the long run.

Third, and most important, is the character and brains of management. I'd rather have good management and less money than poor managers with a lot of money. Poor managers can ruin even a good proposition. The quality of the management is particularly important in appraising the prospects of future growth. Is the management inventive and resourceful, imbued with a determination to keep itself young in a business way? Or does it have a sit-and-die attitude? I have learned to give less weight to big financial names at the head of a company than to the quality of its engineering staff.

These basic economic facts about various enterprises, to repeat, must be checked and rechecked constantly. Sometimes I have made mistakes and yet, by abandoning my position in time, still was able to emerge with a net profit.

Lynch, along with Warren Buffett, Benjamin Graham, and George Soros, has been called one of the greatest investors of all time by the *Wall Street Journal*. Like many other renowned businesspeople, he led a humble life in the beginning and had to earn his status. Lynch's father died when was only 10, so the young boy began caddying on the weekends to bring in extra money for his struggling family. It proved lucrative in more ways than one; Lynch attended Boston College on a scholarship awarded to caddies. While an undergraduate, he made his first great stock pick, which ultimately paid his way to the Wharton School of Business. He joined Fidelity Investments after a brief stint with the Army. Coincidentally, he had regularly caddied for D. George Sullivan, who was then the president of Fidelity.

Lynch took over Fidelity's renown Magellan Fund in 1977. The portfolio included some 45 stocks worth about $20 million. By the time he retired from active duty at Fidelity in 1990, the fund had diversified into more than 1,200 businesses and was worth almost $13 billion. His investment philosophy was simple: "Go for a business that any idiot can run—because sooner or later any idiot probably is going to run it." It wasn't that easy. Lynch visited more than 500 companies every year, interviewing executives and learning about their businesses. This tremendous effort was a result of another favorite maxim, "Know what you own and be able to explain it to a twelve-year-old in a minute."

During his outstanding run as the Magellan Fund manager, Lynch took on the qualities of a hollywood star. His name alone brought in customers and cash like a star packs the theater with moviegoers. So, when he left the fund at the height of his career, many were surprised. Lynch's reason was simple; when it came to work, his "transmission has a very small gearbox. It has overdrive or off." He desperately wanted to spend more time with his family, ergo the gearbox had to be in the off position. Lynch has remained involved with investing, and has written several best-selling books on the topic, including *Beating the Street* (1993) and *One up on Wall Street* (1990), from which the following excerpt is taken.

Do I Have the Personal Qualities It Takes to Succeed?
Peter Lynch

This is the most important question of all. It seems to me the list of qualities ought to include patience, self-reliance, common sense, a tolerance for pain, open-mindedness, detachment, persistence, humility, flexibility, a willingness to do independent research, an equal willingness to admit to mistakes, and the ability to ignore general panic. In terms of IQ, probably the best investors fall somewhere above the bottom ten percent but also below the top three percent. The true geniuses, it seems to me, get too enamored of theoretical cogitations and are forever betrayed by the actual behavior of stocks, which is more simple-minded than they can imagine.

It's also important to be able to make decisions without complete or perfect information. Things are almost never clear on Wall Street, or when they are, then it's too late to profit from them. The scientific mind that needs to know all the data will be thwarted here.

And finally, it's crucial to be able to resist your human nature and your "gut feelings." It's the rare investor who doesn't secretly harbor the conviction that he or she has a knack for divining stock prices or gold prices or interest rates, in spite of the fact that most of us have been proven wrong again and again. It's uncanny how often people feel most strongly that stocks are going to go up or the economy is going to improve just when the opposite occurs. This is borne out by the popular investment-advisory newsletter services, which themselves tend to turn bullish and bearish at inopportune moments.

According to information published by Investor's Intelligence, which tracks investor sentiment via the newsletters, at the end of 1972, when stocks were about to tumble, optimism was at an all-time high, with only 15 percent of the advisors bearish. At the beginning of the stock market rebound in 1974, investor sentiment was at an all-time low, with 65 percent of the advisors fearing the worst was yet to come. Before the market turned downward in 1977, once again the newsletter writers were optimistic, with only 10 percent bears. At the start of the 1982 sendoff into a great bull market, 55 percent of the advisors were bears, and just prior to the big gulp of October 19, 1987, 80 percent of the advisors were bulls again.

It's also important to be able to make decisions without complete or perfect information. Things are almost never clear on Wall Street, or when they are, then it's too late to profit from them.

The problem isn't that investors and their advisors are chronically stupid or unperceptive. It's that by the time the signal is received, the message may already have changed. When enough positive general financial news filters down so that the majority of investors feel truly confident in the short-term prospects, the economy is soon to get hammered.

What else explains the fact that large numbers of investors (including CEOs and sophisticated business people) have been most afraid of stocks during the precise periods when stocks have done their best (i.e., from the mid-1930s to the late 1960s) while being least afraid precisely when stocks have done their worst (i.e., early 1970s and recently in the fall of 1987). Does the success of Ravi Batra's book *The Great Depression of 1990* almost guarantee a great national prosperity?

It's amazing how quickly investor sentiment can be reversed, even when reality hasn't changed. A week or two before the Big Burp of October, business travelers were driving through Atlanta, Orlando, or Chicago, admiring the new construction and remarking to each other, "Wow. What a glorious boom." A few days later, I'm sure those same travelers were looking at those same buildings and saying: "Boy, this place has problems. How are they ever going to sell all those condos and rent all that office space?"

Things inside humans make them terrible stock market timers. The unwary investor continually passes in and out of three emotional states: concern, complacency, and capitulation. He's concerned after the market has dropped or the economy has seemed to falter, which keeps him from buying good companies at bargain prices. Then after he buys at higher prices, he gets complacent because his stocks are going up. This is precisely the time he ought to be concerned enough to check the fundamentals, but he isn't. Then finally, when his stocks fall on hard times and the prices fall to below what he paid, he capitulates and sells in a snit.

Some have fancied themselves "long-term investors," but only until the next big drop (or tiny gain), at which point they quickly become short-term investors and sell out for huge losses or the occasional minuscule profit. It's easy to panic in this volatile business. Since I've run Magellan, the fund has declined from 10 to 35 percent during eight bearish episodes, and in 1987 alone the fund was up 40 percent in August, down 11 percent by December. We finished the year with a 1 percent gain, thus barely preserving my record of never having had a down year—knock on wood. Recently I read that the price of an average stock fluctuates 50 percent in an average year. If that's true, and apparently it's been true throughout this century, then any share currently selling for $50 is likely to hit $60 and/or fall to $40 sometime in the next twelve months. In other words, the high for the year ($60) is 50 percent higher than the low ($40). If you're the kind of buyer who can't resist getting in at $50, buying more at $60 ("See, I was right, that sucker *is* going up"), and then selling out in despair at $40 ("I guess I was wrong. That sucker's going *down*") then no shelf of how-to books is going to help you.

When E.F. Hutton talks, everybody is supposed to be listening, but that's just the problem. Everybody ought to be trying to fall asleep.

Some have fancied themselves contrarians, believing that they can profit by zigging when the rest of the world is zagging, but it didn't occur to them to become contrarian until that idea had already gotten so popular that contrarianism became the accepted view. The true contrarian is not the investor who takes the opposite side of a popular hot issue (i.e., shorting a stock that everyone else is buying). The true contrarian waits for things to cool down and buys stocks that nobody cares about, and especially those that make Wall Street yawn.

When E.F. Hutton talks, everybody is supposed to be listening, but that's just the problem. Everybody ought to be trying to fall asleep. When it comes to predicting the market, the important skill here is not listening, it's snoring. The trick is not to learn to trust your gut feelings, but rather to discipline yourself to ignore them. Stand by your stocks as long as the fundamental story of the company hasn't changed.

If not, your only hope for increasing your net worth may be to adopt J. Paul Getty's surefire formula for financial success: "Rise early, work hard, strike oil."

HENRY CLEWS
1834 – 1923

You cannot pick up a well-researched book on late nine-teenth-century American business without finding Clews in the footnotes. In addition to being one of the most successful financiers of his time, he also authored several works that offer keen insight into (or clues to understanding) the period. Clews was born in England to parents who were intent on their son joining the ministry. However, when he accompanied his father, a manufacturer of china, on a visit to New York in 1850, he became enthralled with the American lifestyle. Clews said, "I began to perceive the possibilities that presented themselves to a young man, who had the courage to push, to compete for a place in the race for wealth and position." He did not return to England with his father.

Clews found a clerk position with a large importer and soon moved into the financial side of the business. It wasn't long before he and several partners opened a private bank on Wall Street. Ever ambitious, Clews had his eye on joining the New York Stock Exchange; however, membership had to be facili-tated by a very powerful patron, of which he had not one. To attract attention, he advertised that he would conduct stock and bond trades for his clients at one half the cost of the other firms (i.e., he used discount brokerage services long before Fidelity or Schwab). The response by the staid firms of the exchange, according to Clews, was comical. "This was such a bombshell in the camp of these old fogies that they were almost para-lyzed." He subsequently was granted membership to the exchange so the old guard could keep an eye on him.

Flamboyance has often been a trait of top moneymen, as it was for Clews. However, he was a disciplined, value investor who diligently studied the market. He understood that "at the bottom of all this turbulent mass of facts there are natural laws at work which, if we study them in relation to the objects which they control, will be found to be as sure in their operation as sunrise." In *How to Make Money on Wall Street,* he expounds on not only how to invest, but also how to avoid adventurous rascals looking to steal your swag.

How to Make Money
on Wall Street
Henry Clews

B ut few gain sufficient
experience in Wall Street to command success until they
reach that period of life in which they have one foot in the
grave. When this time comes these old veterans of the Street
usually spend long intervals of repose at their comfortable
homes, and in times of panic, which recur sometimes oftener
than once a year, these old fellows will be seen in Wall Street,
hobbling down on their canes to their brokers' offices.

Then they always buy good stocks to the extent of their
bank balances, which have been permitted to accumulate for
just such an emergency. The panic usually rages until
enough of these cash purchases of stock is made to afford a
big "rake in." When the panic has spent its force, these old
fellows, who have been resting judiciously on their oars in
expectation of the inevitable event, which usually returns
with the regularity of the seasons, quickly realize, deposit
their profits with their bankers, or the overplus thereof, after
purchasing more real estate that is on the up grade, for permanent investment, and retire for another season to the qui-
etude of their splendid homes and the bosoms of their happy
families.

If young men had only the patience to watch the speculative signs of the times, as manifested in the periodical

egress of these old prophetic speculators from their shells of
security, they would make more money at these intervals
than by following up the slippery "tips" of the professional
"pointers" of the Stock Exchange all the year round, and
they would feel no necessity for hanging at the coat tails,
around the hotels, of those specious frauds, who pretend to
be deep in the councils of the big operators and of all the new
"pools" in process of formation. I say to the young speculators, therefore, watch the ominous visits to the Street of
these old men. They are as certain to be seen on the eve of a
panic as spiders creeping stealthily and noiselessly from
their cobwebs just before rain. If you only wait to see them
purchase, then put up a fair margin for yourselves, keep out
of the "bucket shops" as well as the "sample rooms," and only
visit Delmonico's for light lunch in business hours, you can
hardly fail to realize handsome profits on your ventures.

The habit of following points which are supposed to
emanate from the big operators, nearly always ends in loss
and sometimes in disaster to young speculators. The latter
become slavish in their methods of thought, having their
minds entirely subjected to others, who are presumed to do
the thinking for them, and they consequently fail to cultivate
the self-reliance that is indispensable to the success of any
kind of business.

To the question often put, especially by men outside of
Wall Street, "How can I make money in Wall Street?" there
is probably no better answer than the one given by old
Meyer Rothschild to a person who asked him a similar question. He said, "I buys 'sheep' and sells 'dear.' "

Those who follow this method always succeed. There has
hardly been a year within my recollection, going back nearly
thirty years, when there have not been two or three squalls
in "the Street," during the year, when it was possible to purchase stocks below their intrinsic value. The squall usually
passes over in a few days, and then the lucky buyers of
stocks at panic prices come in for their profits ranging from
five to ten per cent on the entire venture.

The question of making money, then, becomes a mere matter of calculation, depending on the number of the squalls that may occur during any particular year.

If the venture is made at the right time—at the lucky moment, so to speak—and each successive venture is fortunate, as happens often to those who use their judgment in the best way, it is possible to realize a net gain of fifty per cent per annum on the aggregate of the year's investments.

In this way it is easy to see how the rich will get richer, and the poor poorer. . . .

My advice to speculators who wish to make money in Wall Street, therefore, is to ignore the counsel of the barroom "tippers" and "tipplers," . . .

The common delusion, that expert knowledge is not required in speculation, has wrecked many fortunes and reputations in Wall Street, and is still very influential in its pernicious and illusory achievements.

When a man wants correct advice in law he goes to a professional lawyer in good standing, one who has made a reputation in the courts, and who has afforded other evidence to the public that he is thoroughly reliable. No man of average common sense would trust a case in law to a bar room "bummer" who would assert that he was well acquainted with Aaron J. Vanderpoel, Roscoe Conkling, and Wm. M. Evarts, and had got all the inside "tips" from these legal lights on the law relating to the case in question. The fellow would be laughed at, and, in all probability, if he persisted in this kind of talk, would be handed over to the city physician to be examined in relation to his sanity, but in Wall Street affairs men can every day make similar pretensions and pass for embodiments of speculative wisdom.

If speculators are caught and fleeced by following such counsel, the professional brokers who are members of the Stock Exchange, are no more to blame than the eminent lawyers to whom I have referred would be for the upshot of a case that had been taken into court on the advice which some irresponsible person had pretended to receive from these celebrities of the New York Bar.

Professional advice in Wall Street, as in legal affairs, is worth paying for, and costs far less in the end than the cheap "points" that are distributed profusely around the Street, thick as autumn leaves in Vallombrosa, and which only allure the innocent speculator to put his money where he is almost certain to lose it.

People forget that the business of speculation requires special training, and every fool who has got a few hundred dollars cannot begin to deal in stocks and make a fortune.

My advice to speculators who wish to make money in Wall Street, therefore, is to ignore the counsel of the barroom "tippers" and "tipplers," turn their backs on "bucket shops," and when they want "points" to purchase, let them go to those who have established a reputation for giving sound advice in such matters, and who have ample resources for furnishing correct information on financial topics, as well as a personal interest in making all the money they can for their clients.

There is no difficulty in finding out such reliable men and firms in the vicinity of Wall Street, if speculators will only read the newspapers, or make inquiry of the first messenger boy they may happen to meet. . . .

It is true the honor of Wall Street is sometimes slightly tarnished, especially in the eyes of those who reside at a great distance, owing to the occasional delinquencies of dishonorable men, who consider Wall Street men and Wall Street money fair game for swindling operations. These are for the most part outsiders, who pounce upon the Street as their illegitimate prey, after probably making a show of doing business there.

There is no place, of course, where confidence men have the opportunity of reaping such a rich harvest when they can succeed in establishing the confidential relations that help them to secure their swag. But Wall Street proper is not any more responsible for such men than the Church, whose sacred precincts are used and abused by the same social pariahs in a similar manner. The Street is the victim of these adventurers, and has no more to do with nurturing and aiding them than the Church has.

What should be said of a financier who would have the temerity to assert that the Church was an asylum for swindlers, and that thence they issued forth to commit their lawless depredations on society? He would be tabooed by all intelligent people. Yet there would be about as much truth in such a statement as in most of the eloquent anathemas and objurations launched from the pulpit every Sunday against Wall Street.

There is no place on this earth where adventurous thieves have fewer sympathizers than in Wall Street, except perhaps in Pinkerton's and Byrnes' detective bureaux.

There is another popular delusion with regard to those who don't succeed in Wall Street. Their failure is frequently attributed to sharp practice on the part of the old habitues of the Street. People forget that the business of speculation requires special training, and every fool who has got a few hundred dollars cannot begin to deal in stocks and make a fortune. The men who don't succeed are usually those who have spent their early life elsewhere, and whose habits have been formed in other grooves of thought.

The business of Wall Street requires long and close training in financial affairs, so that the mind may attain a flexible facility with the various ins and outs of speculative methods.

If this training is from youth upward, all the better. It is among this class that many of our most successful men are to be found, though there are some eminent examples of success among those who began late in life. It will be found, however, that the latter must have a special genius for the business, and genius, of course, discounts all the usual conditions and auxiliaries; but among ordinary intellects early training is generally indispensable to financial success.

It seldom happens, moreover, that the early trained man from youth up does any great wrong.

Ferdinand Ward may seem an exception to this rule, but he had a born genius for evil, and though he had all the early advantages of Timothy and Samuel the Prophet, with a higher civilization thrown in, so utterly incorrigible was his nature that nothing but prison walls and iron bars could prescribe bounds to his rascality. He is an extraordinary exception, a genius of the other extreme, against whose subtle operations society must always be on its guard; but he is only one of the dangerous exceptions that prove the rule for which I am contending, the rule that early training in finance more, perhaps, than in any other field of human energy, is the great desideratum.

The most successful men of Wall Street, . . . are . . . those who have received severe training, who have had some sledgehammer blows applied to their heads to temper them, like the conversion of iron into steel.

If such a man is unsuccessful, dishonor seldom accompanies his misfortunes. He may pass through the whole catalogue of financial disasters and their natural results. He may fall to the gutter through over-indulgence in liquor and the despair attendant on a run of bad luck or unfortunate connection with wicked partners, but he is still capable of rising from the very ashes of his former self. He will never stoop to swindle, no matter how low the rest of his moral condition may be brought.

No great business can be built up except upon honest and moral principles. It may flourish for a time, but it will topple down eventually. The very magnitude to which the business of Wall Street has grown is a living proof of its moral stamina. It is impossible, in the social and moral nature of things, to unite a large number of men, representing important material interests, except on principles of equity and fair dealing. A conspiracy to cheat must always be confined to a small number.

The most successful men of Wall Street, to my own personal knowledge, are those who came to the Street young, and have "gone through the mill," so to speak; those who have received severe training, who have had some sledge-hammer blows applied to their heads to temper them, like the conversion of iron into steel.

These are some of the prerequisites of a successful financial career.

One of the most common delusions incident to human nature in every walk of life is that of a man who has been successful in one thing imagining he can succeed in anything and everything he attempts. In general, overweening conceit of this kind can be cured by simple experiments that bring men to a humiliating sense of their mortal condition and limited capacity. When the experiment is tried in Wall Street, however, to these healthy admonitions are frequently added irreparable disaster and overwhelming disgrace.

MURIEL SIEBERT

In 1967 Siebert became the first woman to buy a seat on the New York Stock Exchange. Later she also bought a seat on the London Exchange, but was only the second woman to do so (the Queen was the first). There were no laws in the Exchange's constitution that prevented a woman from buying a seat prior to Siebert doing so. The prospective buyer had to be 21, have a business purpose, and be able to finance it. The only problem for Siebert was an unwritten rule that was the collective hostility toward any woman attempting it. After creating Muriel Siebert & Company, she realized, "You can't break a tradition that was 175 years old and have everybody love you." She subsequently broke several other traditions as well. Her brokerage firm offered discounted transaction fees and placed advertisements that attacked her fat-cat rivals.

Siebert knew how to play tough with the boys. For example, she said, "Part of this business still involves sitting down and drinking with people, and God help you if you can't drink." The characteristically brash Siebert could match men scotch for scotch, and then make a deal, which soon earned their respect. After a stint as New York State Superintendent of Banks from 1977 to 1982, Siebert returned to Wall Street determined to revolutionize the policies guiding her own industry.

Siebert has always considered herself a pioneer, from her business practices, to opening doors for other women, to establishing charitable foundations. Money-getting has never been a driving force. She says, "when you have X dollars, you don't need X dollars more. There is a group downtown; their only sense of accomplishment is, are they worth more money this month than they were last month. I don't understand some of these people. I feel sorry for them." As for her own firm's current direction, she is pleased, and her confidence in her peoples' ability is very high. "With the staff and business I have now, I could take a years vacation and it wouldn't bother things a bit." Siebert's refreshing views on business are further illuminated in the following selection.

You've Got to Take Chances
Muriel Siebert

W hen a friend suggested to
me that I buy a seat on the New York Stock Exchange I said,
"Don't be ridiculous." He said, "There's no law against it."
Then it became a challenge and a game. It took me about six
months until I got up the guts to do it. I kept going over it in
my mind: "Gee, I want to do it, no, I don't want to do it.". . . I
was "hocking" myself. Four hundred and forty-five thousand
dollars is a lot of money for something that isn't tangible. I
also didn't know how many of my customers would still continue to do business with me. I was earning my living on the
commissions I got from institutions based on the research I
did for them, and it would mean I would have to go from an
existing brokerage firm, although a small firm, to being on
my own. I would still clear through a major firm so there was
no risk for my customers, but until you take a step like that
you don't know how people will react. You just don't know.

I applied for a loan to buy a seat and I was turned down
even though the loan had been completely collateralized, yes
ma'am, by one of the major banks in this city, the bank that I
had had an account with for a long time, and had borrowed
from to buy securities, and knew me. They loaned me my
deposit but they would not loan me the purchase price. I later

got a loan from another bank. I found out later there was a bet going around that the bank would never have to make the loan because the Stock Exchange was not going to sell me the seat.

You know, whenever you break a tradition that's 187 years old, not everybody's going to love you. People who had volunteered to sponsor me, when the time came, ran out the door. On the other hand, some of the toughest people turned out to be my best friends. My two sponsors were both upstairs members. I could not get anybody from the floor to sponsor me, and some of those people had promised me. That was pretty tough. That's hard to take.

When I finally got my seat, everyone said that the reason there had never been a woman on the floor of the Stock Exchange before was because no lady could stand the language (so I learned the language) and because there was no ladies room on the floor—which is a lie. There is a ladies room, it's been there since the war days. I received three portable johns that weekend from friends—I said I never had so many people concerned about my toilet habits before in my life.

I spent twenty days down there on the floor of the exchange as a trainee, with my little square badge, and test by test, I qualified to do any piece of work I wanted to do on the floor of the New York Stock Exchange.

My family lived in Cleveland, Ohio. I was going to college there, but instead of going to class I was playing bridge. I guess I'm a lousy student if I have to do certain things I don't like to do. Things I like to do, I do very well. I probably didn't have the discipline then to force myself to stay in school. I dropped out.

I'd been to New York once on a vacation. I had visited on the balcony of the Stock Exchange. It seemed very, very exciting. They used to give tourists their names in ticker tape as souvenirs. It said, "Welcome to the New York Stock Exchange," with your name and date on it. Well, I took that home and, strangely enough, I saved it. I have that tape at home in my den now, framed. I told myself then that if I ever came back to New York, I'd like to work on Wall Street.

... everyone said that the reason there had never been a woman on the floor of the Stock Exchange before was because no lady could stand the language (so I learned the language) and because there was no ladies room on the floor ...

You have no idea what New York is to people who aren't from New York. There's a fascination, it beckons. I thought I'd go, stay a few months and come home. I was prepared to work there for a few months to support myself, just to see New York.

I have a feeling for accounting and for numbers. I used to cut classes in college and get A's in accounting. I think you're born with different talents. Then you capitalize on them, you define them. Why can some people pick up a pencil and draw? Sure it can be taught, but the great artists didn't have to be taught. In my case, I was very good with numbers.

So I first applied for a job at Merrill Lynch, the stockbrokers. They asked, "College degree?" I said, "No." So they said, "No job." The next day I applied to Bache and when they asked, "College degree?" I said "Yes." It was an instant degree. If I hadn't been lucky enough to be hired, I would have been a bookkeeper somewhere or an accountant. Luck plays a part that they didn't check.

Every time you sign an application to become a partner of a firm, they put a detective firm on you, but it never came out. That was luck. Otherwise I would not have been able to become a partner and I might have lost the opportunity to make the kind of money I did, which enabled me to buy a seat on the Stock Exchange.

The Stock Exchange checks very thoroughly on people. I put down the right information when I bought my seat on the exchange because I realized that was an historic application, and you are dealing with people's money and trust. The exchange wrote the college and I guess some clerk at the college said I had attended the school for four years, which I really hadn't done, and they took it as a degree.

This world is the only world I know. To me it's represented a constant challenge. I've seen things I've wanted to do and I've done them. In some cases being a woman was an obstacle, but it probably gave me more incentives than I would have had if I'd been a man. It's possible, because when I wasn't being paid as much as a man, I changed jobs, found a firm who'd pay me as much. When I went down on the scale I changed again. I always found a new job before I left the old one. Once I didn't do that and I'll never make the same mistake twice. You can be sought after, but if you quit first, before you get the job, you're not as valuable. I've given that advice out to people. Employers feel much better if they are the aggressive ones and take you out of a job. I think anybody who is successful takes risks. I think you have to analyze and study the situation.

I first applied for a job at Merrill Lynch, the stockbrokers. They asked, "College degree?" I said, "No." So they said, "No job." The next day I applied to Bache and when they asked, "College degree?" I said "Yes." It was an instant degree.

I was a partner for two different small brokerage firms for three years each. I found I was doing a lot of business, concentrating on only a few stocks in aviation and transportation. I developed a reputation for knowing these stocks very well, and I knew the management of these companies.

I'd go to see the management four or five times a year and I might talk to them once a week. When you're with a small firm and you've done the research on Beech Aircraft and written a report, and an institution goes and buys 200,000 shares and you handle the order, you're going to get the credit. If you are with a big firm, let's say you are working for Merrill Lynch, or E. F. Hutton, the credit is going to go partly to the salesman who's covering the account, partly to the man on the trading desk, maybe you'll get a cut of a piece of the research pie, but you're not going to get that credit directly, which is why I decided to work for small firms.

I think one of my strengths is that I'm very sensitive to people. It enabled me to be successful on Wall Street because when I was doing research I was depending on my relationships with my clients and with the companies I was following. My clients were the biggest institutions in the country, and they had faith in me. When I went into business for myself, I did three financings the first two years that came from larger Wall Street firms. That means that I raised $30 million for Seaboard World Airlines, jointly with two other companies. I wasn't even incorporated then. You just don't get those kinds of ratings, but Seaboard World Airlines was a company I'd followed, they had faith in me, and I found a way to do their financing and brought in two larger firms. When companies have that kind of faith, they're buying your ability but they also trust you as a person.

When I started my own business, I also decided to change policy and give discounts to individuals instead of just corporations. The commission structure was changing then so that instead of having a fixed commission base, commissions became negotiable on everything. So I realized there was a market. I saw the way the rates were developing, and I saw that they were staying the same for the individuals but that they had come down sharply for the institutions. The individuals were paying ten times per share basis what the institutions were paying. For example, I was doing business with one hundred shares of stock at ten cents a share for the banks on hundred-share lots. We'd go down six or seven cents a share for the institutions, but the individuals were paying fifty cents or sixty cents a share. So I just felt that individuals weren't being treated fairly. If the larger firms had lowered the rates for the individuals then I never would have gone into that business, but they didn't.

I'd say a woman does have to work harder, put more passion and commitment into what she does, than a man in this business.

So when I realized that this was a trend that was not going to change, I decided that everybody would pay the same for the same size order in the firm. This meant giving the individuals a shot at lower commissions. I thought it would be profitable. You don't know when you take a step like that. I was not loved when I did that, by the Wall Street firms, but I did it. They wouldn't have minded if I had done it without the advertising, but I was running some very powerful ads and it worked out. We got an enormous response. Then a lot of companies followed suit. There are a lot of people in this business now, maybe ten or fifteen members of the Stock Exchange are doing it.

I'd say a woman does have to work harder, put more passion and commitment into what she does, than a man in this business. I don't know if it's going to be that way ten years from now. I think women are coming out of some of the graduate schools and being given at least an even opportunity. In some cases, because the institutions are playing "catch-up," women are being given an advantage. I think ten years from now they'll just be treated equally. It won't be a game to them, it will be work. I think for a lot of us, during the years that I made it, it was a game, but a serious game.

I'm the first woman superintendent of banks in New York State and I was the first woman member on the New

York Stock Exchange. As such, I've filled two of the highest financial jobs in the country that any woman's ever had. Sometime down the road when there have been maybe five or six women superintendents, will the next one work as hard? That's what I mean by a game. It's work but it's also a challenge to dig in and do something well.

I don't think it would have been possible to have had the career I have and been married. Maybe in today's environment it would be because people accept it. I see it in the younger people. People did not accept it twenty years ago. It was very rare. If women worked, it was as schoolteachers. I have to do an awful lot of traveling, calling on the companies and my clients. Twenty years ago a lot of people would not have accepted that.

I was growing pretty fast in my career and, when I look at the various people that I dated seriously over the years, they haven't kept up with me. I mean I've changed terribly as I've grown; because I was succeeding pretty fast, I grew and changed as a person. So I might have had a couple of divorces behind me, too. I would say that most of the women that I know who have been successful do have a divorce or two behind them, because you end up growing sometimes so much faster than your husband. If you're lucky, you're married to someone who's also changing, and changing in the same direction. I don't regret that marriage wasn't possible in my time. You can't have everything.

I don't think ahead. I don't know what I want to do next, whenever I do it. I don't know what other possibilities there are. I wasn't looking for the superintendent job, it came along. There was no guarantee I'd do a good job. I think I've squeaked through. You don't have guarantees in this world. You've got to take chances.

CARL C. ICAHN
1936 –

Born in Brooklyn and raised in Queens, Icahn has used his New York attitude and skepticism to its fullest in building his fortune. Ironically, he was raised by a mother and father who despised the rich. Instead of playing ball with his son, the elder Icahn often read him the writings of philosopher Carl Schopenhauer, who expounded on the primordial drive to endure. Certainly the trait of endurance is embedded in Icahn, as he repeatedly has been attacked over the years for being a corporate raider. Schopenhauer also influenced Icahn's decision to enter Princeton University as a premed philosophy major. Medical school, however, turned out to be a disaster and as Icahn said, "One of the greatest things I did for the human race was not to become a doctor." After dropping out, he entered the Army, which, in an amusing manner, paved his way to Wall Street. Icahn became a cardshark in the barracks, and used a stake of $4,000 from his poker winnings to play the stock market.

In the 1960s Icahn found himself in the risky world of options trading, which leveraged his philosophical studies in empiricism. As Icahn explains, "Empiricism says knowledge is based on observation and experience, not feelings." The philosophy was a critical element in Icahn's ability to determine the true value of a company. He also followed his instincts and relied on no one, understanding that, "If you want a friend on Wall Street, get a dog." In 1978 he initiated his first takeover attempt against a real estate investment trust, and from that point on there was no pretense of being friends, as he subsequently attacked B. F. Goodrich, Marshall Field, Phillips Petroleum, and TWA, among many others.

Before Icahn launched the first takeover attempt, he clearly stated his strategic manifesto to partners, "It is our contention that sizeable profits can be earned by taking large positions in 'undervalued' stocks and then attempting to control the destinies of the companies in question by: a) trying to convince management to liquidate or sell the company to a 'white knight'; b) waging a proxy contest; c) making a tender offer and/or; d) selling back our position to the company." Icahn further depicts his motivations in *What Makes Me Tick?*

What Makes Me Tick?
Carl C. Icahn

People ask, what makes me tick? Sometimes I wonder the same thing myself. No question, I enjoy collecting money. Obviously, I've got more than I'm going to spend and more material comforts than I need. But I love winning. I'm a very competitive person and very obsessive about everything I do. You might as well ask a mountaineer, 'Why do you keep trying to get to the top of the Himalayas?' or a hunter why he keeps going after tigers.

I proselytize—and I know a lot of what I say sounds self-serving—but I believe that I'm doing something that must be done. Productivity in the U.S. continues to decline. If managements don't shape up, the problems of the economy will get worse. Our pension plans won't be able to support the growing number of retirees. I get really angry at the managements of many U.S. corporations. Outrage is probably what drives me the most.

I think I learned it from my father. He was a lawyer—and a damn fine musician—but he didn't really work very much and generally stayed home. He never played ball or anything with me, so when I was 8 or 9 we'd just sit home for hours at a time and talk. He'd read Schopenhauer to me. Or we'd argue, almost as two adults. He was very dogmatic and expressed his beliefs with a kind of fury. He'd have very set opinions on very many things—whether Laurel and Hardy were funnier than Abbott and Costello, whether Caruso sang better than Gigli, or whether socialism was better than capitalism. If you disagreed, you were stupid.

Very wealthy people outraged him the most, and he used to lecture me on how terrible it was that the poor people were starving and the rich people had everything. But I think he would approve of all that I've got because I got it by taking on the establishment. In fact, I think he'd be proud of me.

I get really angry at the managements of many U.S. corporations. Outrage is probably what drives me the most.

He and my mother always worried about their security. He died ten years ago, and she is a retired school teacher who could have been greatly successful if she hadn't had so many fears. They were brought up in tough times and never forgot the Depression. She always worried, 'They're going to take everything away.' She believed if you were Jewish, middle-class, and had hardly any money, you had three strikes against you.

I'm a sort of one-track, single-minded kind of guy. I've always been obsessively interested in anything I'm doing, such as philosophy, which I majored in at Princeton [Icahn won a scholarship there in 1953, the first to do so from his Queens high school]. I was intrigued by the way people thought about things, the concepts of knowledge. My thesis was 'An Explication of the Empiricist Criterion of Meaning,' and it was really good.

Empiricism says knowledge is based on observation and experience, not feelings. In a funny way, studying 20th-century philosophy trains your mind for takeovers. You take out your emotions and your ego—and you sure as hell don't believe your press clips. There's a strategy behind everything. Everything fits. Thinking this way taught me to compete in many things, not only takeovers but chess and arbitrage. It even helped when I studied organic chemistry.

My mother wanted me to be a doctor, and in 1957 I enrolled in medical school at New York University. I hated it, even though my grades were okay. And when they started to take the students out on the wards to see the sick people, I developed the exact symptoms of whatever disease we were studying. After a couple of years I was sent into a tuberculosis ward. This guy coughs all over me and I said, 'I got it!' So I quit and joined the Army.

After six months in the service—which you could do back then—I joined Dreyfus as a trainee broker. Those were bull years: Everyone made money and everyone thought he was a genius. In 1962 the market broke and I lost basically all I had made. I even had to sell my white convertible. That hurt more than the money. I really loved that car.

The fact I had to start all over again made me realize that I really had to go to work. I signed up for a few courses at night school to learn basic accounting, basic security analysis, things like that. And I went into options. I worked hard, day and night, put out a regular newsletter, the *Midweek Option Report*, and built up a big following of clients. By 1968, I had a good business going with three or four assistants, so I decided to buy my own seat on the stock exchange.

In a funny way, studying 20th-century philosophy trains your mind for takeovers. You take out your emotions and your ego—and you sure as hell don't believe your press clips.

In those days a seat was a risk, of course. I borrowed some money, from my uncle Elliott [Elliott Schnall, now a TWA director] and others, put up some of my own, and founded Icahn & Co. Then I got into arbitrage—bona fide, no-risk arbitrage, not the merger stuff they do today. That business worked out well. The next logical step was a jump into what I call asset arbitrage, buying big blocks of shares in companies whose stock was greatly undervalued in relation to their assets. As I saw it then — and still do — my job was to bring those values together. If this means shaking up incompetent, bureaucratic management, so be it. . . .

I'm no managerial genius. But I keep my eye on the bottom line and my people know it. As for management style, I go in with no nonsense. Tom Watson said an interesting thing in FORTUNE ["The Most Successful Capitalist in History," August 31, 1987] when he wrote about how he built IBM: Give me the abrasive guys, he says. I go along with that. They'll tell me the truth, and they're tough. Perhaps I wouldn't want to go fishing with these guys or go on a long vacation with them. Perhaps they feel the same way about me. But they're the ones I have at my right hand. You only have to find one or two. They'll find people just like them to work for them.

I'm no managerial genius. But I keep my eye on the bottom line and my people know it. As for management style, I go in with no nonsense.

These are the guys who never really make it to the top of most corporations, because they don't fit in. Most CEOs got their jobs because their predecessors and the directors liked them. They slapped the right backs and laughed at the right jokes. It's reverse Darwinism: Once a backslapper gets the top job, he sure as hell isn't going to have somebody better than him as his heir apparent. So management gets worse and worse. . . .

One of the hidden 'assets' in many companies is top management: Get rid of some of them, and the value goes up. The companies I won't go near are the ones where the stock is close to the true value. That's a company's best defense.

Managements say stock prices are low because they're doing a lot of research. Bull! Or they say the market only rewards companies that go for short-term profits. But good managements do long-term planning and security analysts give them a multiple if the plans are any good.

Most CEOs got their jobs because their predecessors and the directors liked them. They slapped the right backs and laughed at the right jokes. It's reverse Darwinism . . .

What's going on in companies all over the country these days is absurd. It's like a corporate welfare state. We're supporting managements who produce nothing. No, it's really worse than that. Not only are we paying these drones not to produce, but we're paying them to muck up the works.

From humble beginnings in Hannibal, Missouri, Moore made his way to Yale, and then became president of Citibank in 1959. He subsequently built the company into the world's largest bank. Moore hardly envisioned such a future while at Yale. "I took my classes and took my exams. They were the price I paid for what I wanted to do. They didn't have much relevance to what I planned to do in the future, because the fact was that . . . I didn't have much idea of what I wanted to do in the future." From these ambivalent feelings materialized one useful realization: "What Yale really taught me was how to communicate, and you can't learn anything more important."

While at Yale, Moore had to scrape by on little money, earn what he could in small enterprises, and finagle free meals whenever possible. This modest living unwittingly won him a job when a banking firm recruiting on campus asked which student was the "most successful at self-support." Initially, Moore was hesitant to enter banking, considering it dull. However, the recruiter charmingly explained to him "that being a banker was much better than being a businessman, because a businessman made decisions only about his own business while a banker made decisions about everybody's business." Less than three years later the Great Depression would consume everyone's business.

Somehow, through the astounding financial and employment losses of the period, Moore found himself in 1933 as assistant to the chairman of the bank with a salary increase to boot. The Great Depression dramatically instilled in Moore the first rule of banking, which is don't ever make a loan you can't afford to lose. Obviously for many banks it has been easier said than done. In the following excerpt from his book, *The Banker's Life,* Moore opens by modestly stating that banking is "a simple business, perfect for a C student like Moore." However, he is far above average, and it quickly becomes obvious why he excelled in an industry that demands personable character, as well as keen analytical skills.

The Craft of Lending
George S. Moore

Speaking from a perspective of sixty years in banking and in business, I have to say that banking is the surest, safest, easiest business I have seen or known. I've told people for years that it's a simple business, perfect for a C student like Moore. If you're not actually stupid or dishonest it's hard not to make money in banking. But it's also true that nobody was born a banker, and even more true that you can't become a banker by taking courses in business school. Lending money and getting it back is not an art that takes genius, or a science that takes penetrating study. It's a craft, which you learn by doing, like playing the piano. I have long thought that Citicorp should have a degree-granting institute (as General Motors and IBM do) to finish the training of its younger officers. The reason for setting up such a school inside the bank is that you can't teach banking effectively unless you couple theory with practice.

A banker has to be both a salesman and an analyst. If you let the credit men, the analysts, run the bank, you won't have any customers; if you let the salesmen run the bank, you go bankrupt. When I was hiring lending officers, I'd try to assign them where their temperament *wouldn't* naturally take them. If a man was a natural salesman, I'd send him to the credit analysis department, where he'd learn to add and subtract and be careful. If he seemed to have talent as an analyst, I'd put him out on the street, to get brushed off by

---

If you're not actually stupid or dishonest it's hard not to make money in banking.

---

secretaries and receptionists. He comes back and he says, "I couldn't get in," and you tell him, "Go back until you do get in." Eventually he learns. I used to say that a good salesman was worth ten thousand a year, and a good analyst was worth ten thousand a year, but a man who was both a good salesman and a good analyst was worth a hundred thousand a year. If he can say No and sell, too, he's qualified to be a senior executive.

If you're going to run a man through that sort of course, however, he probably should be twenty-eight or less; certainly, if he's much over thirty, his habits will be too deep to change. And some people are hopeless. One day when I was executive vice-president in charge of the domestic division, my secretary said, "There's a young man from the credit department who insists on seeing you." I saw him, and he said he'd been an analyst in the credit department for three years, and he had time on his hands, he wanted to get into lending. I said, "Well, tell me how the bank's doing—our annual report came out the other day." He hadn't read it. I said, "What do you think of business conditions; do you think our economists got it right in that bulletin we put out yesterday?" He hadn't read that, either. I said, "Are you up on the changes in the banking laws? What's our limit on loans for real estate?" We drew a blank again—nobody, he said, had told him to do that reading. I said, "Nobody around here is going to have time to tell you what to do. Why don't you just leave the bank and find another job?"

To be a banker, you need a good head for numbers, and it helps to have a good memory, and you have to be prepared to work some long hours and get along with people some of whom you may not like very much. One of the first lessons Perkins taught me was, "You have to play the ball, not the man." I criticized my people, and I know some of them resented it on occasion, but it was always about something they had done, not about them personally, and they knew it. The fact is that we didn't lose the people we promoted throughout the years when I could be rough on those who worked for me. I can't think of a single guy who ever left me.

A banker has to be both a salesman and an analyst. If you let the credit men, the analysts, run the bank, you won't have any customers; if you let the salesmen run the bank, you go bankrupt.

Many people think that successful bankers never make a bad loan, but the truth is that nobody ever made a living or performed a service for his society—by betting on sure things. You have to have a little imagination, and you have to be willing to make mistakes once in a while. The important lesson of banking is that you don't make *big* bad loans or too many bad loans, you don't take a risk you can't afford to be wrong with. Any well-run bank must have losses, but they'll be kept within bounds. One of the training documents prepared under my direction was a brief report of the twenty or thirty biggest mistakes we had made—the bad loans, the Russian branches, our largest losses. The people who wrote up those reports usually made it clear that the fellow who'd made the loan or the mistake was a fool, and I would send them back to work on it again, telling them to find the original lending officer's reasons for thinking this would be a good loan, see what it looked like in the environment of the time, *before* anybody knew it was going sour. Ivar Kreuger, the Swedish match king, was the biggest name in Scandinavia and a world financial leader before his empire collapsed; most bankers who lent him money didn't think they were doing anything risky. (As it happened, City Bank had no major involvement with Kreuger, probably because of our close links to the Wallenbergs, who also didn't lend to Kreuger.) While I was president and chairman of Citibank, nobody could get a senior credit initial until he'd read that file. My friend Rainer Gut, who became the head of Credit Suisse a few years ago, told me that one of the things he'd done in his first months was to commission a history of the largest bad loans or credit mistakes his bank ever made, and require that his senior credit officers read that file. He was amused to learn I'd done the same thing.

Many people think that successful bankers never make a bad loan, but the truth is that nobody ever made a living . . . by betting on sure things.

The fact is that in banking, history does repeat itself. If the officers responsible for Mexico and Brazil and Argentina in the 1970s had known some of the past mistakes Citibank had made through taking excessive sovereign risks, such as the German "standstill agreement" of the 1930s, they wouldn't have made the loans they made. After I left the bank, my successors apparently stopped keeping that bad-debt history current, and stopped requiring that credit officers study it.

Knowing what loans to avoid does not necessarily mean a lending officer has to be hard on his customers. Part of the skill of being a man's partner is knowing how to discourage him. I've often claimed that I never just said No to anybody.

If I didn't want to make a loan, after all, what it meant was that I thought the businessman who wanted it was going to get in trouble, make problems not only for the bank but also for himself and his business. He doesn't want that any more than we do. Sometimes I would be able to find a way that he could change his plans so the bank could help him, sometimes I could persuade him not to buy that company or expand that plant. The important thing is that you want him to feel that you've been constructive. He may have a better deal to offer you, some day.

EDWARD C. JOHNSON, III
1930 –

Fidelity Investments was founded in 1946, and in 1957 Johnson joined his father's firm as an analyst. In the 1960s he managed several mutual funds, including the renown multibillion dollar Magellan Fund (only then it had a mere $500,000 in assets). When Johnson took over as president in 1972, and chairman in 1977, he transformed Fidelity into a major player in financial services by offering discounted brokerage services and by building the largest mutual fund company in the United States. The size of their investments soon wielded serious power not only on the stock exchange, but also in corporate board rooms. As Johnson explains, "If we think that a company is clearly off in the wrong direction, we owe it to our shareholders to express our viewpoint." Fidelity has been responsible for more than one termination of a CEO.

Although other securities firms have gone public, Fidelity has remained private because Johnson believes it is most beneficial to the customers and employees. He, like Carl Icahn, has also concluded that "in America too many large corporations are the property no longer of shareholders but of management and investment bankers. Together they are having a ball and sometimes clearly at the expense of their common shareholders." For Johnson, customers (or shareholders) are a number one priority; he frankly claims, "You could run Fidelity if you read all the letters from our customers. You can find out what the heck is wrong with the company with no difficulty at all."

In terms of defining his role in the company, Johnson says, "The job I have, really, is to work in the parts of the business that need strengthening, where the company itself needs to have a greater understanding of what it's doing." To manage the many facets of the business, he has chosen to employ *kaizen*, a Japanese philosophy "that involves gradual but continuous improvement." In *Adventures of a Contrarian*, Johnson delves further into kaizen and the challenges of running an investment firm, and divulges why he never "shoots for the obvious profit."

Adventures of a Contrarian
Edward C. Johnson, III

I f my father, who founded Fidelity Investments in 1946, could see the company today, he might say that we are too big and try to do too many things. But I am sure he would marvel at what we have become.

When he retired in 1974, the company was managing about $2 billion in fourteen funds; twenty years later, we were managing $262 billion in 209 funds and had total customer assets of $380 billion. During that time, we also added many appendages to our basic investment business, ranging from a car service to a chain of art galleries to a telecommunications company in London.

All of this growth certainly has continued to challenge us, which would have delighted my father. He believed that being too secure led to trouble. From the firm's earliest years, he encouraged us to oppose orthodox thinking. This philosophy has given us the freedom to try out new ideas, learn from our mistakes, and build on our successes; it is deeply ingrained in me and in Fidelity today.

STARTING OUT

My father was fascinated by the stock market and had a natural talent for investing. He believed that personal success came from doing what you enjoy and what you are good at, and he counseled me to pursue a career in whatever interested me most, just as he had done.

I was not sure if I would find the investment business interesting. My father had given me a healthy respect for the market—a respect that came from his own experience watching a whole generation lose money in the late 1920s and 1930s. As a child, I knew you were not to play with the market, in the same way I knew not to play with matches, unless you knew what you were doing.

This is a business in which you come to know what you are doing either by buying and selling stocks on your own or buying and selling them professionally; there is no substitute for experience. I had no firsthand experience until I came to work for Fidelity in 1957, first as an analyst and later as a portfolio manager. My father believed that managers should have the freedom to take a certain amount of risk, so we learned mostly through trial and error. Some of the best money managers I have known—my father, Gerry Tsai, and Peter Lynch—developed a unique investment approach by trying out their own ideas.

When it came to the business of investing, my father offered me just a few pieces of direct advice. First, he said, make only the investment decisions about which you have a reasonably high level of conviction. It is a simple but often overlooked lesson: you cannot turn a profit if you are always second-guessing yourself. In and out traders usually enrich their brokers, not themselves. Second, cut your losses and cut them fast; do not listen to reason or emotion, just say goodbye. That was a lesson he had also learned from the 1920s.

This advice proved invaluable for the investing I was beginning to do then and for the building of the business that would come later. Also of great value was the discovery that you can look at the market, as well as the companies in it, in more than one way.

Understanding the cycles of the stock market was of great interest to my father. He liked technical analysis, an objective approach that involves the measuring and charting of market information over extended periods. (Technical analysis is probably the forerunner to today's more sophisticated total quality control; in both cases, the emphasis is on

---

As a child, I knew you were not to play with the market, in the same way I knew not to play with matches, unless you knew what you were doing.

---

measurement.) Like my father, I was also intrigued by market cycles and psychological effects on the market. But my real interest was in what made one particular company good and another not as good, something called fundamental analysis. While money managers seemed to favor one form of analysis or the other, I realized very early that each discipline had enormous benefits as well as some shortcomings. I began to think that if you knew both, you would do better than if you knew just one. This belief soon affected my investing decisions and developed into the idea that the whole company should excel in both, with individual managers deciding which to use and when.

As an analyst, I visited many companies to evaluate their management and their earnings prospects. But I found myself more interested in the philosophy of how they ran the business and why they ran it in a particular way than the statistics I was being given. Over the years, I have learned a lot from studying other companies, which I have been able to apply to our business.

I also saw that sometimes the best stock buys are those that go against market psychology. Doing the opposite of what most investors are doing at any particular time is known as contrary opinion. I have found that being a contrarian works even better in business than in the stock market.

When my father turned over the day-to-day operation of the business to me in 1972, he again let me learn largely by doing. There were things I decided to do that I know he disagreed with, but he never interfered. All he wanted to know were two things: whether I was truly interested in the business and whether I shared his strong sense of personal responsibility to the shareholders — some of whom were relatives and close friends with substantial investments in the funds.

He had a certain confidence in me, despite my reputation in the family as the one who liked to spend money (a reputation that, in fact, has proven to be true). My father knew I could spend the money we made; he just did not know whether it would come back again. There was one year in the mid-1960s when the company made $5.5 million. I remember how guilty my father felt. He said, "A company like ours should never make this much money," whereas my attitude was, "This is wonderful! Boy, are we going to have fun with this money!"

. . . cut your losses and cut them fast; do not listen to reason or emotion, just say good-bye.

To me business is fascinating. It is like a game; sometimes you win, sometimes you lose. There is no formula for success. Sometimes there are big rewards and sometimes no rewards; it is a matter of taking risks — the right risks, those where you believe the probabilities are in your favor. Shooting for the obvious profit seems like the best way to lose money because then you are always riding on someone else's coattails.

TAKING THE CONTRARIAN APPROACH

People have often asked me if it was a tough decision to get into the money market business. In fact, it was easy. It was a matter of survival.

Looking back at the fund industry, it had a wonderful period in the mid-to-late 1960s. Then, with the exception of money market funds, the industry basically died between 1969 and 1982. In the 1960s the fund managers at Fidelity could do no wrong. Everybody loved us. We were oriented toward supergrowth stocks—those with the best prospects of producing earnings quickly—and owned many secondary securities, which did well in the mid-to-late 1960s but poorly beginning in 1969. We went from being the most loved to being the most hated. Our sales fell about 95 percent. In the early 1970s, the assets we managed dropped from $5.5 billion to less than $1.7 billion. We were fighting for survival.

At the time, people were not interested in common stocks or stock funds, and two companies were ahead of us in launching money market funds. We needed to offer a service that was better and different. I thought that if we could provide investors with an easy way to take their money out through check writing, they would be more apt to put their money in. Some of my colleagues and competitors must have thought I was asking for trouble. But, in 1974, we introduced our first money market fund with check writing, called Fidelity Daily Income Trust, and we were surprised at how quickly the money started to pour in. We saw the money funds as a way to gather assets that hopefully would move into our stock funds once the market started to improve, giving us a head start on sales; we never saw them as a business in themselves. Dreyfus, which had launched a money market fund in 1972, promoted its product heavily and gathered the biggest share of assets. I learned from them that even if you have a good product, unless you promote it heavily, you will not gain market share.

A second thing we did that probably raised some eyebrows in the industry was to change our distribution. For thirty years we had sold our funds through broker-dealers. For a variety of reasons, that method of distribution was no longer working.

When I looked at the competition, I saw two strategies that gave me some ideas about how we could take a different approach to selling. First, I was impressed with how Dreyfus used clever marketing and advertising to create demand for its products. Second, Dreyfus had offered the first mutual fund that was aggressively managed for top performance. Fidelity's Capital and Trend funds followed the same style of investing. Our strategy was to buy stocks we perceived to be cheap and sell them when they became overpriced on a relatively short-term basis. The turnover was quite high, so it was considered somewhat scandalous at the time. But in the mid-1960s, the results were excellent. In both cases, we saw performance create sizable demand for the funds.

Many brokers believed that they were solely responsible for creating the demand for the funds, which may not have been totally correct. Investment performance and the investor's desire to make money was the mixture that produced explosive sales. It seemed to me that if our funds performed well, they would sell themselves. In some situations, we could eliminate the broker from the selling process and offer our funds directly to individual investors. That meant we could maintain a lower sales charge on the funds—or, in some cases, even remove it—because we did not have to pay commissions. Thus came our decision in the mid-1970s to sell our funds directly to individual investors through direct response advertising and a toll-free telephone line.

At the time, this was a radical departure from the way most funds were sold. Nobody else had tried to set up an operation that allowed customers to transact their business completely by phone. But we thought it would prove to be a cost-effective distribution system, and it has become just that. Nevertheless, a majority of people still prefer to buy funds with a full commission or sales charge. In fact, stock fund sales today are 60 percent full commission. Many people need the assistance of a salesperson to make their investment decisions. So we support and believe in both approaches—selling funds through brokers and selling them directly.

Despite the stock market's downturns in the 1970s, I remained optimistic because history was on our side. Looking back as far as the Civil War, I knew that the stock market was cyclical, and I had little doubt that it would start to move up again; I just did not know when. (I suppose if I had known in 1969 that we would have to wait thirteen years for another bull market, we might have moved into another business entirely!) At the time, we did not care about maximizing earnings or improving the income statement; we just did not want to lose cash. Remembering my father's experience in the 1920s and 1930s, I knew you could not run a business for long on borrowed money.

Business was so bad in the 1970s that it was actually a wonderful time to take over the company. There were no illusions about anything; we had to live by our wits. Based on that experience, I began to see stock market declines and economic recessions as opportunities to build the company and to make it stronger. They provided a chance for us to look at what we were doing and to try to do it better.

We decided in the 1970s to build and improve our investment department. In the mid-1970s, we did some major pruning and subsequently added to the group, even though our equity assets under management were not growing. Thus, when the bull market started up again in 1982, we had the talent to produce top-performing funds. I do not think that we would have been as well prepared if we had not laid the groundwork in the 1970s.

Another strategy was to bring the shareholder processing operations inside, a decision that added to the complexity of the business and may have caused people within the company to think that I was a little mad. Even my father had always thought that bankers knew best how to keep track of the books. If something went wrong, they would be responsible. It seemed to me that we were always at a great disadvantage if we were unable to communicate directly with our shareholders. If something went wrong and we said it was the bank's fault, the people who did business with us would say, "Well, who hired the bank?" Since we did, we had the ultimate responsibility when there was an error. A third-party outside servicing agent did not have the same stake in the success of the business as we did.

It had not gone unnoticed that Keystone—one of our Boston-based competitors—had a reputation for always providing good service to its broker-dealers and shareholders, largely because Keystone did its own servicing. It occurred to me that the major reason it sold a lot of shares was not investment performance so much as this high level of service. Of course, I knew from my experience as an investment analyst that successful companies usually had good marketing and sales departments as well as good products. To optimize both, it seemed to me we needed control over the service function in addition to the ability to produce top investment results.

Once we made the decision to develop shareholder servicing skills in-house, we did it one step at a time. The first function we brought in was that of the transfer agent, who handles shareholder record keeping; this includes tracking who owns shares of which fund and how many, when the shares were purchased, and what dividends are owed. Once we mastered that process, it seemed logical to next bring in-house the fund bookkeeping and accounting, which we did in 1973. By that time, we already had a history of gradually adding new skills and services. Before this, we had developed our ability to make money in stocks, then our ability to make money in bonds. After fully embracing shareholder servicing, we focused on learning to use the available technology effectively.

At times, our technology investments seemed contrarian. For example, although the company had little cash in the 1970s, we spent money on computers to enable us to handle our shareholder processing operations more efficiently. But it was not until the early 1980s that we started investing heavily in technology. Some of our competitors thought we spent excessively in order to have the latest technology. However, we viewed—and still view—the effective use of technology as essential.

We have tried to be timely in using new technologies, although I have found that if you are the first to use something new, you usually end up spending a lot of time working out the bugs. On the other hand, you cannot wait too long or your competition will get too far ahead of you, and you will never catch up. We have also tried not to fall in love with the technology itself. The technology may be fascinating, but we need to determine if it achieves the goal we want—quality service at a competitive price. In fact, the limiting factor today is not the technology itself but rather the training of people who are using it and writing creative software designs that do more than imitate old processing techniques. After all, technology is just a tool; the hand that guides the tool determines its performance. It is like putting a Stradivarius violin in the hands of an average six-year-old; he or she may love the instrument, but the chances of hearing beautiful music are very slight.

Technology has allowed us to do many things, such as build a two-thousand-person telephone sales and service force. But I believe we are still in the early innings of the game of learning what technology can do and how we can most effectively use it. The steam engine is an analogy. It was invented in 1825. Yet it was not until 1869—almost forty-five years later—that the transcontinental railroad was completed. Just as the steam engine changed the country by opening up new real estate, so technology will continue to revolutionize the way we do business. Any company that wants to be successful must, in my opinion, be part of that revolution; if it is not, another company will be.

Speaking of revolutionary, when we went into the discount brokerage business in 1979, everyone said I must be crazy. Mutual funds is a respectable business, they said. Why do you want to be in a business like discount brokerage, a business with a small profit margin? But there are advantages. Branch offices, for example, would allow us to build a distribution system with national visibility, something that would never be affordable with just mutual funds. And a brokerage system would allow investors to consolidate their stock, bond, and mutual fund investments into a single account. We could never offer that level of convenience with a mutual fund shareholder system. As it turns out, starting a discount brokerage business—we were the only mutual fund company to do so—was a good decision.

SWIMMING UPSTREAM

One of my distant nineteenth-century relatives once said, "Any fish can swim downstream, but only a live fish can swim upstream." This made sense to me as I thought about Fidelity's growth. We wanted to stay lively. We did not want to become entrenched in bureaucracy or to remain satisfied with our achievements. A company is constantly changing; it must be able to adapt. When a company stops changing and believes it has the secrets to everything, it has the secrets to nothing. Small companies know this. They are constantly changing. They face numerous challenges each day. To survive, they have to be nimble and creative.

Many companies, including banks, brokerage houses, and insurance firms, have diversified into mutual funds. But we were one of the first and only mutual fund companies to go into other businesses and to build them from scratch. Of the 1,500 mutual fund companies in the United States today, we are one of the only ones, for example, to start a discount brokerage service. Starting and developing new businesses has always been a key part of Fidelity's culture. Unfortunately, our first diversification efforts were venture capital investments in the 1960s that did not work out well. But this idea of Fidelity doing more than just managing mutual funds was something I had always wanted to do. And so we began diversifying into other businesses in earnest in the 1970s.

My father always felt that running an investment company was not a real business because it was "just a business of ideas." You pick up the telephone to call someone in; he buys the stock. You get in touch with the bank; it settles the trade. You call the bank again; it pays the dividend. Just ideas. It seemed to me that investing in other businesses could give us another possible service. In addition, each new business gave us an opportunity to try out some of our ideas and hopefully acquire new skills to help our basic business. Sometimes we tried to apply the skills learned in our basic business to start up derivative businesses, although we were not always successful.

In the early 1970s, for example, we decided to go into the mini-counseling business. I thought it was a wonderful idea because of the high fees associated with managing individual accounts. Most people did not manage individual accounts well, but I thought we could mechanize that with the help of computers. We bought a small company and put one of our portfolio managers in charge. The whole experience was a failure. We could not control the size of the accounts—they were all smaller than we had hoped. In addition, the investment results were bad. But we learned two important lessons.

First, we learned that it is nearly impossible to have a portfolio manager who can successfully handle individual accounts as well as deal with individual clients. A great investment manager is not necessarily an expert in customer relations.

Second—and this was before computers really were involved—we learned that bookkeeping impediments can kill a business. Keeping track of individual accounts, making sure all the right securities were in the right accounts, calculating the right percentage in each account—the mechanics of running the business—were a disaster. We lacked the necessary shareholder servicing skills.

So, the mini-counseling business failed. But it helped to push us to develop the skills we needed. In the 1980s, it seemed that the cost of venture capital deals had become too high. So we decided that instead of investing our excess cash in other companies, we would actively spawn our own small businesses. The name for these fledgling concerns is Fidelity Capital; among them are a car service, a chain of art galleries, a group of telecommunications companies, an insurance company, an executive search firm, and various publishing operations. The advantage that we have been able to offer the Fidelity Capital companies is an infrastructure that can supply capital, along with motivational and technical skills. These start-ups are free to use the knowledge and skills we have built into our basic business to help launch their efforts.

Growing, Learning, Changing

People wonder why we build small businesses when we have such a strong basic business. There are many reasons, but the best one is building small businesses teaches you a lot about yourself and your organization. You keep alive, in an organization that has ever-increasing numbers of people, a skill that is essential—the ability to start something new and run it well. Starting out as an underdog and having to do a superior job is good practice for a growing company; the skills you learn can be applied to some of your "old" businesses to keep them alive and vibrant. Many of the businesses that we have developed can add something to Fidelity. What we learn in the telecommunications business, for example, can improve the marketing and sales department of our mutual fund operation, which depends heavily on computers and telephones. Plus, telecommunications is an industry with which we are familiar, so it makes sense to further our skills in that area rather than in an industry we know nothing about. Today it takes a whole group of skills — including investment, legal, technology, and general management — to make our business successful.

. . . a new venture cannot simply be intertwined with the old. Since the old brings all the money in, and the new brings in none, a new business may not get the nourishment it needs.

As Fidelity has grown, we have learned how important it is to work like a small company. One way we accomplish that is by continually breaking our basic business down into manageable units. We start a new company within Fidelity when we believe a particular business offers unusual opportunity for growth. Our 401(k) business, for example, which sells services for defined contribution plans to corporations, used to be part of our institutional business. In the mid-1980s, our institutional business had a fast-growing market selling mutual funds to bank trust departments. The 401(k) market, which was a much harder sale, was being ignored. So we broke it off and started a new company dedicated to that area alone. As the 401(k) business took off, it became apparent that the different markets it serviced needed to be treated differently — the needs of *Fortune* 500 companies with thousands of employees were quite different from those of small, emerging businesses. So we carved out separate subsidiaries to better serve each area. By breaking the business up into smaller units, people at all levels were able to take ownership and learn about the different aspects of a particular market in greater detail. We have found that if we do not carve our big businesses into separate small businesses, nobody takes responsibility for anything.

From our start-up companies at Fidelity Capital, we have learned that a new venture cannot simply be intertwined with the old. Since the old brings all the money in, and the new brings in none, a new business may not get the nourishment it needs. It is like trying to grow a little tree under a big tree — the little tree never gets enough sunshine. We can focus best on areas with the most opportunity by moving assets and people from other parts of the business. That way we can nourish the new area completely and hopefully make it to market with a better product faster than the competition.

To keep growing, we have to build new businesses and maintain and improve our old ones. In mutual funds, for example, we learned how to seed new funds and make them grow while keeping the older funds well-nourished so that they, too, produce competitive investment results. Whether starting a new, small business or running a part of the older, larger business, the basics are still the same. In either case, you have to understand exactly what will make the business successful.

. . . a business has to be good for the customer (quality), good for the company (profitable), and good for the employees (rewarding). If we only achieve two out of three, we have not succeeded.

With a small start-up business, we may try to do one or two things exceedingly well. With a bigger business, the goal might be twenty, thirty, or forty things done exceedingly well. In either instance, quality has to precede profit. But once we have succeeded in producing and maintaining a high-quality product or service, we have to make it profitable. Cutting corners, which may be a short-term solution to the profit part of the equation, hurts quality in the long run. No money is saved if quality is sacrificed; working smarter is what brings the two together. That means we have to be willing to try new ideas. My own rule of thumb is that a business has to be good for the customer (quality), good for the company (profitable), and good for the employees (rewarding). If we only achieve two out of three, we have not succeeded.

No matter the business, a good product is essential. That means determining what the customers want and then figuring out what we can provide. Over a long period, we have found that close communication with customers can mean the difference between success or failure. They give us the best feedback about our service; they tell us what they like or dislike about what we offer and what we do not offer that they wish we did. We try to respond to their requests whenever feasible, which is why building a spirit of change into the company is so important. It is also why paying attention to details is critical.

One way we have tried to do both is by implementing a Japanese philosophy known as *kaizen,* which had its beginnings in rice farming. *Kaizen,* a process that involves gradual but continuous improvement, has helped us build into the company the spirit that everything we do can be done better. Looking at the general quality of service that Fidelity provides its customers, it is fair to say we do a good job. But in closely examining some particular things that we do, especially in new areas, one finds that there are many rough edges. We are not as good as we think we are. *Kaizen* has helped us to strive for improvement when we might otherwise have been content with what we had already achieved. That is how we must continue if we want to remain a leader.

One of the best ways to become better at what you do is to learn how other people go about producing a better product or service. When Japan came out with superior products in the late 1960s and early 1970s, I wondered whether the difference could be attributed to a cultural factor or some process they were using. It fascinated me, for instance, that the Japanese could build cameras comparable to the German models at about one-third the cost. Over the years, I had read a lot about Japanese business practices. On a trip there in the mid-1980s, I picked up a book at the Okura Hotel called *Kaizen — The Key to Japan's Competitive Success* by Masaaki Imai. If *kaizen* worked so well in production facilities in Japan, I thought it might work just as well in servicing operations like ours.

We started with *kaizen*'s premise that how well we do little things daily could determine our success. If every employee strived to do his or her job better, that could translate into major improvements in how we as a company did business. The wonderful thing about making small changes is that you can see the effect they have on the total system. If a small change does not work well, it can easily be reversed. If it does work, then you can make another change, until cumulatively a tremendous change has been created. Of course, in order to detect improvement, objective measures of performance are needed for every aspect of a job.

In the spirit of *kaizen*, we continually look at what to measure, how to measure it, and what the results mean. Measuring the quality of what you produce in the service business is much more difficult than if you sell a widget that is supposed to last for ten years and breaks in ten days. So we measure a lot of things, from the quality of our investment results to the length of time it takes us to solve customer problems; once we have consistently met our benchmarks, we set new ones. Measurement is not an end in itself. It is a means to higher quality, timeliness, and lower costs.

Our company is good at coming up with products and services that customers like; making our businesses profitable is always harder and more time-consuming. My father started Fidelity in 1946, but the company never made a decent profit until 1960. Reaching profitability often takes perseverance. Still, businesses that do not turn a profit in good times are going to create losses in bad times. My opinion is that either we need to improve them so that they are profitable or leave them. To me, the willingness to trim businesses is as important as the willingness to build them. We do not want to trim them too soon, but if a business is not profitable, we need to look at it carefully to determine whether there is a real need for this service. If there is, we must decide whether someone will pay us enough to eventually make a profit.

Fidelity's biggest challenge these days is not fighting for survival; it is fighting against obesity. Stable companies run the risk of a metaphorical hardening of the arteries.

The profit motive becomes important for the people who run our operations. Like my father, I believe in putting one person in charge and letting him or her go. If the person who runs a business is the right person—and, of course, if it is a good business—then there is a good chance of success. This is especially true of small start-up businesses. If you want a good entrepreneur—someone with singleness of purpose, love of the business, and absolute patience—you have to give him or her an entrepreneurial profit. The people who manage our start-up companies at Fidelity Capital have an agreement with us. If they build the business to a certain level, which we define in terms of sales and earnings, then they will receive a meaningful financial reward. The investment side of our business works the same way. We try to motivate people with a reward structure that is tied to producing results. Since Fidelity is a private company, the earnings can go to the people who produce the profit.

At all levels of the company, we have set up reward structures that encourage people to strive for improvements.

Sometimes attempts at improvement fail; if they are sincere, intelligent attempts, the reward structure should accept that. On the other hand, we have to be careful that we do not go too far—experimenting with everything at once can spell trouble. We adjust one thing, prove that it works, and then move on to try other things.

We have been fortunate in finding good people and figuring out how to motivate them. Part of the motivation is financial, but part of it comes through making the jobs interesting and demanding. Pride is a factor. The most highly motivated, enthusiastic people take pride in their work, the same way a craftsman takes pride in the chair he has built. The realization that you are doing something important—something that adds value to yourself and to others—is a strong motivation. In fact, having talented and motivated people has helped us succeed more than any other single factor. Obviously, the best ideas in the world amount to nothing if you do not have the right people to execute them.

LOOKING AHEAD

Fidelity's biggest challenge these days is not fighting for survival; it is fighting against obesity. Stable companies run the risk of a metaphorical hardening of the arteries. But there are also dangers in running at high speed. When you grow fast, you work first on increasing capacity and then on improving the quality of the product; there is not time to develop real benchmarks. Yet those benchmarks are exactly what is needed to see improvements and to determine where you are making (or losing) money. Compared to a smaller enterprise, a larger company like ours has to be more organized, with good measurement and internal information systems. When we were small, our information systems were our personal relationships; as we grew bigger, we could no longer manage by gut feelings alone. Having the right measurements is critical now.

How big can Fidelity become? Who knows? A crystal ball might predict our involvement with a few more businesses. There are certainly many areas into which we could still expand—but only those businesses where we can do an excellent job. Whatever Fidelity looks like in the future, however, it will include quality products, quality service to our customers, and the satisfaction of the people who work here. We might not have the dominant market share in all our businesses, but it will be an important market share. What really matters is our ability to run our business exceedingly well.

Any company can fall into the trap of doing things badly—just look at how few companies have been around for twenty, thirty, or forty years. Every industry goes through growth phases and shakeouts. Many companies shrink or disappear after a shakeout; the survivors are the ones that can improve their products and cut their expenses. I live on a piece of land once owned by Sterling Elliot, who owned and ran Elliot Addressograph. The company was the leading automation firm in 1920—twice the size of IBM. It was also quite creative, and Elliot probably had as many inventions in the printing and automation area as any man in America. But who today has heard of him or Elliot Addressograph? Both are totally forgotten. The lesson is that it is very easy to go backward—easier than going forward.

If there was a simple formula for success and it was easy to follow, everybody would be doing it.

The element of personal satisfaction is critical for moving ahead. The business world is like a game. The question is not how well you play golf, for example; it is whether you enjoy playing it. You may be the best golfer in the world, but it means little if you do not play your best to beat your opponent. It is the same with business. Do the profits feel good or do they feel bad? And how about the losses? You can lose money without worry if the losses are part of the cycle and if the company is growing stronger. So it is a matter of balancing the desire to win against the sense of personal satisfaction you need to be enthusiastic about the job. If there was a simple formula for success and it was easy to follow, everybody would be doing it.

Who knows what the future holds? Bull markets or bear markets, I do not know, nor am I sure I want to. Certainly the power of computers opens up enormous new opportunities for processing and servicing in a wide range of businesses, including the financial industry. Asked what the future had in store in 1970, my father said, "Oh, heavens, you don't care about that. I guess my viewpoint on the future is very strong: I ignore it. It's so silly. You can't love the future. You can't hear it. You can't drink it. By thinking about the future, you suck all the vitality out of it. Aim to do whatever you're doing better and let all that take care of itself." I agree.

Chronology

Author Index

Acknowledgments

The Book of Business Wisdom would not have been possible without Ruth Mills, my editor at John Wiley & Sons. I thank her foremost, and will always be grateful to her. Throughout the project, Ruth's enthusiasm and flexibility were exceptional and inspirational. I am also deeply in debted to Ed Knappman of New England Publishing Associates. As a literary agent, he is efficient and direct, and provided important feedback in the development of the project.

The immeasurable importance of family support in any endeavor must be acknowledged and appreciated. Diana, my wife, provided essential encouragement and poignant criticism. She has sacrificed much for the family over the years and I hope I will be able to repay her with more than just a book. Pierson and Alex, our boys, were in charge of music to keep dad going, and their eagerness to help was motivation alone.

Many faceless editors and writers must be applauded for their foresight in capturing on paper the ideas of these great leaders of industry. One of the most interesting periodicals I discovered was *System: The Magazine of Business*, published between 1900 and 1935. It provided a wealth of material and I strongly encourage every historian of business to examine its contents. To the many reference librarians whom I annoyed with my questions—thank you. Thanks also to Bob Atwan, Dan Burstein, Bob Kennedy, and everyone else who donated a suggestion or two.

Notes

The biographical sketches were drawn using the following sources.

J. Ogden Armour:
Forbes, B. C. *Men Who Are Making America.* New York: B. C. Forbes Publishing Co., 1918.

Mary Kay Ash:
Ash, Mary Kay. *Mary Kay.* New York: Harper & Row, Publishers, 1981.

P. T. Barnum:
Barnum, Phineas Taylor. *Struggles and Triumphs; or, Forty Years' Recollections of P. T. Barnum.* New York: Penguin Books, 1981.
Harris, Neil. *Hum Bug: The Art of P. T. Barnum.* Boston: Little, Brown and Company, 1973.

Bernard M. Baruch:
Baruch, Bernard M. *Baruch, My Own Story.* New York: Henry Holt and Company, 1957.
Grant, James. *Bernard Baruch: The Adventures of a Wall Street Legend.* New York: Simon and Schuster, 1983.

Marvin Bower:
Byrne, John A., and Gary McWilliams. "The McKinsey Mystique." *Business Week:* September 20, 1993.

Andrew Carnegie:
Wall, Joseph Frazier. *Andrew Carnegie.* New York: Oxford University Press, 1970.

Henry Clews:
Clews, Henry. *The Wall Street Point of View.* ca. 1900.
Clews, Henry. *Fifty Years in Wall Street.* Irving Publishing, 1908.
Dictionary of American Biography. New York: Charles Scribner's Sons, 1930.

Thomas Alva Edison:
Baldwin, Neil. *Edison: Inventing the Century*. New York: Hyperion, 1995.
Edison, Thomas Alva. "How I would Double the Volume of Business." *System: The Magazine of Business 44*: September 1923.

Benjamin F. Fairless:
Current Biography Yearbook, 1957. New York: The H. W. Wilson Company.
Fairless, Benjamin F. "What Democracy Did for Me." *The American Magazine 145*: February 1948.

Harvey S. Firestone:
Firestone, Harvey S., with Samuel Crowther. *Men and Rubber: The Story of Business*. Garden City, New York: Doubleday, Page & Company.

Julius Fleischmann:
Fucini, Joseph J., and Suzy Fucini. *Entrepreneurs: The Men and Women behind Famous Brand Names and How They Made It*. Boston: G. K. Hall & Co., 1985.

Milton S. Florsheim:
Clark, Neil M. "Builders of Business." *System: The Magazine of Business*: November 1921.

B. C. Forbes:
Winans, Christopher. *Malcolm Forbes: The Man Who Had Everything*. New York: St. Martin's Press, 1990.

Malcolm S. Forbes:
Winans, Christopher. *Malcolm Forbes: The Man Who Had Everything*. New York: St. Martin's Press, 1990.

Henry Ford:
Ford, Henry, with Samuel Crowther. *My Life and Work*. New York: Doubleday, Page & Company, 1922.
Gelderman, Carol. *Henry Ford: The Wayward Capitalist*. New York: The Dial Press, 1981.

Henry Ford, II:
Lasky, Victor. *Never Complain, Never Explain: The Story of Henry Ford II*. New York: Richard Marek Publishers, 1981.

Benjamin Franklin:
Van Doren, Carl. *Benjamin Franklin: A Biography*. New York: Viking Press, 1938.

Harold Geneen:
Geneen, Harold, and Alvin Moscow. *Managing*. New York: Doubleday, 1984.

Sampson, Anthony. *The Sovereign State of ITT.* New York: Stein and Day, 1973.

J. Paul Getty:
Getty, J. Paul. *As I See It: The Autobiography of J. Paul Getty.* New York: Prentice Hall, 1976.
Lenzner, Robert. *The Great Getty: The Life and Loves of J. Paul Getty, Richest Man in the World.* New York: Crown Publishers, 1985.

Horace Greeley:
Hale, William Harlan. *Horace Greeley: Voice of the People.* New York: Harper & Brothers, 1950.

Crawford H. Greenewalt:
Colby, Gerald. *Du Pont Dynasty: Behind the Nylon Curtain.* Secaucus, New Jersey: Lyle Stuart Inc., 1984.
"The Wizards of Wilmington." *Time:* April 16, 1951.

Andrew S. Grove:
Grove, Andrew S. "Managing: Ideas & Solutions." *Fortune:* September 18, 1995.
Hof, Robert D. "The Education of Andrew Grove." *Business Week:* January 16, 1995.

Lee Iacocca:
Iacocca, Lee, with William Novak. *Iacocca: An Autobiography.* New York: Bantam Books, 1984.
Levin, Doron P. *Behind the Wheel at Chrysler: The Iacocca Legacy.* New York: Harcourt Brace & Company, 1995.

Carl C. Icahn:
Stevens, Mark. *King Icahn: The Biography of a Renegade Capitalist.* New York: Dutton, 1993.

Edward C. Johnson, III:
The Editors of Institutional Investor, ed. *The Way It Was: An Oral History of Finance: 1967–1987.* New York: William Morrow and Company, Inc., 1988.
"The Big Bear From Beantown?" *Newsweek:* March 14, 1994.

John J. Johnson:
Johnson, John J., with Lerone Bennett, Jr. *Succeeding Against the Odds.* New York: Warner Books, 1989.
Sobel, Robert, and David B. Sicilia. *The Entrepreneurs: An American Adventure.* Boston: Houghton Mifflin Company, 1986.

Victor Kiam:
Kiam, Victor. *Going for It! How to Succeed as an Entrepreneur.* New York: William Morrow and Company, Inc., 1986.

Kiam, Victor. *Live to Win: Achieving Success in Life and Business*. New York: Harper & Row, Publishers, 1988.

Estée Lauder:
Israel, Lee. *Estée Lauder: Beyond the Magic: An Unauthorized Biography*. New York: Macmillan, 1985.
Lauder, Estée. *Estée: A Success Story*. New York: Random House, 1985.

David E. Lilienthal:
Lilienthal, David. *The Road to Change: 1955–1959: The Journals of David E. Lilienthal, Volume IV*. New York: Harper & Row, Publishers, 1969.

Henry R. Luce:
Swanberg, W. A. *Luce and His Empire*. New York: Scribner, 1972.

Peter Lynch:
Current Biography Yearbook, 1994. New York: H. W. Wilson Company.
Spragins, Ellyn E. "Hard Times for the Mutual Fund King." *Newsweek:* April 10, 1995.

Alfred E. Lyon:
America's Twelve Master Salesmen. New York: B. C. Forbes & Sons Publishing Co., Inc., 1952.
Kluger, Richard. *Ashes to Ashes: America's Hundred-Year War, the Public Health, and the Unabashed Triumph of Philip Morris*. New York: Alfred A. Knopf, 1996.

John L. McCaffrey:
"McCaffrey of International Harvester." *Fortune:* December 1951.
Marsh, Barbara. *A Corporate Tragedy*. Garden City, New York: Doubleday & Company, Inc., 1985.

J. Irwin Miller:
Harris, T. George. "Egghead in the Diesel Industry." *Fortune:* October, 1957.

Tom Monaghan:
Monaghan, Tom, with Robert Anderson. *Pizza Tiger*. New York: Random House, 1986.

George S. Moore:
Moore, George S. *The Banker's Life*. New York: Norton, 1987.

David Ogilvy:
Ogilvy, David. *Blood, Brains & Beer: The Autobiography of David Ogilvy*. New York: Atheneum, 1978.
Ogilvy, David. *On Advertising*. New York: Crown Publishers, Inc., 1983.

J. C. Penney:
Penney, J. C. *The Man with a Thousand Partners.* New York: Harper & Row, 1931.

George W. Perkins:
Forbes, B. C. *Men Who Are Making America.* New York: B. C. Forbes Publishing Co., 1918.
Sinclair, Andrew. *Corsair: The Life of J. Pierpont Morgan.* Boston: Little, Brown and Company, 1981.

T. Boone Pickens:
Pickens, T. Boone. *Boone.* Boston: Houghton Mifflin Company, 1987.

John D. Rockefeller:
Rockefeller, John D. *Random Reminiscences of Men and Events.* New York: Doubleday, Page & Company, 1909.

Willard F. Rockwell, Jr.:
"Rockwell Trims North American." *Business Week:* January 31, 1970.
"The Rockwells Take Off for Outer Space." *Fortune:* June 1, 1967.

Charles M. Schwab:
Wall, Joseph Frazier. *Andrew Carnegie.* New York: Oxford University Press, 1970.
Schwab, Charles. "How to Succeed." Speech delivered to Princeton University.

E. W. Scripps:
Scripps, E. W. *Damned Old Crank.* New York: Harper & Brothers, 1951.

Richard W. Sears:
Emmet, Boris, and John E. Jeuck. *Catalogues and Counters: A History of Sears Roebuck and Company.* Chicago: The University of Chicago Press, 1950.
Katz, Donald R. *The Big Store: Inside the Crisis and Revolution at Sears.* New York: Viking, 1987.

Muriel Siebert:
The Editors of Institutional Investor. *The Way It Was: An Oral History of Finance: 1967–1987.* New York: William Morrow and Company, Inc., 1988.
Wyatt, Edward. *Wall St.'s Top Woman Slips in the Backdoor. New York Times,* February 11, 1996.

Igor I. Sikorsky:
Sikorsky, Igor I. *The Story of the Winged-S: Late Developments and Recent Photographs of the Helicopter, an Autobiography.* Dodd, Mead, 1958.

479

Alfred P. Sloan:

Langworth, Richard M., and Jan P. Norbye. *The Complete History of General Motors 1908–1986.* Skokie, IL: Publications International, Ltd., 1986.

Sloan, Alfred P. *My Years With General Motors.* New York: Doubleday, 1963.

Sam Walton:

Vance, Sandra S., and Roy V. Scott. *Wal-Mart: A History of Sam Walton's Retail Phenomenon.* New York: Twayne Publishers, 1994.

Walton, Sam, with John Huey. *Sam Walton: Made in America: My Story.* New York: Doubleday, 1992.

Thomas J. Watson:

Watson, Thomas J., Jr., with Peter Petre. *Father, Son & Co.: My Life at IBM and Beyond.* New York: Bantam Books, 1990.

Thomas J. Watson, Jr.:

Watson, Thomas J., Jr., with Peter Petre. *Father, Son & Co.: My Life at IBM and Beyond.* New York: Bantam Books, 1990.

John F. Welch, Jr.:

Slater, Robert. *The New GE: How Jack Welch Revived an American Institution.* Homewood, IL: Business One Irwin, 1993.

Tichy, Noel M., and Stratford Sherman. *Control Your Destiny or Someone Else Will: How Jack Welch Is Making General Electric the World's Most Competitive Corporation.* New York: Doubleday, 1993.

Robert W. Woodruff:

Pendergrast, Mark. *For God, Country and Coca-Cola: The Unauthorized History of the Great American Soft Drink and the Company that Makes It.* New York: Charles Scribner's Sons, 1993.

Owen D. Young:

Case, Josephine Young. *Owen D. Young and American Enterprise: A Biography.* D.R. Godine, 1982.

Tarbell, Ida M. *Owen D. Young, A New Type of Industrial Leader.* New York, The Macmillan Company, 1932.

Credits and Sources

"Armour Men Who Got Ahead—and Why" by J. Odgen Armour, from *American Magazine*, March 1917.

"The Art of Listening" from *Mary Kay on People Management* by Mary Kay Ash. Copyright © 1984 by Mary Kay Cosmetics, Inc. All rights reserved.

"The Art of Money-Getting" by Phineas Taylor Barnum, from *My Life Story*, and *Golden Rules for Money Making*, 1886.

"My Investment Philosophy" from *My Own Story* by Bernard Baruch. Copyright © 1957 by Bernard M. Baruch. Reprinted by permission of Henry Holt & Co., Inc.

"Leadership" from *The Will to Manage* by Marvin Bower. Reprinted by permission of Marvin Bower. Copyright © 1966 by Marvin Bower.

"The Road to Business Success" by Andrew Carnegie, from a speech at Curry Commercial College, June 23, 1885.

"How to Make Money on Wall Street" from *Fifty Years in Wall Street* by Henry Clews. Irving Publishing, 1908.

"They Won't Think" from *The Diary and Assundry Observations* by Thomas Edison. The Philosophical Library, 1948.

"What Democracy Did for Me" by Benjamin F. Fairless, from *American Magazine*, February 1948.

"What I have Learned About Men" by Harvey S. Firestone, from *American Magazine*, April 1919.

"My Three Essentials of Management" by Julius Fleischmann, from *System: The Magazine of Business*, July 1924.

"Planning for the Business You Are Going to Have" by Milton S. Florsheim, from *System: The Magazine of Business*, January 1924.

"In Budgeting Your Days, Allow Time for Thinking" from *How to Get the Most Out of Business* by B. C. Forbes. Reprinted by Permission of Forbes, Inc. Copyright © Forbes, Inc., 1927.

"A Vital Ingredient of Sustained Success" and "Dispensibility Precedes Indispensibility" from *Fact and Comment* by Malcolm S. Forbes.

"Succeeding with What You Have" by Charles M. Schwab, from *American Magazine*, November 1916.

"Some Outlandish Rules for Making Money" from *Damned Old Crank* by E. W. Scripps. Copyright © 1951 by Harper & Brothers. Reprinted by permission of HarperCollins Publishers, Inc.

"The Men Behind the Guns of Business" by Richard W. Sears, from *Personality in Business*. First published by The System Company in 1910.

"You've Got to Take Chances" by Muriel Siebert, from *Particular Passions: Talks with Women who Have Shaped Our Times* edited by Lynn Gilbert and Gaylen Moore. Copyright © 1981 by Lynn Gilbert. Used by permission of Lynn Gilbert.

"A Mysterious Faculty" from *The Story of the Winged-S* by Igor Sikorsky. First published by Dodd, Mead & Company, 1958.

"The Most Important Thing I Ever Learned About Business" by Alfred Sloan, from *System: The Magazine of Business*, August 1924.

"Running a Successful Company: Ten Rules that Worked for Me" from *Sam Walton: Made in America* by Sam Walton. Copyright © 1992 by Estate of Samuel Moore Walton. Used by permission of Doubleday, a division of Bantam Doubleday Dell Publishing Group, Inc.

"Sell with Sincerity" by Thomas J. Watson, from *America's Twelve Master Salesmen*. Reprinted by permission of Forbes, Inc. Copyright © Forbes, Inc., 1952.

"The Greatest Capitalist in History" by Thomas J. Watson from *Fortune*, August 31, 1987. Copyright © 1987 by Time, Inc. All rights reserved.

"Lessons for Success" by Jack Welch, from *Control Your Own Destiny or Someone Else Will* by Noel M. Tichy and Stratford Sherman. Copyright © 1993 by Noel M. Tichy and Stratford Sherman. Used by permission of Doubleday, a division of Bantam Doubleday Dell Publishing Group, Inc.

"You in a Career of Selling" by Robert Woodruff, from *Listen to Leaders in Business* edited by Albert Love and James Saxon Childers. Copyright © 1963 by Tupper & Love, Inc. Reprinted by permission of Henry Holt & Co., Inc.

"Interpreting the Weather Signs of Business" by Owen Young, from *System: The Magazine of Business*, September 1924.

Index